Official
Rules of
Sports &
Games

Official Rules of Sports & Games

1982–83

EDITED BY
REGINALD MOORE

KAYE & WARD · KINGSWOOD

First published 1949
Fifteenth edition 1982

Published by
Kaye & Ward Ltd

ISBN 0 7182 3960 1

All enquiries and requests relevant to this title
should be sent to the publisher,
Kaye & Ward Ltd,
The Windmill Press,
Kingswood, Tadworth, Surrey

Printed in Great Britain by
Butler & Tanner Ltd, Frome and London

CONTENTS

ACKNOWLEDGEMENTS

The publishers wish to acknowledge with thanks the very helpful co-operation which they have received from the following associations, who should be consulted over any queries about the games concerned. Without the assistance which these associations and their officials have given, which includes the permission to reproduce these copyright rules and laws and a great deal of help over the illustrations, the publication of this book would not have been possible.

Grand National Archery Society,
    National Agricultural Centre, Stoneleigh, Kenilworth, Warwicks., CV8 2LG.
Amateur Athletic Association,
    Francis House, Francis Street, London, SW1P 1DL.
The Badminton Association of England,
    Bradwell Road, Loughton Lodge, Milton Keynes, MK8 9LA.
English Basket Ball Association,
    Calomax House, Lupton Avenue, Leeds, LS9 7EE.
English Bowling Association,
    2A Iddesleigh Road, Bournemouth, BH3 7JR.
Marylebone Cricket Club,
    Lord's Ground, London, NW8 8QN.
The Croquet Association,
    The Hurlingham Club, Ranelagh Gardens, London, SW6 3PR.
The Eton Fives Association,
    The Moor House, Lane End, High Wycombe, Bucks.
Rugby Fives Association,
    Hollow Oak, Priors Heath, Goudhurst, Kent.
The Football Association,
    16 Lancaster Gate, London, W2 3LW.

Rugby Football Union,
  Twickenham, TW2 7RQ.
Rugby Football League,
  180 Chapeltown Road, Leeds, LS7 4HT.
The Royal and Ancient Golf Club of St. Andrews,
  Fife, KY16 9JD.
Hockey Rules Board,
  26 Stompond Lane, Walton-on-Thames, Surrey.
British Ice Hockey Association,
  48 Barmouth Road, Shirley, Croydon, Surrey, CR0 5EQ.
All England Women's Lacrosse Association,
  Room 235, 70 Brompton Road, London, SW3 1EQ.
English Lacrosse Union,
  Room 1, Bell Field House, Bell Field Ave., Cheadle Hulme,
  Cheshire SK8 7AG.
All England Netball Association,
  Francis House, Francis Street, London, SW1P 1DL.
National Rounders Association,
  4 Gloucester Close, Desford, Leicestershire.
Squash Rackets Association,
  Francis House, Francis Street, London, SW1P 1DL.
Tennis and Rackets Association,
  c/o The Queen's Club, Palliser Road, London, W14 9EQ.
The International Tennis Federation,
  Barons Court, West Kensington, London, W14 9EG.
The International Table Tennis Federation,
  53 London Road, St. leonards-on-Sea, E. Sussex,
  TN37 6AY.
Amateur Swimming Association,
  Water Polo Committee,
  Harold Fern House, Derby Square, Loughborough, Leices-
  tershire.
English Volleyball Association,
  128 Melton Road, West Bridgford, Nottingham, NG2 6EP.

The Rules of
Archery

Archery
RULES OF SHOOTING
FITA Article numbers quoted are those used in FITA Constitution and Rules

INTRODUCTION

(*See Note* on p. 56)

G.N.A.S. Laws

3. The shooting regulations as prescribed in its Rules of Shooting shall be accepted as governing the relevant branches of the sport of archery throughout the area under the Society's jurisdiction. The Rules of Shooting are the responsibility of the National Council.

4. No Regional Society, County Association, archery club or similar organisation recognised by the Society shall include in its Constitution or Shooting Regulations any provisions which conflict with those of the Society. A copy of each County Association's and Regional Society's Constitution shall be deposited with National Council.

12. All members, affiliated clubs, associated organisations, associations, county associations and regional societies shall accept the jurisdiction of the Society and shall conform to such conditions, shooting rules and regulations as may be determined from time to time.

14. (*a*) No archer, other than a member of the Society or one whose national society is affiliated to the Federation Internationale de Tir a l'Arc may compete or officiate at any of the Society's meetings or at any meeting of a Regional Society or a County Association or at a Club or Association affiliated to a Regional Society. This clause does not apply to Ladies Paramount.

(*b*) No archer, other than a British National of the United Kingdom may be the holder of a British National Championship or of any of the challenge trophies offered at the British

National Target Championship Meetings and the Grand National Archery meeting.

(c) A professional archer may not hold a Championship title or challenge trophy nor may he receive any prize in connection with any tournament organised by or held under the auspices of the Grand National Archery Society or any affiliated body unless specifically offered for competition for professional archers only, not shooting in competition with amateurs.

A professional archer is one who uses his skill in shooting with the bow and arrow as a means of making his living.

Declaration of professionalism or reinstatement of amateur status shall be dealt with by the National Council at its discretion. (N.B. For purposes of international competition the attention of members is drawn to the Rules of Amateur Status laid down from time to time by the Federation Internationale de Tir a l'Arc.)

Amateur Status

An amateur in archery practises the sport in all or one of the various branches as a leisure pursuit.

1. He shall observe the rules of the IOC, his International Federation and his National Federation.

2. He shall not have received any financial rewards or material benefits in connection with his sport participation except:

(a) He may be a physical education or sport teacher giving elementary instruction.

(b) Accept, subject to certain limitation:

(i) assistance administered through his National Olympic Committee or National Federation.

(ii) compensation authorised by his NOC or National Federation, in case of necessity, to cover financial loss resulting from his absence from work.

(c) Accept prizes or trophies not to exceed 700 Swiss francs in value. Cash prizes are not allowed.

(d) Accept academic and technical scholarships.

3. Full details of amateur status and the IOC Eligibility Code, etc. are to be found in FITA Rules and Regulations Articles 201–205 inclusive.

I. TARGET ARCHERY

100. Target Faces

(*a*) The standard British target face is circular, 122 cm (4 ft) in diameter. This British target face is composed as follows:

A circle in the centre 24.4 cm diameter, ringed by four concentric bands the breadth of each, measured radially, being 12.2 cm.

The colours of the target face are: (from the centre outwards) gold, red, blue, black, and white.

The centre of the gold is termed the "pinhole".
The standard FITA face is as above but each colour is divided into two zones of equal width by a line not exceeding 2 mm in width.

(*b*) Any dividing line which may be used between colours shall be made entirely within the higher scoring zone.

(*c*) Any line marking the outermost edge of the white shall be made entirely within the scoring zone.

(*d*) Tolerances on British faces are permitted as follows:

4 mm on the full 122 cm diameter

3 mm in any one zone of 12.2 cm

3 mm on the 24.4 cm diameter of the Gold.

101. Range Layout

(*a*) The targets shall be set up at one end of the ground. They shall be inclined at an angle of about 15 degrees, with the pinholes 130 cm (4 ft 3 in) above the ground.

(*b*) Minimum spacing of target centres shall be:

Archers shooting singly			2.44 m	(8 ft)
,,	,,	in pairs	3.05 m	(10 ft)
,,	,,	in threes	3.66 m	(12 ft)

(*c*) Each target shall be securely anchored so that it cannot blow off its stand. Likewise stands shall be anchored to prevent them from blowing over.

(*d*) All targets shall be clearly numbered.

(*e*) The shooting line (over which the archers shall take up their shooting positions) shall be measured from points vertically below the pinholes.

(*f*) Shooting marks, consisting of discs or other flat

markers, shall be positioned opposite the targets at the appropriate distances. The shooting marks are to bear the number of the target opposite which they are placed.

(g) Lines at right angles to the shooting line and extending from the shooting line to the target line making lanes containing one, two or three bosses may be laid down.

(h) A waiting line shall be placed at least five yards behind the shooting line.

(i) On grounds where the public have right of access an area shall be roped off to indicate that no one can pass behind the targets within 50 yards of them. Where an efficient backstop netting, a bank or other similar device (not a hedge or penetrable fence) high enough for the top of the stop as seen from the shooting line to be at least as far above the top of the target as the gold is below the top of the target, then this distance may be reduced to 25 yards. The area to be roped shall extend from the ends of the "safety line" so that no one can pass within 20 yards of the ends of the target line, 10 yards of the shooting line and 15 yards behind the shooting line.

102. Equipment

Three types of bow are recognised:

(a) Bows and their accessories which conform in all respects to the following:

(i) A bow of any type may be used provided it subscribes to the accepted principle and meaning of the word bow as used in Target Archery; e.g. an article consisting of a handle (grip), riser and two flexible limbs each ending in a tip with a string nock.

The bow is braced for use by a single bowstring attached directly between the two string nocks only and, in operation, is held in one hand by its handle (grip) while the fingers of the other hand draw, hold back and release the string.

(ii) A bowstring may be made up of any number of strands of the material chosen for the purpose, with a centre serving to accommodate the drawing fingers, a nocking point to which may be added serving(s) to fit the arrow nock as necessary, and to locate this point one or two nock locators may be positioned and in each of the two ends of the bowstring a loop to be placed in the string nocks of the bow when braced.

In addition, one attachment which may not exceed a diameter of one centimetre in any direction is permitted on the string to serve as nose or lip mark.

The serving on the string must not end within the archer's vision at full draw. A bowstring must not in any way offer aid in aiming through "peephole", marking or any other means.

(iii) An arrowrest, which can be adjustable, any movable pressure button, pressure point or arrowplate and draw check indicator may all be used on the bow provided they are not electric or electronic and do not offer an additional aid in aiming.

(iv) A bowsight, a bowmark or a point of aim on the ground for aiming is permitted, but at no time may more than one such device be used.

(1) A bowsight as attached to the bow for the purpose of aiming may allow for windage adjustment as well as elevation setting but it is subject to the following provision:

it shall not incorporate a prism or lens or other magnifying device, levelling or electric devices nor shall it provide for more than one sighting point.

An attachment to which the bowsight is fixed is permitted.

The length of any sight (ring, barrel, conical, etc.) shall not exceed the minimum inside diameter of the aperture. A hood is not to exceed a length of 1 cm irrespective of shape.

(2) A bowmark is a single mark made on the bow for the purpose of aiming. Such mark may be made in pencil, tape or any other suitable marking material.

A plate or tape with distance markings may be mounted on the bow as a guide but must not in any way offer any additional aid.

(3) A point of aim on the ground is a marker placed in the shooting lane between the shooting line and the target. Such marker may not exceed a diameter of 7.5 cm and must not protrude above the ground more than 15 cm.

(v) Stabilisers and torque flight compensators on the bow are permitted provided they do not:

(1) serve as a string guide

(2) touch anything but the bow

(3) represent any obstacle to other archers as far as place on the shooting line is concerned.

(vi) Arrows of any type may be used provided they subscribe to the accepted principle and meaning of the word arrow as used in Target Archery, and that such arrows do not cause undue damage to target faces and buttresses.

An arrow consists of a shaft with head (point), nock, fletching and, if desired, cresting and/or numbers. The arrows of each archer shall be marked with the archer's name, initials or insignia and all arrows used for the same end of 3 or 6 arrows shall carry the same pattern and colour(s) of fletching, nocks and cresting (if any).

(vii) Finger protection in the form of finger stalls or tips, gloves, shooting tab or tape (plaster) to draw, hold back and release the string is permitted, provided they are smooth and with no device to help to hold and/or release the string.

Shooting tabs may be built up of several layers of any materials suitable for their use and allow for the part of the tab behind that used for drawing the string to be stiff using different materials for this build-up (the latter can be leather, plastic, metal, etc.). No shapes have been specified and no limitations in respect of size.

A separator between the fingers to prevent pinching the arrow may be used.

On the bow hand an ordinary glove, mitten or similar may be worn.

(viii) Field glasses, telescopes and other visual aids may be used for spotting arrows.

Ordinary spectacles as necessary or shooting spectacles provided they are fitted with the same lenses normally worn by the archer, and sun glasses may be worn.

None may be fitted with microhole lenses, glasses or similar marked in any way which can assist aiming.

(ix) Accessories are permitted such as bracers, dress shield, bowsling, belt or ground quiver, tassel and foot markers not protruding above the ground more than one centimetre.

(*b*) Crossbows which conform to the Rules and Conditions stated in Part V.

(*c*) Compound and other bows and their accessories which do not meet the requirements of para. 102 (a).

103. Separate Styles and Conditions

(*a*) Bows conforming to 102 (*a*).

(i) Free Style: As 102 (*a*).

(ii) Barebow:

(1) As 102 (*a*) (i) and the bow must be free from any protrusions, marks or blemishes or laminated pieces which could be used in aiming. The inside of the upper limb shall be without trade marks.

(2) As 102 (*a*) (ii).

(3) An arrowrest and arrowplate which are part of the bow (i.e. not movable) and provided they do not offer any aid in aiming.

(4) As 102 (*a*) (vi) except that in Field Archery the arrows need be numbered by rings only, approx. 5 mm wide and 5 mm apart.

(5) As 102 (*a*) (vii).

(6) As 102 (*a*) (ix) except footmarkers.

(7) As 102 (*a*) (viii) except that field glasses and other visual aids may not be used when shooting Field Rounds with unmarked distances.

(8) The following are not permitted:

> Any aid for estimating distances
> Any memoranda that assist in improving scores
> Sights, draw check indicator and mounted stabilisers—the bow must be bare.

(iii) Traditional—As barebow except that the arrows shall be made of wood except for the fletchings and may comprise a metallic pile and a plastic nock.

(*b*) Crossbows (see Part V).

(*c*) Bows conforming to 102 (*c*).

(i) Unlimited – No restrictions as to accessories, but the bow must be free and held in the hand.

(ii) Limited – The bow must be held in the hand and the string must be drawn, held back and released by the fingers of the other hand. A level, peepsight and pressure button are permitted but a scope is not allowed. A cable guard may be fitted.

(iii) Bowhunter – No marking or attachment may appear on the bow or string which may be used as an aid to aiming. A cable guard, pressure button and an adjustable arrow plate are permitted. Only one stabiliser not longer than 30.5 cm (12 in) overall may be fitted. No release aid may be used.

(*a*) Shooting, except in the case of permanently or semi-permanently disabled archers, shall be from an unsupported standing position, placing one foot on each side of the shooting line.

(*b*) (i) The order in which archers shall shoot at their respective targets shall be the order in which they appear on the target list and the drawing up of the target list shall be a matter for arrangement by the Tournament Organisers. Unless otherwise directed, No. 3 on each target shall be the Target Captain, and No. 4 the Lieutenant. The Captain shall be responsible for the orderly conduct of shooting in accordance with the Rules of Shooting.

(ii) The order of shooting in all Tournaments of Record Status shall rotate. For other Tournaments, including Club Target Days, rotation shall be optional. (This rule does not apply to the Worcester Round.)

(*c*) Six arrows shall be shot at an end. Each archer shall shoot three arrows and immediately retire and, when all on a target have shot, shall shoot three more. If an archer persists in shooting more than three arrows consecutively he may be disqualified by the Judge.

(*d*) In the event of an archer shooting more than six arrows at an end, the archer shall be penalised by losing the value of his best arrow(s) in the target, and such arrow(s) shall not be measured for a Gold prize.

(*e*) An arrow shall be deemed not to have been shot, if the archer can touch it with his bow without moving his feet from their normal position in relation to the shooting line. In which case another arrow may be shot in its place. If another arrow is not available he may only retrieve his misnocked arrow with the Judge's permission.

(*f*) If from any cause an archer is not prepared to shoot before all have shot, such archer shall lose the benefit of that end.

(*g*) Archers arriving late shall not be allowed to make up any ends that they have missed.

(*h*) An archer shall retire from the shooting line as soon as his last arrow has been shot. The last archer on a target may, however, remain on the shooting line to keep company with another archer still shooting.

(*i*) Two and half minutes shall be the maximum time for an archer to shoot three arrows, the time to start from when the archer steps on to the shooting line.

(*j*) Whilst an archer is on the shooting line, he shall receive no information by word or otherwise from anyone except the Judge or Field Captain(s).

(*k*) At any Meeting no practice is allowed on the ground the same day, except that one end of six arrows may be shot as sighters before the beginning of each day's shooting, but only after competitors have come under the Judge's orders at the Assembly. Such sighters shall not be recorded.

(*l*) If for any reason an archer is alone on a target he must notify the Judge who shall arrange for him to be transferred to another target or another archer to be transferred to join him.

(*m*) The maximum number of archers on a target shall be six.

105. Control of Shooting

(*a*) The Lady Paramount shall be the supreme arbitrator on all matters connected with the Tournament at which she officiates.

(*b*) At all times, whenever shooting takes place, it must be under the control of a Field Captain.

At larger meetings a Judge shall be appointed to take charge of the shooting. Field Captains, to whom the Judge may delegate his authority, may be appointed as necessary. If a Field Captain has not been appointed previously, the Judge may appoint any experienced archer to act in this capacity.

At Tournaments the Judge and Field Captains shall be non-shooting.

(*c*) The Judge shall be in sole control of the shooting and shall resolve all disputes (subject to the supreme authority of the Lady Paramount) in accordance with the Rules of Shooting.

106. Scoring

(*a*) The scoring points for hits on the target face for G.N.A.S. Rounds are:

Gold 9, Red 7, Blue 5, Black 3, White 1.

The scoring points for hits on the target face for F.I.T.A. Rounds are:

Inner Gold 10, Outer Gold 9, Inner Red 8, Outer Red 7, Inner Blue 6, Outer Blue 5, Inner Black 4, Outer Black 3, Inner White 2, Outer White 1.

The value shall be determined by the position of the arrow shaft.

(*b*) Archers shall identify their arrows by pointing at the nocks. Neither the arrow nor the target face shall be touched until the final decision as to score has been given and any such interference with the target or arrow shall disqualify the archer from scoring the higher value.

The Lieutenant will identify the arrows with the score called and will assist the Captain in any way that may be required. No. 1 on the target shall identify the Lieutenant's score.

The duty of entering the scores on the score sheet may be shared by the archers on each target, but the Target Captain shall remain responsible for ensuring that scores are correctly recorded. The Target Captain and Lieutenant will check the score sheet and the Target Captain and the archer shall sign it as correct. The Lieutenant shall sign the Target Captain's score sheet. The attention of archers is drawn to their responsibility for ensuring that when signing score sheets the score, etc., that they sign for is correct.

(*c*) If an arrow touches two colours or any dividing line it shall be scored as being of that of the higher value.

(*d*) If any doubt or dispute shall arise it shall be decided by the Target Captain subject to appeal to the Judge.

(*e*) No alteration shall be made in the value of any arrow as entered on the score sheet, to the advantage of its owner, after such arrow has been drawn from the target.

Any alteration to the recorded score must be initialled by the Judge in a differing coloured ink prior to the withdrawal of the arrow from the target. No arrows shall be withdrawn from the target (without the express direction of the Captain) until all the archers' scores have been entered on the score sheet and the Captain is satisfied that they are correctly entered.

(*f*) If an arrow is observed to rebound from a target, the archer concerned shall draw the attention of the Judge to the fact after having shot his sixth arrow (or third if shooting in ends of 3 only) by retiring two paces from the shooting line and holding his bow above his head.

Upon the Judge satisfying himself that the claim is justified, the archer shall be permitted to shoot another arrow separately in the same end after all archers on that target have completed their normal shooting, such arrow to be numbered or preferably marked by the Judge.

To prevent frivolous bouncer claims, the archer is to be warned individually that if six original arrows were shot not including a bouncer, then his highest scoring arrow may, at the discretion of the Judge on repetition of a false claim, be deducted from that end's score. The Judge shall take part in that competitor's scoring to ensure that only the correct number of arrows are scored, and that the bouncer was not caused by striking another arrow already in the target. An arrow passing through a target cannot be scored.

(*g*) An arrow passing through the target face but remaining in the boss shall be withdrawn by the Captain or Lieutenant and shall be inserted from the back in the same place and at the assumed angle of original penetration until the pile is visible in the target face, when the score shall be determined.

(*h*) An arrow hitting and remaining embedded in another arrow shall be scored the same as the arrow struck.

(*i*) An arrow in the target, which has or may have been deflected by another arrow already in the target, shall be scored according to the position of its shaft in the target face.

(*j*) An arrow on the ground believed to have hit and

rebounded from another arrow shall be scored the value of the struck arrow, if the latter is found in the target with its nock damaged in a compatible manner.

(*k*) If an arrow fails to enter the buttress and is hanging in the target face it shall be pushed in by the Judge or shall be removed and the Judge will ensure that the appropriate score is recorded when scoring takes place.

(*l*) The F.I.T.A. Rule that bouncers shall only be scored if arrow holes on the target face are marked applies to all F.I.T.A. Rounds shot including those shot at Club Target Days, inter-county matches, etc.

(*m*) An archer may delegate another archer on the same target to record his score and pick up his arrows.

(*n*) An incapacitated archer may nominate an assistant, who shall be under the control and discipline of the Judge, to record his score and pick up his arrows.

(*o*) In the event of a tie for a score prize the winner shall be the one of those who tie who has the greatest number of hits. Should this result in a tie the prize shall be awarded to the archer among those who tie who has the greatest number of Golds. Should this number also be the same the archers shall be declared joint winners. Where the prize is for (i) most hits, or (ii) most Golds, ties shall be resolved on the above principle in the following order (i) highest score, most Golds, (ii) highest score, most hits.

(*p*) When a shoot (other than the annual Grand National Archery Meeting) is abandoned due to adverse weather con-ditions, the placings and prizes shall be awarded on the cumu-lative score at the conclusion of the last full end shot by the competitors, by instruction of the Judge.

(*q*) Bows which are recognised in Rule 102 (*b*) and (*c*) MAY NOT BE USED IN DIRECT COMPETITION with bows recognised in Rule 102 (*a*). Archers using bows recognised in Rule 102 (*b*) and (*c*) shall not be eligible for any prize, medal, trophy or other award, classification, handicap or other dis-tinction which has not been specifically devised or designated for archers using such bows.

The allocation of any prize, medal, trophy or other award shall be a matter for each individual tournament organiser.

Classification, handicap or other distinction shall remain the sole prerogative of the Grand National Archery Society.

107. Dress Regulations

(*a*) At all Tournaments with National Record Status members of the Society shooting and officiating are required to wear the accepted dress.

(*b*) (i) Ladies are required to wear a dress or skirt or trousers (slacks) with suitable blouse.

(ii) Gentlemen are required to wear full length trousers and long or short sleeved shirts.

(iii) Sweaters/cardigans/blazers may be worn.

Each garment shall be plain dark green or white. There is no objection to wearing green and white garments together.

Waterproof clothing worn only during inclement weather is not subject to these regulations, but both white and green waterproofs are available and are recommended.

(*c*) Footwear must be worn by all competitors at all times during the Tournament.

(*d*) Advertising material must not be carried or worn. The name/emblem of an archer's Country, Regional or County Association or Club may be worn on the uniform or shooting clothes.

(*e*) Any archer not conforming to the above regulations shall be requested by the Judge and Organiser to leave the shooting line and will not be permitted to shoot.

108. Recognised Rounds for Record Classification and Handicap Purposes

(*a*) The following Rounds are recognised by the Society:

York: 6 dozen arrows at 100 yd.; 4 dozen arrows at 80 yd.; 2 dozen arrows at 60 yd.

Western: 4 dozen arrows at 60 yd.; 4 dozen arrows at 50 yd.

St. George: 3 dozen arrows at 100 yd.; 3 dozen arrows at 80 yd.; 3 dozen arrows at 60 yd.

National: 4 dozen arrows at 60 yd.; 2 dozen arrows at 50 yd.

New Western: 4 dozen arrows at 100 yd.; 4 dozen arrows at 80 yd.

Windsor: 3 dozen arrows at 60 yd.; 3 dozen arrows at 50 yd.; 3 dozen arrows at 40 yd.

New National: 4 dozen arrows at 100 yd.; 2 dozen arrows at 80 yd.

American: 30 arrows at 60 yd.; 30 arrows at 50 yd.; 30 arrows at 40 yd.

Hereford: 6 dozen arrows at 80 yd.; 4 dozen arrows at 60 yd.; 2 dozen arrows at 50 yd.

Albion: 3 dozen arrows at 80 yd.; 3 dozen arrows at 60 yd.; 3 dozen arrows at 50 yd.

Long Western: 4 dozen arrows at 80 yd.; 4 dozen arrows at 60 yd.

Long National: 4 dozen arrows at 80 yd.; 2 dozen arrows at 60 yd.

Long Metric (Gentlemen): 3 dozen arrows at 90 m.; 3 dozen arrows at 70 m.

F.I.T.A. (Gentlemen): 3 dozen arrows at 90 m., 3 dozen arrows at 70 m., 3 dozen arrows at 50 m., 3 dozen arrows at 30 m.

F.I.T.A. (Ladies): 3 dozen arrows at 70 m., 3 dozen arrows at 60 m., 3 dozen arrows at 50 m., 3 dozen arrows at 30 m.

Short Metric: 3 dozen arrows at 50 m., 3 dozen arrows at 30 m.

Long Metric (Ladies): 3 dozen arrows at 70 m., 3 dozen arrows at 60 m.

(*b*) in every round the longer, or longest distance is shot first, and the shorter, or shortest distance last.

(*c*) When F.I.T.A. and Metric Rounds are shot, F.I.T.A. Rules apply.

(*d*) (i) A F.I.T.A. Round may be shot in one day or over two consecutive days under F.I.T.A. Rules.

(ii) All other Rounds to be shot in one day. (Except in accordance with Rule for Championships of more than one day's duration.)

(*e*) In addition any "local" round made up of other numbers of arrows at specified distances may be used in Clubs and Tournaments provided the Rules of Shooting are adhered to in all respects and subjects to their non-recognition by the G.N.A.S. for Record, Classification or Handicap purposes.

109. Club Events

(a) Club Target Day

(i) A Target Day is any day and time appointed under the Rules of the Club and previously announced to the Members.

(ii) There is no statutory limit to the number of officially appointed Target Days in any one week.

(iii) All scores made must be entered in the Club Record Book.

(iv) Target Days should commence punctually at the announced time.

(v) All shooting shall be in accordance with G.N.A.S. Rules of Shooting.

(vi) On any Club Target Day there shall be a minimum of two archers shooting, not necessarily on the same Target, each recording the other's scores in order that these scores may be recognised. An archer shooting alone may claim his score provided that it has been recorded throughout by a non-shooting archer.

(b) Open Meeting

An Open Meeting is an event run as a competition open to all Members of G.N.A.S. and F.I.T.A. Affiliated Members, with all the necessary organisation, advertising of the event, judging, etc., run under G.N.A.S. Rules of Shooting.

(c) Tournament

A Tournament is an Event at which awards are given. This may be an Open or Closed Meeting.

110. Six Gold Badge

(a) The award, which is for six consecutive arrows shot at one end into the gold, is open to Members of the Society.

(b) The shortest distances at which it may be gained are:
Gentlemen — 80 yd.   Ladies — 60 yd.

(c) In the F.I.T.A. Round the badge will be awarded for six consecutive arrows at one end shot into the Gold zone at:
Gentlemen — 90 or 70 metres   Ladies — 70 or 60 metres

(d) The Six Gold End must be made at a Meeting organised by the Society or by any of its associated bodies, or in competition at an Associated Club's Target Day, under G.N.A.S. Rules of Shooting.

(*e*) Claims for the award must be submitted to the G.N.A.S. Secretary on the appropriate form, accompanied by the original score sheet duly signed by the Club Secretary or Meeting Organiser.

111. F.I.T.A. Star Badge

The award is open to Members of the Society according to qualifications and applications as laid down in F.I.T.A. Rules. Claims for the award must be submitted to the G.N.A.S. Secretary on the appropriate form.

120. Regulations for the Grand National Archery Meeting

(*a*) The meeting shall consist of not less than three days' shooting, weather permitting, during which a Handicap Meeting may be held.

(*b*) A lady shall be invited to officiate as Lady Paramount by the Secretary after consultation with the National Council.

(*c*) The Judges shall be appointed by National Council.

121. Rounds

(*a*) The Ladies' Meeting shall consist of: Two Hereford Rounds. Ladies may enter for the National Round only.

(*b*) The Gentlemen's Meeting shall consist of: Two York Rounds.

122. Winners

The winner shall be those Archers obtaining the greatest scores over the Double Hereford and York Rounds respectively.

In the event of a tie the archer making the greatest number of hits amongst those who have ties shall be the winner. In the event of this resulting in a tie the winner shall be the one of those who tie who has the greatest number of Golds. Should this number also be the same the archers shall be declared joint winners.

123. Shooting

If, owing to the state of the weather, the full number of arrows is not shot on the first or second day, the remaining arrows shall, if possible, be shot on the next day, providing that not more than eighteen dozen arrows are shot in any one day. The Judge in consultation with the Secretary (Organiser) and Field Captain shall decide whether any other Competitions shall be cancelled.

124. Challenge Trophies and Prizes

(a) The Challenge Trophies are open only to British Nationals of the United Kingdom. Unless the winner is permanently resident in the United Kingdom the trophy shall remain in the custody of the Society. Any question as to the residence of the winner shall be decided by the National Council, whose decision shall be final.

(b) No awards shall be made unless one complete Round is shot, and if the Double Round be incomplete, the prizes and Challenge Trophies shall be awarded on the one round only that has been completed.

(c) Certain Challenge Trophies, i.e. those of the original National Round Championships, will be awarded on the two National Rounds. All Ladies will be competing for these.

(d) (i) The County Challenge Trophies shall be awarded to the County Teams making the highest aggregate scores at the Championship Meeting. The archer making the highest score in a winning team shall be entitled to hold the Trophy until the next meeting.

(ii) Each County's teams score shall consist of the four, or fewer, highest scores made by the Ladies and Gentlemen respectively competing at the Championship Meeting.

(iii) Archers competing who are affiliated to the Society through one of its Affiliated Clubs (Associate Member) shall shoot for the County through which their G.N.A.S. Affiliation Fees are paid.

Archers competing who are Ordinary Members of the Society, or whose G.N.A.S. Affiliation Fees are paid through an Associated Organisation of G.N.A.S. shall notify the G.N.A.S. Secretary and the Secretary of the County concerned by 1st January in each year of the County for which they wish to shoot.

140. Regulations for the British National Target Championship

(*a*) The Annual Championship shall consist of not less than two days shooting, weather permitting.

(*b*) A lady shall be invited to officiate as Lady Paramount by the Secretary after consultation with the National Council.

(*c*) The Judges shall be appointed by National Council.

141. Rounds

(*a*) The Ladies' Championship shall consist of two Hereford Rounds.

(*b*) The Gentlemen's Championship shall consist of two York Rounds.

142. Titles

The Championship Titles are open only to British Nationals of the United Kingdom and shall be awarded to the archers obtaining the greatest scores over the Double Hereford and York Rounds respectively. In the event of a tie the archer making the greatest number of hits amongst those who have ties shall be the Champion. In the event of this resulting in a tie the Champion shall be the one of those who tie who has the greatest number of Golds. Should this number also be the same the archers shall be declared joint Champions.

143. Shooting

If, owing to the state of the weather, the full number of arrows is not shot on the first day, the remaining arrows, shall, if possible, be shot on the second day, If, owing to the state of the weather, a full Round cannot be shot the Judge in consultation with the Tournament Organiser and Field Captain shall determine at which point the Champions shall be declared.

144. Challenge Trophies

(*a*) The Challenge Trophies are open only to British Nationals of the United Kingdom.

(*b*) The Regional and County Challenge Trophies and/or medals shall be awarded to the respective teams making the highest aggregate scores at the Championship Meeting. The archer making the highest score in a winning team shall be entitled to hold the trophy until the next meeting.

Each team's score shall consist of the four, or fewer, highest scores made by Ladies and/or Gentlemen competing at the Championship Meeting.

(*c*) The County and Region for which an archer shall shoot shall be determined by applying Rule 124 (*d*) (iii).

160. Regulations for the UK Masters' Tournament

The UK Masters' Tournament is held annually, usually during the second weekend in June. The Tournament is by invitation only to:

(*a*) All Grand Master Bowmen, Master Bowmen and Junior Master Bowmen.

(*b*) Archers from F.I.T.A. Member Associations.

(*c*) Archers nominated by the G.N.A.S. Target Selection Committee.

161. Rounds

A single F.I.T.A. Round shall be shot over two consecutive days under F.I.T.A. Target Archery Rules.

162. Titles

No titles are awarded.

163. Challenge Trophies

The Challenge Trophies are open to all competitors under the conditions stated in 124 (*a*).

180. Indoor Target Archery

181. Recognised Rounds

The following Rounds are recognised by the Society:

(*a*) **Stafford Round:** 6 dozen arrows at 30 metres at an 80 cm target face.

(*b*) **Portsmouth Round:** 5 dozen arrows at 20 yards at a 60 cm target face.

(*c*) **Worcester Round:** 5 dozen arrows at 20 yards at a 40.64 cm (16 in) target face.

(*d*) **F.I.T.A. Round I:** 30 arrows at 18 metres at a 40 cm target face.

(*e*) **F.I.T.A. Round II:** 30 arrows at 25 metres at a 60 cm target face.

(*f*) In addition any "local" round made up of other numbers of arrows at specified distances may be used in Clubs and Tournaments provided the Rules of Shooting are adhered to in all respects and subject to their non-recognition by the G.N.A.S. for record, classification or handicap purposes.

182. Regulations for the Stafford and Portsmouth Rounds

The Rules of Target Archery shall apply with the following exceptions.

(*a*) **Target Faces.** The target faces used shall be:

(i) Stafford Round: 80 cm diameter 10 zone at a distance of 30 metres (standard F.I.T.A. target face).

(ii) Portsmouth Round: 60 cm diameter 10 zone at a distance of 20 yards (standard coloured and zoned).

(iii) Tolerances on 80 cm and 60 cm target faces shall not exceed 2 mm on any one zone and 3 mm on the diameter of each target face.

(*b*) **Range Layout.** Target centres shall be placed so as to allow archers to stand at a minimum of 0.91 m (3 ft) intervals while shooting.

(*c*) **Shooting**

(i) Archers may shoot singly or in pairs provided that Rule 182 (*b*) is complied with. Archers shall rotate the order of shooting when shooting singly, and alternate when shooting in pairs.

(ii) An end shall consist of 3 arrows.

(iii) 3 Sighter arrows shall be shot.

(*d*) **Scoring**

The scoring points for hits on the target, reading from the inner Gold to the outer White are 10, 9, 8, 7, 6, 5, 4, 3, 2, 1.

183. Regulations for the Worcester Round

The Rules of Target Archery shall apply with the following exceptions:

(*a*) **Target Faces**

(i) The target faces used shall be circular 40.64 cm (16 in) in diameter.

This target face is composed as follows:

A circle in the centre 8.13 cm ($3\frac{1}{5}$ in) diameter ringed by four concentric bands, the breadth of each measured radially being 4.064 cm ($1\frac{3}{5}$ in).

The centre circle shall be coloured white and the four concentric bands black. The concentric bands shall be divided by white lines. Each of the white dividing lines shall be of no greater width than 1 mm (0.04 in).

(ii) Tolerances on target faces are permitted as follows:

2 mm (0.08 in) on each zone and 2 mm (0.08 in) on full 40.64 cm (16 in) diameter.

(*b*) **Range Layout**

(i) The centres of the target bosses on which the target faces are affixed shall be placed so as to allow archers to stand at a minimum of 0.91 m (3 ft) intervals while shooting.

(ii) The shooting line (over which the archers shall take up their shooting positions) shall be measured from points vertically below the centre of the target boss on which target faces are affixed.

(*c*) **Shooting**

(i) Five arrows shall be shot at an end. Each archer will shoot his five arrows before retiring from the shooting line.

(ii) In the event of an archer shooting more than five arrows at an end the archer shall be penalised by losing the value of his best arrow(s) in the target.

(iii) At any meeting no practice is allowed except that one end of five arrows may be shot as sighters.

(iv) The maximum number of archers on a target boss shall be four.

(v) Five minutes shall be the maximum time for an archer to shoot an end. The time to start from when the archer steps on to the shooting line.

(*d*) **Scoring**

The scoring points for hits on the target face are: 5, 4, 3, 2, 1, reading from the centre white circle.

(*e*) **Recognised Round**

(i) The Round shall consist of 12 ends (60 arrows).

(ii) The distance to be shot is twenty yards.

(iii) Each boss shall hold four target faces.

(iv) Target faces shall be arranged thus:

$$\begin{array}{cc} 1 & 2 \\ 3 & 4 \end{array}$$

(v) Two archers of a group shall shoot five arrows when the second group shall then shoot their five arrows.

(vi) The first group of two archers shall shoot at the higher targets; the second group at the lower targets.

(vii) When all archers have shot 30 arrows those who have been shooting at the lower targets shall change to the higher targets and those who have been shooting at the higher targets shall shoot at the lower targets, thus:

Those who have been shooting on targets 1 and 2 shall shoot the remaining 30 arrows on targets 3 and 4 retaining their same shooting positions.

184. Regulations for the F.I.T.A. Rounds I and II

(*a*) F.I.T.A. Rules 950–954 will apply.

(*b*) **Shooting and Scoring**

(i) Each archer shall shoot his arrows in ends of three.

(ii) Two ends of sighter arrows are permitted each day preceding the commencement of shooting.

(iii) Scoring shall take place after each end of three arrows.

(*c*) **Other Rules and Regulations**

In all other aspects the rules of Target Archery shall apply except that the two and a half minute time limit for shooting three arrows may not be extended.

If space does not permit a waiting line may be omitted.

185. Regulations for the National Indoor Championship Meeting

(*a*) The Stafford Round shall be shot at the National Championship Meeting.

(*b*) Regulations for National Championship Meetings, Rules 140–144 apply as appropriate.

(*c*) National Records may be established according to Part VIII.

II. FIELD ARCHERY

200. Regulations

(*a*) G.N.A.S. Rules of Shooting 102, 103, 201–206 shall apply to G.N.A.S. recognised Rounds and any other traditional or local round run under the G.N.A.S. Rules of Shooting.

(*b*) F.I.T.A. Constitution and Rules Part VIII shall apply generally to the F.I.T.A. recognised Rounds, i.e. the Hunter and the Field, and to the F.I.T.A. Combination Round. The F.I.T.A. Combination Round shall consist of one unit of Unmarked F.I.T.A. Hunter Targets and one unit of Marked F.I.T.A. Field Targets, shot not over the same ground. The use of binoculars, or the carrying of them, is not permitted during the Hunter Round.

(*c*) At National Record Status and other F.I.T.A. Round events at and above County Championship level there shall be an initial equipment inspection. At other F.I.T.A. Round meetings an archer's equipment shall be liable to inspection at any time.

201. General Field Archery Rules

(*a*) A Field Captain shall be appointed to be in control of the shoot.

(*b*) The duties of the Field Captain shall be:

(i) to ensure that adequate safety precautions have been observed in the lay-out of the course and practice area (if any).

(ii) to address the assembled competitors before the shoot commences on safety precautions and any other appropriate matter including method of starting the event, the starting points of each group, etc.

(iii) to ensure that all competitors are conversant with the rules of the competition and the method of scoring.

(iv) to resolve disputes or queries that may arise in interpretation of the rules or other matters.

(*c*) Each shooting group shall consist of not more than five and not less than three archers, one of whom shall be designated Target Captain and two others as scorers.

(*d*) The Target Captain shall be responsible for the orderly conduct of shooting within the group, and have the ultimate responsibility for scoring the arrows.

(*e*) Each scorer shall be supplied with and complete a separate set of score cards for the shooting group and the duties of scorers shall be as follows:

(i) to write down the score of each competitor in the group.

(ii) to complete the score card at the end of the shooting.

(iii) to be responsible for deciding the value of each arrow, in the case of a dispute the Target Captain shall make the final decision.

(*f*) The score cards shall be signed by the scorer at the end of shooting, and by the archer as an acceptance of the final score.

(*g*) Should the two score cards not agree, then the lower score shall be taken as the result.

(*h*) The use of binoculars and other visual aids is not permitted in G.N.A.S. Field Archery rounds.

(*i*) The archer's more forward foot must be in contact and behind the shooting post while shooting.

(*j*) Arrows bouncing from or passing through the target may not be scored.

202. Specific Rules Relating to the G.N.A.S. "Recognised" Rounds

(*a*) Foresters Round

The standard Unit shall consist of the following 14 shots:

Three 24″ diameter faces at a distance of up to 70 yd.

Four 18″ diameter faces at a distance of up to 50 yd.

Four 12″ diameter faces at a distance of up to 40 yd.

Three 6″ diameter faces at a distance of up to 20 yd.

Targets. The target faces shall be of animal or bird design, and shall have inscribed on them an outer circle of fixed diameter, an inner circle of half that diameter, and a spot of one-sixth that diameter.

Thus: 24″ Face	12″ Inner Circle.	4″ Spot
18″ Face	9″ Inner Circle.	3″ Spot
12″ Face	6″ Inner Circle.	2″ Spot
6″ Face	3″ Inner Circle.	1″ Spot

Shooting Rules. At a 24″ Target, four arrows are shot, one from each of four posts. At an 18″ Target, three arrows are shot, one from each of three posts. At a 12″ Target, two arrows are shot, one from each of two posts. At a 6″ Target, only one arrow is shot from one post. Multi-post shots may be equidistant from the target or 'walk-up' or 'walk-away'.

Scoring Aiming spot 15 points
Inner circle 10 points
Outer circle 5 points

Range Marking. In either Marked or Unmarked distances.

(b) **Four Shot Foresters Round**

Shooting: On Forester animal faces, over unmarked Forester distances.

Shots: Four walk-up shots at each face.

Scoring: 15, 10, and 5 for spot, inner and outer respectively.

Unit: Fourteen faces in each unit ($3 \times 24″$; $4 \times 18″$; $4 \times 12″$; $3 \times 6″$)—112 shots, maximum possible score 1680.

Dimensions of Scoring Zones: Spot: one-sixth of the outer diameter.
Inner: half the outer diameter.

(c) **Big Game Round**

The standard Unit shall consist of the following 14 shots, at the suggested ranges:

Three group 1 Targets at a distance of 70 to 40 yd.
Three group 2 Targets at a distance of 50 to 30 yd.
Four group 3 Targets at a distance of 40 to 20 yd.
Four group 4 Targets at a distance of 30 to 10 yd.

Targets. The target faces shall be of animal or bird design, with the scoring area divided into two parts. The high-scoring area, is the smaller area, situated in the "heart/lung" region of the animal, and is known as the "kill" zone. The low-scoring area, is the remainder of the animal within the marked perimeter, and is known as the "wound" zone.

Targets are classed into groups one, two, three and four, according to size.

Group 1. $40″ \times 28″$—Bear, deer, moose, elk, caribou.

Group 2. $28″ \times 22″$—Antelope, small deer, wolf, mountain lion.

Group 3. $22'' \times 14''$—Coyote, javelina, turkey, fox, goose, wildcat, pheasant.

Group 4. $14'' \times 11''$—Turtle, duck, grouse, crow, skunk, jackrabbit, wood-chuck.

Any animal or bird consistent in size with a particular group may be used.

Shooting Rules. Three shots are permitted at each target, one from each of three posts, each successive post being closer to the target than the previous pone.

Arrows shall be identifiable as to order of shooting. The archer shall stop shooting as soon as a hit is considered to have been made.

Scoring. The score is decided by the position of the arrow in the Target (i.e. in the "kill" or "wound" zone) and the number of arrows shot.

	kill	wound
1st arrow score	20	16
2nd arrow score	14	10
3rd arrow score	8	4

Only the score of the first "scoring" arrow counts.

Range Marking. In either Marked or Unmarked distances.

203. Other Rounds

Traditional or local rounds involving differing targets and methods of scoring may be shot in either Club or Open Competition providing that the G.N.A.S. rules affecting safety are observed and that the rules are made known to all competitors before shooting starts.

204. Separate Classes and Styles

(*a*) There shall be separate classes for Ladies, Gentlemen and Juniors (see Rule 704).

(*b*) Styles as defined in Rule 103.

205. Juniors

Where Juniors under 15 years of age shoot in a group containing archers above this age, the Juniors shall shoot last. *For other Junior Rules see Part VII and 806 (c) in G.N.A.S. Rules.*

206. Regulations for the National Field Championship Meeting

(*a*) The Championship shall be known as:
G.N.A.S. ALL BRITISH AND OPEN FIELD CHAMPION-
SHIP.

(*b*) The Championship shall be according to F.I.T.A. Field
Championship Regulations and the same Programme (Articles
350, 354 and 812).

(*c*) Exception may be made in not marking all arrow holes
in which case for Championship purposes bouncers or arrows
passing through the face shall **not** be scored.

(*d*) The Championship Titles and Awards are open to all
competitors from F.I.T.A. Member Associations under the
conditions set out in 124 (*a*).

207. Interpretation of F.I.T.A. Rules

(*a*) The serving of the string must not end within the archer's
vision at full draw. A clear guideline on the above is to ensure
that the top end of the serving finishes either BELOW the point
of the nose, or ABOVE the eyebrow in the archer's full-draw
position. This is applicable to both Free Style and Barebow
archers. Both face-walking and string-walking are forbidden in
Barebow Shooting.

(*b*) An arrow rest may be used of any type provided it does
not offer aid in aiming, but it must be securely fixed to the bow
and stay in the same place throughout the shoot. It must not be
possible to peel it off and re-locate it in the course of a shoot.
Some extra gluing or form of fixing may be required for some
designs (Barebow). See 102 (*a*) (iii) for Free Style.

(*c*) Ordinary spectacles as necessary or shooting spectacles
provided they are fitted with the same lenses normally worn by
the archer, and sun glasses may be worn.

None may be fitted with microhole lenses, glasses or similar
marked in any way which can assist aiming.

(*d*) Bowsights may be provided with distance markings in
F/S, in the same way as for bow-marks, so long as they offer no
additional aid.

(*e*) An archer may have as many sets of arrows as he likes,
subject to inspection where required, but those he shoots at any
one target (i.e. numbered target) must be of the same fletching

and nock colour(s). Fur-fletch is permitted provided that all the arrows shot at one target are fletched in the same way. Each arrow shall be numbered by the use of plainly visible rings of approximately 5 mm width and 5 mm spacing.

(*f*) The Rule about no Stabilisers in B/B is made more explicit. **Mounted** stabilisers are not allowed. Sights and draw-checks are not allowed. The bow must be BARE.

(*g*) The following equipment is not permitted:

(i) Field glasses and other visual aids when shooting Rounds with Unmarked distances.

(ii) Any aids for estimating distances.

(iii) Any memoranda that assist in improving scores.

(*h*) Archers shall shoot in groups of not less than three nor more than five and shall shoot in pairs which shall rotate. Five archers shall rotate in pairs in sequence.

III. FLIGHT SHOOTING

300. Basis

(*a*) The three classes for which competitions may take place are:

    A. Target Bows.

    B. Flight Bows.

    C. Free-style.

Ladies, Gentlemen and Juniors may compete equally in each class.

(*b*) The Classes may be subdivided into bow weights, as follows:

    1—16 kg (35 lb).

    2—23 kg (50 lb).

    3—Unlimited.

Except for the target bow and unlimited classes flight bows shall be weighed as follows:

(i) Bows shall be weighed just prior to commencement of shooting. Weight of bow, length of arrow, and the class for which this combination is eligible, shall be recorded on a label affixed to the face of the bow.

(ii) The weight of the bow shall be taken at two inches less than the length of the longest arrow, and again at one inch less than the length of this arrow. The difference in these weights shall be added to the last weight of the bow at full draw.

Weighing bows at full draw is optional with the competitor. When an overdraw device is used and permits a draw in excess of one inch from the back of the bow, this excess shall be considered a portion of the arrow length for bow weighing purposes.

(c) For classes A and B only hand bows may be used and the bow must be held in the unsupported hand.

(d) If competitions for both Target and Flight Bows are being held on the same occasion, all shooting with Target Bows must be completed first.

301. Range Layout

(a) The Range Line, at right angles to the shooting line shall be clearly marked at 150 yards then at 50 yard intervals to at least 50 yards beyond the existing National Record Distance.

(b) Red warning flags shall be placed at each side of the range at 75 yards from the line of distance markers at a distance of 150 yards from the shooting line.

302. Equipment

(a) A Target Bow is any bow with which the user has shot at least two standard Target or Field Rounds. In the event of a breakage, a similar bow may be used as replacement.

(b) Any type of bow, other than a cross-bow, may be entered for Classes B and C.

(c) In the Target Bow class competitors must use their own length standard Target arrows and normal tab or shooting glove.

(d) In Classes B and C any type of arrow may be used.

(e) Sipurs are not permitted in Class A.

(f) Mechanical releases, inter-moving drawing and/or re-lease aids are prohibited.

The following may be used in Classes B and C:

Six-gold ring, Flipper or Strap (single or double), block sipur, and angle measuring device.

(g) In the event of a breakage a substitute bow or limb may be used providing it is checked for conforming to its class. In the event of this not being done the archer will automatically be transferred to the unlimited class.

303. Shooting

(*a*) Competitors should be at least six feet apart, and must not advance their leading foot over the shooting line.

(*b*) Each competitor may have one assistant or adviser, who must keep at least one yard behind the shooting line.

(*c*) (i) At least four ends, each of three arrows, will be shot.

(ii) After all classes have shot the first end competitors and officials will go forward. Competitors will stand by their furthest arrow. A marker with a label attached bearing the name of the competitor and class will then be placed at the pile end of the furthest arrow in each class.

(iii) Arrows will then be withdrawn.

(iv) Succeeding ends will then be shot and markers adjusted where necessary.

304. Control of Shooting

There shall be a Range Captain in charge who will act as Referee and Judge. His decision shall be final. He will also be responsible for the safety of spectators, who must at all times, when shooting is in progress, be not less than 10 yards behind the shooting line.

305. Measurements

Measurement of distances shall be made with a steel tape along the range line. The distances shot shall be measured to that point on the range line at which a line at right angles to the range line passes the point where the arrow enters the ground. If the arrow is lying on the ground the line should pass through the pile end of the arrow.

IV. CLOUT SHOOTING

400. Regulations

The Rules of Target Archery shall apply except as enumerated in the following paragraphs.

The Organisers shall take all reasonable steps to ensure that there be no risk occasioned to people, animals or property from arrows that miss the target area by overshot or to either side (N.B. a distance of 75 yards from the Clout centre to the boundary of any land to which the public has access is deemed reasonable).

401. Targets

The centre of the Target shall be marked by a brightly coloured distinctive flag 12″ square, set as close as practicable to ground level on a smooth vertical stick. The stick should not project above the flag.

402. Shooting

(*a*) Shooting may be either "two way" or "one way".

(*b*) Six sighter arrows shall be shot in each direction when shooting two ways.

(*c*) The Organiser, after considering general safety, archers' comfort and the duties of scorers, shall use his discretion as to the number of archers allocated to each target.

403. Scoring

(*a*) Scores shall be determined according to the distance of arrows at point of entry in ground from centre of flag stick.

Within a radius of 18 inches—5 points

3 feet—4 points

6 feet—3 points

9 feet—2 points

12 feet—1 point.

Arrows which have hit and remain embedded in the Clout shall score 5 provided they are not embedded in a lower scoring ring whereupon they shall score according to the ring in which they are embedded.

(*b*) Rings of the above radii may be marked on the ground, the lines drawn being wholly within each circle.

(*c*) Where it is not practical to draw lines on the ground, scores shall be determined with a non-stretch cord or tape looped round the centre stick and clearly marked to measure the various radii.

(*d*) No person other than the appointed scorers shall enter the target area until all arrows have been withdrawn and placed in their respective scoring groups. An arrow withdrawn by any other than an appointed scorer shall not be scored.

404. Round

(*a*) A Clout Round consists of 36 arrows.

(*b*) Distances to be shot shall be determined by the organisers. These would normally be:

>for Gentlemen—9 score yards
>for Ladies   —7 score yards

405. National Championship Round

The National Championship shall be decided over a Double Clout Round.

V. CROSSBOW ARCHERY

500. Regulations

The Rules of Target Archery shall apply with the following exceptions:

(*a*) Crossbowmen shall shoot on separate targets from other archers and not compete with them.

(*b*) No person under 16 years of age may shoot unless in adult care and no person less than 12 years of age may shoot or manipulate a crossbow.

501. Equipment

(*a*) A crossbow stock and mechanism may be made from any material. No mechanical aids or rests are permitted. Prods may be made of any other material except metal. The length measured along the curves shall not exceed 36 inches.

(*b*) The draw-length shall be measured from the back of the prod to the string latch. Draw-weight shall not exceed 1280 lb/in with a maximum draw of 18 inches. (To determine the lb/in multiply the draw-length by the draw-weight.) The draw-weight shall be marked on the prod, e.g. 70 lb @ 18″.

(*c*) A string may be made of any non-metallic material.

(*d*) Bolts may be made of any material and of such design as not to cause unreasonable damage to the target. Bolt length is minimum 12 inches, maximum 15 inches. Three fletchings, feather or plastic, shall be fitted.

(*e*) Telescopic or magnifying sights are not allowed.

(*f*) Stirrups attached to the stock or ground are permitted, provided that Rule 501 (*b*) is complied with.

(*g*) Pistol crossbows are not permitted.

(*h*) The use of safety catches is recommended and will become mandatory in 1983.

502. Recognised Rounds

(*a*) Windsor Round shot on a 60 cm F.I.T.A. face scoring 9, 7, 5, 3, 1. The Championship Round shall be a Double Windsor.

(*b*) American Round shot on a 60 cm F.I.T.A. face scoring 10, 9, 8, 7, 6, 5, 4, 3, 2,1.

(*c*) Western Round shot on an 80 cm F.I.T.A. face scoring 10, 9, 8, 7, 6, 5, 4, 3, 2, 1.

(*d*) Any recognised G.N.A.S. or F.I.T.A. Round.

503. Field Archery

(*a*) Current Field Archery Rules shall apply with those exceptions detailed in 500 (*a*) and (*b*).

(*b*) Targets shall be fixed below skyline.

(*c*) Field Rounds as recognised by G.N.A.S. or F.I.T.A. shall be shot.

504. The Crossbow and the Law

When travelling on public transport or walking in a public thoroughfare it is essential that the prod be removed and the stock and prod be carried in a case or cover.

505. Safety Rules

If shooting is interrupted for any reason, crossbows shall be lowered immediately so that they are directed at the ground immediately in front of the shooting line and the bolt removed. Safety catches, where fitted, shall be applied.

VI. OTHER FORMS OF ARCHERY

600. Popinjay Shooting

Set-up for Popinjay

(*a*) The full complement of a Popinjay "roost" shall consist of:

> One Cock Bird
> Four Hens
> Minimum of twenty-four Chicks.

(*b*) Body size of all birds shall be $1\frac{1}{2}''$ long $\frac{3}{4}''$ in diameter—only the plumage shall differ:

—that of the Cock Bird being most resplendent and $10''$–$12''$ high.

—that of the Hen Birds being shorter $6''$–$8''$ high and less colourful.

—that of the Chicks being shortest $3''$–$4''$ high.

(*c*) The Chicks shall be perched on spikes $6''$ long, not less than $4''$ apart, in three rows, the vertical height between rows being not less than 3 feet. The Hen Birds shall be perched on spikes $18''$ above the top row and shall be spaced not less than $8''$ apart.

The Cock Bird shall be perched on a central spike not less than $30''$ above the top row.

(*d*) The perches may be attached to, or hauled up, a mast or wall to a height of 90 feet (measured to the Cock Bird).

Arrangements must be made to ensure that when in position the perches are firmly held against movement by wind.

(*e*) All obstructions on and within the framework of perches must be softened with rubber or sponge rubber (or similar resilient material) to lessen the risk of arrow breakage.

(*f*) No hard and fast shooting position is dictated, although it should be pointed out to all competitors that a near vertical, close to mast attitude will offer a better target to the archer, inasmuch as a greater number of birds will be in line of the arrow flight path.

(*g*) Each and every part of the Popinjay Mast and Framework of Perches must be made to be safe from breakage and/or dislodgement by arrow or the elements.

(*h*) Whenever possible a shelter should be provided for com-

ARCHERY

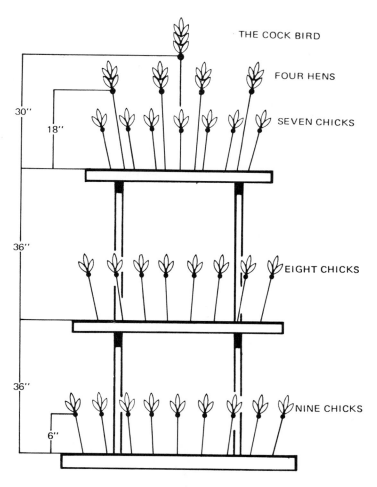

Typical Popinjay "roost" showing minimum complement.

petitors, a temporary structure approx. 7′6″ high covered on top with ½″ wire mesh is sufficient for this purpose. If no shelter is available competitors waiting to shoot must be made to wait outside the arrow fall-out area.

601. Arrows

Only arrows with blunts ¾″ to 1″ in diameter shall be used.

602. Shooting

(*a*) Archers will draw for order of shooting.

(*b*) Only one archer shall shoot at a time.

(*c*) Archers must shoot in rotation—only one arrow being shot per end.

(*d*) Disabled archers may shoot with the aid of a prop.

603. Mast Captain

A Mast Captain shall be appointed to ensure that shooting is conducted in a safe and proper manner.

604. Scoring

(*a*) The scoring points for hits are:

  Cock Bird—5 points
  Hen Bird —3 points
  Chick   —1 point

(*b*) Birds must be struck with the arrow and be dislodged and fall to the ground to score.

605. "Round"

Results may be determined by time limit or by a declared number of arrows.

606. Regulations for Tournaments

Popinjay Tournament Schedules shall bear the following information:

(*a*) Whether competition is determined by time limit or by number of arrows shot her person.

(*b*) Maximum number of archers that will be accepted.

Note: The G.N.A.S. Insurance Scheme does not cover for risks attendant on the erection and dismantling of Popinjay Masts.

620. Archery Golf
Regulations

(*a*) Only one bow shall be used throughout a round. In case of breakage it may be replaced.

(*b*) Any arrows may be used.

(*c*) The archer shall "hole out" by hitting a white cardboard disc 4″ in diameter, placed on the ground at least one yard within the edge of the green level with the hole.

(*d*) An arrow landing off the fairway or in a bunker shall incur one extra stroke.

(*e*) The archer must stand immediately behind where his arrow lands to shoot the next arrow.

(*f*) A lost arrow incurs the normal penalty (as in golf) for stroke play but loses the hole in match play.

(*g*) The winner of the previous "hole" takes the first shot for the next hole.

(*h*) The current Golf Rules and local Course Regulations shall apply in all cases not covered by the foregoing rules.

640. Archery Darts
Regulations

The Rules of Target Archery shall apply with the following exceptions:

Target Faces

Archery Darts Faces 76.2 cm (2′ 6″) in diameter shall be used.

General Rules

(*a*) The Targets shall be set up so that the centre of the Bull is at the centre of a 122 cm minimum diameter boss 130 cm from the ground.

(*b*) The minimum shooting distance shall be 13.7 m (15 yds).

(*c*) An End shall consist of three arrows unless a game is finished in less.

(*d*) The order of starting shall be determined by the toss of a coin.

(*e*) Each match must start and finish on a Double (the narrow outer ring). The inner ring counts treble; the inner Bull counts 50; and the outer Bull 25.

(*f*) A practice end of three arrows must be shot at the Bull.

(*g*) The value of an arrow shall be determined by the position of the greater part of the shaft.

(*h*) Scoring shall be by the subtraction method, so that the score required for the completion of each game is always shown.

(*i*) If the score required to complete the game is exceeded in the course of an End, then that End ceases, and no account is taken of the score obtained during that End.

Note: Local variations may be used.

VIII. RECORDS

800. National Record

A National Record may be established and submitted to National Council for ratification at:

(*a*) Any Meeting organised by F.I.T.A., F.I.T.A. Members, G.N.A.S., Regional Societies.

(*b*) Any Meeting which has applied to National Council by 31st December for prior recognition and has been granted such status. It shall be a condition that such meeting shall be open to all members of G.N.A.S.

801. Submission of Claims

Claims for National Records shall be submitted to the G.N.A.S. Secretary on the appropriate form except for National Championships and U.K. Masters Tournament when the Secretary will submit claims to National Council.

The claim forms must be completed prior to the dispersal of the Meetings at which the record has been made, one copy shall be handed to the archer and one copy retained by the Tournament Organiser. Both copies must be sent to the Secretary within 28 days of the date on which the record was made.

The claim form sent by the Tournament Organiser shall be accompanied by the original score sheet (or a photo copy) and the results sheet as circulated.

802. Target Archery

(*a*) A world record may be established for the F.I.T.A.

Round and each distance of the F.I.T.A. Round according to qualifications laid down in F.I.T.A. Rules.

Claims for World Records shall be submitted to the G.N.A.S. Secretary supported by the necessary documents for onward transmission to F.I.T.A. for ratification.

(b) National Records may be claimed for any single or double round shot at recognised Record Status Meetings but where a Double Round is shot on the one day the second Round will not be accepted for Record purposes.

803. Field Archery

Record Rounds are restricted to Unmarked Hunter, Marked Field and F.I.T.A. Combination Rounds.

804. Flight Shooting

(a) National records may be claimed in all classes. The measurements must be checked and witnessed by the Range Captain and one other responsible person. In addition the Range Captain must certify that the ground over which the shot was made was reasonably flat and level.

(b) A new record may be established when the measurement is at least one yard longer than an existing record.

805. Clout Shooting

National records may be established for "one way" and "two way" when shooting is at the following distances:

Gentlemen—9 score yards
Ladies   —7 score yards

IX. CLASSIFICATION AND HANDICAP SCHEMES

900. Classification Regulations for all Disciplines

(a) The use of the Classification Scheme by Clubs is optional and the administration of it shall be in the hands of Club officials.

(b) Initial grading or subsequent upgrading occurs immediately the necessary scores have been made in the calendar year.

(*c*) The qualification holds for one year immediately following that in which it is gained. If it is not maintained during that year, reclassification shall be on the scores made during the year.

(*d*) The scheme shall apply only to those archers using equipment defined in Clause 102 (*a*).

901. Target Archery

(*a*) To gain Class I, II or III a member must shoot during the calendar year and under G.N.A.S. Rules of Shooting, three Rounds of, or better than, the scores set out in Table A at a meeting organised by G.N.A.S. or a body affiliated to G.N.A.S. or at an Associated Club Target Day when a minimum of two archers are shooting together.

(*b*) **Master Bowman**

(i) Qualifying Rounds: York, F.I.T.A. (Gentlemen); Hereford, F.I.T.A. (Ladies).

(ii) Number of Rounds: Four, including at least one York/Hereford and one F.I.T.A.

(iii) Any two of the Rounds must be shot at a meeting organised by F.I.T.A., F.I.T.A. Members, G.N.A.S., a Regional Society or County Association. The remainder may be shot at any of the above or at any Associated Club Tournament or Target Day when a minimum of two archers are shooting together on the same target.

(*c*) **Grand Master Bowman**

(i) Qualifying Rounds: York, F.I.T.A. (Gentlemen); Hereford, F.I.T.A. (Ladies).

(ii) Number of Rounds: 2 F.I.T.A., 1 York/Hereford.

(iii) All Rounds must be shot at Meetings organised by F.I.T.A., F.I.T.A. Members, G.N.A.S. or a Regional Society, including Regional Inter-County Tournaments whether such meetings are open or closed.

(*d*) **Junior Master Bowman**

(i) Qualifying Rounds: York, Bristol I, Men's F.I.T.A., Ladies' F.I.T.A., Metric I (Boys); Hereford, Bristol II, Ladies' F.I.T.A., Metric I, Metric II (Girls).

(ii) Number of Rounds: Four of the Rounds must be shot,

Table A   Qualifying Scores—Senior

	G.M.B.	M.B.	1st Class	2nd Class	3rd Class
Gentlemen:					
York	1085	1000	798	560	342
F.I.T.A.	1223	1153	980	753	512
St. George			646	475	304
New Western			512	347	202
New National			368	243	139
Long Metric			431	302	181
Short Metric				451	331
Hereford				760	519
Albion				614	436
Long Western				494	330
Long National				351	228
Western					455
National					330
Windsor					568
American					473
Ladies:					
Hereford	1112	1033	843	606	378
F.I.T.A.	1198	1121	933	688	439
Albion			672	502	325
Long Western			551	389	236
Long National			395	272	161
Long Metric			443	312	187
Short Metric				376	253
Western				516	348
National				375	249
Windsor				631	450
American				525	375

with a minimum of one and a maximum of three F.I.T.A./ Metric Rounds.

(iii) One Round must be shot at a meeting organised by F.I.T.A., F.I.T.A. Members, G.N.A.S., a Regional Society or County Association. The other three Rounds may be shot at the above or at a Club Tournament or Target Day with a minimum of two archers shooting supervised by a Senior.

902. Field Archery

(*a*) Qualifying Rounds: F.I.T.A. Hunter, F.I.T.A. Field and F.I.T.A. Combination.

(*b*) Qualifying scores: As in Table below.

(*c*) **Grand Master Bowman**

(i) Number of Rounds (each Round must be of the required standard):

> 2 Hunter, 2 Field
>
> 2 Hunter, 1 Field, 1 Combination
>
> 1 Hunter, 2 Field, 1 Combination

(ii) All Rounds must be shot at Meetings organised by F.I.T.A., F.I.T.A. Members, G.N.A.S., a Regional Championship Meeting, a Regional Inter-Counties Meeting, County Championship or any competition granted National Record Status (only two scores shot at the same venue may be used for this qualification).

(*d*) **Master Bowman**

(i) Number of Rounds (each Round must be of the required standard):

> 3 Hunter, 1 Field
>
> 2 Hunter, 2 Field
>
> 1 Hunter, 3 Field
>
> 2 Hunter, 1 Field, 1 F.I.T.A. Combination
>
> 1 Hunter, 2 Field, 1 F.I.T.A. Combination

(ii) Two Rounds must be shot at Meetings detailed in (*c*)(ii) above. The remainder may be shot at any of the above or at any Associated Club Open Tournament when a minimum of three archers are shooting together on one target.

(*e*) **Classes I, II & III**

N.B. Qualifying scores may be obtained by shooting the same Unit twice.

(i) Number of Rounds:

1st Class:	As for Master Bowman
2nd & 3rd Class:	Two Rounds, each of which must be of the required standard

(ii) Rounds must be shot at any of the Meetings detailed in (d) (ii) above or at a Classification Shoot when a minimum of three archers are shooting together on the same target.

TABLE C Qualifying score tables

	GMB	MB	1st CLASS	2nd CLASS	3rd CLASS
Freestyle:					
Ladies	400	350	300	230	160
Gentlemen	440	400	350	270	180
Girls		300	250	180	100
Boys		350	300	230	150
Barebow:					
Ladies	350	300	230	160	110
Gentlemen	400	350	300	230	160
Girls		230	180	110	60
Boys		300	250	180	100
Traditional:					
Ladies	300	230	160	110	60
Gentlemen	350	300	230	160	110
Girls		180	110	60	40
Boys		230	180	110	60

(There is no separate scheme for those under 15 years of age. Should such Juniors wish to enter the classification scheme they must shoot the full distance.)

903. Flight Shooting

(a) Archers can qualify as Master Flight Shot or 1st Class Flight Shot at any Flight Shoot organised by G.N.A.S., a Regional Society or County Association under G.N.A.S. Rules of Shooting.

(b) Archers can qualify as Grand Master Flight Shot at any of the above except that the County Association Meeting must be the County Championships.

(c) Minimum distances:

	Ladies	Gentlemen
Grand Master Flight Shot	450 yards	550 yards
Master Flight Shot	340 yards	440 yards
1st Class Flight Shot	275 yards	375 yards

904. Crossbow Shooting

Using the Windsor Round.

Qualifying Scores

Master Arbalist	780	3 scores	(2 and 1)	
Arbalist 1st Class	630	3 scores	(1 and 2)	see
Arbalist 2nd Class	480	3 scores	(1 and 2)	below

Qualifying Meetings

For the Master Arbalist 2 and for the 1st and 2nd Class Arbalist 1, scores must be made at a Meeting organised by F.I.T.A., F.I.T.A. Members, G.N.A.S., a Regional Society, or County Association. The remainder may be shot at any of the above or at any Associated Club Tournament or Target Day when a minimum of two archers are shooting together on the same Target.

905. Submission of Claim

(a) Claims for the title of Grand Master and Master in all disciplines shall be submitted to the G.N.A.S. Secretary on the appropriate form. The Secretary will, on behalf of the National Council:

(i) Satisfy himself as to the validity of the claim.

(ii) Notify the claimant and send him the appropriate badge.

(iii) Publicise the award.

(b) It shall be the responsibility of the archer concerned to submit the claim together with the following documents of proof.

(i) **Rounds shot at Club Meetings.** The original score sheet endorsed by an Officer of the Club to the effect that the Round was shot at a Club Tournament or Target Day.

(ii) **Rounds shot at any other Meeting.** The official Result Sheet sent out by the Organiser(s) of the Meeting.

(*c*) Any such claim shall also include a certificate that the archer was using a bow recognised as in Rule 102 (*a*).

920. Handicap Scheme

Copies of the G.N.A.S. Handicap Tables, which include the Rules for the operation of the Scheme, can be obtained from the G.N.A.S. Secretary.

921. Handicap Improvement Medal

(*a*) The medals are Challenge Trophies and remain the property of the G.N.A.S.

(*b*) One medal will be loaned on application to any Club having not less than ten shooting members, which has been an Associated Club of the Society for at least twelve months.

(*c*) In the event of a Club ceasing to function, the Secretary thereof will be personally responsible for returning the medal to the Society.

(*d*) The Club will notify to the Secretary the name and address of the winner of the medal each year immediately it has been awarded (giving old and new handicap figures) or, if it has not been duly competed for, will return it to the Society.

(*e*) (i) The medal is to be awarded to the member, lady or gentleman, who having been a member of the Club for not less than six months prior to January 1st attains the greatest improvement in handicap during the following calendar year provided that he or she shall have shot not fewer than twelve rounds on his or her own Club Target Days during that period, in addition to any eligible rounds shot elsewhere. If owing to adverse weather, no member has shot twelve rounds on Club Target Days during the period, the Club Committee has discretion to make the award on a slightly lesser number of rounds.

(ii) In the event of a tie, those who tied shall shoot it off on a day and round to be decided by the Club, or, at the Club's discretion, the medal may be awarded to the member with the greatest number of attendances during the period amongst those who have tied.

(*f*) The G.N.A.S. Handicap Regulations and Tables must be used for assessing all handicaps in connection with the award of these medals.

(*g*) The holder of the medal should wear it on all Club Target Days at which he or she is present. It is left to each Club to impose any penalty in this connection.

Printed by permission of the Grand National Archery Society. Many of the Rules have here been abbreviated for reasons of space. Copies of the complete Rules and Regulations, including those for Junior Archery, can be obtained from the Society.

The Rules of
Athletics

Athletics

These are extracts from the official Rules for Competitions under the Laws of the A.A.A. (see Note on p. 82). The following terms, used throughout, have the following meanings:

Area Association: Northern Counties A.A.A., Midland Counties A.A.A., Southern Counties A.A.A., Welsh A.A.A., and such other 'Area' Associations as may be formed by the A.A.A. from time to time.

"District": A District of the N.C.A.A., a group of Counties or similar geographical sub-divisions of an "Area" having a separate Committee for administrative purposes.

"Club": Club, Business House Club, University, College, School, Service Unit, Pre-Service Unit or other Society or Association of Amateur Athletes.

AMATEUR DEFINITION

1. All competitions held under the Laws of the Association are confined to amateurs under the following definitions:

(1) An amateur is a person of the male sex who competes for the love of sport and as a means of recreation, without any motive of securing any material gain from such competition.

(2) Competition under A.A.A. Laws is restricted to amateur athletes who are under the jurisdiction of a Member of the I.A.A.F. and who are eligible to compete under the rules laid down by the A.A.A.

(3) Persons ineligible to take part in competitions under A.A.A. Rules *are listed in detail under this heading in "A.A.A. Rules for Competition".*

An athlete who is a qualified teacher of Physical Education recognised by the Ministry of Education does not lose his amateur status by being so employed.

The *expenses* of any athlete may be paid by the body responsible for the entry, *subject to the detailed provisions set out in "A.A.A. Rules for Competition" under this heading.*

GENERAL CONDITIONS

2. (1) In these Rules the term "14 years of age" on a given date refers to an athlete whose 14th birthday falls on or before the date, but who has not reached his 15th birthday. Similarly for "15 years of age", etc.

(2) Open Competitions:

(*a*) Individual:

(i) An Open Competition is one which is open to all athletes who have reached the age of 18 years and which is not confined to members of Closed Clubs.

(ii) After one year of Open Competition, after having reached the age of 18, a competitor must become a member of a Club or Association affiliated directly or indirectly to the A.A.A.

(iii) A competitor taking part in an Open Competition must have reached the age of 18 years on the day of competition. Competitors who are under 18 may compete in certain Open Competitions, as specified in Rules 20, 21 and 22 below. Competitors who are 18, 19 and 20, taking part in Cross Country, Road Running and Road Relay Running, are governed by Rule 21 (2) and (3). Competitors who are 15 and 16 may compete in certain Open Competitions, as specified in Rule 20 (1).

(*b*) Team:

(i) Open Team Competitions, Team Contests, Relay Races, Team Races and Tugs-of-War are competitions open to all clubs and not confined to Closed Clubs.

(ii) Invitation inter-club competitions are not Open Competitions unless more than 6 teams are invited. The promoters may make such qualifying conditions as they think fit, including the right to stipulate that the competition is for first-claim members only.

(3) The following are *not* Open Competitions: events confined to H.M. Services; events confined to employees of a particular trade or occupation; events promoted in rural areas and confined to residents within 10 miles radius from the ground.

(4) Every Club, Society and Managing Body promoting an

athletic meeting under A.A.A. Laws, and every person tendering an entry, shall be deemed to have submitted to the jurisdiction of the Association on all questions which may arise.

3. No club or member under the jurisdiction of the A.A.A. may compete outside the United Kingdom, and no foreign club or member may compete within England and Wales, without the permission of the General Committee, except in the International Cross-Country Race.

No British athlete resident in England and Wales may compete under A.A.A. Laws as a member of a foreign athletic club.

REGISTRATION

5. Anyone competing in any open athletic competition in England or Wales promoted by a Club, Association or Managing Body which is not affiliated to an Area Association (or the British Cycling Federation), or in possession of a Certificate of Registration for that particular competition, shall thereby disqualify himself from competing under A.A.A. Laws.

The following do not require registration: events confined to members of any particular club or firm; events promoted by and confined to H.M. Services; events confined to employees of a County or Local Authority; events open to pre-Service Organisations, combinations of Schools, Boy Scouts, Youth Clubs and other Juvenile Organisations.

Open Cross-Country Races and Tug-of-War competitions may be held only by organisations holding permits from those sports associations.

ENTRIES

6. Every entry shall be made to the Secretary of the promoting body, who has the right to refuse an entry without giving a reason.

7. No entry either for individual or team events may be made except upon the form approved, which must be dated and completed with all the particulars required.

8. Every entry must be made in the real name of the competitor, which shall appear on the programme.

9. Every individual entry shall be signed by the intending competitor, who shall be responsible for all statements therein.

10. Every entry for a Colts', Boys', Youths', Juniors' or Veterans' race shall state the date of birth and present age in years and months of the intending competitor.

11. Every entry for a team competition shall be signed by the Secretary of the club on whose behalf the entry is made.

12. No entry may be accepted unless accompanied by the stipulated entrance fee.

13. *Spare*.

14. When an athlete is a member of two or more Clubs, the Club he has belonged to for the longest unbroken period shall have first claim upon his services. While at school an athlete remains first claim to his school.

15. An Open Club is a Club whose membership is not confined to persons in a particular occupation or business organisation. All other Clubs, societies and organisations affiliated directly or indirectly to an Area Association shall be deemed Closed Clubs.

16. Ineligibility of a competitor in an Inter-Club or Inter-Team competition does not necessarily disqualify the club he represents and in such a case the competition shall be decided as if the ineligible competitor had not taken part.

17. In open team competitions, consisting of several events, the total entry of each competing club shall not exceed twice the number allowed to compete. All entrants are eligible to compete in any of the events comprising the competition.

In an open relay race, clubs shall not be allowed to enter more than three times the number entitled to compete. A club entering more than one team in a race shall be allowed to select their teams from the Club Entry for that event. Teams must be declared before the start of the race.

No one shall be allowed to compete in a team unless his name appears on the programme in the Club Entry. If it is impracticable to issue a programme, it is recommended that a complete list of the entries should be provided for the information of the Referee.

RULES FOR COMPETITIONS CONFINED TO PARTICULAR CLASSES

18. Colts:

(1) Track (excluding Track Walking) and Field Events for Colts shall be confined to competitors who have reached their 11th but not their 13th birthdays by midnight August 31st/ September 1st in the year of competition. Colts shall not be allowed to compete in more than three individual events on one day. This rule does not apply to Pentathlon and Decathlon competitions. Colts may compete in events up to 3,000 m. (but not the steeplechase). Colts may not compete against Youth/ Juniors or Seniors in any events.

(2) Road running and Road Relay running for Colts shall be confined to competitors who are 12 and 13 years of age on April 1st for competitions held between April 1st and August 31st, or on August 31st for competitions held between September 1st and March 31st. The distance shall not exceed $2\frac{1}{2}$ miles.

(3) Cross Country running for Colts shall be confined to competitors who are 11 or 12 years of age on September 1st prior to the competition. The distance shall not exceed $2\frac{1}{2}$ miles.

19. Boys:

(1) Track (excluding Track Walking) and Field events for Boys shall be confined to competitors who have reached their 13th but not their 15th birthdays by midnight August 31st/ September 1st in the year of competition. Boys shall not be allowed to compete in more than three individual events on one day. This rule does not apply to Pentathlon and Decathlon competitions. Boys may not compete in steeplechases.

(2) Road running and Road Relay running for Boys shall be confined to competitors who are 14 and 15 on April 1st (for competitions held between April 1st and August 31st) or August 31st (for competitions between September 1st and March 31st). The distance shall not exceed 3 miles.

(3) Cross Country running for Boys shall be confined to competitors who are 13 or 14 on September 1st prior to the competition. The distance shall not exceed 3 miles.

(4) Track and Road Walking for Boys shall be confined to competitors who have reached their 12th but not their 15th birthdays on August 31st in the year of competition. The distance shall not exceed 3 miles.

20. Youths:

(1) Track (including Track Walking) and Field events for Youths shall be confined to competitors who have reached their 15th but not their 17th birthdays by midnight August 31st/September 1st in the year of competition. They shall not be allowed to compete in more than three individual events on any one day. This rule does not apply to Pentathlon and Decathlon competitions.

(2) Road Running and Road Relay Running for Youths shall be confined to competitors who are 16 and 17 on April 1st (for competitions held between April 1st and August 31st) or August 31st (for competitions between September 1st and March 31st). The distance shall not exceed 4 miles.

(3) Cross Country Running for Youths shall be confined to competitors who are 15 or 16 on September 1st prior to the competition. The distance shall not exceed 4 miles.

(4) Road Walking for Youths shall be confined to competitors who have reached their 15th but not their 17th birthdays on August 31st in the year of competition. The distance should not exceed 3 miles for first year Youths nor 5 miles for second year Youths.

21. Juniors:

(1) Track (including Track Walking) and Field events for Juniors shall be confined to competitors who have reached their 17th birthdays by midnight August 31st/September 1st but not their 20th birthdays by midnight December 31st in the year of competition. They shall not be allowed to compete in more than three individual events on any one day. This rule does not apply to Pentathlon and Decathlon competitions.

(2) Road Running and Road Relay Running for Juniors shall be confined to competitors aged 18 and 19 on April 1st (for competitions held between April 1st and August 31st) or August 31st (for competitions between September 1st and March 31st). The distance shall not exceed 6 miles.

(3) Cross Country running for Juniors shall be confined to

competitors who are 17, 18 or 19 on September 1st prior to competition. The distance shall not exceed 6 miles.

(4) Road Walking for Juniors shall be confined to competitors who have reached their 17th but not their 21st birthdays on August 31st in the year of competition. The distance should not exceed 7 miles if the competitors are 17.

22. Seniors:

(1) In Track (including Track Walking) and Field events a Senior is a competitor aged at least 19 on September 1st in the year of competition. A competitor aged at least 18 on the day of competition may be allowed to take part in any Senior event.

(2) A competitor in a Senior Road Race or Senior Road Relay Race where the Race or Section does not exceed 15 km ($9\frac{1}{2}$ miles) must be at least 17 on the day of competition. Where the Race or Section exceeds 15 km, he must be at least 18.

23. Veterans:

Events for Veterans shall be confined to competitors aged at least 40 on the day of competition.

24. Novices:

(1) For the purposes of Novice Competitions, Track and Field events are divided into: (a) Running, Hurdling and Steeplechase; (b) Jumping and Vaulting; (c) Throwing; and (d) Walking.

(2) A competition advertised as a Novice Competition for Track and Field events other than Walking shall be confined to competitors who, at the time, have never won a prize in an open competition of the same class. A Walking Novice is one who has not reached the age of 16 or won a prize in any walking event. A Cross Country Novice is one who has not, since the age of 16, won a prize in a running event of 1 mile and upwards.

25. Competitors in Consolation Races must have competed without winning a prize in an event at the meeting.

RULES FOR PROMOTING BODIES

33. Any Club or Association desirous of obtaining a Certificate of Registration for a Sports Meeting must make application to the Hon. Sec. of the County Association or District Committee in whose area the event is to be held. Applications

for the registration of Cross-Country races must be made to the Hon. Sec., E.C.C.U.

Where any open event for women or girls is included, a permit must be obtained from the W.A.A.A. unless the promoting body is affiliated thereto.

No Club, Association or Managing Body shall permit any athletic event to be televised, either live or subsequently, without prior permission of the A.A.A.

34. All advertisements, programmes, etc. shall state that the Meeting is held "under A.A.A. Laws". This does not apply to International Meetings.

35. If an open team event is included, full particulars shall be clearly stated. In the case of a relay race, the distance of each section, and the order in which the sections are to be run, must be similarly stated.

36. Every club or committee to which a permit has been granted must exhibit it in a conspicuous place in the competitors' dressing-room.

37. Every programme shall state: (*a*) the value of each prize offered for competition; (*b*) the date on which the handicaps were made; and (*c*) the name and club, or, if unattached, the place of residence, of each person whose entry has been accepted, and his handicap mark or time allowance (if any).

38. Within seven days after the competition, a programme marked with the names of the winners, etc., shall be sent to the Hon. Sec. of the Area Association, who shall keep it for reference.

39. No individual or team shall be allowed to compete in any event unless a properly completed entry form has been accepted.

40. In scratch competitions where the composition of heats is printed in the programme, no competitor shall be allowed to compete in any heat other than that in which his name appears; but the Referee shall have power, if he thinks the circumstances justify it, to permit a departure from this rule.

PRIZES

41. Money, saving certificates, bonds, stamps or cheques *must*

not be offered as prizes; nor may vouchers or orders on tradesmen, except for book or record tokens and athletic clothing or equipment.

42. No prize of a greater value than the equivalent of 100 U.S. Dollars shall be offered, except as a Challenge Prize which cannot be won outright in a single competition.

43. The amount actually paid (after deducting any discount) shall be considered the value of the prize.

44. Every objection by a competitor to the value of a prize shall be made within 14 days.

45. Every prize at a meeting where open events are decided shall be publicly presented on the ground on the day of the meeting.

46. Any competitor who receives a prize to which he is not entitled shall return it forthwith on being asked to do so.

47. A Challenge Prize belongs to the promoting body until won outright and must be returned by the holder on request.

48. A Challenge Prize holder who is in all respects eligible to compete has an interest in the trophy and the right to enter the next competition.

49. If properly entered according to the governing conditions, the accidental omission of the holder's name from the programme does not debar him from competing.

DRESSING ACCOMMODATION

50. (*a*) Every promoting body shall provide sufficient and convenient accommodation for the competitors.

(*b*) Where a competition for colts or boys is included, separate dressing accommodation shall whenever possible be provided.

BETTING

51. Open betting must be rigorously suppressed, and notices stating that betting is prohibited must be conspicuously displayed at every entrance.

COMPETITION RULES

Clothing and Footwear

52. In all events competitors must wear at least a vest and shorts which are clean and so designed and worn as not to be objectionable.

53. Competitors may compete in bare feet or with shoes on one or both feet. The purpose of shoes is to give protection and stability to the feet and a firm grip of the ground; they must not be constructed so as to give the competitor any additional assistance.

Numbers

54. Every competitor shall be supplied with and wear during competition a distinctive number corresponding with his number in the programme.

Assistance

55. A competitor shall not receive any assistance, except as provided in these Rules.

Tracks and Measurements

56. The inner edge of all tracks must be distinctly marked, cinder and other permanent tracks preferably by a raised border of concrete or other suitable material 2 in (5 cm) high, otherwise by a chalk line or white tape.

Races up to 120 yd (110 m) must be run on a straight course, in lanes, so as to allow a separate course for each competitor. The width between the lanes must be not less than 4 ft (1.22 m).

Stations

57. In scratch races, stations for competitors shall be drawn, the competitor drawing No. 1 taking, in straight sprint races, the station on the left facing the winning post and, in races on a circular track, the station nearest the centre of the ground.

58. Starting blocks are permissible in races up to and including 400 m. They must be approved by the Starter.

The Start

59. The start of a race shall be denoted by a line marked in chalk 2 in (5 cm) wide at right angles to the inner edge of the track. In all races not run in lanes the starting line shall be curved, so that all competitors cover the same distance.

60. All questions concerning the start shall be in the absolute discretion of the Starter, whose decision shall be final.

61. Competitors must be placed in their respective stations by marksmen. In scratch races, an assembly line shall be drawn 10 ft (3 m) behind the starting line. Marksmen shall place competitors on the assembly lines and signal to the Starter when all is ready. A competitor must not touch either the startline or the ground in front of it with his hands or his feet when on his mark.

62. All races shall be started by the report of a pistol or any similar apparatus. The pistol shall be fired upwards into the air and it is essential that it should give a satisfactory flash which can be seen clearly by the Timekeepers. The time will be taken from the flash.

63. When the Starter has received the signal from the marksman, he shall give the competitors the following commands:

(i) For competitors running a distance up to and including 400 m:

(a) "On your marks";

(b) "Set",

and when all competitors are Set, i.e. motionless on mark, the pistol shall be fired.

(ii) For competitors running, or walking, a distance greater than 400 m:

"On your marks"

and when all competitors are steady the pistol shall be fired.

If for any reason the Starter has to speak to any competitor after the order "On your marks" and before the pistol is fired, he shall order all competitors to stand up and the marksman shall place them on the assembly line again.

If a competitor leaves his mark with hand or foot before the pistol is fired, it shall be considered a false start. Any competitor making a false start shall be warned; if responsible for two false starts, he shall be disqualified.

Winners of Preliminary Heats

65. In the preliminary heats of scratch races, the winners and seconds or fastest loser should qualify for the next round. (A fastest loser is not necessarily the second in the fastest heat.)

66. The following minimum rest must be allowed between the last heat of the round and the first heat of the subsequent round or final:

Up to 100 m	20 min.
100–200 m	40 min.
200–400 m	60 min.
400–800 m	80 min.
Over 800 m	100 min.

The Race

67. Any competitor jostling, running across or obstructing another so as to impede his progress shall be liable to disqualification. The Referee shall have power, in such cases, to order the race to be re-run.

In all races run in lanes, each competitor should keep in his allotted lane from start to finish.

68. A competitor after voluntarily leaving the track shall not be allowed to continue in the race. A competitor who leaves the course of a road race shall not be allowed to continue if by going off course he lessens the distance to be covered.

69. (a) No attendant shall accompany any competitor on the mark or in the race, nor shall any competitor be allowed to receive assistance or refreshment from anyone during a race of 15 km or less.

(b) No official or other person within the arena, except an official timekeeper appointed to do so, shall indicate intermediate times to competitors.

The Finish

70. The finish shall be a line 2 in (5 cm) wide drawn across the track at right angles to the inner edge. Worsted (white 2-ply Botany wool) shall, if possible, be stretched over this line at breast height and fastened to white posts placed at each side. The competitors shall be placed in the order in which any part of the body (i.e. 'torso', as distinguished from neck, head, arms,

legs, hands or feet) reaches the vertical plane of the nearer edge of the Finish Line.

71. Any protest or objection must be made to the Referee or Judges immediately after the competition. *Protests are governed by the regulations set out in detail in Rules 71 to 74 of "A.A.A. Rules for Competition".*

75. Doping before or during competition is forbidden.

FIELD EVENTS

Competition Rules

General

76. A draw shall be made to decide the order in which competitors shall take their trials and this order should be printed on the programme. The Judges shall have power to alter this order.

A competitor cannot hold over any of his trials to a subsequent round, except in the High Jump and Pole Vault. A competitor in a field event who unreasonably delays making a trial renders himself liable to disqualification after warning.

77. (1) Ties in scratch events shall be decided as follows:

(*a*) In jumping or vaulting for height: the competitor with the lowest number of jumps at the height *at which the tie occurs* shall be awarded the higher place; if the tie still remains, the competitor with the lowest total of failures throughout the competition up to the height last cleared shall be awarded the higher place; if the tie still remains, the competitors tying shall have one more jump at the lower height at which they failed, and if no decision is reached the bar should be lowered or raised 1 cm at a time—8 cm in the pole vault—with one jump at each height until the tie is decided.

(*b*) In throwing or jumping for distance: the second best performance of the competitors tying shall decide the tie; if the tie remains, the third best and so on. If the tie still remains and it concerns the first place, the competitors shall have such additional number of extra trials as is required.

High Jump

78. (a) The uprights or posts shall not be moved during the competition unless the Judges consider the take-off or landing ground has become unsuitable. Such a change shall be made only after a round is completed.

(b) Unless such details are specified on the programme, the Judges shall decide the height at which the competition shall start, and the different heights to which the bar will be raised at the end of each round. The competitors shall be informed of the details before the competition begins.

(c) A competitor may commence jumping at any height above the minimum height and may jump at his own discretion at any subsequent height. Three consecutive failures, regardless of the height at which any of them occurs, disqualify from further jumping.

N.B. The effect of this Rule is that a competitor may forgo his second and third jumps or vaults at a particular height (after failing once or twice) and still jump at a subsequent height.

(e) Even after all the other competitors have failed, a competitor is entitled to continue jumping until he has forfeited his right to compete further and his best jump shall be recorded as the winning height.

(e) The employment of weights or grips of any kind is forbidden.

(f) A competitor may place marks to assist him in his run up and take-off and a handkerchief on the cross-bar for sighting purposes. The distance of the run is unlimited.

(g) All measurements shall be made perpendicularly from the ground to the upper side of the cross-bar where it is lowest. A steel or fibre-glass measure should be used. Any measurements of a new height should be made before competitors attempt that height. In the case of records the officials must check the measurement after the height has been cleared. The height shall be recorded to the nearest $\frac{1}{4}$ in (1 cm) below the height measured; i.e. fractions less than $\frac{1}{4}$ in (1 cm) must be ignored.

N.B. Judges should ensure, before commencing the competition, that the under-side and front of the cross-bar are distinguishable, and that the bar is always replaced in a similar manner.

(*h*) A competitor fails if he: (i) in the course of a jump dislodges the bar so that it falls from the pegs; or (ii) touches the ground or landing area beyond the plane of the uprights without clearing the bar; or (iii) takes off from both feet.

79. Any style of uprights or posts may be used provided they are rigid. *See further details under this Rule in "A.A.A. Rules for Competition"*.

80. Ties in High Jump and Pole Vault: *see details in "A.A.A. Rules"*.

Pole Vault

81. No marks shall be placed on the runway, but a competitor may place marks alongside the runway. Any competitor may have the uprights moved in either direction, but they must not be moved more than 2 ft (60 cm) from the prolongation of the inside edge of the top of the stop-board. If the uprights are moved, the Judges should make a remeasurement to ensure there is no variation in the height.

The take-off for the pole shall be from a wooden or metal box.

A competitor fails if he: (i) in the course of a vault dislodges the bar so that it falls from the pegs; (ii) without first having cleared the bar, touches with any part of his body, or with the pole, the ground (including the landing area) beyond the vertical plane of the upper part of the stop-board; (iii) leaves the ground to make a vault and fails to clear the bar; or (iv) at the moment he makes a vault, or after leaving the ground, places his lower hand above the upper one or moves the upper hand higher up on the pole.

82. Any style of uprights or posts may be used provided they are rigid. *Details of specifications are given in "A.A.A. Rules"*.

Long Jump

83. (*a*) The competition may be decided *either* by each competitor being allowed from 3 to 6 trials *or* by each being allowed 3 trials and the three to six best competitors allowed 3 more.

(*b*) Each competitor shall be credited with the best of all his trials.

(*c*) The take-off shall be from a board the edge of which nearer the landing area shall be called the "scratch line". If a competitor takes off before reaching the board, it shall not for that reason be counted as a failure.

(*d*) The distance of the run is unlimited. No marks shall be placed on the runway, but a competitor may place marks alongside the runway. No competitor may place, or cause to be placed, any mark beyond the scratch line.

(*e*) If any competitor touches the ground beyond the scratch line or scratch line extended, with any part of his body, whether running up without jumping or in the act of jumping, it shall be counted as a failure.

(*f*) It shall be counted as a failure if a competitor, after completing a jump, walks back through the landing area.

(*g*) The measurement of the jumps shall be made at right angles from the nearest break in the ground in the landing area made by any part of the competitor's body to the scratch line. If, in the course of landing, a competitor touches the ground outside the landing area nearer to the scratch line than the break in the ground to which the measurement of the jump would have been made, such jump shall not be measured but shall count as a failure. The distance shall be measured to the nearest $\frac{1}{4}$ in (1 cm) below the distance covered.

(*h*) The employment of weights or grips of any kind is forbidden.

Details of Long Jump Specifications are given in Rules 84 and 85 in "A.A.A. Rules".

Triple Jump

86. The *hop* shall be made so that the competitor first lands upon the foot with which he took off, in the *step* he shall land on the other foot, from which subsequently the *jump* is performed. If the competitor while jumping touches the ground with the "sleeping" leg, it shall be considered as a failure.

87. *Details of Triple Jump Specifications are given in "A.A.A. Rules".*

Putting the Shot

88. In order to avoid accidents, competitors must be given instructions that implements must be thrown during practice only from the circles or scratch line or the immediate vicinity, and must be returned during practice or competition by hand and not thrown back to the starting area.

No competitor may place, or cause to be placed, any mark within the throwing sector.

89. Gloves may not be worn.

No device of any kind—e.g. the taping of fingers—which in any way assists a competitor when making a throw shall be allowed. But the use of tape to cover hand injury will be allowed if the Referee is satisfied on medical or other evidence that it is necessary.

A competitor must commence the throw from a stationary position within the circle.

It shall be a foul throw if the competitor, after he has stepped into the circle and started to make the throw, touches with part of his body the ground outside the circle, the top of the stop-board or the top of the circle. The competitor must not leave the circle until the implement has touched the ground, and shall leave from the rear half, indicated by a line across the circle and extended outside.

A foul throw or letting go of the implement in an attempt shall be reckoned as a trial.

The circle must be clearly marked on the ground by chalk, or otherwise, and all measurements must be made from the nearer edge of the mark first made in the ground by the implement to the inner edge of the circle along a line drawn from the mark to the centre of the circle.

In making his puts the competitor may rest his feet against but not on top of the stop-board.

The shot shall be put from the shoulder with one hand only. At the time the competitor takes a stance in the ring, the shot shall touch or be in close proximity to the chin and the hand shall not be dropped below this position during the action of putting. The shot must not be brought behind the line of the shoulders.

For a valid put, the shot must fall so that the point from which measurement is to be made is within the inner edges of lines marking a sector of 40° set out on the ground so that the radii lines cross at the centre of the circle.

All measurements should be made immediately after each put.

Details of Putting the Shot Specifications are given in Rules 89 and 90 in "A.A.A. Rules".

Throwing the Hammer

91. All hammer throws shall be made from an enclosure or cage.

The competitor in his starting position prior to the preliminary swings or turns is allowed to put the head of the hammer on the ground inside or outside the circle.

It shall not be considered a foul throw if the head of the hammer touches the ground when the competitor makes the preliminary swings or turns. But if, after having so touched the ground, he stops throwing so as to begin the trial again, this shall count as a failure.

Details of Throwing the Hammer Specifications are given in Rules 92 and 93 in "A.A.A. Rules".

Throwing the Discus

94. All discus throws shall be made from an enclosure or cage.

For a valid throw the discus must fall so that the point from which measurement is to be made is within the inner edges of lines marking a sector of 40° set out on the ground so that the radii lines cross at the centre of the circle.

95. *Throwing the Discus Specifications are detailed in "A.A.A. Rules".*

Throwing the Javelin

96. The length of the runway shall be not more than 120 ft (36.5 m) but not less than 98 ft 6 in (30 m) and shall be marked by 2 parallel lines 2 in (5 cm) wide and 13 ft 1½ in (4 m) apart.

The throw shall be made from behind an arc of a circle drawn with a radius of 26 ft 3 in (8 m); such arc shall consist of a strip made of wood or metal 2¾ in (7 cm) wide, painted white and

ATHLETICS

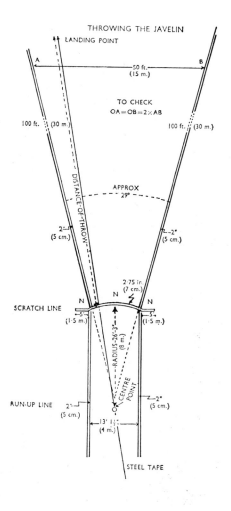

THROWING THE JAVELIN

LANDING POINT

A   50 ft.   B
(15 m.)

TO CHECK

OA = OB = 2 × AB

100 ft.   (30 m.)   100 ft.   (30 m.)

DISTANCE OF THROW

APPROX
29°

2″
(5 cm.)   2″
(5 cm.)

2·75 in.
(7 cm.)

N   N   N

SCRATCH LINE

5′
(1·5 m.)   5′
(1·5 m.)

RADIUS 26′·3″
(8 m.)

CENTRE POINT

RUN-UP LINE   2″
(5 cm.)   2″
(5 cm.)

O

13′ 1½″
(4 m.)

STEEL TAPE

77

sunk flush with the ground. Lines shall be drawn from the extremities of the arc at right angles to the parallel lines marking the runway. These lines shall be 5 ft (1.5 m) long and 2¾ in (7 cm) wide.

All throws to be valid must fall within the inner edge of lines marking the sector set out on the ground by extending for a distance of 95 yd (90 m) the lines from the centre of the circle, of which the arc is a part, through the points at which the arc joins the lines marking the runway. A competitor's throw must not be marked and measured if he steps on the arc or extended scratch lines, or if he crosses the scratch line on the ground marked N (*see diagram*) at any time, before a fair throw has been indicated by the judge at the throwing end. He is allowed to run on or outside the run-up lines provided that at the moment of throwing he is behind the arc and between the run-up lines.

The javelin must be held with one hand only, and at the grip, so that the little finger is nearest to the point. The javelin shall be thrown over the shoulder or upper part of the throwing arm, and must not be slung or hurled. *Non-orthodox styles are not permitted.*

In throwing the javelin no marks shall be placed on the runway but competitors may place marks at the side of the runway.

No throw shall be valid in which the tip of the metal head does not strike the ground before any other part of the javelin, or if the competitor crosses the scratch line or its extension. The competitor must not place his foot or feet upon the scratch line or board.

Javelin Specifications are detailed in Rule 97 of "A.A.A. Rules". Rules 98–100 are spare.

RULES FOR PARTICULAR EVENTS

Hurdle Races

101. A hurdle should consist of two uprights, or standards, supporting a rectangular frame or gate and should have a level top rail. The hurdle may be adjustable in height, but must be rigidly fastened at the required height for each event.

102. All races shall be run in lanes and each competitor shall run in his own lane throughout. He shall be disqualified if he trails his foot or leg alongside any hurdle, or jumps any hurdle not in his own lane, or deliberately knocks down any hurdle by hand or foot.

Hurdle races for Seniors should be over 10 flights of hurdles as follows:

Distance of Race	Height of Hurdles	From Start to First Hurdle	Between Hurdles	From Last Hurdle to Finish
110 m	106.7 cm	13.72 m	9.14 m	14.02 m
200 m	76.2 cm	18.29 m	18.29 m	17.10 m
400 m	91.4 cm	45 m	35 m	40 m

In Women's 100 m hurdles, over 10 flights, height of hurdles should be 84 cm, 13 m from start to first hurdle, 8.5 m between hurdles, and 10.5 m from last hurdle to finish.

Steeplechases

103. (*a*) The standard distances shall be: (i) 3,000 m (1 mile 1,520 yd 2 ft 8 in). There shall be 28 hurdles and 7 water jumps. (ii) 2,000 m (1 mile 427 yd 0 ft 9 in). There shall be 18 hurdles and 5 water jumps. (iii) 1,500 m (1,640 yd 1 ft 4 in). There shall be 13 hurdles and 3 water jumps.

(*b*) The hurdles shall be 3 ft (91.4 cm) high. Each flight shall be at least 12 ft (3.66 m) in total width. The water jump shall be 12 ft (3.66 m) in width and length, the water being 2 ft 3·5 in (70 cm) deep at the hurdle end and sloping to field level at the farther end.

(*c*) Every competitor must go over or through the water. He shall be disqualified if he jumps to the right or left of the water jump or trails his leg or foot alongside any obstacle. He may jump or vault over each hurdle and may place a foot on each hurdle and on the hurdle at the water jump.

Pentathlon and Decathlon

104. The Pentathlon (men) consists of 5 events in the following order: Long Jump, Throwing the Javelin, 200 Metres, Throwing

the Discus, and 1,500 Metres; (women) 100 m Hurdles, the Shot, High and Long Jumps and 800 Metres. The Decathlon consists of 10 events in the following order: 100 Metres, Long Jump, Putting the Shot, High Jump and 400 Metres on the first day; 110 Metres Hurdles, Throwing the Discus, Pole Vault, Throwing the Javelin and 1,500 Metres on the following day. It is permissible to decide all the events on the same day and in that case the order may be varied. Any athlete failing to take part in any of the events shall be considered to have abandoned the competition.

Relay Races

105. (*a*) Chalk lines shall be drawn across the track to mark the distance of the stages and to denote the scratch line.

(*b*) Chalk lines shall also be drawn 11 yd (10 m) before and after the scratch line to denote the take-over zone.

(*c*) The positions of the teams at the start of the race shall be drawn and shall be retained at each take-over zone, except that in races where lanes are not used, or have ceased to operate, waiting runners can move to the inside position as incoming team-mates arrive, provided this can be done without fouling.

(*d*) When relay races up to 400 m are contested on a circular track, each team should, if possible, have a separate lane and each lane must be the full distance.

(*e*) Except for the first runner, where the stage to be run does not exceed 200 m the outgoing runner may commence his run not more than 11 yd (10 m) outside the take-over zone: where the stage exceeds 200 m the outgoing runner must commence his run within the take-over zone. Additional chalk lines in a different colour from that used for the take-over zone markings should be drawn to indicate the additional 11 yd (10 m) zone at all change-over points.

(*f*) In events where the first lap only is run in lanes, competitors after leaving the take-over zone are free to take up any positions on the track.

(*g*) In sprint relay races up and down a track, the take-over is by touch, contact being made within a clearly defined area of 1 yd (1 m) beyond, and at each end of, the relay distance.

(*h*) The baton must be carried in the hand throughout the

race, and if dropped must be recovered by the athlete who dropped it. The baton must be passed only within the take-over zone.

(*i*) Competitors after handing over the baton should remain in their lanes or zones until the course is clear. Should any competitor wilfully impede a member of another team, he is liable to cause his own team to be disqualified.

(*j*) Assistance by pushing-off or any other method will cause disqualification.

(*k*) When a relay race is being run in lanes, a competitor may place a check mark on the track within his own lane but may not place, or cause to be placed, any marking object on or alongside the track.

(*l*) Once a team has competed in the preliminary round(s) of an event its composition must not be altered, except in the case of injury or illness.

(*m*) It is permissible for the order of running to be changed between heats and succeeding round or final.

(*n*) No competitor may run two sections for a team.

(*o*) The baton shall be a smooth hollow tube circular in section made of any rigid material in one piece, not more than 1 ft (30 cm) and not less than 11 in (28 cm) long. The circumference shall be $4\frac{3}{4}$–5 in (12–13 cm) and the weight not less than $1\frac{3}{4}$ oz (50 gm).

Team Races

106. The composition of a team must not be changed after a heat has been run, except through injury or illness. Only competitors finishing the full distance are eligible to compete in the final.

The team scoring the least number of points, according to the positions in which the members of the team finish whose positions are to count, shall be the winner. In the case of a tie on points, the team whose last scoring member finished nearest the first place shall be the winner.

Road Running

107. Road races, including Marathon races, shall be run on roads. Runners must follow the traffic rules of the road,

especially at roundabouts; when traffic makes it unsuitable, the course may be on a bicycle path or footpath alongside the road, but should not be on soft ground such as verges. The start and finish may be in an enclosed ground or arena.

The term 'Marathon Race' shall only be applied to a race of 26 miles 385 yd (42,195 m).

Walking Races

108. Walking is progression by steps so taken that unbroken contact with the ground is maintained, i.e. the advancing foot must make contact with the ground before the rear foot leaves it. Any competitor disqualified by a walking Judge must at once retire from the competition.

Tug-of-War Rules

The complete rules for Tug-of-War are included in the Tug-of-War Association Handbook.

109. Teams shall consist of an equal number of pulling members with a maximum of 8 per team. In Senior competitions no pulling member shall be under 17. All heats shall be won by two pulls out of three.

The rope shall not be less than 4 in (10 cm) and not more than 5 in (12.5 cm) in circumference, and the minimum length not less than 35 yd (32 m).

The rope shall have a coloured tape or marking at the centre; two white ones each 6 ft 6¾ in (2 m) on either side of the centre marking; and two additional coloured ones each 16 ft 6 in (5 m) on either side of the centre marking. Ground markings shall consist of three lines parallel to each other, the distance between the centre line and each of the others being 6 ft 6¾ in (2 m).

A Pull shall be won when one of the side markings on the rope is pulled over the side ground line farthest from it.

Printed by permission of the A.A.A. It should be noted that many of the Rules given above have here been abbreviated for reasons of space. Copies of the current edition of the A.A.A. Handbook, containing the complete A.A.A. Rules for Competitions, are available from the Association, price £2.25 including packing and postage.

The Laws of
Badminton

DIAGRAM (A).

Measurements are quoted in Feet (') and Inches ('') and in Metres.

DIAGRAM (B). Singles Court.

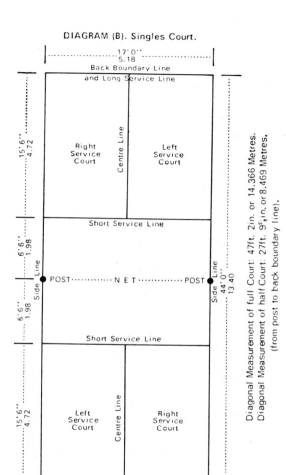

Measurements are quoted in Feet (') and Inches ('') and in Metres.

Badminton

Court

1. (*a*) The Court shall be laid out as in Diagram 'A' (except in the case provided for in paragraph (*b*) of this Law) and to the measurements there shown, and shall be defined preferably by white or yellow lines or, if this is not possible, by other equally distinguishable lines, $1\frac{1}{2}$ in (40 mm) wide.

In marking the court, the width, $1\frac{1}{2}$ in (40 mm) of the centre lines shall be equally divided between the right and left service courts; the width, $1\frac{1}{2}$ in (40 mm) each, of the short service line and the long service line shall fall within the 13 ft (3.96 m) measurement given as the length of the service court; and the width, $1\frac{1}{2}$ in (40 mm) each, of all other boundary lines shall fall within the measurements given.

(*b*) Where space does not permit of the marking out of a court for doubles, a court may be marked out for singles only as shown in Diagram "B". The back boundary lines become also the long service lines, and the posts, or the strips of material representing them as referred to in Law 2, shall be placed on the side lines.

Posts

2. The posts shall be 5 ft 1 in (1.55 m) in height from the surface of the court. They shall be sufficiently firm to keep the net strained as provided in Law 3, and shall be placed on the side boundary lines of the court. Where this is not practicable, some method must be employed for indicating the position of the side boundary line where it passes under the net, e.g. by the use of a thin post or strip of material, not less than $1\frac{1}{2}$ in (40 mm) in width, fixed to the side boundary line and rising vertically to the net cord. Where this is in use on a court marked for doubles it shall be placed on the boundary line of the doubles court irrespective of whether singles or doubles are being played.

Net

3. The net shall be made of fine natural cord or artificial fibre of a dark colour and even thickness with a mesh not less than $\frac{5}{8}$ in (15 mm) and not more than $\frac{3}{4}$ in (20 mm). It shall be firmly stretched from post to post, and shall be 2 ft 6 in (0.76 m) in depth. The top of the net shall be 5 ft (1.524 m) in height from the floor at the centre, and 5 ft 1 in (1.55 m) at the posts, and shall be edged with a 3 in (75 mm) white tape doubled and supported by a cord or cable run through the tape and strained over and flush with the top of the posts.

Shuttle

4. (*a*) *General Design.* A shuttle shall have from 14 to 16 feathers fixed in a cork base, 1 to $1\frac{1}{8}$ in (0.025 to 0.028 m) in diameter. The feathers shall be from $2\frac{1}{2}$ to $2\frac{3}{4}$ in (0.064 to 0·070 m) in length from the tip to the top of the cork base. The tips of the feathers shall form a circle with a diameter within the range from $2\frac{1}{8}$ to $2\frac{1}{2}$ in (0.054 to 0.064 m) spread at the top and shall be firmly fastened with thread or other suitable material.

(*b*) *Weight.* A shuttle shall weigh from 73 to 85 grains (4.73 to 5.50 gm).

(*c*) *Pace and Flight.* A shuttle shall be deemed to be of correct pace if, when it is hit by a player with a full underhand stroke from a spot immediately above one back boundary line in a direction parallel to the side lines, and at an upward angle, to fall not less than 1 ft (0·30 m) and not more than 2 ft 6 in (0.76 m) short of the other back boundary line.

(*d*) Subject to there being no substantial variation in the general design, pace, weight and flight of the shuttle, modifications in the above specifications may be made, subject to the approval of the national organisation concerned: (*i*) in places where atmospheric conditions, due either to altitude or climate, make the standard shuttle unsuitable; or (*ii*) if special circumstances exist which make it otherwise necessary in the interests of the game.

Players

5. (*a*) The word "Player" applies to all those taking part in a game.

(*b*) The game shall be played, in the case of the doubles game, by two players a side, and in the case of the singles game, by one player a side.

(*c*) The side for the time being having the right to serve shall be called the "In" side, and the opposing side shall be called the "Out" side.

The Toss

6. Before commencing play the opposing sides shall toss, and the side winning the toss shall have the option of: (*a*) Serving first; or (*b*) Not serving first; or (*c*) Choosing Ends.

The side losing the toss shall then have choice of any alternative remaining.

Scoring

7. (*a*) The doubles and men's singles game consists of 15 points. Provided that when the score is 13-all, the side which first reaches 13 has the option of "Setting" the game to 5, and that when the score is 14-all, the side which first reached 14 has the option of "Setting" the game to 3. After a game has been "Set" the score is called "Love-All", and the side which first scores 5 or 3 points, according as the game has been "Set" at 13 or 14-all, wins the game. In either case the claim to "Set" the game must be made before the next service is delivered after the score has reached 13-all or 14-all.

(*b*) The ladies' singles game consists of 11 points. Provided that when the score is 9-all the player who first reached 9 has the option of "Setting" the game to 3, and when the score is 10-all the player who first reached 10 has the option of "Setting" the game to 2.

(*c*) A side rejecting the option of "Setting" at the first opportunity shall not be thereby barred from "Setting" if a second opportunity arises.

(*d*) Notwithstanding para. (*a*) above, it is permissible by prior arrangement for only one game to be played and also for this to consist of 21 points, in which case "Setting" shall be as for the game of 15 points with scores of 19 and 20 being substituted for 13 and 14 respectively.

(e) In handicap games, "Setting" is not permitted.

8. The opposing sides shall contest the best of three games, unless otherwise agreed. The players shall change ends at the commencement of the second game and also of the third game (if any). In the third game the players shall change ends when the leading score reaches:

(a) 8 in a game of 15 points;

(b) 6 in a game of 11 points.

Or, in handicap events, when one of the sides has scored half the total number of points required to win the game (the next highest number being taken in case of fractions). When it has been agreed to play only one game the players shall change ends as provided above for the third game.

In a game of 21 points, the players shall change ends when the leading score reaches 11 or in handicap games as indicated above.

If, inadvertently, the players omit to change ends as provided in this Law at the score indicated, the ends shall be changed immediately the mistake is discovered, and the existing score shall stand.

Doubles Play

9. (a) It having been decided which side is to have the first service, the player in the right-hand service court of that side commences the game by serving to the player in the service court diagonally opposite. If the latter player returns the shuttle before it touches the ground it is to be returned by one of the "In" side, and then returned by one of the "Out" side, and so on, till a fault is made or the shuttle ceases to be "In Play" (*vide* paragraph (b)). If a fault is made by the "In" side, its right to continue serving is lost, as only one player on the side beginning a game is entitled to do so (*vide* Law 11), and the opponent in the right-hand service court then becomes the server; but if the service is not returned, or the fault is made by the "Out" side, the "In" side scores a point. The "In" side players then change from one service court to the other, the service now being from

the left-hand service court to the player in the service court diagonally opposite. So long as a side remains "In", service is delivered alternately from each service court into the one diagonally opposite, the change being made by the "In" side when, and only when, a point is added to its score.

(b) The first service of a side in each innings shall be made from the right-hand service court. A "Service" is delivered as soon as the shuttle is struck by the server's racket. The shuttle is thereafter "In Play" until it touches the ground, or until a fault or "Let" occurs, or except as provided in Law 19. After the service is delivered, the server and the player served to may take up any positions they choose on their side of the net, irrespective of any boundary lines.

10. The player served to may alone receive the service, but should the shuttle touch, or be struck by, his partner, the "In" side scores a point. No player may receive two consecutive services in the same game, except as provided in Law 12.

11. Only one player of the side beginning a game shall be entitled to serve in its first innings. In all subsequent innings each partner shall have the right, and they shall serve consecutively. The side winning a game shall always serve first in the next game, but either of the winners may serve and either of the losers may receive the service.

12. If a player serves out of turn, or from the wrong service court (owing to a mistake as to the service court from which service is at the time being in order), *and his side wins the rally*, it shall be a "Let", provided that such "Let" be claimed and allowed, or ordered by the umpire, before the next succeeding service is delivered.

If a player of the "Out" side standing in the wrong service court is prepared to receive the service when it is delivered, *and his side wins the rally*, it shall be a "Let", provided that such "Let" be claimed and allowed, or ordered by the umpire, before the next succeeding service is delivered.

If in either of the above cases the side at fault *loses the rally*, the mistake shall stand and the players' positions shall not be corrected.

Should a player inadvertently change sides when he should not do so, and the mistake not be discovered until after the next succeeding service has been delivered, the mistake shall stand, and a "Let" cannot be claimed or allowed, and the players' positions shall not be corrected.

Singles Play

13. In singles, Laws 9 and 12 hold good, except that:

(*a*) The players shall serve from and receive service in their respective right-hand service courts only when the server's score is 0 or an even number of points in the game, the service being delivered from and received in their respective left-hand service courts when the server's score is an odd number of points. Setting does not affect this sequence.

(*b*) Both players shall change service courts after each point has been scored.

Faults

14. A fault made by a player of the side which is "In" puts the server out; if made by a player whose side is "Out", it counts a point to the "In" side.

It is a fault:

(*a*) If, in serving, (i) any part of the shuttle at the instant of being struck be higher than the server's waist, or (ii) if at the instant of the shuttle being struck the shaft of the racket be not pointing in a downward direction to such an extent that the whole of the head of the racket is discernibly below the whole of the server's hand holding the racket.

(*b*) If, in serving, the shuttle does not pass over the net, or falls into the wrong service court (i.e., into the one not diagonally opposite to the server), or falls short of the short service line or beyond the long service line, or outside the side boundary lines of the service court into which service is in order.

(*c*) If the server's feet are not in the service court from which service is at the time being in order, or if the feet of the player receiving the service are not in the service court diagonally opposite until the service is delivered. (*Vide* Law 16.)

(*d*) If, once the service has started, any player makes preliminary feints or otherwise intentionally baulks his opponent, or if any player deliberately delays serving the shuttle or in getting ready to receive it so as to obtain an unfair advantage.

(When the server and receiver have taken up their respective positions to serve and to receive, the first forward movement of the server's racket constitutes the start of the service and such must be continuous thereafter.)

(*e*) If, either in service or play, the shuttle falls outside the boundaries of the court, or passes through or under the net, or fails to pass the net, or touches the roof or side walls, or the person or dress of a player. (A shuttle falling on a line shall be deemed to have fallen in the court or service court of which such line is a boundary.)

(*f*) If, when in play, the initial point of contact with the shuttle is not on the striker's side of the net. (The striker may, however, follow the shuttle over the net with his racket in the course of his stroke.)

(*g*) If, when the shuttle is "In Play", a player touches the net or its supports with racket, person or dress.

(*h*) If the shuttle be caught and held on the racket and then slung during the execution of a stroke; or if the shuttle be hit twice in succession by the same player with two strokes; or if the shuttle be hit by a player and his partner successively.

(*i*) If, in play, a player strikes the shuttle (unless he thereby makes a good return) or is struck by it, whether he is standing within or outside the boundaries of the court.

(*j*) If a player obstructs an opponent.

(*k*) If Law 16 be transgressed.

GENERAL

15. The server may not serve till his opponent is ready, but the opponent shall be deemed to be ready if a return of the service be attempted.

16. The server and the player served to must stand within the limits of their respective service courts (as bounded by the short and long service, the centre, and side lines), and some part of both feet of these players must remain in contact with the surface of the court in a stationary position until the service is delivered. A foot on or touching a line in the case of either the server or the receiver shall be held to be outside his service court. (*Vide* Law 14 (*c*).) The respective partners may take up

any position, provided they do not unsight or otherwise obstruct an apponent.

17. (*a*) If, in the course of service or rally, the shuttle touches and passes over the net, the stroke is not invalidated thereby. It is a good return if the shuttle having passed outside either post drops on or within the boundary lines of the opposite court. A "Let" may be given by the umpire for any unforeseen or accidental hindrance.

(*b*) If, in service, or during a rally, a shuttle, *after passing over the net*, is caught in or on the net, it is a "Let".

(*c*) If the receiver is faulted for moving before the service is delivered, or for not being within the correct service court, in accordance with Laws 14 (*c*) or 16, and at the same time the server is also faulted for a service infringement, it shall be a "Let".

(*d*) When a "Let" occurs, the play since the last service shall not count, and the player who served shall serve again, except when Law 12 is applicable.

18. If the server, in attempting to serve, misses the shuttle, it is not a fault; but if the shuttle be touched by the racket, a service is thereby delivered.

19. If, when in play, the shuttle strikes the net and remains suspended there, or strikes the net and falls towards the surface of the court on the striker's side of the net, or hits the surface outside the court and an opponent then touches the net or shuttle with his racket or person, there is no penalty, as the shuttle is not *then* in play.

20. If a player has a chance of striking the shuttle in a downward direction when quite near the net, his opponent must not put up his racket near the net on the chance of the shuttle rebounding from it. This is obstruction within the meaning of Law 14 (*j*).

A player may, however, hold up his racket to protect his face from being hit if he does not thereby baulk his opponent.

21. It shall be the duty of the umpire to call "Fault" or "Let" should either occur, without appeal being made by the players, and to give his decision on any appeal regarding a point in dispute, if made before the next service; and also to appoint linesmen and service judges at his discretion. An umpire's

decision shall be final, but he shall uphold the decision of a linesman or service judge. This shall not preclude the umpire also from faulting the server or receiver. Where, however, a referee is appointed, an appeal shall lie to him from the decision of an umpire on questions of law only.

Continuous Play

22. (*a*) Play shall be continuous from the first service till the match be concluded; except that (i) in international competitive events there shall be allowed an interval not exceeding five minutes between the second and third games of a match; (ii) in countries where conditions render it desirable, there shall be allowed, subject to the previously published approval of the national organisation concerned, an interval not exceeding five minutes between the second and third games of a match, in singles or doubles, or both; and (iii) when necessitated by circumstances not within the control of the players, the umpire may suspend play for such a period as he may consider necessary. If play be suspended, the existing score shall stand and play be resumed from that point. (*b*) Under no circumstances shall play be suspended to enable a player to recover his strength or wind, or to receive instruction or advice. (*c*) Except in the case of an interval provided for above, no player shall be allowed to receive advice during a match or to leave the court until the match be concluded without the umpire's consent. (*d*) The umpire shall be the sole judge of any suspension of play and he shall have the right to disqualify an offender.

The Rules of
Basketball

REGULATION SIZE COURT

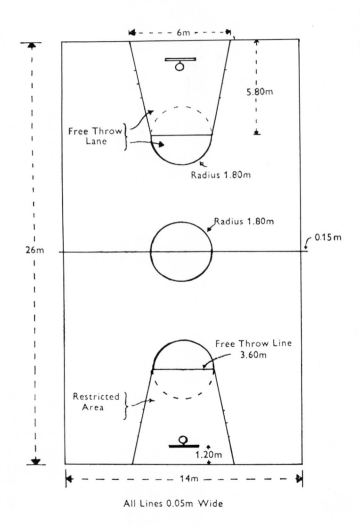

All Lines 0.05m Wide

Basketball

The Game

1. Definition

Basketball is played by two teams of five players each. The purpose of each team is to throw the ball into the opponents' basket and to prevent the other team from securing the ball or scoring. The ball may be passed, thrown, batted, rolled or dribbled in any direction, subject to the restrictions laid down in the following Rules.

RULE 2

Equipment

2. Court—Dimensions

The playing court shall be a rectangular hard surface free from obstructions and shall have dimensions of 26 m in length by 14 m in width, measured from the inside edge of the boundary lines.

The following variations in the dimensions are permitted: plus or minus 2 m on the length and plus or minus 1 m on the width, the variations being proportional to each other.

The height of the ceiling should be at least 7 m. The playing surface should be uniformly and adequately lighted. The light units should be placed where they will not hinder the vision of players.

3. Boundary Lines

The playing court shall be marked by well defined lines, which shall be at every point at least 1 m from any obstruction. The lines of the long sides of the court shall be termed the Side Lines, those of the short sides, the End Lines. The distance between these lines and the spectators should be at least 2 m.

REGULATION FREE THROW LANE

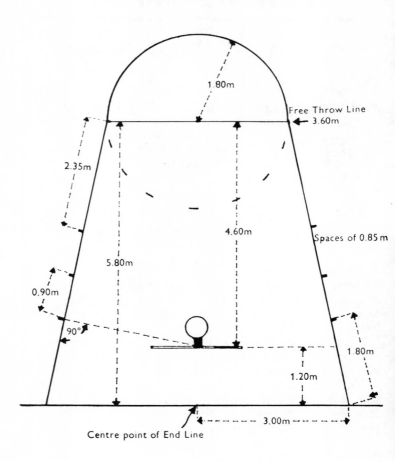

1.80m

Free Throw Line
◄ 3.60m

2.35m

4.60m

Spaces of 0.85 m

5.80m

0.90m

90°

1.80m

1.20m

Centre point of End Line

3.00m

When the margin of out-of-bounds free from obstruction is less than 1 m a fine line should be drawn in the court 1 m from the boundary line.

The lines mentioned in this article and in the following must be drawn so as to be perfectly visible and be 5 cm in width.

4. Centre Circle

The centre circle shall have a radius of 1.80 m and it shall be marked in the centre of the court. The radius shall be measured to the outer edge of the circumference.

5. Centre Line—Front Court, Back Court

A Centre Line shall be drawn, parallel to the end lines, from the mid-points of the side lines and shall extend 15 cm beyond each side line.

A team's Front Court is that part of the court between the end line behind the opponents' basket and the nearer edge of the Centre Line. The other part of the court, including the Centre Line, is the team's Back Court.

6. Free Throw Lines

A free throw line shall be drawn parallel to each end line. It shall have its further edge 5.80 m from the inner edge of the end line, and it shall be 3.60 m long and its mid-point shall lie on the line joining the mid-points of the two end lines.

7. Restricted Areas and Free Throw Lanes

The restricted areas shall be spaces marked in the court which are limited by the end lines, the free throw lines and by lines which originate at the end lines, their outer edges being 3 m from the mid-points of the end lines, and terminate at the ends of the free throw lines.

The free throw lanes are the restricted areas extended in the playing court by semi-circles with a radius of 1.80 m, their centres at the mid-points of the free throw lines. Similar semi-circles shall be drawn with a broken line within the restricted areas.

Spaces along the free throw lanes, to be used by players during free throws, shall be marked as follows:

The first space shall be situated 1.80 m from the inside edge of the end line, measured along the line at the side of the free throw lane, and shall be 85 cm in width. The second space shall be adjacent to the first and shall also be 85 cm in width. The lines used to mark these spaces shall be 10 cm long and be perpendicular to the side line of the free throw lane and shall be drawn outside the space they are delimiting.

8. Backboards—Size, Material and Position

Each of the two backboards shall be made of hard wood, 3 cm thick, or of a suitable transparent material (made in one piece and of the same degree of rigidity as those made of wood), and their dimensions shall be 1.80 m horizontally and 1.20 m vertically. The front surface shall be flat and unless it is transparent, it shall be white. This surface shall be marked as follows: a rectangle shall be drawn behind the ring and marked by a line 5 cm wide. The rectangle shall have outside dimensions of 59 cm horizontally and 45 cm vertically. The top edge of its base line shall be level with the ring.

Borders of the backboards shall be marked with a line, 5 cm wide. These lines shall be of a colour contrasting with the background. Normally, if the backboard is transparent, it shall be marked in white; in other cases in black. The edges of the backboards and the rectangles marked on them should be of the same colour.

The backboards shall be rigidly mounted in a position at each end of the court at right-angles to the floor, parallel to the end lines, and with their lower edges 2.75 m above the floor. Their centres shall lie in the perpendiculars erected at the points in the court 1.20 m from the mid-points of the end lines. The uprights supporting the backboards shall be at a distance of at least 40 cm from the outer edge of the end lines in the out-of-bounds area (it is strongly recommended that whenever possible this distance should be 1 m) and shall be of a bright colour in contrast with the background in such a manner that they will be clearly visible to the players. In addition, they should be suitably padded to prevent injury.

9. Baskets

The basket shall comprise the rings and the nets. The rings shall be constructed from solid iron, 45 cm in inside diameter, painted orange. The metal of the rings shall be 20 mm in diameter, with the possible addition of small-gauge loops on the under-edge or similar device for attaching the nets. They should be rigidly attached to the backboards and should lie in a horizontal plane 3.05 m above the floor, equidistant from the two vertical edges of the backboard. The nearest point of the inside edge of the rings shall be 15 cm from the faces of the backboards.

The nets shall be of white cord suspended from the rings and constructed so as to check the ball momentarily as it passes through the basket. They shall be 40 cm in length.

10. Ball—Material, Size and Weight

The ball shall be spherical; it shall be made of a rubber bladder covered with a case of leather, rubber or synthetic material; it shall be not less than 75 cm nor more than 78 cm in circumference; it shall weigh not less than 600 gm nor more than 650 gm; and it shall be inflated to an air pressure such that when it is dropped on to a solid wooden floor from a height of about 1.80 m measured to the bottom of the ball, it will rebound to a height, measured to the top of the ball, of not less than about 1.20 m nor more than about 1.40 m.

The home team shall provide a new ball or two good used balls satisfactory to the Referee. If used balls are provided, the Referee shall choose the one with which the game shall be played, and the visiting team shall have it as their practice ball. If a new ball is provided, neither team shall use it in practice. If the ball provided by the home team is unsatisfactory to the Referee, he is hereby given authority to order the game to be played with the visiting team's ball if the latter is in a better condition.

11. Technical Equipment

The following Technical Equipment shall be provided by the home team and shall be at the disposal of the Officials and their assistants:

(*a*) The Game Watch and the time-out watch. The Time-keeper shall be provided with at least two stopwatches, one of which shall be the game watch. It shall be placed on the table so that both the Timekeeper and the Scorer can see it.

(*b*) A suitable device, visible to players and spectators, shall be provided for the administration of the 30-seconds Rule and shall be operated by the 30-seconds Operator.

(*c*) The official Score Sheet shall be the one approved by the International Amateur Basketball Federation, and it shall be filled in by the Scorer before and during the game as provided for in these Rules.

(*d*) There shall be suitable equipment for all signals provided for in these Rules, including a Score Board visible to players, spectators and the Scorer's Table.

(*e*) Markers numbered 1 to 5 shall be at the disposal of the Scorer. Every time a player commits a foul, the Scorer shall raise in a manner visible to both Coaches the marker with the number corresponding to the number of fouls committed by that player. The markers shall be white with black numbers from 1 to 4 and red for number 5.

(*f*) The Scorer shall be provided with two Team Foul Markers. These shall be red flags constructed in such a way that when positioned on the Scorer's Table, they are easily visible to players, Coaches and Officials. The moment the ball goes into play following the eighth player foul by a team, a flag shall be positioned on the Scorer's Table at the end nearer the bench of the team that has committed the eighth player foul.

RULE 3

Players, Substitutes and Coaches

12. Teams

Each team shall consist of ten players, one of whom shall be the captain, and of a Coach who may be seconded by an Assistant Coach. (See also art. 15.) In tournaments where a team has to play more than five games the number of players in each team shall be increased to twelve.

Five players from each team shall be on the court during

playing time (for exceptions see art. 33) and may be substituted within the provisions contained in these Rules.

Each player shall be numbered on the front and back of his shirt with plain numbers of solid colour contrasting with the colour of his shirt, and made of material not less than 2 cm wide. The numbers on the back shall be at least 20 cm high and those on the front at least 10 cm high. Teams shall use numbers from 4 to 15. Players on the same team shall not wear duplicate numbers.

13. Player Leaving Court

A player may not leave the playing court during playing time without permission of an Official.

14. Captain—Duties and Powers

The Captain shall be the representative of his team and shall control its play. (See also art. 90.) The Captain may address an Official on matters of interpretation or to obtain essential information when necessary, if it is done in a courteous manner. No other player may address an Official except as provided in article 46.

Before leaving the playing court for any valid reason, the Captain shall inform the Referee regarding the player who will replace him during his absence.

15. Coaches

Before the game is scheduled to begin, the Coach shall furnish the Scorer with names and numbers of players who are to play in the game, and with the name and number of the Captain of the team. If a player changes his number during the game he shall report the change to the Scorer and Referee. Requests for charged time-outs shall be made by the Coach. When a Coach decides to request a substitution, he shall instruct the substitute to report to the Scorer. The player must be ready to play immediately. (See art. 41, 46.)

If there is an Assistant Coach, his name must be inscribed on the Score Sheet before the beginning of the game. He shall assume the responsibilities of the Coach if for any reason the Coach is unable to continue.

The team captain may act as Coach. If he must leave the playing court for any valid reason, he may continue to act as Coach. However, if he must leave following a disqualifying foul, or if he is unable to act as Coach owing to severe injury, his substitute as Captain shall also replace him as Coach.

RULE 4

Officials and their Duties

16. Officials and their Assistants

The Officials shall be a Referee and an Umpire, who shall be assisted by a Timekeeper, a Scorer and a 30-seconds Operator.

It cannot be too strongly emphasised that the Referee and the Umpire of a given game should not be connected in any way with either of the organisations represented on the court, and that they should be thoroughly competent and impartial. The Officials have no authority to agree to changes in the Rules. They shall wear a uniform consisting of basketball or tennis shoes, long trousers, shirt or pullover, grey in colour.

17. Duties and Powers of Referee

The Referee shall inspect and approve all equipment, including all the signals used by the Officials and their Assistants. He shall designate the official timepiece and recognise its operator, and shall also recognise the Scorer and the 30-seconds Operator. He shall not permit any player to wear objects which in his judgment are dangerous to other players.

The Referee shall toss the ball at the centre to start the game. He shall decide whether a goal shall count if the Officials disagree. He shall have power to forfeit a game when conditions warrant. He shall decide matters upon which the Timekeeper and the Scorer disagree. At the end of each half and of each extra period, or at any time he feels necessary, he shall carefully examine the Scoresheet, approve the score and confirm the time that remains to be played. His approval at the end of the game terminates the connection of the Officials with the game.

The Referee shall have power to make decisions on any point not specifically covered in the Rules.

18. Duties of Officials—Referee and Umpire

The Officials shall conduct the game in accordance with the Rules. This includes: putting the ball in play, determining when the ball becomes dead and killing it with the whistle when necessary or blowing the whistle to stop action after the ball has become dead, administering penalties, ordering time-out, beckoning substitutes to come on the court, handing (not tossing) ball to a player when such player is to make a throw-in from out-of-bounds whenever this is provided for in these Rules (see art. 67 and 80), and silently counting seconds to administer provisions contained in art. 31, 55, 58, 59, 60, 67 and 72.

Before the beginning of the game, the Officials shall agree upon a division of the playing court, to be covered by each of them. After each foul and jump-ball decision, the Officials shall exchange their positions.

The Officials shall blow their whistles and simultaneously give the signal to stop the clock (signal 2 or 11), followed by all the signals, to make known a decision.

The Officials shall not whistle after a goal from the field or resulting from a free throw, but shall clearly indicate that a goal has been scored by using signal 23.

If verbal communication is necessary to make a decision clear, this must be done in English for all international games.

19. Time and Place for Decisions

The Officials shall have power to make decisions for infractions of the rules committed either within or outside the boundary lines; these powers shall start when they arrive on the court, which shall be 20 minutes before the game is scheduled to begin and shall terminate with the expiration of playing time as approved by the Referee.

Penalties for fouls committed before the game or during intervals of play shall be administered as described in article 74.

If during the period between the end of playing time and the signing of the Score Sheet there is any unsportsmanlike behaviour by players, Coaches, Assistant Coaches or team followers, the Referee must record on the Score Sheet that an incident has occurred and ensure that a detailed report is submitted to the responsible authority which shall deal with the matter with appropriate severity.

Neither Official shall have authority to set aside or question decisions made by the other within the limits of his respective duties as outlined in these Rules.

If the Officials make approximately simultaneous decisions on the same play and the infractions involve different penalties, the more severe penalty shall be imposed. This does not prevent a double foul as defined in article 83.

20. Calling of Fouls

When a foul is committed, the Official shall indicate the offender, signalling his number to the Scorer with his fingers. If it is a personal foul involving a free throw penalty, the Official shall signal this clearly by indicating the free throw line; he shall also indicate the player who is to attempt the free throws. At this point, the Officials shall exchange their positions as provided for in article 18. One of the Officials shall then administer the free throws or, if no throw is involved, the Official shall hand the ball to the player who is to put it into play from the side line.

The Officials shall penalise unsportsmanlike conduct by any player, Coach, substitute or team follower, If there is a flagrant case of such conduct, the Officials shall penalise it by removing any offending player from the game and banishing any offending substitute, Coach, attendant or team follower.

21. Duties of Scorer

The Scorer shall keep a chronological running summary of the points scored; he shall record the field goals made and the free throws made or missed. He shall record the personal and technical fouls called on each player and shall notify the Referee immediately when the fifth foul is called on any player. He shall record the time-outs charged to each team, and shall notify a Coach through an Official when he has taken a second time-out in each half. He shall also indicate the number of fouls committed by each player by using the numbered markers as provided in article 11 (*e*).

The Scorer shall keep a record of the names and numbers of

players who are to start the game and of all substitutes who enter the game. When there is an infraction of the Rules pertaining to submission of line-up, substitutions or numbers of players, he shall notify the nearer Official as soon as possible when the infraction is discovered.

The sounding of the Scorer's signal does not stop the game. He should be careful to sound his signal only when the ball is dead and the game watch is stopped, and before the ball is again in play.

It is essential that the Scorer's signal be different from that of the Timekeeper and of the Officials.

22. Duties of Timekeeper

The Timekeeper shall note when each half is to start and shall notify the Referee more than three minutes before this time so that he may notify the teams, or cause them to be notified, at least three minutes before the half is to start. He shall signal to the Scorer two minutes before starting time. He shall keep record of playing time and time of stoppage as provided in these Rules.

For a charged time-out the Timekeeper shall start a time-out watch and shall direct the Scorer to signal the Referee when it is time to resume play.

The Timekeeper shall indicate with a gong, pistol or bell the expiration of playing time in each half, or extra period. This signal terminates actual playing time in each period. If the Timekeeper's signal fails to sound, or if it is not heard, the Timekeeper shall go on the court or use other means to notify the Referee immediately. If, in the meantime, a goal has been made or a foul has occurred, the Referee shall consult the Timekeeper and the Scorer. If they agree that the time was up before the ball was in the air on its way to the basket or before the foul was committed, the Referee shall rule that the goal does not count, or in the case of a foul, that it shall be disregarded, but if they disagree, the goal shall count or the foul be penalised unless the Referee has knowledge that would alter this ruling.

23. Duties of 30-seconds Operator

The 30-seconds Operator shall operate the 30-seconds device or watch (see art. 11(*b*)) as provided in article 62 in these rules.

The signal of the 30-seconds Operator causes the ball to become a dead ball.

RULE 5

Playing Regulations

24. Playing Time

The game shall consist of two halves of 20 minutes each, with an interval of 10 minutes between halves.

Note. *If local conditions warrant it, the organisers may increase this interval to 15 minutes. This decision must be made known to all concerned before the beginning of the game. In tournaments lasting several days, the decision must be taken, and made known to all concerned, at the latest one day before the tournament is due to start.*

25. Beginning of Game

The game shall be started by the Referee, who shall toss the ball up for a centre jump between two opponents in the centre circle; the same procedure shall be followed at the beginning of the second half and, eventually, of each extra period.

The visiting team shall have choice of baskets in the first half; on neutral courts teams shall toss for baskets. For the second half the teams shall change baskets.

The game cannot begin if one of the teams is not on the court with five players ready to play. If 15 minutes after the starting time the defaulting team is not present, the other team wins the game by forfeit.

26. Jump-Ball

A jump-ball takes place when the Official tosses the ball between two opposing players.

During a jump-ball the two jumpers shall stand with their feet inside that half of the circle which is nearer to their own baskets, with one foot near the centre of the line that is between them. The Official shall then toss the ball upward (vertically) in a plane at right angles to the side lines between the jumpers, to a height greater than either of them can reach by jumping and so that it will drop between them. The ball must be tapped by one or both of the jumpers *after* it reaches its highest point. If it touches the floor without being tapped by at least one of the jumpers, the Official shall put it into play again in the same place.

Neither jumper shall tap the ball before it reaches its highest point, nor leave their positions until the ball has been tapped. Either jumper may tap the ball twice only. After the second tap by a jumper, he shall not touch the ball again until it has touched one of the eight non-jumpers, the floor, the basket, or the backboard. Under this provision, four taps are possible, two by each jumper. When a jump-ball takes place, the eight non-jumpers shall remain outside the circle (cylinder) until the ball has been tapped. Team-mates may not occupy adjacent positions around the circle if an apponent desires one of the positions.

During a jump-ball the Officials shall see that the other players are in such positions that they do not interfere with the jumpers.

27. Violation during Jump-Ball

A player shall not violate provisions governing jump-ball. If, before the ball is tapped, a jumper leaves the jumping position or if a non-jumper enters the circle (cylinder), the Officials are authorised to give the violation arm signal but to withhold the whistle, to give opportunity for the opposing jumper to tap the ball into the basket or to tap it in such a way that one of his team-mates is first to touch the ball. If either of these occurs, the violation is disregarded. If both teams violate the jumping rule, or if the Official make a bad toss, the toss shall be repeated.

Penalty. See article 65.

28. Goal—When Made and its Value

A goal is made when a live ball enters the basket from above and remains in or passes through.

A goal from the field counts 2 points; a goal from a free throw counts 1 point. A goal from the field counts for the team attacking the basket into which the ball is thrown.

If the ball accidentally enters the basket from below, it shall become dead and play shall be resumed by a jump-ball at the nearest free throw line.

If, however, a player deliberately causes the ball to enter the basket from below, it is a violation and play shall be resumed by an opponent throwing the ball in from the side line at the point nearest to where the violation occurred.

29. Interfere with Ball in Offence

An offensive player may not touch the ball when it is in its downward flight above the level of the ring and is directly above the restricted area, whether it is a shot for goal or a pass. This restriction applies only until the ball touches the ring.

An offensive player shall not touch his opponent's basket or backboard while the ball is on the ring during a shot for goal.

Penalty. No point can be scored and the ball is awarded to opponents for a throw-in from out-of-bounds at a position on the side line nearest the point where the violation occurred (see art. 65).

30. Interfere with Ball in Defence

A defensive player shall not touch the ball after it has started its downward flight during an opponent's shot for goal and while the ball is above the level of the ring. This restriction applies only until the ball touches the ring or until it is apparent it will not touch it.

A defensive player shall not touch his own basket or backboard while the ball is on the ring during a shot for goal, or touch the ball or basket while the ball is within such basket.

Penalty. The ball becomes dead when violation occurs. The thrower is awarded one point if during a free throw as in article 73, and 2 points if during a shot for goal. Ball is awarded out-of-bounds from behind the end line as though the shot had been successful and there had been no violation.

31. Ball in Play after Goal

After a goal from the field, any opponent of the team credited with the score shall put the ball in play from any point out-of-bounds at the end of the court where the goal was made. He may throw it from any point behind the end line, or he may pass it to a team-mate behind the end line. Not more than five seconds may be consumed in getting the ball in play, the count starting the instant the ball is at the disposal of the first player out-of-bounds.

The Official should not handle the ball unless by so doing he can get the ball in play more quickly. Opponents of the player who is to put the ball in play shall not touch the ball. Allowance may be made for touching the ball accidentally or instinctively, but if a player delays the game by interfering with the ball, it is a technical foul.

After the last free throw, the ball shall be thrown in from out-of-bounds:

(*a*) by any opponent of the free thrower from behind the end line if the throw is successful, or

(*b*) by any player of the free thrower's team from out-of-bounds at mid-court if the free throw is for a technical foul by Coach or substitute, whether or not the throw is successful (see art. 78—penalty).

32. Decision of Game

A game shall be decided by the scoring of the greater number of points in the playing time.

33. Game to be Forfeited

Captains shall be notified three minutes before the termination of the interval between halves. If either team is not on the floor ready to play within one minute after the Referee calls play, either at the beginning of the second half or after time has been taken out for any reason, the ball shall be put in play in the same manner as if both teams were on the floor ready to play, and the absent team shall forfeit the game.

A team shall forfeit the game if it refuses to play after being instructed to do so by the Referee. When during a game the number of players of a team on the court shall be less than two, the game shall end, and that team shall lose the game by forfeit. If the team to which the game is forfeited is ahead, the score at the time of forfeiture shall stand. If this team is not ahead, the score shall be recorded as 2–0 in its favour.

34. Tie Score and Extra Periods

If the score is a tie at the expiration of the second half, play shall be continued for an extra period of five minutes or as many such periods of five minutes as may be necessary to break the tie. Before the first extra period the teams shall toss for baskets and shall change baskets at the beginning of each additional extra period. An interval of two minutes shall be allowed before each extra period. At the beginning of each extra period, the ball shall be put in play at the centre.

35. When Game is Terminated

The game shall terminate at the sounding of the Timekeeper's signal indicating the end of playing time.

When a foul is committed simultaneously with or just previous to the Timekeeper's signal ending a half or an extra period, time shall be allowed for the free throw or throws, if any are involved in the penalty.

When a shot (see art. 57) is taken near the end of playing time the goal, if made, shall count if the ball was in the air before time expired. All provisions contained in articles 29 and 30 shall apply until the ball touches the ring. If the ball strikes the ring, rebounds and then enters the basket, the goal shall count. If, after the ball has touched the ring, a player of either team touches the ball, it is a violation. If a defensive player commits such a violation, 2 points shall be awarded. If an offensive player commits such a violation, the ball becomes dead and the goal, if scored, shall not count. These provisions apply until it is apparent the shot will not be successful.

RULE 6

Timing Regulations

36. Game Watch Operations

The Game Watch shall be started when the ball, after having reached its highest point on a toss at the beginning of a half or extra period, is tapped by the first player.

The Game Watch shall be stopped at the expiration of time for each period of play.

37. Ball Goes into Play

The ball goes into play (is in play) when:

(*a*) the Official enters the circle to administer a jump-ball, or

(*b*) the Official enters the free throw lane to administer a free throw (see art. 72), or

(*c*) when in an out-of-bounds situation the ball is at the disposal of the player who is at the point of the throw-in.

38. Ball Becomes Alive

The ball becomes alive when:

(*a*) after having reached its highest point in a jump-ball it is tapped by the first player, or

(*b*) when the Official places it at the disposal of a free thrower (see art. 72), or

(*c*) when on a throw-in from out-of-bounds, it touches a player in the court.

39. Dead Ball

The ball becomes dead when:

(*a*) Any goal is made (see art. 28).

(*b*) Any violation occurs.

(*c*) A foul occurs while the ball is alive or in play.

(*d*) Held ball occurs or ball lodges on the basket support.

(*e*) It is apparent that the ball will not go into the basket; on a free throw for a technical foul by Coach, Assistant Coach, substitute or team follower, or a free throw which is to be followed by another throw.

(*f*) Official's whistle is blown while the ball is alive or in play.

(*g*) The 30-seconds Operator's signal is sounded while the ball is alive.

(*h*) Time expires for a half or extra period.

Exceptions: The ball does not become dead at the time of the listed act and goal, if made, counts if:

(1) ball is in flight on a free throw or shot for goal when (*c*), (*f*), (*g*) or (*h*) occurs, or

(2) an opponent fouls while the ball is still in control of a player who is shooting for goal and who finished his shot with a continuous motion which started before the foul occurred, or

(3) penalty for a jump-violation is ignored.

40. Time-out

Time-out occurs and the Game Watch shall be stopped when an Official signals:

(*a*) A violation;

(*b*) A foul;

(*c*) A held ball;

(*d*) Unusual delay in getting a dead ball into play;

(*e*) Suspension of play for an injury, or for removal of a player, such removal being ordered by an Official;

(*f*) Suspension of play for any reason, ordered by the Officials;

(*g*) When the 30-seconds signal is sounded; or

(*h*) When a basket is scored against the team of a Coach who has requested a charged time-out.

41. Charged Time-out

A Coach has the right to request a charged time-out. He shall do so by going in person to the Scorer and asking clearly for a "time-out", making the proper conventional sign with his hands. Electrical devices enabling Coaches, if they so wish, to request a time-out without leaving their places may be used. Such devices may not, under any circumstances, be used to request a player substitution.

The Scorer shall indicate to the Officials that a request for charged time-out has been made by sounding his signal as soon as the ball is dead and the Game Watch is stopped *but before the ball is again in play* (see art. 37).

A Coach may also be granted a charged time-out if, after a request from him for a time-out, a field goal is scored by his opponents. In this case the Timekeeper shall immediately stop the Game Watch. The Scorer shall then sound his signal and indicate to the Officials that a charged time-out has been requested.

A charged time-out shall not be granted from the moment the ball is in play for the first or only free throw until the ball becomes dead after being alive again after the free throw or throws.

A time-out shall be charged to a team for each minute consumed under these provisions. If the team responsible for the time-out is ready to play before the end of the charged time-out the Referee is hereby given authority to start the game immediately.

Exceptions: No time-out is charged if an injured player is ready to play immediately or is substituted as soon as possible or if a disqualified player, or a player who has committed his fifth foul is replaced within one minute, or if an Official permits a delay.

42. Legal Charged Time-out

Two charged time-outs may be granted to each team during each half of playing time, and one charged time-out for each extra period. Unused time-outs may not be carried over to the next half or extra period.

43. Time-out in Case of Injury

The Officials may order time-out in case of injury to players or for any other reason, although not for trifles. If the ball is alive when an injury occurs, the Officials shall withhold their whistles until the play has been completed, that is, the team in possession of the ball has thrown for goal, lost possession of the ball, has withheld the ball from play, or the ball has become a dead ball.

When necessary to protect an injured player, the Officials may suspend play immediately.

If the injured player cannot continue to play immediately, he must be substituted within one minute or as soon as possible, should the injury prevent an earlier substitution. If free throws have been awarded to the injured player, they must be attempted by his substitute. If this occurs, the provisions contained in the last paragraph of article 46, *Exception*, shall not apply. If an injured player is not substituted as set out in this article, his team shall be charged with a time-out except in the case of a team having to continue with fewer than five players. If his team has no charged time-outs left, a technical foul shall be charged against the Coach.

44. Time-in

After time has been out, the Game Watch shall be started:

(*a*) If play is resumed by a jump-ball, when the ball after having reached its highest point is tapped by the first player.

(*b*) If a free throw is not successful and ball is to continue in play, when the ball touches a player in the court.

(*c*) If play is resumed by a throw-in from out-of-bounds, when the ball touches a player in the court.

45. How Play is Resumed

After time-out or after the ball has become dead for any other reason ball is put in play as follows: (*a*) If a team has control of the ball, any player of that team shall throw it in from the point out-of-bounds on the side lines nearest the point where the ball became dead. (*b*) If neither team has control, the ball is put in play by a jump-ball at the circle nearest where the ball became dead. (*c*) After a foul, ball is put in play by placing it at the disposal of the offended team (out-of-bounds on the side line) or of the free thrower or by a jump-ball at the nearest circle. (See also art. 80—Penalty, *b*(i).) (*d*) After a held ball, or the ending of a half period; or a field goal or an out-of-bounds, or the ending of a free throw, or a violation; ball is put in play as prescribed in the relevant Rule.

RULE 7

Players' Regulations

46. Substitutions

A substitute before going upon the court shall report to the

Scorer and must be ready to play immediately. The Scorer shall sound his signal immediately if the ball is dead and the Game Watch stopped, or as soon as the ball becomes dead and the Game Watch is stopped, but before the ball is again in play (see art. 37), as the consequence of one of the following situations:

(a) a held ball has been called,

(b) a foul has been called,

(c) a charged time-out has been granted, or

(d) game has been stopped, to attend an injured player, or for any other reason, ordered by the Officials.

Following a violation, only the team who has possession of the ball for the throw-in from out-of-bounds may effect a substitution. If such a situation occurs, the opponents may also effect a substitution.

The substitute shall remain outside the boundary line until an Official beckons him to enter, whereupon he shall report immediately to the nearer Official, indicating the number of the player he replaces. When a substitute enters at the beginning of the second half, he is not required to report to an Official but he must report to the Scorer. Substitutions shall not take more than 20 seconds, regardless of the number of substitutions effected by one team. If more time is taken, it shall count as a time-out, and shall be charged against the offending team. A player involved in a jump-ball may not be substituted by another player. A substitution is not permitted from the moment that the ball is in play for the first or only free throw until the ball becomes dead after being alive again after the free throw or throws.

Exception: After a successful last free throw only the player who was attempting the free throw may be substituted provided such substitution was requested before the ball went into play for the first or only free throw, in which case the opponents may be granted one substitution provided the request is made before the ball goes into play for the last free throw.

47. Location of Player and Official

The location of a player is determined by where he is touching the floor. When he is in the air from a leap, he retains the same status as when he last touched the floor as far as the boundary lines, the centre line, the free throw line or the lines limiting the free throw lanes are concerned (except as provided in article 68 (*b*)).

The location of an Official is determined in the same manner as that of a player. When the ball touches an Official it is the same as touching the floor at the Official's location.

48. How Ball is Played

In Basketball the ball is played with the hands. *Kicking or striking it with the fist is a violation. For penalty see article 65.*

Kicking the ball is a violation only when it is a positive act; accidently striking the ball with the foot or leg is not a violation.

49. Control of the Ball

A player is in control of the ball when he is holding or dribbling a live ball or in an out-of-bounds situation when the ball is at his disposal for a throw-in (see art. 37c). A team is in control when a player of that team is in control and also when the ball is being passed between team mates. Team control continues until an opponent secures control or the ball becomes dead or on a shot for goal when the ball is no longer in contact with the hand of the shooter.

50. Player Out-of-Bounds — Ball Out-of-Bounds

A player is out-of-bounds when he touches the floor on or outside of the boundary lines.

The ball is out-of-bounds when it touches a player who is out-of-bounds, or any other person, the floor or any object on or outside a boundary line, or the supports or back of the backboard.

51. How Ball Goes Out-of-Bounds

If the ball is out-of-bounds because of touching something other than a player, it is caused to go out by the last player to touch it before it goes out. If it is out-of-bounds because of touching a player (on or outside boundary), such a player causes it to go out. If a player deliberately throws or taps the ball on to an opponent, thus causing it to go out-of-bounds, the ball shall be awarded to the opponents, even though it was last touched by that team. (See art. 62.) An Official shall clearly indicate the team which shall put the ball in play from out-of-bounds. Out-of-bounds decisions should be clearly signalled by the Officials. If there is doubt about players understanding the decision, the Official should secure the ball and delay the throw-in until the decision has been made clear. (See also art. 56.)

To cause the ball to go out-of-bounds is a violation. For penalty see article 65.

Officials should declare jump-ball when they are in doubt as to which team caused the ball to go out-of-bounds.

52. Pivot

A pivot takes place when a player who is holding the ball steps once or more than once in any direction with the same foot, the other foot, called the pivot foot, being kept at its point of contact with the floor.

53. Dribbling

A dribble is made when a player, having gained control of the ball, gives impetus to it by throwing, tapping or rolling it, and touches it again before it touches another player. In a dribble the ball must come in contact with the floor. After giving impetus to the ball as described in the foregoing, the player completes his dribble the instant he touches the ball simultaneously with both hands, or permits the ball to come to rest in one or both hands. There is no limit to the number of steps a player may take when the ball is not in contact with his hand; he may take as many steps as he wishes between bounces of a dribble.

A player is entitled to a dribble each time he gains control of the ball. After completing a dribble he may not dribble again until he has lost and then regained control of the ball. He loses control the moment the ball leaves his hand(s) on a shot or a pass, or has been batted or taken out of his possession by an opponent.

A player who throws the ball against a backboard and touches it before it touches another player commits a second dribble violation unless in the opinion of the Official it was a shot.

Exception: The following are not dribbles: Successive tries for goal, fumbles, attempts to gain control of the ball by tapping it from the vicinity of other players striving for it, batting it from the control of another player, blocking a pass and recovering the ball, or tossing the ball from hand(s) to hand(s) and permitting it to come to rest before touching the floor, provided he does not commit a progressing-with-the-ball violation.

To make a second dribble is a violation. For penalty see article 65.

54. Progressing with the Ball

A player may progress with the ball in any direction within the following limits:

ITEM 1. A player who receives the ball while standing still may pivot, using either foot as the pivot foot.

ITEM 2. A player who receives the ball while he is progressing or upon completion of a dribble may use a two-count rhythm in coming to a stop or in getting rid of the ball. The first count occurs:

(*a*) as he receives the ball if either foot is touching the floor at the time he receives it, or

(*b*) as either foot touches the floor or as both feet touch the floor simultaneously after he receives the ball if both feet are off the floor when he receives it.

The second count occurs when, after the count of one, either foot touches the floor or both feet touch the floor simultaneously.

When a player comes to a legal stop if one foot is in advance of the other he may pivot but the rear foot only may be used as the pivot foot. However, if neither foot is in advance of the other he may use either foot as the pivot foot.

ITEM 3. A player who receives the ball while standing still, or who comes to a legal stop while holding the ball, (*a*) may lift the pivot foot or jump when he throws for goal or passes, but the ball must leave his hands before one or both feet again touch the floor; (*b*) may not lift the pivot foot in starting a dribble before the ball leaves his hands.

To progress with the ball in excess of these limits is a violation. For penalty see article 65.

55. Held Ball

A held ball shall be declared when two or more players of opposing teams have one or both hands firmly on the ball.

Officials should not declare held ball too quickly, thereby interrupting the continuity of the game, and unjustly taking the ball from the player who gained or is about to gain possession. Under the first clause of this article, held ball should not be called until at least one player from each team has one or both hands firmly on the ball so that neither player could gain possession without undue roughness. A held ball decision is not warranted merely on the grounds that the defensive player gets his hands on the ball. Usually such a decision is unfair to the player who has firm possession of the ball. If a player is lying or sitting on the floor while in possession of the ball, he should have opportunity to play it, but held ball should be called if there is danger of injury.

When held ball is called, the ball shall be tossed up between the two contending players at the nearest circle. In case of doubt as to which is the nearest circle, the ball shall be tossed up at the centre. If there are more than two players involved, the ball shall be tossed up between two contending players of approximately the same height.

56. Jump-Ball in Special Situations

If the ball goes out-of-bounds and was last touched simultaneously by two opponents, or if the Official is in doubt as to who last touched the ball, or if the Officials disagree, play shall be resumed by a jump-ball between the two involved players at the nearest circle.

Whenever the ball lodges on the basket supports, it shall be put in play by a jump-ball between any two opponents on the nearer free throw line, except when such a situation arises during a free throw following a technical foul by Coach, Assistant Coach, substitute or team follower (see art. 78), in which case the ball shall be put in play in the prescribed manner.

57.   Player in the Act of Shooting

A player is in the act of shooting when in the judgment of an Official he starts an attempt to score by throwing, dunking, or tapping the ball and it continues until the ball has left the player's hand(s).

Exceptions: Players who tap the ball towards the basket directly from a jump-ball are not considered to be in the act of shooting.

58.   Three-seconds Rule

A player shall not remain for more than three seconds in that part of the opponents' restricted area, between the end line and the further edge of the free throw line, while the ball is in control of his team. The three-seconds restriction is in force in all out-of-bounds situations, and the count shall start at the moment the player throwing-in is out-of-bounds and has control of the ball.

The lines bounding the restricted area are part of it and a player touching one of these lines is in the area. The three-seconds restriction does not apply while the ball is in the air on a shot for goal, or while it is rebounding from the backboard or is dead, because the ball is not in control of either team at such times. Allowance may be made for a player who, having been in the restricted area for less than three seconds, dribbles in to throw for goal.

An infraction of this rule is a violation. For penalty see article 65.

59.   Five-seconds Rule

Held ball shall be called when a closely guarded player who is holding the ball does not pass, shoot, roll or dribble the ball within five seconds.

60.   Ten-seconds Rule

When a team gains control of the ball in its back court, it must, within ten seconds, cause the ball to go into its front court.

The ball goes into a team's front court when it touches the court beyond the centre line or touches a player of that team who has part of his body in contact with the court beyond the centre line.

An infraction of this rule is a violation. For penalty see article 65.

61. Ball Returned to Back Court

A player in his front court may not cause the ball to go into his back court. It is caused to go into the back court by the last player to touch it before it goes into the back court. This restriction applies to all situations occurring in a team's front court, including a throw-in from out-of-bounds, rebounds and interceptions. It does not apply, however, to jump-ball situations at the centre circle or to the situation described in article 78 (Penalty) and in article 89.

A player in his front court who gains control of the ball directly from a jump-ball at the centre circle, may pass the ball into his back court.

The ball goes into a team's back court when it touches a player of that team who has part of his body in contact with the centre line or with the court beyond the centre line, or is touched by a player of that team after it has touched the back court.

Penalty. The ball is awarded to an opponent for a throw-in from the mid-point of a side line and he shall be entitled to pass the ball to a player at any point on the playing court.

62. 30-seconds Rule

When a team gains control of a live ball on the court, a shot for goal must be made within 30 seconds. *Failure to do so is a violation of this rule. For penalty see article 65.*

If the ball goes out-of-bounds during the 30-seconds period, and if the ball is awarded to the same team, a new 30-seconds period shall begin. The mere touching of the ball by an opponent does not start a new 30-seconds period if the same team remains in control of the ball.

If a player deliberately throws or bats the ball into an opponent, causing it to go out-of-bounds, the ball shall be awarded to the opponents, even though it was last touched by that team. This provision is made to prevent a team from illegally obtaining a new 30-seconds period.

All regulations concerning the end of playing time shall apply to violations of the 30-seconds rule.

RULE 8

Infractions and Penalties

63. Violations and Fouls

A violation is an infraction of the Rules, the penalty for which is the loss of the ball.

When an infraction involves a personal contact with an opponent or unsportsmanlike conduct, *the violation becomes a foul*, which will be inscribed against the offender and the consequences of which is a penalty administered according to the provisions contained in the relevant article of these Rules.

64. Ball in Play after Violation or Foul

After the ball has become dead following an infraction of the Rules, the ball is put in play (*a*) by a throw-in from out-of-bounds, or (*b*) by a jump-ball at one of the circles, or (*c*) by one or more free throws.

65. Procedure when a Violation is Called

When a violation is called the ball becomes dead. The ball is awarded to a nearby opponent for a throw-in from the side line at the point nearest that where the violation occurred. If the ball goes into a basket during the dead ball which follows such a violation, no point can be scored.

66. Procedure When Foul is Called

When a player foul is called the Official shall signal to the Scorer the number of the offender. The player thus indicated shall turn to face the Scorer's Table and shall immediately raise his hand above his head. For failure to do so, after having been warned once by the Official, a technical foul may be called against the offending player.

If the foul was committed on a player who was not in the act of shooting, the Official shall hand the ball to him or to one of his team-mates for a throw-in from the side line at a spot nearest the place of the foul.

If the foul was committed on a player in the act of shooting, (*a*) if the goal is made it shall count and in addition one free throw shall be awarded, (*b*) if the goal is missed, the Official shall take the ball to the free throw line and shall put it at the disposal of the free-thrower unless play is to be resumed by a jump-ball, as in the case of a double foul.

67. How Ball is Put in Play from Out-of-Bounds

The player who is to throw the ball in from out-of-bounds shall stand out-of-bounds at the side line at a spot nearest the point where the ball left the court or the violation or foul was committed. Within five seconds from the time the ball is at his disposal, he shall throw, bounce or roll the ball to another player within the court. While the ball is being passed into the court, no other player shall have any part of his body over the boundary line. When the margin of out-of-bounds territory free from obstruction is less than 1 m, no player of either team shall be within 1 m of the player who is putting the ball in play.

Whenever the ball is awarded to a team out-of-bounds at the side line in its front court, an Official must hand the ball to the player who is to put it in play. The purpose of this is to make the decision clear, and not to delay the game until the defensive team gets "set".

Whenever the ball is awarded to a team out-of-bounds at the side line in its back court, the Official, if there is confusion as to the decision, shall hand the ball to the thrower-in at the side line closest to the violation.

68. Violation of Out-of-Bounds Play

A player shall not violate provisions governing a throw-in from out-of-bounds. These provisions:

(*a*) forbid a player who has been awarded the ball for a throw-in to touch it in the court before it has touched another player, or to step on the line of the court whilst releasing the ball, or to consume more than five seconds in putting the ball in play;

(*b*) forbid any other player to have any part of his person over the boundary line before the ball has been thrown across the line, or to put the ball in play after the Official has awarded it to the other team. (*Penalty:* If infraction is of (*a*) see art. 65; if of (*b*) see art. 77.)

69. How Ball is Put in Play with Jump-Ball

Whenever the ball must be put in play with a jump-ball, this will be done in the manner described in article 26.

70. Free Throws

A free throw is a privilege given a player to score one point by an unhindered throw for goal from a position directly behind the free throw line (see art. 72).

71. Player to Attempt Free Throw

When a personal foul is called, and a free throw penalty is awarded, the player upon whom the foul was committed shall be designated by the Official to attempt the free throws. If any other player attempts the throw, it shall not count if made, and whether made or missed the ball shall be awarded to an opponent out-of-bounds at the side line opposite the free throw line.

Should a player, by mistake, execute a free throw into his own basket, the try shall be annulled, whether successful or not, and a new try shall be granted at the right basket.

If the designated player must leave the game because of injury, his substitute must attempt the free throws. If the player who has been fouled is to leave the game because of a substitution, he shall attempt the free throws before leaving (see art. 46).

When there is no substitute available, the free throws may be attempted by the Captain or any player designated by him.

When a technical foul is called, the free throw or throws may be attempted by any player of the opposing team.

72. How a Free Throw is Attempted

The throw for goal shall be made within five seconds after the ball has been placed at the disposal of the free thrower at the free throw line. This shall apply to each free throw.

The player who is to attempt the free throws shall take a

position immediately behind the free throw line and shall be free to use any system in throwing the ball, but he shall not touch the free throw line or the court beyond the line until the ball touches the ring.

Players may not attempt to disconcert the thrower by their action. Neither Official shall stand in the free throw area (restricted area) or behind the backboard.

When a player is attempting a free throw, the other players shall be entitled to take the following position:

(a) two players from the opposing team the two places nearer the basket,

(b) the other players shall take alternate positions,

(c) all other players may take any other position, provided that:

(i) they neither disturb nor are in the way of the free thrower and of the Officials,

(ii) they do not move from their positions before the ball has touched the ring,

(iii) they do not occupy the places along the free throw lane next to the end line.

On free throws following technical fouls by Coach or substitutes, players shall not line up along the free throw lane (see art. 78—penalty).

73. Violation of Free Throw Provisions

After the ball has been placed at the disposal of the free thrower:

(a) he shall throw within five seconds, and in such a way that the ball enters the basket or touches the ring before it is touched by a player;

(b) neither he nor any other player shall touch the ball or basket while the ball is on its way to the basket or is on or within the basket;

(c) he shall not touch the floor on or across the free throw line and no other player of either team shall touch the free throw lane or disconcert the thrower. This restriction applies until the ball touches the ring or until it is apparent it will not touch it.

Penalty: (1) If the violation is by the free thrower only, no point can be scored. Ball becomes dead when violation occurs. Ball is awarded out-of-bounds on the side line, to the free thrower's team opposite centre circle after a technical foul by Coach, Assistant Coach, substitute or team followers, and to the free thrower's opponents opposite the free throw line after a player foul.

(2) If violation of (b) is by a team-mate of the free thrower, no point can be scored and violation shall be penalised as above. If violation (b) is by both teams, no point can be scored and play shall be resumed by a jump-ball on the free throw line. If violation of (b) is by the free thrower's opponents only, violation is penalised as indicated in article 30.

(3) If violation of (c) is by a team-mate of the free thrower and the free throw is successful, the goal shall count and violation be disregarded. If the free throw is not successful, violation shall be penalised as above. However, if the ball misses the ring and goes out-of-bounds or falls within bounds, it shall be put in play by the opponents from the side line opposite the free throw line.

(4) If violation of (c) is by the free thrower's opponents only, and if the throw is successful, the goal counts and violation is disregarded; if it is not successful, a substitute throw shall be attempted by the same thrower.

(5) If there is a violation of (c) by both teams, and the free throw is successful, the goal shall count and violation be disregarded. If the free throw is not successful play shall be resumed by a jump-ball on the free throw line.

If there is a multiple throw, the out-of-bounds and jump-ball provisions apply only to a violation during the last free throw.

74. Technical Foul before the Game or during an Interval of Play

If a technical foul is called before the game, during the half-time or during an interval before an extra period, the penalty shall be two free throws and play shall be started or resumed by a jump-ball at centre after the throws have been attempted.

75. Ball in Play if Free Throw is Missed

If the goal is missed, the ball shall continue in play after the last free throw following a player foul. If the ball misses the ring, it is a violation (see art. 73) and the ball shall be put in play from the side line at the point opposite the free throw line by the opposing team. In case of a free throw following a technical foul by Coach, Assistant Coach, substitute or team followers, see article 31(*b*).

RULE 9

Rules of Conduct

A. RELATIONSHIPS

76. Definition

The proper conduct of the Game demands the full and loyal co-operation of members of both teams, including Coaches and substitutes, with the Officials and their assistants.

Both teams are entitled to do their best to secure victory, but this must be done in a spirit of sportsmanship and fair play.

An infringement of this co-operation or of this spirit, when deliberate or repeated, should be considered as a Technical Foul and penalised as provided in the following articles of these Rules.

77. Technical Foul by Player

A player shall not disregard admonitions by Officials or use unsportsmanlike tactics such as:

(*a*) disrespectfully addressing or contacting an Official,

(*b*) using language or gestures likely to give offence,

(*c*) baiting an opponent or obstructing his vision by waving hands near his eyes,

(*d*) delaying the game by preventing ball from being promptly put in play,

(*e*) not raising his hand properly when a foul is called on him (see art. 66),

(*f*) changing his playing number without reporting to Scorer and to Referee,

(*g*) entering the court as a substitute without reporting to Scorer, or without reporting promptly to an Official (unless between halves) or during a time-out after having withdrawn during the same time-out,

(*h*) grasping the ring; a player who violates this provision must be promptly penalised by a technical foul awarded against him.

Technical infractions which are obviously unintentional and have no effect on the game, or are of an administrative character, are not considered technical fouls unless there is a repetition of the same infraction after a warning by an Official to the offending player and to his Captain.

Technical infractions which are deliberate or are unsportsmanlike or give the offender an unfair advantage should be penalised promptly with a technical foul.

Penalty. A foul shall be charged and recorded for each offence and two free throws awarded the opponents for each foul and the Captain shall designate the thrower. For flagrant or persistent infraction of this article, a player shall be disqualified and removed from the game.

If discovery of foul is after ball is in play following the foul, penalty should be administered as if foul had occurred at the time of discovery. Whatever occurred in the interval between the foul and its discovery shall be valid.

78. Technical Foul by Coaches, Substitutes or Team Followers

The Coach, Assistant Coach, substitutes or team followers shall not enter the court unless by permission of an Official to attend an injured player, nor leave their place to follow the action on the court from the boundary lines, nor disrespectfully address Officials (including Scorer, Timekeeper and 30-seconds Operator) or opponents.

A Coach may address players of his team during a charged time-out, provided he does not enter playing court and players do not cross boundary line, unless permission is first obtained from an Official. Substitutes may also listen-in provided they do not enter the playing court.

The distinction between unintentional and deliberate infractions (see art. 77) applies also to infractions committed by Coaches, Assistant Coaches, substitutes and team followers.

Penalty. A foul shall be charged and inscribed against the

Coach and one free throw awarded for each offence, and the opposing Captain shall designate the thrower. During the free throw players shall not line up along the free throw lanes. After the throw, the ball shall be put in play by any player of the free thrower's team from out-of-bounds at mid-court on the side line, whether or not the throw is successful.

Technical fouls may be called during intervals of play (see art. 74). If called against the Coach, the assistant Coach or team follower, the penalty shall be two free throws. If called against a player or a substitute, a technical foul shall be charged against him and two free throws awarded to the opponents.

For a flagrant infraction of this article, or when a Coach is charged with three technical fouls as a result of unsportsmanlike conduct by the Coach, Assistant Coach or team follower, the Coach shall be disqualified and banished from the vicinity of the court. He shall be replaced by the assistant Coach, or in the event of there not being an Assistant Coach, by the Captain.

B. PERSONAL CONTACTS

79. Personal Contact

Although Basketball is theoretically a "no-contact game", it is obvious that personal contact cannot be avoided entirely when ten players are moving with great rapidity over a limited space. For instance, the ball is free; two opponents start quickly for the ball and collide. The personal contact may be serious, yet, if both were in favourable positions from which to get the ball and were intent only upon getting it, an unavoidable accident, and not a foul, occurs. On the other hand, if one player is about to catch the ball and an opponent behind him, jumping in an attempt to get the ball, strikes him in the back, the opponent commits a foul even though he is "playing the ball". In this case, as in "guarding from the rear", the player behind is usually responsible for the contact because of his unfavourable position relative to the ball and to his opponent. In short, if personal contact results from a "bona fide" attempt to play the ball, if the players are in such positions that they could reasonably expect to gain the ball without contact and if they use due care to avoid contact, such contact may be classified as accidental and need not be penalised.

80. Personal Foul

A personal foul is a player foul which involves contact with an opponent.

Blocking is personal contact which impedes the progress of an opponent who is not in control of the ball.

Holding is personal contact with an opponent that interferes with his freedom of movement.

Pushing is personal contact that takes place when a player forcibly moves or attempts to move an opponent. Contact caused by a player approaching the ball holder from behind may be a form of pushing.

Guarding from the rear which results in personal contact is a personal foul. Officials should give special attention to this type of infraction. The mere fact that the defensive player is attempting to play the ball does not justify him in making contact with an opponent who controls the ball.

Charging is personal contact which occurs when a player, with or without the ball, makes his way forcibly and contacts an opponent in his path.

Illegal use of hands occurs when a player contacts an opponent with his hand(s) unless such contact is only with the opponent's hand while it is on the ball and is incidental to an attempt to play the ball.

Screening is an attempt to prevent an opponent who does not control the ball from reaching a desired position.

A dribbler shall not charge into nor contact an opponent in his path nor attempt to dribble between opponents or between an opponent and a boundary line, unless there is a reasonable chance for him to go through without contact. If a dribbler, without causing contact, passes an opponent, sufficiently to have head and shoulders in advance of him, the greater responsibility for subsequent contact is on the opponent. If a dribbler has established a straight line path, he may not be forced out of that path but, if an opponent is able to establish a legal guarding position in that path, the dribbler must avoid contact by stopping or changing direction.

A player who screens has the greater responsibility if contact occurs: (a) if he takes a position so near an opponent that pushing or charging occurs when normal movements are made by him, or (*b*) if he takes a position so quickly in a moving opponent's path that pushing or charging cannot be avoided.

Penalty. A personal foul shall be charged to the offender in all cases. In addition:

(1) If a foul is committed on a player who is not in the act of shooting, the ball shall be put in play by the non-offending team from out-of-bounds on the side line nearest the place of the foul. As soon as the foul is called, the Official shall signal the Scorer the number of the offender and shall then hand the ball to the opponents for a throw-in from the side line (for exception, see art. 92 and also art. 90 and 93).

(2) If a foul is committed on a player who is in the act of shooting, (i) if the goal is made, it shall count and in addition one free throw shall be awarded, (ii) if the goal is missed, two free throws shall be awarded (see art. 89 and 90). As soon as the foul is called, the Official shall signal the Scorer the number of the offender and shall then place the ball at the disposal of the free thrower (see also art. 90).

81. Intentional Foul

An intentional foul is a personal foul which in the opinion of the Official was committed deliberately by a player.

A player who deliberately disregards the ball and causes personal contact with an opponent who controls the ball commits an intentional foul. This is generally true also of fouls committed on a player who does not have the ball. A player who controls the ball may also commit an intentional foul if he deliberately contacts an opponent. A player who repeatedly commits intentional fouls may be disqualified.

Penalty. A personal foul shall be charged to the offender and in addition two free throws are awarded. However if the foul is committed on a player who is in the act of shooting and who scores, the basket shall count and in addition one free throw shall be awarded (see art. 66, 80 and 89).

If the foul is committed on a player in the act of shooting who fails to score, two free throws shall be awarded (see art. 66, 80, 89 and 90).

82. Disqualifying Foul

Any flagrantly unsportsmanlike infraction of articles 77 and 80 is a disqualifying foul. A player who commits such a foul must be disqualified and removed immediately from the game and a foul shall be charged against him. *Penalty:* same as article 81.

83. Double Foul

A double foul is a situation in which two opponents commit fouls against each other at approximately the same time. *Penalty:*

In the case of a double foul, no free throw shall be awarded but a personal foul shall be charged against each offending player.

The ball shall be put in play at the nearest circle by a jump-ball between the two players involved, unless a valid basket is scored at the same time, in which case the ball shall be put into play from the end line.

84. Multiple Foul

A multiple foul is a situation in which two or more team-mates commit personal fouls against the same opponent at approximately the same time. *Penalty:*

When two or more personal fouls are committed against a player by opponents, one foul shall be charged to each offending player and the offended player shall be awarded two free throws, irrespective of the number of fouls (see art. 89). If the fouls are committed on a player in the act of shooting, the goal if made shall count, and in addition one free throw shall be awarded.

85. Foul on a Player in the Act of Shooting

Whenever a foul is called on the opponent of a player who, as part of a continuous motion which started before the foul occurred, succeeds in making a field goal, the goal shall count even if the ball leaves the player's hands after the whistle blows, provided the whistle did not affect the game. The player must be shooting for goal or starting an effort to shoot for goal when the whistle blows; the goal does not count if he makes an entirely new effort after the whistle blows.

C. GENERAL PROVISIONS

86. Basic Principle

Each Official has power to call fouls independently from the other, and this at any time during the Game, whether the ball is in play, alive or dead.

Fouls committed during the dead ball that follows a foul and until the moment when the ball is again in play (see art. 37) are considered as being committed at the time the ball became dead because of the first foul.

Any number of fouls may therefore be called at the same time against one or both teams.

Irrespective of the penalty, a foul shall be inscribed on the Score Sheet against the offenders for each foul.

87. Double and Multiple Foul

When a double foul and another foul are committed at the same time, the double foul shall be dealt with as in article 83, and the other foul dealt with according to the respective Rule above. Play shall be resumed, after the fouls have been charged and the eventual penalty administered, as though the double foul had not occurred.

88. Fouls in Special Situations

Situations other than those foreseen in these Rules may occur when fouls are committed at approximately the same time or during the dead ball that follows a foul, a double foul or a multiple foul. As a general direction to Officials, the following principles may be applied in such situations:

(a) a foul shall be charged for each offence;

(b) fouls that involve penalties of about the same gravity against both teams shall not be penalised by awarding free throws, and the ball shall be put in play by a jump-ball at the nearest circle or, in case of doubt, at the centre;

(c) penalties that are not compensated by similar penalties against the other team shall be maintained, but under no circumstances shall a team be awarded more than two free throws and possession of the ball.

89. Three-for-Two Rule

Whenever two free throws are awarded to a player who was fouled while in the act of shooting, if either or both these throws are unsuccessful, one additional free throw shall be awarded.

90. Right of Option

A team that has been awarded two free throws (see also art. 89) shall have the option of either attempting the throws or of putting the ball in play from out-of-bounds at the mid-point of a side line.

The decision shall rest with the Captain of the team, who shall take the initiative to indicate immediately and clearly to the Official in charge that the ball is to be put in play from the side line. A delay by the Captain is using the right of option shall forfeit this right, and the two free throws shall be attempted.

The player who is to put the ball in play from out-of-bounds shall be entitled to pass the ball to a player at any point on the playing court.

The right of option shall not apply if a team has been awarded one or two free throws and possession of the ball (see art. 78 and 88-c).

91. Disqualifying Foul

Any flagrantly unsportsmanlike infraction of articles 77 and 80 is a disqualifying foul. A player who commits such a foul must be disqualified and removed immediately from the game.

92. Five Fouls by Player

A player who has committed five fouls either personal or technical must automatically leave the game.

93. Eight Fouls by Team

After a team has committed eight player fouls, personal or technical, in a half (extra periods are considered to be part of the second half) all subsequent player fouls shall be penalised by two free throws (for exceptions, see art. 80, Penalty (2), and art. 89 and 93).

94. Foul by Player whilst His Team is in Control of the Ball

A foul committed by a player whilst his team is in control of ball shall always be penalised by recording the foul against the offender and awarding the ball to an opponent at the nearest point out of bounds at a side-line (for exceptions, see art. 77 and 81). For definition of team in control of the ball, see art. 49.

These Rules, adopted by the International Amateur Basketball Federation, continue in operation until the end of the season 1984.

The Laws of
Bowls

Bowls

1. (*a*) "Controlling Body" means the body having immediate control of the conditions under which a match is played. The order shall be:

   (i) The International Bowling Board;

   (ii) The National Bowling Association;

   (iii) The State, Division, Local District or County Association;

  (iv) The Club on whose Green the Match is played.

(*b*) "Skip" means the Player, who, for the time being, is in charge of the head on behalf of the team.

(*c*) "Team" means either a four, triples or a pair.

(*d*) "Side" means any agreed number of Teams, whose combined scores determine the results of the match.

(*e*) "Four" means a team of four players whose positions in order of playing are named Lead, Second, Third, Skip.

(*f*) "Bowl in Course" means a bowl from the time of its delivery until it comes to rest.

(*g*) "End" means the playing of the Jack and all the bowls of all the opponents in the same direction on a rink.

(*h*) "Head" means the Jack and such bowls as have come to rest within the boundary of the rink and are not dead.

(*i*) "Mat Line" means the edge of the Mat which is nearest to the front ditch. From the centre of the Mat Line all necessary measurements to Jack or bowls shall be taken.

(*j*) "Master Bowl" means a bowl which has been approved by the I.B.B. as having the minimum bias required, as well as in all other respects complying with the Laws of the Game and is engraved with the words "Master Bowl".

   (i) A Standard Bowl of the same bias as the Master Bowl shall be kept in the custody of each National Association.

   (ii) A Standard Bowl shall be provided for the use of each official Licensed Tester.

(*k*) "Jack High" means that the nearest portion of the Bowl referred to is in line with and at the same distance from the Mat Line as the nearest portion of the Jack.

(*l*) "Pace of Green" means the number of seconds taken by a bowl from the time of its delivery to the moment it comes to rest, approximately 30 yd from the Mat Line.

(*m*) "Displaced" as applied to a Jack or Bowl means "disturbed" by any agency that is not sanctioned by these laws.

THE GREEN

2. Area and Surface

The green should form a square of not less than 40 yd and not more than 44 yd a side. It shall have a suitable playing surface, which shall be level. It shall be provided with suitable boundaries in the form of a ditch and bank.

3. The Ditch

The green shall be surrounded by a ditch and shall have a bowling surface not injurious to bowls and be free from obstacles. The ditch shall be not less than 8 in nor more than 15 in wide and it shall be not less than 2 in nor more than 8 in below the level of the green.

4. Banks

The banks shall be not less than 9 in above the level of the green, preferably upright, or alternatively at an angle of not more than 35 degrees from the perpendicular. The surface of the face of the bank shall be non-injurious to bowls. No steps likely to interfere with play shall be cut in the banks.

5. Division of the Green

The green shall be divided into spaces called rinks, each not more than 19 ft nor less than 18 ft wide. They shall be numbered consecutively, the centre line of each rink being marked on the bank at each end by a wooden peg or other suitable device. The four corners of the rink shall be marked by pegs made of wood or other suitable material, painted white, and fixed to the face of the bank and flush therewith, or alternatively fixed on the bank not more than 4 in back from the face thereof. The corner pegs shall be connected by a green thread drawn tightly along the surface of the green, with sufficient loose thread to reach the corresponding pegs on the face or surface of the bank, in order to define the boundary of the rink.

White pegs or discs shall be fixed on the side banks to indicate a clear distance of 27 yd from the ditch on the line of play. Under no circumstances shall the boundary thread be lifted while the bowl is in motion.

The boundary pegs of an outside rink shall be placed at least 2 ft from the side ditch.

6. Permissible Variations of Laws 2 and 5

(*a*) National Associations may admit Greens in the form of a square not longer than 44 yd nor shorter than 33 yd, or of a rectangle of which the longer side should not be more than 44 yd and the shorter side not less than 33 yd.

(*b*) For domestic play the green may be divided into rinks not less than 14 ft nor more than 19 ft wide. National Associations may dispense with the use of boundary threads.

MAT, JACK, BOWLS, FOOTWEAR

7. Mat

The mat shall be of a definite size, namely 24 in long and 14 in wide.

8. Jack

The Jack shall be round and white, with a diameter of not less than $2\frac{15}{32}$ in nor more than $2\frac{17}{32}$ in, and not less than 8 oz nor more than 10 oz in weight.

9. Bowls

(*a*) (i) Bowls shall be made of wood, rubber or composition and shall be black or brown in colour. Each bowl of the set shall bear the member's individual and distinguishing mark on each side. The provision relating to the distinguishing mark on each side of the bowl need not apply other than in International Matches, World Bowls Championships and Commonwealth

Games. Bowls made of wood (Lignum Vitae) shall have a maximum diameter of $4\frac{3}{4}$ in (120.65 mm) and the weight shall not exceed 3 lb 8 oz (1.59 kg). Loading of bowls made of wood is strictly prohibited.

(ii) For all International and Commonwealth Games Matches a bowl made of rubber or composition shall have a maximum diameter of $5\frac{1}{8}$ in and a minimum diameter of $4\frac{3}{4}$ in and the weight shall not exceed 3 lb 8 oz. Subject to bowls bearing a current stamp of the Board, and/or a current stamp of a Member National Authority, and/or the current stamp of the B.I.B.C. and provided they comply with the Board's Laws, they may be used in all matches controlled by the Board, or by any Member National Authority. Notwithstanding the aforegoing provisions, any Member National Authority may adopt a different scale of weights and sizes of bowls to be used in matches under its own control—such bowls may not be validly used in International Matches, World Championships, Commonwealth Games, or other matches controlled by the Board, if they differ from the Board's Laws, and unless stamped with a current stamp of the Board or any Member National Authority or the B.I.B.C.

(iii) The controlling body may, at its discretion, supply and require players to temporarily affix an adhesive marking to their bowls in any competition game. Any temporary marking under this Law shall be regarded as part of the bowl for all purposes under these Laws.

(*b*) *Bias of Bowls*. The master bowl shall have a bias approved by the International Bowling Board. A bowl shall have a bias not less than that of the master bowl and shall bear the imprint of the stamp of the International Bowling Board or that of its National Association. National Associations may adopt a standard which exceeds the bias of the master bowl. To ensure accuracy of bias and visibility of stamp, all bowls shall be re-tested and re-stamped at least once every 15 years, or earlier if the date of the stamp is not clearly legible.

(c) *Objection to Bowls.* A challenge or any intimation thereof shall not be lodged with any opposing player during the progress of a match. A challenge may be lodged with the Umpire at any time during a match, provided the Umpire is not a player in that or in any other match of the same competition.

If a challenge be lodged it shall be made not later than ten minutes after the completion of the final end in which the bowl was used. Once a challenge is lodged with the Umpire, it cannot be withdrawn.

The challenger shall immediately lodge a fee of £1 with the Umpire. The challenge shall be based on the grounds that the bowl does not comply with one or more of the requirements set out in Law 9(a) and 9(b).

The Umpire shall request the user of the bowl to surrender it to him for forwarding to the controlling body. If the owner of the challenged bowl refuses to surrender it to the Umpire, the match shall thereupon be forfeited to the opponent. The user or owner, or both, may be disqualified from playing in any match controlled or permitted by the controlling body, so long as the bowl remains untested by a licensed tester.

On receipt of the fee and the bowl, the Umpire shall take immediate steps to hand them to the Secretary of the controlling body, who shall arrange for a table test to be made as soon as practicable, and in the presence of a representative of the controlling body.

If a table test be not readily available, and any delay would unduly interfere with the progress of the competition, then, should an approved green testing device be available, it may be used to make an immediate test on the green. If a green test be made, it shall be done by, or in the presence of the Umpire, over a distance of not less than 25 yards. The comparison shall be between the challenged bowl and a standard bowl, or if it be not readily available then a recently stamped bowl of similar size, or nearly so, should be used.

The decision of the Umpire, as a result of the test, shall be final and binding for that match.

The result of the subsequent table test shall not invalidate the decision given by the Umpire on the green test.

If a challenged bowl, after an official table test, be found to comply with all the requirements of Law 9(*a*) and (*b*), it shall be returned to the user or owner and the fee paid by the challenger shall be forfeited to the controlling body.

If the challenged bowl be found not to comply with Law 9(*a*) and (*b*), the match in which it was played shall be forfeited to the opponent, and the fee paid by the challenger shall be returned to him.

If a bowl in the hands of a licensed tester has been declared as not complying with Law 9, (*a*) and (*b*), by an official representative of the controlling body, then, with the consent of the owner, and at his expense, it shall be altered so as to comply before being returned to him.

If the owner refuses his consent, and demands the return of his bowl, any current official stamp appearing thereon shall be cancelled prior to its return.

(*d*) *Alteration to Bias.* A player shall not alter, or cause to be altered other than by an official bowl tester, the bias of any bowl bearing the imprint of the official stamp of the Board, under penalty of suspension from playing for a period to be determined by the Council of the National Association of which his club is a member. Such suspension shall be subject to confirmation by the Board or a committee thereof appointed for that purpose and shall be operative among all Associations in membership with the Board.

10. Footwear

Players, umpires and markers shall wear white, brown or black smooth-soled, heel-less footwear while playing on the green, or acting as umpires or markers. (*E.B.A. Ruling: Brown footwear only will be worn.*)

ARRANGING A GAME

11. General Form and Duration

A game of bowls shall be played on one rink or on several rinks. It shall consist of a specified number of shots or ends, or shall be played for any period of time as previously arranged. The ends of the game shall be played alternatively in opposite directions excepting as provided in Laws 38, 42, 44, 46 and 47.

12. Selecting the Rinks for Play

When a match is to be played, the draw for the rinks to be played on shall be made by the Skips or their representatives.

In a match for a trophy or where competing Skips have previously been drawn, the draw to decide the numbers of the rinks to be played on shall be made by the visiting Skips or their representatives.

No player in a competition or match shall play on the same rink on the day of such competition or match before play commences, under penalty of disqualification.

This law shall not apply in the case of open tournaments.

13. Play Arrangements

Games shall be organised in the following play arrangements:
- (*a*) As a single game.
- (*b*) As a team game.
- (*c*) As a sides game.
- (*d*) As a series of single games, team games or side games.
- (*e*) As a special tournament of games.

14. A single game shall be played on one rink of a green as a single-handed game by two contending players, each playing two, three or four bowls singly and alternately.

15. A pairs game by two contending teams of two players called lead and Skip according to the order in which they play, and who at each end shall play four bowls, alternately, the leads first, then the Skips similarly. (For other than Internationals and Commonwealth Games, players in a pairs game may play two, three or four bowls each, as previously arranged by the controlling body.)

16. A triples game by two contending teams of three players, who shall play two or three bowls singly and in turn, the leads playing first.

17. A fours game by two contending teams of four players, each member playing two bowls singly and in turn.

18. A team game shall be played by two contending sides, each composed of an equal number of teams/players.

19. Games in series shall be arranged to be played on several and consecutive occasions, as:

(*a*) A series or sequence of games organised in the form of an eliminating competition and arranged as singles, pairs, triples, or fours.

(*b*) A series or sequence of side matches, organised in the form of a league competition, or an eliminating competition, or of inter-association matches.

20. A special tournament of games: Single games and team games may also be arranged in group form as a special tournament of games in which the contestants play each other in turn; or they may play as paired-off teams of players on one or several greens in accordance with a common time-table, success being adjudged by the number of games won, or by the highest net score in shots in accordance with the regulations governing the tournament.

21. For International Matches, World Bowls, and Commonwealth Games, in matches where played,

   (i) Singles shall be 21 shots up (shots in excess of 21 shall not count) four bowls each player, played alternately.
  (ii) Pairs shall be 21 ends, four bowls each player, played alternately.
 (iii) Triples shall be 18 ends, three bowls each player, played alternately.
 (iv) Fours shall be 21 ends, two bowls each player, played alternately.

Provided that pairs, triples and fours may be of a lesser number of ends, but in the case of pairs and fours there shall not be less than 18 ends, but in the case of triples not less than 15 ends, subject in all cases to the express approval of the Board as represented by its most senior officer present. If there be no officer of the Board present at the time, the decision shall rest with the "Controlling Body" as defined in Law 1. Any decision to curtail the number of ends to be played shall be made before the commencement of any game, and such decision shall only be made on the grounds of climatic conditions, inclement weather, or shortage of time to complete a programme.

22. Awards

No cash prize or monetary stake shall be played for, presented or received.

All prizes shall be in kind.

STARTING THE GAME

23. (*a*) Trial Ends

Before start of play in any competition, match or game, or on the resumption of an unfinished competition, match or game on another day, not more than one trial end each way shall be played.

(*b*) Tossing for Opening Play

The captains in a side game or Skips in a team game shall toss to decide which side or team shall play first, but in all singles games the opponents shall toss, the winner of the toss to have the option of decision. In the event of a tied (no score) or a dead end, the first to play in the tied end or dead end shall again play first.

In all ends subsequent to the first the winner of the preceding score end shall play first.

24. Placing the Mat

At the beginning of the first end the player to play first shall place the mat lengthwise on the centre line of the rink, the back edge of the mat to be 4 ft from the ditch.

Where ground sheets are in use, the mat at the first and every subsequent end shall be placed at the back edge of the sheet, the mat's back edge being 4 ft from the ditch.

25. The Mat and its Replacement

After play has commenced in any end the mat shall not be moved from its first position. If the mat be displaced during the progress of an end it shall be replaced as nearly as is practicable in the same position. If the mat be out of alignment with the centre line of the rink, it may be straightened at any time during the end.

After the last bowl in each end has come to rest in play, or has sooner become dead, the mat shall be lifted and placed wholly beyond the face of the rear bank. Should the mat be picked up by a player before the end has been completed, the opposing player shall have the right of replacing the mat in its original position.

26. The Mat in Subsequent Ends

(*a*) In all subsequent ends the back edge of the mat shall be not less than 4 ft from the rear ditch, and the front edge not less than 27 yd from the front ditch, and on the centre line of the rink of play.

(*b*) Should the Jack be improperly delivered under Law 30, the opposing player may then move the mat in the line of play, subject to clause (*a*) above, and deliver the Jack, but shall not play first. Should the Jack be improperly delivered for the second time in any end, the back edge of the mat shall be placed 4 ft from the rear ditch, and no further movement of the mat shall be permitted until the completion of the end.

27. Stance on Mat

A player shall take his stance on the mat and, at the moment of delivering the Jack or his bowl, shall have one foot remaining entirely within the confines of the mat. The foot may be either in contact with or over the mat. Failure to observe this law constitutes foot-faulting.

28. Foot-faulting

Should a player infringe the law on foot-faulting, the Umpire may, after having given a warning, have the bowl stopped and declared dead. If the bowl has disturbed the head, the opponents shall have the option of either re-setting the head, leaving the head as altered, or declaring the end dead.

29. Delivering the Jack

The players to play first shall deliver the Jack. If the Jack in its original course comes to rest at a distance of less than 2 yd from the opposite ditch, it shall be moved out to that distance and be centred. If the Jack during its original course be obstructed or deflected by a neutral object or neutral person, or by a marker, opponent, or member of the opposing team, it shall be redelivered by the same player, but if it be obstructed or deflected by a member of his own team, it shall be redelivered by the Lead of the opposing team.

30. Jack Improperly Delivered

Should the Jack in any end be not delivered from a proper stance on the mat, or if it ends its original course in the ditch or outside the side boundary of the rink or less than 25 yd in a straight line of play from the front edge of the mat, it shall be returned and the opposing player shall deliver the Jack, but shall not play first.

The Jack shall be returned as often as it is improperly delivered, but the right of the player first delivering the Jack in that end, to play the first bowl of the end, shall not be affected (see Law 26(*b*) above).

No player shall be permitted to challenge the legality of the original length of the Jack after each player in a singles game, or the leads in a team game, have each bowled one bowl.

31. Variations to Laws 24, 26, 29 and 30

Notwithstanding anything contained in Laws 24, 26, 29 and 30, any National Authority may for domestic purposes, but not in any International Matches, World Bowls Championships or Commonwealth Games, vary any of the distances mentioned in these Laws.

MOVEMENT OF BOWLS

32. "Live" Bowl

A bowl which, in its original course on the green, comes to rest within the boundaries of the rink, and not less than 15 yd from the front edge of the mat, shall be accounted as a "live" bowl and shall be in play.

33. "Touchers"

A bowl which, in its original course on the green, touches a Jack, even though such bowl passes into the ditch within the boundaries of the rink, shall be accounted as a live bowl, and shall be called a "toucher". If after having come to rest a bowl falls over and touches the Jack before the next succeeding bowl is delivered, or if in the case of the last bowl of an end it falls and touches the Jack within the period of half-minute invoked under Law 53, such bowl shall also be a "toucher". No bowl shall be accounted a "toucher" by playing on to, or by coming into contact with, the Jack while the Jack is in the ditch. If a "toucher" in the ditch cannot be seen from the mat, its position may be marked by a white or coloured peg about 2 in broad placed upright on the top of the bank and immediately in line with the place where the "toucher" rests.

34. Marking a "toucher"

A "toucher" shall be clearly marked with a chalk mark by a member of the player's team. If, in the opinion of either Skip, or opponent in singles, a "toucher" or a wrongly chalked bowl comes to rest in such a position that the act of making a chalk mark, or of erasing it, it likely to move the bowl or to alter the head, the bowl shall not be marked or have its mark erased but shall be "indicated" as a "toucher" or "non-toucher" as the case may be. If a bowl is not so marked or not so "indicated" before the succeeding bowl comes to rest, it ceases to be a "toucher". If both Skips or opponents agree that any subsequent movement of the bowl eliminates the necessity for continuation of the "indicated" provision, the bowl shall thereupon be marked or have the chalk mark erased as the case may be. Care should be taken to remove "toucher" marks from all bowls before they are played, but should a player fail to do so, and should the bowl not become a "toucher" in the end in play, the marks shall be removed by the opposing Skip or his deputy or marker immediately the bowl comes to rest, unless the bowl is "indicated" as a "non-toucher" in circumstances governed by earlier provisions of this Law.

35. Action of "Touchers"

Movement of "Touchers"—a "toucher" in play in the ditch may be moved by the impact of a Jack in play or of another "toucher" in play, and also by the impact of a "non-toucher" which remains in play after the impact, and any movement of the "toucher" by such incidents shall be valid. However, should the "non-toucher" enter the ditch at any time after the impact, it shall be dead, and the "toucher" shall be deemed to have been displaced by a dead bowl, and the provisions of Law 38(*e*) shall apply.

36. Bowl Accounted "Dead"

(*a*) Without limiting the application of any other of these Laws, a bowl shall be accounted dead if it:

- (i) not being a "toucher", comes to rest in the ditch or rebounds on to the playing surface of the rink after contact with the bank or with the Jack or a "toucher" in the ditch, or
- (ii) after completing its original course, or after being moved as a result of play, it comes to rest wholly outside the boundaries of the playing surface of the rink, or within 15 yd of the front of the mat, or
- (iii) in its original course, passes beyond a side boundary of the rink on a bias which would prevent its re-entering the rink. (A bowl is not rendered "dead" by a player carrying it whilst inspecting the head.)

(*b*) Skips, or opponents in singles, shall agree on the question as to whether or not a bowl is "dead", and having reached agreement, the question shall not later be subject to appeal to the Umpire. Any member of either team may request a decision from the Skips but no member shall remove any bowl prior to the agreement of the Skips. If Skips or opponents are unable to reach agreement as to whether or not a bowl is "dead" the matter shall be referred to the Umpire.

37. Bowl Rebounding

Only "touchers" rebounding from the face of the bank to the ditch or the rink shall remain in play.

38. Bowl Displacement

(*a*) Displacement by rebounding "non-toucher": A bowl displaced by a "non-toucher" rebounding from the bank shall be restored as near as possible to its original position, by a member of the opposing team.

(*b*) Displacement by participating player: If a bowl, while in motion or at rest on the green or a "toucher" in the ditch, be interfered with or displaced by one of the players, the opposing Skip shall have the option of:

- (i) Restoring the bowl as near as possible to its original position;
- (ii) Letting it remain where it rests;
- (iii) Declaring the bowl "dead"; or
- (iv) Declaring the end "dead".

(*c*) Displacement by a neutral object or neutral person— (other than as provided in Clause (*d*) hereof):

- (i) of a bowl in its original course: if such a bowl be displaced within the boundaries of the rink of play without having disturbed the head, it shall be replayed.

   If it be displaced and it has disturbed the head, the Skips, or the opponents in singles, shall reach agreement on the final position of the displaced bowl and on the replacement of the head, otherwise the end shall be "dead". These provisions shall also apply to a bowl in its original course displaced outside the boundaries of the rink of play provided such bowl was running on a bias which would have enabled it to re-enter the rink.

- (ii) of a bowl at rest, or in motion as a result of play after being at rest—if such a bowl be displaced the Skips, or opponents in singles, shall come to an agreement as to the position of the bowl and of the replacement of any part of the head disturbed by the displaced bowl, otherwise the end shall be "dead".

(*d*) Displacement inadvertently produced: If a bowl be moved at the time of its being marked or measured it shall be restored to its former position by an opponent. If such displacement is caused by a Marker or an Umpire, the Marker or Umpire shall replace the bowl.

(*e*) Displacement by a "dead" bowl: If a "toucher" in the ditch be displaced by a "dead" bowl from the rink of play, it shall be restored to its original position by a player of the opposite team or by the Marker.

39. "Line bowls"

A bowl shall not be accounted as outside any circle or line unless it be entirely clear of it. This shall be ascertained by looking perpendicularly down upon the bowl or by placing a square on the green.

MOVEMENT OF JACK

40. A "live" Jack in the Ditch

A Jack moved by a bowl in play into the front ditch within the boundaries of the rink shall be deemed to be "live". It may be moved by the impact of a "toucher" in play and also by the impact of a "non-toucher" which remains in play after the impact; any movement of the Jack by such incidents shall be valid. However, should the "non-toucher" enter the ditch after impact, it shall be "dead" and the Jack shall be deemed to have been "displaced" by a "dead" bowl and the provisions of Law 48 shall apply. If the Jack in the ditch cannot be seen from the mat its position shall be marked by a white peg about 2 in broad and not more than 4 in in height, placed upright on top of the bank and immediately in line from the place where the Jack rests.

41. A Jack accounted "Dead"

Should the Jack be driven by a bowl in play and come to rest wholly beyond the boundary of the rink, i.e., over the bank or over the side boundary or into any opening or inequality of any kind in the bank or rebound to a distance less than 22 yd in a direct line from the centre of the front edge of the mat to the Jack in its rebounded position, it shall be accounted "dead".

(National Associations have the option to vary the distance to which a Jack may rebound and still be playable for games other than International and Commonwealth Games.)

42. "Dead" End

When the Jack is "dead", the end shall be regarded as a "dead" end and shall not be accounted as a played end, even though all the bowls in that end have been played. All "dead" ends shall be played anew in the same direction unless both Skips or opponents in singles agree to play in the opposite direction.

43. Playing to a Boundary Jack

The Jack, if driven to the side boundary of the rink and not wholly beyond its limits, may be played to on either hand and if necessary a bowl may pass outside the side limits of the rink. A bowl so played which comes to rest within the boundaries of the rink shall not be accounted "dead".

If the Jack be driven to the side boundary line and come to rest partly within the limits of the rink, a bowl played outside the limits of the rink and coming to rest entirely outside the boundary line, even though it has made contact with the Jack, shall be accounted "dead" and shall be removed to the bank by a member of the player's team.

44. A Damaged Jack

In the event of a Jack being damaged, the Umpire shall decide if another Jack is necessary and, if so, the end shall be regarded as a "dead" end and another Jack shall be substituted and the end shall be replayed anew.

45. A Rebounding Jack

If the Jack be driven against the face of the bank and rebound on to the rink, or after being played into the ditch it be operated on by a "toucher" so as to find its way on to the rink, it shall be played to in the same manner as if it had never left the rink.

46. Jack Displaced by Player

If the Jack be diverted from its course while in motion on the green or displaced while at rest on the green or in the ditch by any one of the players, the opposing Skip shall have the Jack restored to its former position, or allow it to remain where it rests and play the end to a finish, or declare the end "dead".

47. Jack Displaced by Non-player

(*a*) If the Jack, whether in motion or at rest on the rink or in the ditch, be displaced by a bowl from another rink or by any object or by any individual not a member of the team, the two

Skips shall decide as to its original position, and if they are unable to agree, the end shall be declared "dead".

(b) If a Jack be displaced by a Marker or Umpire, it shall be restored by him to its original position, of which he shall be the sole judge.

48. Jack Displaced by "Non-toucher"

A Jack displaced in the rink of play by a "dead" bowl rebounding from the bank shall be restored, or as near as possible, to its original position by a player of the opposide team. Should a Jack however, after having been played into the ditch, be displaced by a "non-toucher", it shall be restored to its marked position by a player of the opposing team or by the Marker.

FOURS PLAY

The basis of the game of bowls is fours play.

49. The Rink and Fours Play

(a) Designation of players: A team shall consist of four players, named respectively lead, second, third and Skip, according to the order in which they play, each playing two bowls.

(b) Order of play: The leads shall play their two bowls alternately, and so on, each pair of players in succession to the end.

No one shall play until his opponent's bowl shall have come to rest.

Except under circumstances provided for in Law 63, the order of play shall not be changed after the first end has been played, under penalty of disqualification, such penalty involving the forfeiture of the match or game to the opposing team.

50. Possession of the Rink

Possession of the rink shall belong to the team whose bowl is being played.

The players in possession of the rink for the time being shall not be interfered with, annoyed or have their attention distracted in any way by their opponents.

As soon as each bowl shall have come to rest, possession of

the rink shall be transferred to the other team, time being allowed for marking a "toucher".

51. Position of Players

Players of each team not in the act of playing or controlling play shall stand behind the Jack and away from the head or 1 yd behind the mat.

As soon as the bowl is delivered, the Skip or player directing, if in front of the Jack, shall retire behind it.

52. Players and their Duties

(a) The Skip shall have sole charge of his team and his instructions shall be observed by his players. With the opposing Skip he shall decide all disputed points and when both agree their decision shall be final.

If both Skips cannot agree, the point in dispute shall be referred to and considered by an Umpire, whose decision shall be final.

A Skip may at any time delegate his powers and any of his duties to other members of his team, provided that such delegation is notified to the opposing Skip.

(b) The third: The third player may have deputed to him the duty of measuring any and all disputed shots.

(c) The second: The second player shall keep a record of all shots scored for and against his team and shall at all times retain possession of the score card whilst play is in progress. He shall see that the names of all players are entered on the score card, shall compare his record of the game with that of the opposing second player as each end is declared, and at the close of the game shall hand his score card to his Skip.

(d) The lead: The lead shall place the mat and shall deliver the Jack, ensuring that the Jack is properly centred before playing his first bowl.

(e) In addition to the duties specified in the preceding clauses, any player may undertake such duties as may be assigned to him by the Skip in Clause 52(a) hereof.

RESULT OF END

53. "The Shot"

A shot or shots shall be adjudged by the bowl or bowls nearer to the Jack than any bowl played by the opposing player or players.

When the last bowl has come to rest, half a minute shall elapse, if either team desires, before the shots are counted.

Neither Jack nor bowls shall be moved until each Skip has agreed as to the number of shots, except in circumstances where a bowl has to be moved to allow the measuring of another bowl.

54. Measuring Conditions to be Observed

No measuring shall be allowed until the end has been completed.

All measurements shall be made to the nearest point of each object. If a bowl requiring to be measured is resting on another bowl which prevents its measurement, the best available means shall be taken to secure its position, whereupon the other bowl shall be removed. The same course shall be followed where more than two bowls are involved, or where, in the course of measuring, a single bowl is in danger of falling or otherwise changing its position. When it is necessary to measure to a bowl or Jack in the ditch, and another bowl or Jack on the green, the measurement shall be made with the ordinary flexible measure. Calipers may be used to determine the shot only when the bowls in question and the Jack are on the same plane.

55. "Tie"—no shot

When at the conclusion of play in any end the nearest bowl of each team is touching the Jack, or is deemed to be equidistant from the Jack, there shall be no score recorded. The end shall be declared "drawn" and shall be counted a played end.

56. Nothing in these Laws shall be deemed to make it mandatory for the last player to play his last bowl in any end, but he shall declare to his opponent or opposing Skip his intention to refrain from playing it before the commencement of determining the result of the end and this declaration shall be irrevocable.

GAME DECISIONS

57. Games Played on one Occasion

In the case of a single game or a team game or a side game played on one occasion, or at any stage of an eliminating competition, the victory decision shall be awarded to the player, team or side of players producing at the end of the game the higher total score of shots, or in the case of a "game of winning ends", a majority of winning ends.

58. Tournament Games and Games in Series

In the case of tournament games or games in series, the victory decision shall be awarded to the player, team or side of players producing at the end of the tournament or series of contests either the largest number of winning games or the highest net score of shots in accordance with the regulations governing the tournament or series of games. Points may be used to indicate game successes. Where points are equal, the aggregate shots scored against each team (or side) shall be divided into the aggregate shots it has scored. The team (or side) with the highest result shall be declared the winner.

59. Playing to a Finish and Possible drawn Games

If in an eliminating competition consisting of a stated or agreed-upon number of ends, it be found, when all the ends have been played, that the scores are equal, an extra end or ends shall be played until a decision has been reached.

The captains or Skips shall toss and the winner shall have the right to decide who shall play first. The extra end shall be played from where the previous end was completed and the mat shall be placed in accordance with Law 24.

DEFAULTS OF PLAYERS IN
FOURS PLAY

60. Absentee Players in any Team or Side

(*a*) In a single fours game, for a trophy, prize or other competitive award, where a club is represented by only one four, each member of such four shall be a *bona-fide* member of the club. Unless all four players appear and are ready to play at the end of the maximum waiting period of 30 minutes, or should they introduce an ineligible player, then that team shall forfeit the match to the opposing team.

(b) In a domestic fours game: Where in a domestic fours game the number of players cannot be accommodated in full teams of four players, three players may play against three players, but shall suffer the deduction of one-fourth of the total score of each team. A smaller number of players than six shall be excluded from that game.

(c) In a side game: If, within a period of 30 minutes from the time fixed for the game, a single player is absent from one or both teams in a side game, whether a friendly club match or a match for a trophy, prize, or other award, the game shall proceed, but in the defaulting team, the number of bowls shall be made up by the lead and second players playing three bowls each, but one-fourth of the total shots scored by each "four" playing three men shall be deducted from their score at the end of the game. Fractions shall be taken into account.

(d) In a side game: Should such default take place where more fours than one are concerned, or where a four has been disqualified for some other infringement, and where the average score is to decide the contest, the scores of the non-defaulting fours only shall be counted, but such average shall, as a penalty in the case of the defaulting side, be arrived at by dividing the aggregate score of that side by the number of fours that should have been played and not, as in the case of the other side, by the number actually engaged in the game.

61. Play Irregularities

(a) Playing out of turn: When a player has played before his turn, the opposing Skip shall have the right to stop the bowl in its course and it shall be played in its proper turn, but, in the event of the bowl so played having moved or displaced the Jack or a bowl, the opposing Skip shall have the option of allowing the end to remain as it is after the bowl so played has come to rest, or of having the end declared "dead".

(b) Playing the wrong bowl: A bowl played by mistake shall be replaced by the player's own bowl.

(*c*) Changing bowls: A player shall not be allowed to change his bowls during the course of a game, or in a resumed game, unless they be objected to as provided in Law 9(*c*) or when a bowl has been so damaged in the course of play as, in the opinion of the Umpire, to render the bowl (or bowls) unfit for play.

(*d*) *Omitting to play.* (i) If the result of an end has been agreed upon, or the head has been touched in the agreed process of determining the result, then a player who forfeits or has omitted to play a bowl, shall forfeit the right to play it.

(ii) A player who has neglected to play a bowl in the proper sequence shall forfeit the right to play such bowl, if a bowl has been played by each team before such mistake was discovered.

(iii) If before the mistake be noticed a bowl has been delivered in the reversed order and the head has not been disturbed, the opponent shall then play two successive bowls to restore the correct sequence. If the head has been disturbed, Law 61(*a*) shall apply.

62. Play Interruptions

(*a*) Game stoppages: When a game of any kind is stopped, either by mutual arrangement or by the Umpire after appeal to him on account of darkness or the condition of the weather, or any other valid reason, it shall be resumed with the scores as they were when the game was stopped. An end commenced, but not completed, shall be declared null.

(*b*) Substitutes in a resumed game: If in a resumed game any one of the four original players be not available, one substitute shall be permitted as stated in Law 63 below. Players, however, shall not be transferred from one team to another.

INFLUENCES AFFECTING PLAY

63. Leaving the Green

If during the course of a side, fours, triples or pairs game a player has to leave the green owing to illness, or other reasonable cause, his place shall be filled by a substitute, if in the opinion of both Skips (or failing agreement by them, then in the opinion of the Controlling Body) such substitution is necessary. Should the player affected be a Skip, his duties and position in a fours game shall be assumed by a third player and the substitute shall play either as lead, second or third. In the case of triples the substitute may play either as lead or second but not as Skip, and in the case of pairs the substitute shall play as lead only. Such substitute shall be a member of the club to which the team belongs. In domestic play National Associations may decide the position of any substitute.

If during the course of a single-handed game a player has to leave the green, owing to illness or other reasonable cause, the provisions of Law 62(a) shall be observed.

No player shall be allowed to delay the play by leaving the rink or team, unless with the consent of his opponent, and then only for a period not exceeding 10 minutes.

Contravention of this law shall entitle the opponent or opposing team to claim the game or match.

64. Objects on the Green

Under no circumstances, other than as provided in Laws 33 and 40, shall any extraneous object to assist a player be placed on the green, or on the bank, or on the Jack, or on a bowl, or elsewhere.

65. Unforeseen Incidents

If during the course of play the position of the Jack or bowls be disturbed by wind, storm or by any neutral object, the end shall be declared "dead", unless the Skips are agreed as to the replacement of Jack or bowls.

DOMESTIC ARRANGEMENTS

66. In addition to any matters specifically mentioned in these Laws, National Associations may, in circumstances dictated by climate or other local conditions, make such other regulations as are deemed necessary and desirable. Such regulations must be submitted to the International Bowling Board for approval. For this purpose the Board shall appoint a committee, to be known as the Laws Committee, with powers to grant approval or otherwise to any proposal, such decision to be valid until the proposal is submitted to the Board for a final decision.

67. Local Arrangements

Constituent clubs of National Associations shall also, in making their domestic arrangements, make such regulations as are deemed necessary to govern their club competitions, but such regulations shall comply with the Laws of the Game and be approved by the Council of their National Association.

68. National Visiting Teams or Sides

No team or side of bowlers visiting overseas or the British Isles shall be recognised by the International Bowling Board unless it first be sanctioned and recommended by the National Association to which its members are affiliated.

69. Contracting Out

No club, club management committee or any individual shall have the right or power to contract out of any of the Laws of the Game as laid down by the International Bowling Board.

REGULATING SINGLE-HANDED, PAIRS AND TRIPLES GAMES

70. The foregoing Laws, where applicable, shall also apply to single-handed, pairs and triples games.

SPECTATORS

71. Persons not engaged in the game shall be situate clear of and beyond the limits of the rink of play and clear of verges. They shall preserve an attitude of strict neutrality, and neither by word nor act disturb or advise the players.

Betting or gambling in connection with any game or games shall not be permitted or engaged in within the grounds of any constituent club.

DUTIES OF MARKER

72. (*a*) The Marker shall control the game in accordance with the I.B.B. Basic Laws. He shall, before play commences, examine all bowls for the imprint of the I.B.B. stamp, or that of its National Association, such imprint to be clearly visible, and shall ascertain by measurement the width of the rink of play.

(*b*) He shall centre the Jack and shall place a full-length Jack 2 yd from the ditch.

(*c*) He shall ensure that the Jack is not less than 25 yd from the front edge of the mat after it has been centred.

(*d*) He shall stand at one side of the rink and to the rear of the Jack.

(*e*) He shall answer affirmatively or negatively a player's enquiry as to whether a bowl is Jack high. If requested he shall indicate the distance of any bowl from the Jack or from any other bowl, and also, if requested, indicate which bowl he thinks is shot and/or the relative position of any other bowl.

(*f*) Subject to contrary directions from either opponent under Law 34, he shall mark all "touchers" immediately they come to rest, and remove chalk marks from "non-touchers". With the agreement of both opponents he shall remove all dead bowls from the green and the ditch. He shall mark the positions of the Jack and "touchers" which are in the ditch (see Laws 33 and 40).

(*g*) He shall not move, or cause to be moved, either Jack or bowls until each player has agreed as to the number of shots.

(*h*) He shall measure carefully all doubtful shots when requested by either player. If unable to come to a decision satisfactory to the players, he shall call in an Umpire. If an official Umpire has not been appointed, the Marker shall select one. The decision of the Umpire shall be final.

(*i*) He shall enter the score at each end and shall intimate to the players the state of the game. When the game is finished, he shall see that the score card, containing the names of the players, is signed by the players and disposed of in accordance with the rules of the competition.

DUTIES OF UMPIRE

73. An Umpire shall be appointed by the Controlling Body of the Association, Club or Tournament Management Committee. His duties shall be as follows:

(*a*) He shall examine all bowls for the imprint of the I.B.B. stamp or that of its National Association, and ascertain by measurement the width of the rinks of play.

(*b*) He shall measure any shot or shots in dispute, and for this purpose shall use a suitable measure. His decision shall be final.

(*c*) He shall decide all questions as to the distance of the mat from the ditch and the Jack from the mat.

(*d*) He shall decide as to whether or not Jack and/or bowls are in play.

(*e*) He shall enforce the Laws of the Game.

(*f*) In World Bowls Championships and Commonwealth Games the Umpire's decision shall be final in respect of any breach of a Law, except that, upon questions relating to the meaning or interpretation of any Law, there shall be a right of appeal to the Controlling Body.

These Laws, originally formulated by the Scottish Bowling Association and last revised in 1980, may not be published without the consent of the International Bowling Board.

The Laws of
Cricket

Cricket

1. THE PLAYERS

1. Number of Players and Captain

A match is played between two sides each of eleven Players, one of whom shall be Captain. In the event of the Captain not being available at any time a Deputy shall act for him.

2. Nomination of Players

Before the toss for innings, the Captain shall nominate his Players who may not thereafter be changed without the consent of the opposing Captain.

NOTES

(a) More or Less than Eleven Players a Side.

A match may be played by agreement between sides of more or less than eleven players but not more than eleven players may field.

2. SUBSTITUTES AND RUNNERS: BATSMAN OR FIELDSMAN LEAVING THE FIELD: BATSMAN RETIRING: BATSMAN COMMENCING INNINGS

1. Substitutes

Substitutes shall be allowed by right to field for any player who during the match is incapacitated by illness or injury. The consent of the opposing Captain must be obtained for the use of a Substitute if any player is prevented from fielding for any other reason.

2. Objection to Substitutes

The opposing Captain shall have no right of objection to any player acting as Substitute in the field, nor as to where he shall field, although he may object to the Substitute acting as Wicket-Keeper.

3. Substitute Not to Bat or Bowl

A Substitute shall not be allowed to bat or bowl.

4. A Player for whom a Substitute has acted

A player may bat, bowl or field even though a Substitute has acted for him.

5. Runner

A Runner shall be allowed for a Batsman who during the match is incapacitated by illness or injury. The player acting as Runner shall be a member of the batting side and shall, if possible, have already batted in that innings.

6. Runner's Equipment

The player acting as Runner for an injured Batsman shall wear batting gloves and pads if the injured Batsman is so equipped.

7. Transgression of the Laws by an Injured Batsman or Runner

An injured Batsman may be out should his Runner break any one of Laws 33 (Handled the Ball), 37 (Obstructing the Field) or 38 (Run Out). As Striker he remains himself subject to the Laws. Furthermore, should he be out of his ground for any purpose and the wicket at the Wicket-Keeper's end be put down he shall be out under Law 38 (Run Out) or Law 39 (Stumped) irrespective of the position of the other Batsman or the Runner and no runs shall be scored.

When not the Striker, the injured Batsman is out of the game and shall stand where he does not interfere with the play. Should he bring himself into the game in any way then he shall suffer the penalties that any transgression of the Laws demands.

8. Fieldsman Leaving the Field

No Fieldsman shall leave the field or return during a session of play without the consent of the Umpire at the Bowler's end. The Umpire's consent is also necessary if a Substitute is required for a Fieldsman, when his side returns to the field after an interval. If a member of the fielding side leaves the field or fails to return after an interval and is absent from the field for longer than 15 minutes, he shall not be permitted to bowl after his return until he has been on the field for at least that length of playing time for which he was absent. This restriction shall not apply at the start of a new day's play.

9. Batsman Leaving the Field or Retiring

A Batsman may leave the field or retire at any time owing to illness, injury or other unavoidable cause, having previously notified the Umpire at the Bowler's end. He may resume his innings at the fall of a wicket, which for the purposes of this Law shall include the retirement of another Batsman.

If he leaves the field or retires for any other reason he may only resume his innings with the consent of the opposing Captain.

When a Batsman has left the field or retired and is unable to return owing to illness, injury or other unavoidable cause, his innings is to be recorded as "retired, not out". Otherwise it is to be recorded as "retired, out".

10. Commencement of a Batsman's Innings

A Batsman shall be considered to have commenced his innings once he has stepped on to the field of play.

3. THE UMPIRES

1. Appointment

Before the toss for innings two Umpires shall be appointed, one for each end, to control the game with absolute impartiality as required by the Laws.

2. Change of Umpire

No Umpire shall be changed during a match without the consent of both Captains.

3. Special Conditions

Before the toss for innings, the Umpires shall agree with both Captains on any special conditions affecting the conduct of the match.

4. The Wickets

The Umpires shall satisfy themselves before the start of the match that the wickets are properly pitched.

5. Clock or Watch

The Umpires shall agree between themselves and inform both Captains before the start of the match on the watch or clock to be followed during the match.

6. Conduct and Implements

Before and during a match the Umpires shall ensure that the conduct of the game and the implements used are strictly in accordance with the Laws.

7. Fair and Unfair Play

The Umpires shall be the sole judges of fair and unfair play.

8. Fitness of Ground, Weather and Light

(*a*) The Umpires shall be the sole judges of the fitness of the ground, weather and light for play.

    (i) However, before deciding to suspend play or not to start play or not to resume play after an interval or stoppage, the Umpires shall establish whether both Captains (the Batsmen at the wicket may deputise for their Captain) wish to commence or to continue in the prevailing conditions; if so, their wishes shall be met.

    (ii) In addition, if during play, the Umpires decide that the light is unfit, only the batting side shall have the option of continuing play. After agreeing to continue to play in unfit light conditions, the Captain of the batting side (or a Batsman at the wicket) may appeal against the light to the Umpires, who shall uphold the appeal only if, in their opinion, the light has deteriorated since the agreement to continue was made.

(*b*) After any suspension of play, the Umpires, unaccompanied by any of the Players or Officials shall, on their own initiative, carry out an inspection immediately the conditions improve and shall continue to inspect at intervals. Immediately the Umpires decide that play is possible they shall call upon the Players to resume the game.

9. Exceptional Circumstances

In exceptional circumstances, other than those of weather, ground or light, the Umpires may decide to suspend or abandon play. Before making such a decision the Umpires shall establish, if the circumstances allow, whether both Captains (the Batsmen at the wicket may deputise for their Captain) wish to continue in the prevailing conditions: if so their wishes shall be met.

10. Position of Umpires

The Umpires shall stand where they can best see any act upon which their decision may be required.

Subject to this over-riding consideration the Umpire at the Bowler's end shall stand where he does not interfere with either the Bowler's run up or the Striker's view.

The Umpire at the Striker's end may elect to stand on the off instead of the leg side of the pitch, provided he informs the Captain of the fielding side and the Striker of his intention to do so.

11. Umpires Changing Ends

The Umpires shall change ends after each side has had one innings.

12. Disputes

All disputes shall be determined by the Umpires and if they disagree the actual state of things shall continue.

13. Signals

The following code of signals shall be used by Umpires who will wait until a signal has been answered by a Scorer before allowing the game to proceed.

Boundary	by waving the arm from side to side.
Boundary 6	by raising both arms above the head.
Bye	by raising an open hand above the head.

Dead Ball	by crossing and re-crossing the wrists below the waist.
Leg Bye	by touching a raised knee with the hand.
No Ball	by extending one arm horizontally.
Out	by raising the index finger above the head. If not out the Umpire shall call "not out".
Short Run	by bending the arm upwards and by touching the nearer shoulder with the tips of the fingers.
Wide	by extending both arms horizontally.

14. Correctness of Scores

The Umpires shall be responsible for satisfying themselves on the correctness of the scores throughout and at the conclusion of the match. See Law 21.6. (Correctness of Result).

4. THE SCORERS

1. Recording Runs

All runs scored shall be recorded by Scorers appointed for the purpose. Where there are two Scorers they shall frequently check to ensure that the score sheets agree.

2. Acknowledging Signals

The Scorers shall accept and immediately acknowledge all instructions and signals given to them by the Umpires.

5. THE BALL

1. Weight and Size

The ball, when new, shall weigh not less than $5\frac{1}{2}$ oz (155.9 g), nor more than $5\frac{3}{4}$ oz (163 g): and shall measure not less than $8\frac{13}{16}$ in (22.4 cm), nor more than 9 in (22.9 cm) in circumference.

2. Approval of Balls

All balls used in matches shall be approved by the Umpires and Captains before the start of the match.

3. New Ball

Subject to agreement to the contrary, having been made before the toss, either Captain may demand a new ball at the start of each innings.

4. New Ball in Match of 3 or more Days Duration

In a match of 3 or more days' duration, the Captain of the fielding side may demand a new ball after the prescribed number of overs has been bowled with the old one. The Governing Body for cricket in the country concerned shall decide the number of overs applicable in that country which shall be not less than 75 six-ball overs (55 eight-ball overs).

5. Ball Lost or Becoming Unfit for Play

In the event of a ball during play being lost or, in the opinion of the Umpires, becoming unfit for play, the Umpires shall allow it to be replaced by one that in their opinion has had a similar amount of wear. If a ball is to be replaced, the Umpires shall inform the Batsmen.

6. THE BAT

1. Width and Length

The bat overall shall not be more than 38 in (96.5 cm) in length; the blade of the bat shall be made of wood and shall not exceed $4\frac{1}{4}$ in (10.8 cm) at the widest part.

7. THE PITCH

1. Area of Pitch

The pitch is the area between the bowling creases – see Law 9. (The Bowling, Popping and Return Creases). It shall measure 5 ft (1.52 m) in width on either side of a line joining the centre of the middle stumps of the wickets. (See Law 8: The Wickets.)

2. Selection and Preparation

Before the toss for innings, the Executive of the Ground shall be responsible for the selection and preparation of the pitch; thereafter the Umpires shall control its use and maintenance.

3. Changing Pitch

The pitch shall not be changed during a match unless it becomes unfit for play, and then only with the consent of both Captains.

4. Non-Turf Pitches

In the event of a non-turf pitch being used, the following shall apply:
(*a*) *Length:* That of the playing surface to a minimum of 58 ft (17.68 m).
(*b*) *Width:* That of the playing surface to a minimum of 6 ft (1.83 m).

8. THE WICKETS

1. Width and Pitching

Two sets of wickets, each 9 in (22.86 cm) wide, and consisting of three wooden stumps with two wooden bails upon the top, shall be pitched opposite and parallel to each other at a distance of 22 yd (20.12 m) between the centres of the two middle stumps.

2. Size of Stumps

The stumps shall be of equal and sufficient size to prevent the ball from passing between them. Their tops shall be 28 in (71.1 cm) above the ground, and shall be dome-shaped except for the bail grooves.

3. Size of Bails

The bails shall be each $4\frac{3}{8}$ in (11.1 cm) in length and when in position on the top of the stumps shall not project more than $\frac{1}{2}$ in (1.3 cm) above them.

9 THE BOWLING, POPPING AND RETURN CREASES

1. The Bowling Crease

The bowling crease shall be marked in line with the stumps at each end and shall be 8 ft 8 in (2.64 m) in length, with the stumps in the centre.

2. The Popping Crease

The popping crease, which is the back edge of the crease marking, shall be in front of and parallel with the bowling crease. It shall have the back edge of the crease marking 4 ft (1.22 m) from the centre of the stumps and shall extend to a minimum of 6 ft (1.83 m) on either side of the line of the wicket.

The popping crease shall be considered to be unlimited in length.

3. The Return Crease

The return crease marking, of which the inside edge is the crease, shall be at each end of the bowling crease and at right angles to it. The return crease shall be marked to a minimum of 4 ft (1.22 m) behind the wicket and shall be considered to be unlimited in length. A forward extension shall be marked to the popping crease.

10. ROLLING, SWEEPING, MOWING, WATERING THE PITCH AND RE-MARKING OF CREASES

1. Rolling

During the match the pitch may be rolled at the request of the Captain of the batting side, for a period of not more than 7 minutes before the start of each innings, other than the first innings of the match, and before the start of each day's play. In addition, if, after the toss and before the first innings of the match, the start is delayed, the Captain of the batting side shall have the right to have the pitch rolled for not more than 7 minutes.

The pitch shall not otherwise be rolled during the match.

The 7 minutes rolling permitted before the start of a day's play shall take place not earlier than half an hour before the start of play and the Captain of the batting side may delay such rolling until 10 minutes before the start of play should he so desire.

If a Captain declares an innings closed less than 15 minutes before the resumption of play, and the other Captain is thereby prevented from exercising his option of 7 minutes rolling or if he is so prevented for any other reason the time for rolling shall be taken out of the normal playing time.

2. Sweeping
Such sweeping of the pitch as is necessary during the match shall be done so that the 7 minutes allowed for rolling the pitch provided for in 1 above is not affected.

3. Mowing
(*a*) *Responsibilities of Ground Authority and of Umpires*. All mowings which are carried out before the toss for innings shall be the responsibility of the Ground Authority. Thereafter they shall be carried out under the supervision of the Umpires, see Law 7.2 (Selection and Preparation).

(*b*) *Initial Mowing*. The pitch shall be mown before play begins on the day the match is scheduled to start or in the case of a delayed start on the day the match is expected to start. See 3(a) above (Responsibilities of Ground Authority and of Umpires).

(*c*) *Subsequent Mowings in a Match of 2 or More Days' Duration*. In a match of two or more days' duration, the pitch shall be mown daily before play begins. Should this mowing not take place because of weather conditions, rest days or other reasons the pitch shall be mown on the first day on which the match is resumed.

(*d*) *Mowing of the Outfield in a Match of 2 or More Days' Duration*. In order to ensure that conditions are as similar as possible for both sides, the outfield shall normally be mown before the commencement of play on each day of the match, if ground and weather conditions allow.

4. Watering
The pitch shall not be watered during a match.

5. Re-Marking Creases
Whenever possible the creases shall be re-marked.

6. Maintenance of Foot Holes
In wet weather, the Umpires shall ensure that the holes made

by the Bowlers and Batsmen are cleaned out and dried whenever necessary to facilitate play. In matches of 2 or more days' duration, the Umpires shall allow, if necessary, the re-turfing of foot holes made by the Bowler in his delivery stride, or the use of quick-setting fillings for the same purpose, before the start of each day's play.

7. Securing of Footholds and Maintenance of Pitch

During play, the Umpires shall allow either Batsman to beat the pitch with his bat and players to secure their footholds by the use of sawdust, provided that no damage to the pitch is so caused, and Law 42 (Unfair Play) is not contravened.

11. COVERING THE PITCH

1. Before the Start of a Match

Before the start of a match complete covering of the pitch shall be allowed.

2. During a Match

The pitch shall not be completely covered during a match unless prior arrangement or regulations so provide.

3. Covering Bowlers' Run-Up

Whenever possible, the Bowlers' run-up shall be covered, but the covers so used shall not extend further than 4 ft/1.22 m in front of the popping crease.

12. INNINGS

1. Number of Innings

A match shall be of one or two innings of each side according to agreement reached before the start of play.

2. Alternate Innings

In a two innings match each side shall take their innings alternately except in the case provided for in Law 13 (The Follow-On).

3. The Toss

The Captains shall toss for the choice of innings on the field of play not later than 15 minutes before the time scheduled for the match to start, or before the time agreed upon for play to start.

4. Choice of Innings

The winner of the toss shall notify his decision to bat or to field to the opposing Captain not later than 10 minutes before the time scheduled for the match to start, or before the time agreed upon for play to start. The decision shall not thereafter be altered.

5. Continuation After One Innings of Each Side

Despite the terms of 1 above, in a one innings match, when a result has been reached on the first innings the Captains may agree to the continuation of play if, in their opinion, there is a prospect of carrying the game to a further issue in the time left. See Law 21 (Result).

13. THE FOLLOW-ON

1. Lead on First Innings

In a two innings match the side which bats first and leads by 200 runs in a match of five days or more, by 150 runs in a three-day or four-day match, by 100 runs in a two-day match, or by 75 runs in a one-day match, shall have the option of requiring the other side to follow their innings.

2. Day's Play Lost

If no play takes place on the first day of a match of two or more days' duration, 1 above shall apply in accordance with the number of days' play remaining from the actual start of the match.

14. DECLARATIONS

1. Time of Declaration

The Captain of the batting side may declare an innings closed at any time during a match irrespective of its duration.

2. Forfeiture of Second Innings

A Captain may forfeit his second innings, provided his decision to do so is notified to the opposing Captain and Umpires in sufficient time to allow 7 minutes rolling of the pitch. See Law 10 (Rolling, Sweeping, Mowing, Watering the Pitch and Re-Marking of Creases). The normal 10 minute interval between innings shall be applied.

15. START OF PLAY

1. Call of Play

At the start of each innings and of each day's play and on the resumption of play after any interval or interruption the Umpire at the Bowlers' end shall call "play".

2. Practice on the Field

At no time on any day of the match shall there be any bowling or batting practice on the pitch.

No practice may take place on the field if, in the opinion of the Umpires, it could result in a waste of time.

3. Trial Run-Up

No Bowler shall have a trial run-up after "play" has been called in any session of play, except at the fall of a wicket when an Umpire may allow such a trial run-up if he is satisfied that it will not cause any waste of time.

16. INTERVALS

1. Length

The Umpire shall allow such intervals as have been agreed upon for meals, and 10 minutes between each innings.

2. Luncheon Interval – Innings Ending or Stoppage within 10 Minutes of Interval

If an innings ends or there is a stoppage caused by weather or bad light within 10 minutes of the agreed time for the luncheon interval, the interval shall be taken immediately.

The time remaining in the session of play shall be added to

the agreed length of the interval but no extra allowance shall be made for the 10 minutes interval between innings.

3. Tea Interval – Innings Ending or Stoppage within 30 Minutes of Interval

If an innings ends or there is a stoppage caused by weather or bad light within 30 minutes of the agreed time for the tea interval, the interval shall be taken immediately.

The interval shall be of the agreed length and, if applicable, shall include the 10 minute interval between innings.

4. Tea Interval – Continuation of Play

If at the agreed time for the tea interval, nine wickets are down, play shall continue for a period not exceeding 30 minutes or until the innings is concluded.

5. Tea Interval – Agreement to Forego

At any time during the match, the Captains may agree to forego a tea interval.

6. Intervals for Drinks

If both Captains agree before the start of a match that intervals for drinks may be taken, the option to take such intervals shall be available to either side. These intervals shall be restricted to one per session, shall be kept as short as possible, shall not be taken in the last hour of the match and in any case shall not exceed 5 minutes.

The agreed times for these intervals shall be strictly adhered to except that if a wicket falls within 5 minutes of the agreed time then drinks shall be taken out immediately.

If an innings ends or there is a stoppage caused by weather or bad light within 30 minutes of the agreed time for a drinks interval, there will be no interval for drinks in that session.

At any time during the match the Captains may agree to forgo any such drinks interval.

17. CESSATION OF PLAY

1. Call of Time

The Umpire at the Bowler's end shall call "time" on the cessation of play before any interval or interruption of play, at the end of each day's play, and at the conclusion of the match. See Law 27 (Appeals).

2. Removal of Bails

After the call of "time", the Umpires shall remove the bails from both wickets.

3. Starting a Last Over

The last over before an interval or the close of play shall be started provided the Umpire, after walking at his normal pace, has arrived at his position behind the stumps at the Bowler's end before time has been reached.

4. Completion of the Last Over of a Session

The last over before an interval or the close of play shall be completed unless a Batsman is out or retires during that over within 2 minutes of the interval or the close of play or unless the Players have occasion to leave the field.

5. Completion of the Last Over of a Match

An over in progress at the close of play on the final day of a match shall be completed at the request of either Captain even if a wicket falls after time has been reached.

If during the last over the Players have occasion to leave the field the Umpires shall call "time" and there shall be no resumption of play and the match shall be at an end.

6. Last Hour of Match – Number of Overs

The Umpires shall indicate when one hour of playing time of the match remains according to the agreed hours of play. The next over after that moment shall be the first of a minimum of 20 6-ball overs, (15 8-ball overs), provided a result is not reached earlier or there is no interval or interruption of play.

7. Last Hour of Match—Intervals Between Innings and Interruptions of Play

If, at the commencement of the last hour of the match, an interval or interruption of play is in progress or if, during the last hour there is an interval between innings or an interruption of play, the minimum number of overs to be bowled on the resumption of play shall be reduced in proportion to the duration, within the last hour of the match, of any such interval or interruption.

The minimum number of overs to be bowled after a resumption of play shall be calculated as follows:

(*a*) In the case of an interval or interruption of play being in progress at the commencement of the last hour of the match, or in the case of a first interval or interruption a deduction shall be made from the minimum of 20 6-ball overs (or 15 8-ball overs).

(*b*) If there is a later interval or interruption a further deduction shall be made from the minimum number of overs which should have been bowled following the last resumption of play.

(*c*) These deductions shall be based on the following factors:

(i) the number of overs already bowled in the last hour of the match or, in the case of a later interval or interruption in the last session of play.

(ii) the number of overs lost as a result of the interval or interruption allowing one 6-ball over for every full three minutes (or one 8-ball over for every full four minutes) of interval or interruption.

(iii) any over left uncompleted at the end of an innings to be excluded from these calculations.

(iv) any over left uncompleted at the start of an interruption of play to be completed when play is resumed and to count as one over bowled.

(v) an interval to start with the end of an innings and to end 10 minutes later; an interruption to start on the call of "time" and to end on the call of "play".

(*d*) In the event of an innings being completed and a new innings commencing during the last hour of the match, the number of overs to be bowled in the new innings shall be calculated on the basis of one 6-ball over for every three minutes or part thereof remaining for play (or one 8-ball over for every four minutes or part thereof remaining for play); or alternatively on the basis that sufficient overs be bowled to enable the full minimum quota of overs to be completed under circumstances governed by (*a*), (*b*) and (*c*) above. In all such cases the alternative which allows the greater number of overs shall be employed.

8. Bowler Unable to Complete an Over During Last Hour of the Match

If, for any reason, a Bowler is unable to complete an over during the period of play referred to in 6 above, Law 22.7 (Bowler Incapacitated or Suspended during an Over) shall apply.

18. SCORING

1. A Run

The score shall be reckoned by runs. A run is scored:

(*a*) So often as the Batsmen, after a hit or at any time while the ball is in play, shall have crossed and made good their ground from end to end.

(*b*) When a boundary is scored. See Law 19 (Boundaries).

(*c*) When penalty runs are awarded. See 6 below.

2. Short Runs

(*a*) If either Batsman runs a short run, the Umpire shall call and signal "one short" as soon as the ball becomes dead and that run shall not be scored. A run is short if a Batsman fails to make good his ground on turning for a further run.

(*b*) Although a short run shortens the succeeding one, the latter, of completed shall count.

(*c*) If either or both Batsmen deliberately run short the Umpire shall, as soon as he sees that the fielding side have no chance of dismissing either Batsman, call and signal "dead ball" and disallow any runs attempted or previously scored. The Batsmen shall return to their original ends.

(*d*) If both Batsmen run short in one and the same run, only one run shall be deducted.

(*e*) Only if three or more runs are attempted can more than one be short and then, subject to (*c*) and (*d*) above, all runs so called shall be disallowed. If there has been more than one short run the Umpires shall instruct the Scorers as to the number of runs disallowed.

3. Striker Caught

If the Striker is Caught, no run shall be scored.

4. Batsman Run Out

If a Batsman is Run Out, only that run which was being attempted shall not be scored. If, however, an injured Striker himself is run out no runs shall be scored. See Law 2.7 (Transgression of the Laws by an Injured Batsman or Runner).

5. Batsman Obstructing the Field

If a Batsman is out Obstructing the Field, any runs completed before the obstruction occurs shall be scored unless such obstruction prevents a catch being made in which case no runs shall be scored.

6. Runs Scored for Penalties

Runs shall be scored for penalties under Laws 20 (Lost Ball), 24 (No Ball), 25 (Wide Ball), 41.1 (Fielding the Ball) and for boundary allowances under Law 19 (Boundaries).

7. Batsman Returning to Wicket he has Left

If, while the ball is in play, the Batsmen have crossed in running, neither shall return to the wicket he has left even though a short run has been called or no run has been scored as in the case of a catch. Batsmen, however, shall return to the wickets they originally left in the cases of a boundary and of any disallowance of runs and of an injured Batsman being, himself, run out. See Law 2.7 (Transgression of the Laws by an Injured Batsman or Runner).

19. BOUNDARIES

1. The Boundary of the Playing Area

Before the toss for innings, the Umpires shall agree with both Captains on the boundary of the playing area. The boundary shall, if possible, be marked by a white line, a rope laid on the ground, or a fence. If flags or posts only are used to mark a boundary, the imaginary line joining such points shall be regarded as the boundary. An obstacle, or person, within the playing area shall not be regarded as a boundary unless so decided by the Umpires before the toss for innings. Sightscreens within, or partially within, the playing area shall be regarded as the boundary and when the ball strikes or passes within or under or directly over any part of the screen, a boundary shall be scored.

2. Runs Scored for Boundaries

Before the toss for innings, the Umpires shall agree with both Captains the runs to be allowed for boundaries, and in deciding the allowance for them, the Umpires and Captains shall be guided by the prevailing custom of the ground. The allowance for a boundary shall normally be 4 runs, and 6 runs for all hits pitching over and clear of the boundary line or fence, even though the ball has been previously touched by a Fieldsman. 6 runs shall also be scored if a Fieldsman, after catching a ball, carries it over the boundary. 6 runs shall not be scored when a ball struck by the Striker hits a sightscreen full pitch if the screen is within, or partially within, the playing area, but if the ball is struck directly over a sightscreen so situated, 6 runs shall be scored.

3. A Boundary

A boundary shall be scored and signalled by the Umpire at the Bowler's end whenever, in his opinion:

(*a*) A ball in play touches or crosses the boundary, however marked.

(*b*) A Fieldsman with ball in hand touches or grounds any part of his person on or over a boundary line.

(*c*) A Fieldsman with ball in hand grounds any part of his

person over a boundary fence or board. This allows the Fieldsman to touch or lean on or over a boundary fence or board in preventing a boundary.

4. Runs Exceeding Boundary Allowance

The runs completed at the instant the ball reaches the boundary shall count if they exceed the boundary allowance.

5. Overthrows or Wilful Act of a Fieldsman

If the boundary results from an overthrow or from the wilful act of a Fieldsman, any runs already completed and the allowance shall be added to the score. The run in progress shall count provided that the Batsmen have crossed at the instant of the throw or act.

20. LOST BALL

1. Runs Scored

If a ball in play cannot be found or recovered any fieldsman may call "lost ball" when 6 runs shall be added to the score; but if more than 6 have been run before "lost ball" is called, as many runs as have been completed shall be scored. The run in progress shall count provided that the Batsmen have crossed at the instant of the call of "lost ball".

2. How Scored

The runs shall be added to the score of the Striker if the ball has been struck, but otherwise to the score of byes, leg-byes, no-balls or wides as the case may be.

21. THE RESULT

1. A Win—Two Innings Matches

The side which has scored a total of runs in excess of that scored by the opposing side in its two completed innings shall be the winners.

2. A Win—One Innings Matches

(*a*) One innings matches, unless played out as in 1 above, shall be decided on the first innings, but see Law 12.5 (Continuation After One Innings of Each Side).

(*b*) If the Captains agree to continue play after the completion of one innings of each side in accordance with Law 12.5 (Continuation After One Innings of Each Side) and a result is not achieved on the second innings, the first innings result shall stand.

3. Umpires Awarding a Match

(*a*) A match shall be lost by a side which, during the match,
   (i) refuses to play, or
   (ii) concedes defeat,
and the Umpires shall award the match to the other side.

(*b*) Should both Batsmen at the wickets or the fielding side leave the field at any time without the agreement of the Umpires, this shall constitute a refusal to play and, on appeal, the Umpires shall award the match to the other side in accordance with (*a*) above.

4. A Tie

The result of a match shall be a tie when the scores are equal at the conclusion of play, but only if the side batting last has completed its innings.

If the scores of the completed first innings of a one-day match are equal, it shall be a tie but only if the match has not been played out to a further conclusion.

5. A Draw

A match not determined in any of the ways as in 1, 2, 3 and 4 above shall count as a draw.

6. Correctness of Result

Any decision as to the correctness of the scores shall be the responsibility of the Umpires. See Law 3.14 (Correctness of Scores).

If, after the Umpires and Players have left the field, in the belief that the match has been concluded, the Umpires decide that a mistake in scoring has occurred, which affects the result, and provided time has not been reached, they shall order play to resume and to continue until the agreed finishing time unless a result is reached earlier.

If the Umpires decide that a mistake has occurred and time has been reached, the Umpires shall immediately inform both Captains of the necessary corrections to the scores and, if applicable, to the result.

7. Acceptance of Result

In accepting the scores as notified by the scorers and agreed by the Umpires, the Captains of both sides thereby accept the result.

22. THE OVER

1. Number of Balls

The ball shall be bowled from each wicket alternately in overs of either 6 or 8 balls according to agreement before the match.

2. Call of "Over"

When the agreed number of balls has been bowled, and as the ball becomes dead or when it becomes clear to the Umpire at the Bowler's end that both the fielding side and the Batsmen at the wicket have ceased to regard the ball as in play, the Umpire shall call "over" before leaving the wicket.

3. No Ball or Wide Ball

Neither a no ball nor a wide ball shall be reckoned as one of the over.

4. Umpire Miscounting

If an Umpire miscounts the number of balls, the over as counted by the Umpire shall stand.

5. Bowler Changing Ends

A Bowler shall be allowed to change ends as often as desired provided only that he does not bowl two overs consecutively in an innings.

6. The Bowler Finishing an Over

A Bowler shall finish an over in progress unless he be incapacitated or be suspended under Law 42.8. (The Bowling of Fast Short Pitched Balls), 42.9. (The Bowling of Fast High Full Pitches), 42.10. (Time Wasting) and 42.11. (Players Damaging the Pitch). If an over is left incomplete for any reason at the start of an interval or interruption of play, it shall be finished on the resumption of play.

7. Bowler Incapacitated or Suspended During an Over

If, for any reason, a Bowler is incapacitated while running up to bowl the first ball of an over, or is incapacitated or suspended during an over, the Umpire shall call and signal "dead ball" and another Bowler shall be allowed to bowl or complete the over from the same end, provided only that he shall not bowl two overs, or part thereof, consecutively in one innings.

8. Position of Non-Striker

The Batsman at the Bowler's end shall normally stand on the opposite side of the wicket to that from which the ball is being delivered, unless a request to do otherwise is granted by the Umpire.

23. DEAD BALL

1. The Ball Becomes Dead, when:—

(*a*) It is finally settled in the hands of the Wicket Keeper or the Bowler.

(*b*) It reaches or pitches over the boundary.

(*c*) A Batsman is out.

(*d*) Whether played or not, it lodges in the clothing or equipment of a Batsman or the clothing of an Umpire.

(*e*) A ball lodges in a protective helmet worn by a member of the fielding side.

(*f*) A penalty is awarded under Law 20 (Lost Ball) or Law 41.1 (Fielding the Ball).

(*g*) The Umpire calls "over" or "time".

2. Either Umpire Shall Call and Signal "Dead Ball", when:

(*a*) He intervenes in a case of unfair play.

(*b*) A serious injury to a Player or Umpire occurs.

(*c*) He is satisfied that, for an adequate reason, the Striker is not ready to receive the ball and makes no attempt to play it.

(*d*) The Bowler drops the ball accidentally before delivery, or the ball does not leave his hand for any reason.

(*e*) One or both bails fall from the Striker's wicket before he receives delivery.

(*f*) He leaves his normal position for consultation.

(*g*) He is required to do so under Laws 26.3 (Disallowance of Leg-Byes), etc.

3. The Ball Ceases to be Dead, when:

(*a*) The Bowler starts his run up or bowling action.

4. The Ball is Not Dead, when:

(*a*) It strikes an Umpire (unless it lodges in his dress).

(*b*) The wicket is broken or struck down (unless a Batsman is out thereby).

(*c*) An unsuccessful appeal is made.

(*d*) The wicket is broken accidentally either by the Bowler during his delivery or by a Batsman in running.

(*e*) The Umpire has called "no ball" or "wide".

24. NO BALL

1. Mode of Delivery

The Umpire shall indicate to the Striker whether the Bowler intends to bowl over or round the wicket, overarm or underarm, or right or left-handed. Failure on the part of the Bowler to indicate in advance a change in his mode of delivery is unfair and the Umpire shall call and signal "no ball".

2. Fair Delivery—The Arm

For a delivery to be fair the ball must be bowled not thrown. If either Umpire is not entirely satisfied with the absolute fairness of a delivery in this respect he shall call and signal "no ball" instantly upon delivery.

3. Fair Delivery—The Feet

The Umpire at the bowler's wicket shall call and signal "no ball" if he is not satisfied that in the delivery stride:

(*a*) the Bowler's back foot has landed within and not touching the return crease or its forward extension, or

(*b*) some part of the front foot whether grounded or raised was behind the popping crease.

4. Bowler Throwing at Striker's Wicket Before Delivery

If the Bowler, before delivering the ball, throws it at the Striker's wicket in an attempt to run him out, the Umpire shall call and signal "no ball". See Law 42.12 (Batsman Unfairly Stealing a Run) and Law 38 (Run Out).

5. Bowler Attempting to Run Out Non-Striker Before Delivery

If the Bowler, before delivering the ball, attempts to run out the non-Striker, any runs which result shall be allowed and shall be scored as no balls. Such an attempt shall not count as a ball in the over. The Umpire shall not call "no ball". See Law 42.12 (Batsman Unfairly Stealing a Run).

6. Infringement of Laws by a Wicket-Keeper or a Fieldsman

The Umpire shall call and signal "no ball" in the event of the Wicket-Keeper infringing Law 40.1 (Position of Wicket-Keeper) or a Fieldsman infringing Law 41.2 (Limitation of On-side Fieldsmen) or Law 41.3 (Position of Fieldsmen).

7. Revoking a Call

An Umpire shall revoke the call "no ball" if the ball does not leave the Bowler's hand for any reason. See Law 23.2 (Either Umpire Shall Call and Signal "Dead Ball").

8. Penalty

A penalty of one run for a no ball shall be scored if no runs are made otherwise.

9. Runs From a No Ball

The Striker may hit a no ball and whatever runs result shall be added to his score. Runs made otherwise from a no ball shall be scored no balls.

10. Out From a No Ball

The Striker shall be out from a no ball if he breaks Law 34 (Hit the Ball Twice) and either Batsman may be Run Out or shall be given out if either breaks Law 33 (Handled the Ball) or Law 37 (Obstructing the Field).

11. Batsman Given Out Off a No Ball

Should a Batsman be given out off a no ball the penalty for bowling it shall stand unless runs are otherwise scored.

25. WIDE BALL

1. Judging a Wide

If the Bowler bowls the ball so high over or so wide of the wicket that, in the opinion of the Umpire it passes out of reach of the Striker, standing in a normal guard position, the Umpire shall call and signal "wide ball" as soon as it has passed the line of the Striker's wicket.

The Umpire shall not adjudge a ball as being a wide if:

(*a*) The Striker, by moving from his guard position, causes the ball to pass out of his reach.

(*b*) The Striker moves and thus brings the ball within his reach.

2. Penalty

A penalty of one run for a wide shall be scored if no runs are made otherwise.

3. Ball Coming to Rest in Front of the Striker

If a ball which the Umpire considers to have been delivered comes to rest in front of the line of the Striker's wicket, "wide" shall not be called. The Striker has a right, without interference from the fielding side, to make one attempt to hit the ball. If the fielding side interfere, the Umpire shall replace the ball where it came to rest and shall order the Fieldsmen to resume the places they occupied in the field before the ball was delivered.

The Umpire shall call and signal "dead ball" as soon as it is clear that the Striker does not intend to hit the ball, or after the Striker has made one unsuccessful attempt to hit the ball.

4. Revoking a Call

The Umpire shall revoke the call if the Striker hits a ball which has been called "wide".

5. Ball Not Dead

The ball does not become dead on the call of "wide ball"—see Law 23.4 (The Ball is Not Dead).

6. Runs Resulting from a Wide

All runs which are run or result from a wide ball which is not a no ball shall be scored wide balls, or if no runs are made one shall be scored.

7. Out from a Wide

The Striker shall be out from a wide ball if he breaks Law 35 (Hit Wicket) or Law 39 (Stumped). Either Batsman may be Run Out and shall be out if he breaks Law 33 (Handled the Ball) or Law 37 (Obstructing the Field).

8. Batsman Given Out Off a Wide

Should a Batsman be given out off a wide, the penalty for bowling it shall stand unless runs are otherwise made.

26. BYE AND LEG-BYE

1. Byes

If the ball, not having been called "wide" or "no ball" passes the Striker without touching his bat or person, and any runs are obtained, the Umpire shall signal "bye" and the run or runs shall be credited as such to the batting side.

2. Leg-Byes

If the ball, not having been called "wide" or "no ball" is

unintentionally deflected by the Striker's dress or person, except a hand holding the bat, and any runs are obtained the Umpire shall signal "leg-bye" and the run or runs so scored shall be credited as such to the batting side.

Such leg-byes shall only be scored if, in the opinion of the Umpire, the Striker has:

(a) attempted to play the ball with his bat, or

(b) tried to avoid being hit by the ball.

3. Disallowance of Leg-Byes

In the case of a deflection by the Striker's person, other than in 2(a) and (b) above, the Umpire shall call and signal "dead ball" as soon as one run has been completed or when it is clear that a run is not being attempted or the ball has reached the boundary.

On the call and signal of "dead ball" the Batsmen shall return to their original ends and no runs shall be allowed.

27. APPEALS

1. Time of Appeals

The Umpires shall not give a Batsman out unless appealed to by the other side which shall be done prior to the Bowler beginning his run-up or bowling action to deliver the next ball. Under Law 23.1 (g) (The Ball Becomes Dead) the ball is dead on "over" being called; this does not, however, invalidate an appeal made prior to the first ball of the following over provided "time" has not been called. See Law 17.1 (Call of Time).

2. An Appeal "How's That?"

An appeal "How's That?" shall cover all ways of being out.

3. Answering Appeals

The Umpire at the Bowler's wicket shall answer appeals before the other Umpire in all cases except those arising out of Law 35 (Hit Wicket) or Law 39 (Stumped) or Law 38 (Run Out) when this occurs at the Striker's wicket.

When either Umpire has given a Batsman not out, the other Umpire shall, within his jurisdiction, answer the appeal or a further appeal, provided it is made in time in accordance with 1 (Time of Appeals) above.

4. Consultation by Umpires

An Umpire may consult with the other Umpire on a point of fact which the latter may have been in a better position to see and shall then give his decision. If, after consultation, there is still doubt remaining the decision shall be in favour of the Batsman.

5. Batsman Leaving his Wicket under a Misapprehension

The Umpires shall intervene if satisfied that a Batsman, not having been given out, has left his wicket under a misapprehension that he has been dismissed.

6. Umpire's Decision

The Umpire's decision is final. He may alter his decision, provided that such alteration is made promptly.

7. Withdrawal of an Appeal

In exceptional circumstances the Captain of the fielding side may seek permission of the Umpire to withdraw an appeal providing the outgoing Batsman has not left the playing area. If this is allowed, the Umpire shall cancel his decision.

28. THE WICKET IS DOWN

1. Wicket Down

The wicket is down if:

(*a*) Either the ball or the Striker's bat or person completely removes either bail from the top of the stumps. A disturbance of a bail, whether temporary or not, shall not constitute a complete removal, but the wicket is down if a bail in falling lodges between two of the stumps.

(*b*) Any player completely removes with his hand or arm a bail from the top of the stumps, providing that the ball is held in that hand or in the hand of the arm so used.

(*c*) When both bails are off, a stump is struck out of the

ground by the ball, or a player strikes or pulls a stump out of the ground, providing that the ball is held in the hand(s) or in the hand of the arm so used.

2. One Bail Off

If one bail is off, it shall be sufficient for the purpose of putting the wicket down to remove the remaining bail, or to strike or pull any of the three stumps out of the ground in any of the ways stated in 1 above.

3. All the Stumps Out of the Ground

If all the stumps are out of the ground, the fielding side shall be allowed to put back one or more stumps in order to have an opportunity of putting the wicket down.

4. Dispensing with Bails

If owing to the strength of the wind, it has been agreed to dispense with the bails, the decision as to when the wicket is down is one for the Umpires to decide on the facts before them. In such circumstances and if the Umpires so decide the wicket shall be held to be down even though a stump has not been struck out of the ground.

29. BATSMAN OUT OF HIS GROUND

1. When out of his Ground

A Batsman shall be considered to be out of his ground unless some part of his bat in his hand or of his person is grounded behind the line of the popping crease.

30. BOWLED

1. Out Bowled

The Striker shall be out bowled if:

(*a*) His wicket is bowled down, even if the ball first touches his bat or person.

(*b*) He breaks his wicket by hitting or kicking the ball on to it before the completion of a stroke, or as a result of attempting to guard his wicket. See Law 34.1 (Out—Hit the Ball Twice).

31. TIMED OUT

1. Out Timed Out

An incoming Batsman shall be out Timed Out if he wilfully takes more than two minutes to come in—the two minutes being timed from the moment a wicket falls until the new batsman steps on to the field of play.

If this is not complied with and if the Umpire is satisfied that the delay was wilful and if an appeal is made, the new Batsman shall be given out by the Umpire at the Bowler's end.

2. Time to be Added

The time taken by the Umpires to investigate the cause of the delay shall be added at the normal close of play.

32. CAUGHT

1. Out Caught

The Striker shall be out Caught if the ball touches his bat or if it touches below the wrist his hand or glove, holding the bat, and is subsequently held by a Fieldsman before it touches the ground.

2. A Fair Catch

A catch shall be considered to have been fairly made if:

(a) The Fieldsman is within the field of play throughout the act of making the catch.

(i) The act of making the catch shall start from the time when the Fieldsman first handles the ball and shall end when he both retains complete control over the further disposal of the ball and remains within the field of play.

(ii) In order to be within the field of play, the Fieldsman may not touch or ground any part of his person on or over a boundary line. When the boundary is marked by a fence or board the Fieldsman may not ground any part of his person over the boundary fence or board, but may touch or lean over the boundary fence or board in completing the catch.

(*b*) The ball is hugged to the body of the catcher or accidentally lodges in his dress or, in the case of the Wicket-Keeper, in his pads. However, a Striker may not be caught if a ball lodges in a protective helmet worn by a Fieldsman, in which case the Umpire shall call and signal "dead ball". See Law 23 (Dead Ball).

(*c*) The ball does not touch the ground even though a hand holding it does so in effecting the catch.

(*d*) A Fieldsman catches the ball, after it has been lawfully played a second time by the Striker, but only if the ball has not touched the ground since being first struck.

(*e*) A Fieldsman catches the ball after it has touched an Umpire, another Fieldsman or the other Batsman. However a Striker may not be caught if a ball has touched a protective helmet worn by a Fieldsman.

(*f*) The ball is caught off an obstruction within the boundary provided it has not previously been agreed to regard the obstruction as a boundary.

3. Scoring of Runs

If a Striker is caught, no runs shall be scored.

33. HANDLED THE BALL

1. Out Handled the Ball

Either Batsman on appeal shall be out Handled the Ball if he wilfully touches the ball while in play with the hand not holding the bat unless he does so with the consent of the opposite side.

34. HIT THE BALL TWICE

1. Out Hit the Ball Twice

The Striker, on appeal, shall be out Hit the Ball Twice if, after the ball is struck or is stopped by any part of his person, he wilfully strikes it again with his bat or person except for the sole purpose of guarding his wicket: this he may do with his bat or any part of his person other than his hands, but see Law 37.2 (Obstructing a Ball From Being Caught).

For the purpose of this Law, a hand holding the bat shall be regarded as part of the bat.

2. Returning the Ball to a Fieldsman

The Striker, on appeal, shall be out under this Law, if, without the consent of the opposite side, he uses his bat or person to return the ball to any of the fielding side.

3. Runs from Ball Lawfully Struck Twice

No runs except those which result from an overthrow or penalty, see Law 41 (The Fieldsman), shall be scored from a ball lawfully struck twice.

35. HIT WICKET

1. Out Hit Wicket

The Striker shall be out Hit Wicket if, while the ball is in play:—

(*a*) His wicket is broken with any part of his person, dress, or equipment as a result of any action taken by him in preparing to receive or in receiving a delivery, or in setting off for his first run, immediately after playing, or playing at, the ball.

(*b*) He hits down his wicket whilst lawfully making a second stroke for the purpose of guarding his wicket within the provisions of Law 34.1 (Out Hit the Ball Twice).

36. LEG BEFORE WICKET

1. Out L.B.W.

The Striker shall be out L.B.W. in the circumstances set out below:

(*a*) *Striker Attempting to Play the Ball.* The Striker shall be out L.B.W. if he first intercepts with any part of his person, dress or equipment a fair ball which would have hit the wicket and which has not previously touched his bat or a hand holding the bat, provided that:

(i) The ball pitched, in a straight line between wicket and

wicket or on the off side of the Striker's wicket, or in the case of a ball intercepted full pitch would have pitched in a straight line between wicket and wicket.

and

    (ii) the point of impact is in a straight line between wicket and wicket, even if above the level of the bails.

    (b) *Striker Making No Attempt to Play the Ball.* The Striker shall be out L.B.W. even if the ball is intercepted outside the line of the off-stump, if, in the opinion of the Umpire, he has made no genuine attempt to play the ball with his bat, but has intercepted the ball with some part of his person and if the circumstances set out in (a) above apply.

38. RUN OUT

1. Out Run Out

Either Batsman shall be out Run Out if in running or at any time while the ball is in play—except in the circumstances described in Law 39 (Stumped)—he is out of his ground and his wicket is put down by the opposite side. If, however, a Batsman in running makes good his ground he shall not be out Run Out, if he subsequently leaves his ground, in order to avoid injury, and the wicket is put down.

37. OBSTRUCTING THE FIELD

1. Wilful Obstruction

Either Batsman, on appeal, shall be out Obstructing the Field if he wilfully obstructs the opposite side by word or action.

2. Obstructing a Ball from Being Caught

The Striker, on appeal, shall be out should wilful obstruction by either Batsman prevent a catch being made.

    This shall apply even though the Striker causes the obstruction in lawfully guarding his wicket under the provisions of Law 34. See Law 34.1 (Out Hit the Ball Twice).

2. "No Ball" Called

If a no ball has been called, the Striker shall not be given Run Out unless he attempts to run.

3. Which Batsman is Out

If the Batsmen have crossed in running, he who runs for the wicket which is put down shall be out; if they have not crossed, he who has left the wicket which is put down shall be out. If a Batsman remains in his ground or returns to his ground and the other Batsman joins him there, the latter shall be out if his wicket is put down.

4. Scoring of Runs

If a Batsman is run out, only that run which is being attempted shall not be scored. If however an injured Striker himself is run out, no runs shall be scored. See Law 2.7 (Transgression of the Laws by an Injured Batsman or Runner).

39. STUMPED

1. Out Stumped

The Striker shall be out Stumped if, in receiving a ball, not being a no-ball, he is out of his ground otherwise than in attempting a run and the wicket is put down by the Wicket-Keeper without the intervention of another Fieldsman.

2. Action by the Wicket-Keeper

The Wicket-Keeper may take the ball in front of the wicket in an attempt to Stump the Striker only if the ball has touched the bat or person of the Striker.

40. THE WICKET-KEEPER

1. Position of Wicket-Keeper

The Wicket-Keeper shall remain wholly behind the wicket until a ball delivered by the Bowler touches the bat or person of the Striker, or passes the wicket, or until the Striker attempts a run.

In the event of the Wicket-Keeper contravening this Law, the Umpire at the Striker's end shall call and signal "no ball" at the instant of delivery or as soon as possible thereafter.

2. Restriction on Actions of the Wicket-Keeper

If the Wicket-Keeper interferes with the Striker's right to play the ball and to guard his wicket, the Striker shall not be out, except under Laws 33 (Handled the Ball), 34 (Hit the Ball Twice), 37 (Obstructing the Field) and 38 (Run Out).

3. Interference with the Wicket-Keeper by the Striker

If in the legitimate defence of his wicket, the Striker interferes with the Wicket-Keeper, he shall not be out, except as provided for in Law 37.2 (Obstructing a Ball From Being Caught).

41. THE FIELDSMAN

1. Fielding the Ball

The Fieldsman may stop the ball with any part of his person, but if he wilfully stops it otherwise, 5 runs shall be added to the run or runs already scored; if no run has been scored 5 penalty runs shall be awarded. The run in progress shall count provided that the Batsmen have crossed at the instant of the act. If the ball has been struck, the penalty shall be added to the score of the Striker, but otherwise to the score of byes, leg-byes, no balls or wides as the case may be.

2. Limitation of On-Side Fieldsmen

The number of on-side Fieldsmen behind the popping crease at the instant of the Bowler's delivery shall not exceed two. In the event of infringement by the fielding side the Umpire at the Striker's end shall call and signal "no ball" at the instant of delivery or as soon as possible thereafter.

3. Position of Fieldsmen

Whilst the ball is in play and until the ball has made contact with the bat or the Striker's person or has passed his bat, no Fieldsman, other than the Bowler, may stand on or have any part of his person extended over the pitch [measuring 22 yd

$(20.12\,\mathrm{m}) \times 10\,\mathrm{ft}\ (3.05\,\mathrm{m})]$. In the event of a Fieldsman contravening this Law, the Umpire at the bowler's end shall call and signal "no ball" at the instant of delivery or as soon as possible thereafter. See Law 40.1 (Position of Wicket-Keeper).

42. UNFAIR PLAY

1. Responsibility of Captains

The Captains are responsible at all times for ensuring that play is conducted within the spirit of the game as well as within the Laws.

2. Responsibility of Umpires

The Umpires are the sole judges of fair and unfair play.

3. Intervention by the Umpire

The Umpires shall intervene without appeal by calling and signalling "dead ball" in the case of unfair play, but should not otherwise interfere with the progress of the game except as required to do so by the Laws.

4. Lifting the Seam

A Player shall not lift the seam of the ball for any reason. Should this be done, the Umpires shall change the ball for one of similar condition to that in use prior to the contravention. See Note (a).

5. Changing the Condition of the Ball

Any member of the fielding side may polish the ball provided that such polishing wastes no time and that no artificial substance is used. No one shall rub the ball on the ground or use any artificial substance or take any other action to alter the condition of the ball.

In the event of a contravention of this Law, the Umpires, after consultation, shall change the ball for one of similar condition to that in use prior to the contravention.

This Law does not prevent a member of the fielding side from drying a wet ball, or removing mud from the ball.

6. Incommoding the Striker

An Umpire is justified in intervening under this Law and shall call and signal "dead ball" if, in his opinion, any Player of the fielding side incommodes the Striker by any noise or action while he is receiving a ball.

7. Obstruction of a Batsman in Running

It shall be considered unfair if any Fieldsman wilfully obstructs a Batsman in running. In these circumstances the Umpire shall call and signal "dead ball" and allow any completed runs and the run in progress or alternatively any boundary scored.

8. The Bowling of Fast Short Pitched Balls

The bowling of fast short pitched balls is unfair if, in the opinion of the Umpire at the Bowler's end, it constitutes an attempt to intimidate the Striker.

Umpires shall consider intimidation to be the deliberate bowling of fast short pitched balls which by their length, height and direction are intended or likely to inflict physical injury on the Striker. The relative skill of the Striker shall also be taken into consideration.

In the event of such unfair bowling, the Umpire at the Bowler's end shall adopt the following procedure:

(*a*) In the first instance the Umpire shall call and signal "no ball", caution the Bowler and inform the other Umpire, the Captain of the fielding side and the Batsmen of what has occurred.

(*b*) If this caution is ineffective, he shall repeat the above procedure and indicate to the Bowler that this is a final warning.

(*c*) Both the above caution and final warning shall continue to apply even though the Bowler may later change ends.

(*d*) Should the above warnings prove ineffective the Umpire at the Bowler's end shall:

(i) At the first repetition call and signal "no ball" and when the ball is dead direct the Captain to take the Bowler off forthwith and to complete the over with another Bowler, provided that the Bowler does not bowl two overs or part thereof consecutively. See Law 22.7 (Bowler Incapacitated or Suspended during an Over).

(ii) Not allow the Bowler, thus taken off, to bowl again in the same innings.

(iii) Report the occurrence to the Captain of the batting side as soon as the Players leave the field for an interval.

(iv) Report the occurrence to the Executive of the fielding side and to any governing body responsible for the match who shall take any further action which is considered to be appropriate against the Bowler concerned.

9. The Bowling of Fast High Full Pitches

The bowling of fast high full pitches is unfair.

In the event of such unfair bowling the Umpire at the bowler's end shall adopt the procedures of caution, final warning, action against the Bowler and reporting as set out in 8, above.

10. Time Wasting

Any form of time wasting is unfair.

(*a*) In the event of the Captain of the fielding side wasting time or allowing any member of his side to waste time, the Umpire at the Bowler's end shall adopt the following procedure:

(i) In the first instance he shall caution the Captain of the fielding side and inform the other Umpire of what has occurred.

(ii) If this caution is ineffective he shall repeat the above procedure and indicate to the Captain that this is a final warning.

(iii) The Umpire shall report the occurrence to the Captain of the batting side as soon as the Players leave the field for an interval.

(iv) Should the above procedure prove ineffective the Umpire shall report the occurrence to the Executive of the fielding side and to any governing body responsible for that match who shall take appropriate action against the Captain and the Players concerned.

(*b*) In the event of a Bowler taking unnecessarily long to bowl an over the Umpire at the Bowler's end shall adopt the procedures, other than the calling of "no-ball", of caution, final warning, action against the Bowler and reporting.

(c) In the event of a Batsman wasting time other than in the manner described in Law 31 (Timed Out), the Umpire at the Bowler's end shall adopt the following procedure:

(i) In the first instance he shall caution the Batsman and inform the other Umpire at once, and the Captain of the batting side, as soon as the Players leave the field for an interval, of what has occurred.

(ii) If this proves ineffective, he shall repeat the caution, indicate to the Batsman that this is a final warning and inform the other Umpire.

(iii) The Umpire shall report the occurrence to both Captains as soon as the Players leave the field for an interval.

(iv) Should the above procedure prove ineffective, the Umpire shall report the occurrence to the Executive of the batting side and to any governing body responsible for that match who shall take appropriate action against the Player concerned.

11. Players Damaging the Pitch

The Umpires shall intervene and prevent Players from causing damage to the pitch which may assist the Bowlers of either side.

(a) In the event of any member of the fielding side damaging the pitch the Umpire shall follow the procedure of caution, final warning and reporting as set out in 10(a) above.

(b) In the event of a Bowler contravening this Law by running down the pitch after delivering the ball, the Umpire at the Bowler's end shall first caution the Bowler. If this caution is ineffective the Umpire shall adopt the procedures, other than the calling of "no-ball", of final warning, action against the Bowler and reporting.

(c) In the event of a Batsman damaging the pitch the Umpire at the Bowler's end shall follow the procedures of caution, final warning and reporting as set out in 10(c) above.

12. Batsman Unfairly Stealing a Run

Any attempt by the Batsman to steal a run during the Bowler's run-up is unfair. Unless the Bowler attempts to run out either Batsman—see Law 24.4 (Bowler Throwing at Striker's Wicket Before Delivery) and Law 24.5 (Bowler Attempting to Run

Out Non-Striker Before Delivery)—the Umpire shall call and signal "dead ball" as soon as the Batsmen cross in any such attempt to run. The Batsmen shall then return to their original wickets.

13. Players' Conduct

In the event of a player failing to comply with the instructions of an Umpire, criticising his decisions by word or action, or showing dissent, or generally behaving in a manner which might bring the game into disrepute, the Umpire concerned shall, in the first place report the matter to the other Umpire and to the Player's Captain requesting the latter to take action. If this proves ineffective, the Umpire shall report the incident as soon as possible to the Executive of the Player's team and to any Governing Body responsible for the match, who shall take any further action which is considered appropriate against the Player or Players concerned.

Printed by permission of the M.C.C. Copies of the current edition of the official Laws of Cricket with full notes and interpretations can be obtained from Lord's Cricket Ground.

The Laws of
Association
Croquet
and
Golf Croquet

DIAGRAM OF STANDARD COURT AND SETTING

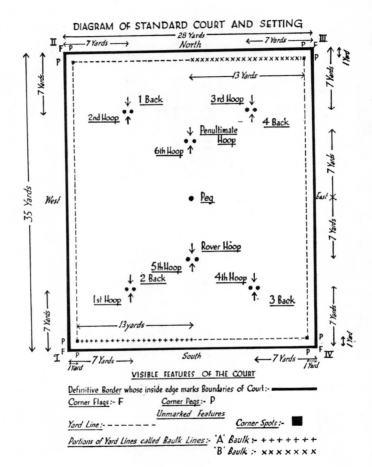

VISIBLE FEATURES OF THE COURT

Definitive Border whose inside edge marks Boundaries of Court :- ▬▬▬▬

Corner Flags :- F   Corner Pegs :- P

Unmarked Features

Yard Line :- – – – – – –   Corner Spots :- ■

Portions of Yard Lines called Baulk Lines :- 'A' Baulk :- + + + + + + +
                                              'B' Baulk :- × × × × × × ×

Association Croquet

I. THE COURT AND SETTING, EQUIPMENT AND COURT ACCESSORIES

1. The Standard Court and Setting

(a) *The Standard Court.* The Standard Court is a rectangle measuring 35 yd by 28 yd. Its boundaries shall be marked out clearly, the *inside* edge of the definitive border being the actual boundary.

(b) *Court references.* The four corners of the Court are known respectively as Corners I, II, III and IV (see Diagram opposite). The four boundaries are known as the South, West, North and East boundaries, regardless of the orientation of the Court.

(c) *Yard-line, Yard-line Area, Corner Spot, Corner Square.* The sides of an inner rectangle parallel to and distant 1 yd from the boundary are called the yard-line, its corners the corner spots, and the space between the yard-line and the boundary the yard-line area. The square yard formed at each corner by the two corner pegs, the corner spot, and the corner flag, is called a corner square.

(d) *Yard-line Balls and Corner Balls.* Balls on the yard-line are called yard-line balls. Balls on the corner spots of the yard-line are in addition known as corner balls.

(e) *Baulk-lines.* Portions of the yard-line, from the corner spots at corners I and III towards corners IV and II respectively, each measuring 13 yd, are called baulk-lines (see Diagram).

(f) *The Standard Setting.* The peg shall be set in the centre of the Court. The hoops shall be set parallel to the north and south boundaries, the centres of the two inner hoops 7 yd to the north and south of the peg; the centres of the four outer hoops 7 yd from their adjacent boundaries.

(g) The Diagram depicts the Standard Setting for a Standard Court and together with the explanations thereon and thereunder shall be part of this Law.

2. Equipment

(a) *Hoops*. The hoops shall be of round iron or aluminium, $\frac{5}{8}$ in in diameter, and of uniform thickness. They shall be 12 in in height above the ground measured to the top of the hoop, vertical, and firmly fixed. The crown shall be straight and at right angles to the uprights, which shall be not less than $3\frac{11}{16}$ in or more than 4 in apart uniformly between the uprights (inside measurement), provided that all the hoops on any one court shall be of the same dimensions. The hoops shall be painted white, the crown of the first hoop coloured blue, and that of the last hoop, which is known as the rover hoop, red.

(b) *The Peg*. The peg shall be of wood, of a uniform diameter above the ground of $1\frac{1}{2}$ in. It shall be 18 in in height above the ground, exclusive of a detachable portion to hold clips, vertical, and firmly fixed. The base shall be painted white.

(c) *The Balls*. The balls shall be coloured respectively blue, red, black and yellow. (Alternative coloured balls, brown, green, pink and white are permitted). They shall be $3\frac{5}{8}$ in in diameter, plus or minus $\frac{1}{32}$ in, and of even weight 16 oz, plus or minus $\frac{1}{4}$ oz. Faulty or damaged balls may be changed.

(d) *Mallets*. The head of the mallet shall be of wood, or any other material, provided that the player shall gain no advantage over wood. Metal may be used for weighting or strengthening it. The two faces shall be parallel and identical in every respect. There may be a bevelled edge which shall not be considered to be part of the face. A player may not change his mallet during a turn, except in the case of damage affecting use.

3. Court Accessories

The following accessories should be supplied for guidance, convenience and decoration. The accessories do not form part of the setting of the court. Accordingly, any such accessories temporarily impeding a striker may be temporarily removed.

(a) *Corner Flags*. Flags coloured blue, red, black and yellow shall be placed in corners I, II, III and IV respectively. The flags shall be mounted on pegs about 1 ft high. The peg shall be touching the boundary but no part shall be on the court.

(b) *Corner Pegs*. Eight white corner pegs, measuring $\frac{3}{4}$ in in diameter and 3 in in height above the ground, shall be placed on the boundary 1 yd from the corner flags, measured to the further side of the corner pegs. The inside edge of the corner pegs shall be in line with the boundary. In addition a peg or mark may define the east end of A baulk and the west end of B baulk.

(c) *Extension in Peg.* A detachable portion to hold the clips shall be attached to the top of the peg.

(d) *Clips.* The function of clips is to indicate the state of the game on the court. The hoop or peg next in order for every ball at the beginning of every turn shall be distinguished by a clip of the colour corresponding with that of the ball. When a ball scores a hoop so distinguished the striker shall remove the clip and at the end of the turn place it upon the appropriate hoop or the peg. When the peg is scored the clip shall be removed from the court. The first six hoops shall be distinguished by placing the clip on the crown of the hoop, the last six by placing it on one of the uprights. Each player should call the attention of the other to a misplaced clip as soon as the mistake is observed and the clip should then be properly placed.

(e) It is also permissible and desirable that a check-fence, just high enough to arrest the progress of balls, be placed round the outside of the court about 1 yd from the boundary.

II. THE LAWS OF ORDINARY LEVEL SINGLES PLAY

(A) AN OUTLINE OF THE GAME

4. Introduction to the Game

(a) *The Object of the Game.* The game is played between two players, of whom one plays the blue and black, the other the red and yellow balls (or brown and green versus pink and white). The object of the game is for a player to make both his balls score the 12 hoop points and the peg point, a total of 26 points, before his adversary. The player wins whose balls first score the 26 points. A ball scores a hoop point by passing through the hoop in the order and in the direction shown on the Diagram on p. 212. This is known as running a hoop. But a ball which has made a roquet cannot thereafter in the same stroke score a point for itself except as provided in Law 16(a).

A ball which has scored all 12 hoop points is known as a rover. It can then score the peg by hitting it. (See Law 39 for handicap play.)

(*b*) *How Play is Made.* Play is made by striking a ball with a mallet. For the essentials of a fair stroke, see Laws 31–2. The player so playing is called the striker and the ball which he strikes, the striker's ball. The striker may never strike an adversary's ball and he may strike only one of his own two balls during any one turn. By striking this ball the striker may cause any other ball to move and to score a point, but only when the striker's ball is a rover can he cause another rover ball to score the peg. (See Law 15.)

(*c*) *The Turn.* The players play alternate turns. A player is initially entitled to one stroke in a turn, after which his turn ends unless in that stroke his striker's ball has scored a hoop point or hit another ball. When a hoop is scored, the striker is entitled to play one continuation stroke. When another ball is hit, the striker is said to have made a roquet on that ball and becomes entitled to two extra strokes. The first of these two strokes is known as the croquet stroke and is made after moving and placing the striker's ball in contact with the roqueted ball which, in the croquet stroke, is now known as the croqueted ball. In the croquet stroke the striker must move or shake the croqueted ball. Further, if in the croquet stroke the croqueted ball is sent off the court or the striker's ball is sent off the court without first having made another roquet, or scored a hoop point for itself, the turn ends. During a turn the striker may roquet each ball once and he may make a further roquet on each ball provided that since he has last roqueted it his striker's ball has scored a hoop point for itself under Laws 14 or 16(*a*). If, at the beginning of a turn, the striker elects to play a ball in contact with another ball, the striker's ball is deemed to have roqueted that ball and the turn starts with a croquet stroke. Thus, by a series of strokes entitling him to continue, the striker may make one or more points. Such a series is known as making a break. But continuation strokes are not cumulative, so that a striker who:

    (i) scores a hoop and makes a roquet in the same stroke immediately takes croquet;

    (ii) makes a roquet in a croquet stroke immediately takes croquet and continues accordingly;

   (iii) scores a hoop for his striker's ball in a croquet stroke plays only one continuation stroke;

   (iv) scores two hoops for his striker's ball in one stroke plays only one continuation stroke.

For amplification of the above, see Comprehensive Laws of Roquet and Croquet, 16–20.

5. Ball in Hand

(*a*) A ball in hand is any ball which has to be moved, and is therefore lifted and given a fresh position on the court in accordance with these Laws. Examples are:

   (i) A ball which has made a roquet (see Law 17(*b*)) or is deemed to have done so (see Law 16(*c*));

  (ii) Balls off the court and certain balls in the yard-line area (see Laws 6, 7, 8 and 18(*b*));

  (iii) A ball lifted under Law 13(*b*) or Law 36.

(*b*) When the striker lifts his balls at the beginning of a turn it immediately becomes in hand. The striker may not then change his mind and play with his other ball; but if he does so and the adversary fails to forestall, the stroke shall be valid.

6. Ball off the Court

A ball off the court is a ball in hand as soon as it goes off the court. Until it is replaced in accordance with Law 8, it is an outside agency. A ball goes off the court as soon as any part of it would touch a straight edge raised vertically from a boundary, that is to say the inside edge of the definitive border. Where more than one marking is visible, the most recent shall be regarded as the true one.

7. Balls in the Yard-line Area

At the end of each stroke all balls in the yard-line area, other than the striker's ball which is played from where it lies, become balls in hand. Only at the end of the turn does the striker's ball in the yard-line area become a ball in hand.

8. Replacement of Balls off the Court and Balls in Hand in Yard-line Area

(*a*) Before the next stroke all balls off the court and balls in hand in the yard-line area, other than the striker's ball entitled to take croquet, shall be placed on the yard-line at the point nearest to which they went off the court, or remained on the court in the yard-line area, as the case may be.

(*b*) If a ball cannot be so placed because of the presence of another ball or balls on the yard-line, including the corner spot, it shall be placed on the yard-line in contact with such ball or one of them on the yard-line on either side; but if one of two such balls be a corner ball the third ball shall be placed on the yard-line on the unoccupied side of the ball on the corner spot.

(*c*) If a ball cannot be so placed because of the presence of a ball outside the yard-line area, it shall be placed on the yard-line on any point in contact with that ball; provided that if the ball to be placed is a corner ball, it shall in addition thereto be placed on the yard-line as near as possible to the corner spot.

(*d*) If two or more balls have to be replaced under this Law and the replacement of one will interfere with the replacement of another the order of replacement is at the option of the striker. (See diagram below.)

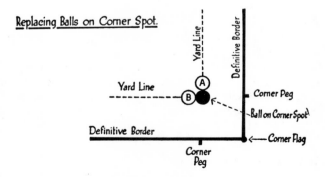

If a ball already occupies the corner spot other balls due for simultaneous replacement thereon must be replaced on the yard-line in contact with such ball. A second ball therefore may be placed either in position "A" or "B".

A third ball must be placed in the position left vacant.

9. The Toss before the Start of the Game

The winner of the toss shall decide whether he will take the choice of lead or the choice of balls. This is known as the right of choice. If he take the choice of lead the adversary has the choice of balls, and *vice versa*. When a match consists of more than one game the right of choice after the initial toss shall alternate.

10. The Start of the Game

At the start the Striker plays either of his balls into the game from any point on either baulk-line. At the end of that turn his opponent does likewise. In the third and fourth turns the remaining two balls are similarly played into the game.

11. Ball in Play

A ball played under Law 10 may immediately score points and make roquets and is known as a ball in play. It continues in play until it has scored the peg, except when it is off the court or, between strokes, in hand.

12. Option of Striker to Play either Ball

After all four balls have been played into the game, the striker may, in any subsequent turn, play with either of his two balls at his option.

13. Wired Balls

   (a) A ball is said to be wired from another ball if:
   (i) any part of an upright of a hoop or the peg would impede the direct course of any part of the striker's ball towards any part of the other ball; or
   (ii) any part of a hoop or the peg so interferes with any part of the swing of the mallet prior to impact between mallet and ball that the striker, with his usual style of play, cannot in order to make a roquet drive his ball freely towards any part of the other ball, when striking the

centre of his ball with any part of the face of the mallet; or if any part of the striker's ball is within the jaws of the hoop. The mere interference of a hoop or the peg with the stance of the striker does not constitute wiring.

(b) If, at the beginning of a turn, the striker elects to play a ball which is wired from all other balls, which is a ball not in contact with another ball, and is a ball for whose position the adversary is responsible, he may elect to lift it. If he does so it immediately becomes in hand and must be played by the striker from any point on either baulk-line. (See Law 5(b).) A player shall be responsible for the position of all balls moved or shaken as a consequence of his play or which he is deemed to have played under Law 31(b).

(B) HOOP POINTS, PEG POINT AND COMPREHENSIVE LAWS OF ROQUET AND CROQUET

14. Hoop Points

In amplification of Law 4(a):

(a) A ball scores a hoop point by passing through the hoop in the order and in the direction shown in the Diagram on p. 212. This is known as running a hoop but a ball which has made a roquet cannot thereafter in the same stroke score a point for itself except as provided in Law 16A.

(b) The front of the hoop as a ball approaches to run it in order is known as the playing side of the hoop; the other side as the non-playing side. The whole of the ball does not have to pass through the whole of the hoop in order to score a point, *because*:

(i) a ball begins to run a hoop only when the front of the ball would touch a straight edge raised vertically against the non-playing side of the hoop;

(ii) but contrariwise a ball completes the running of a hoop as soon as the back of the ball has passed a line made by raising a straight edge against the playing side of the hoop—subject to (iii) below.

(iii) A ball which moves back before it has finally come to

rest does not score the hoop if in its final position it has not completed the running.

(iv) A ball may complete the running of a hoop in two or more turns but, if a ball becomes in hand, it must begin to run the hoop afresh.

(v) If a ball from which the striker is taking croquet lies partly within the jaws of the striker's hoop in order, the striker's ball may run the hoop in that stroke, provided that, when placed in the position from which the striker is about to take croquet, it cannot be touched by a straight edge on the non-playing side.

(c) When the striker's ball has scored a hoop point the striker shall then play a continuation stroke unless he is entitled to take croquet or his turn has ended under Law 19(c).

(d) When a ball, other than the striker's ball, is caused to score a hoop point, it is said to have been peeled through the hoop.

15. The Peg Point

This Law amplifies Law 4(a) and (b).

(a) A ball scores the peg by hitting it; but only when the striker's ball has made all 12 hoop points (and is then known as a rover) can the striker score the peg point or cause another rover ball to do so. (See Law 39 for handicap play.)

(b) If the striker's ball hits the peg in order and simultaneously makes a roquet, the striker shall elect whether to score the point or claim the roquet. If the roquet is not claimed the point is scored.

(c) If the striker's ball, being a rover, hits or causes another ball to hit a rover ball which is in contact with the peg, that ball shall be pegged out unless it is hit in a direction away from the peg. Likewise if the striker at the beginning of a turn play a rover which is in contact with the peg it shall be pegged out unless it is played in a direction away from the peg.

(d) A ball pegged out is deemed to come to rest at the peg and thereafter is an outside agency and any subsequent interference during that stroke shall be rectified in accordance with Law 34(b).

(*e*) Before the next stroke the striker shall remove the pegged-out ball from the court.

16. Roquet

Laws 16–20 hereunder amplify and repeat Laws 4(*a*) and (*c*):

(*a*) *When Roquet may be Made.* During a turn the striker is entitled to roquet each ball, and he may make a further roquet on each ball provided that since he last roqueted it his striker's ball has either scored a hoop point for itself or is deemed to have done so under Law 16A.

(*b*) *Making an Actual Roquet.* The striker makes an actual roquet when his striker's ball, by direct hit or by glancing off a hoop or the peg or a previously croqueted ball, hits a ball which he is entitled to roquet, subject to (i), (ii) and (iii) below:

> (i) When a roquet would have been made under the above Law on two or more balls during one stroke, it shall be deemed only to have been made on the ball first hit; if two or more balls are hit simultaneously the roquet shall be deemed only to have been made on one such ball to be nominated by the striker as the roqueted ball;

> (ii) When the striker's ball simultaneously hits the peg in order and makes a roquet the provisions of Law 15(*b*) apply;

> (iii) After scoring a hoop point for itself, the striker's ball cannot in the same stroke make an actual roquet on a ball from which it started in contact, but if such balls come to rest in contact, a roquet is deemed to have been made under (*c*) (ii) below.

(*c*) *Ball Deemed to have been Roqueted.* The striker shall be deemed to have made a roquet, and his ball becomes in hand, if: (i) at the beginning of a turn he plays a ball in actual contact with another ball; or (ii) during a turn which he is otherwise entitled to continue, his ball is in contact with a ball which he is entitled to roquet.

If in like circumstances the striker's ball be in actual contact with more than one ball, he shall be deemed to have roqueted only one of such balls to be nominated by the striker as the roqueted ball. If in like circumstances the striker plays a ball which is one of a group of balls in mutual contact, any one of which is a yard-line ball, he shall be deemed to have roqueted any one of such balls to be nominated by him as the roqueted ball. The right of nomination is exercised by the act of taking croquet.

16A. Special Case of Hoop and Roquet in Same Stroke

If, while running its hoop, but before completing the running, the striker's ball hits a ball that is clear of the hoop on the non-playing side and finally runs the hoop, it is deemed that the point is scored and the roquet made in that order.

17. The Effect of Making a Roquet

(*a*) Except as provided for in Law 16A, a ball which has made a roquet cannot thereafter in the same stroke score a point for itself.

(*b*) When a roquet is made, unless the striker's turn ends under Law 19(*c*), or unless the ball on which the roquet is made is pegged out in the roquet stroke, the striker's ball at the end of the stroke becomes a ball in hand and the striker takes croquet in accordance with Laws 18 and 19. In the above two exceptions the striker's ball remains in play where it lies and the turn ends.

(*c*) A ball which has made a roquet remains in play throughout the stroke and may only be picked up or arrested in its course to save time if the state of the game will not be affected thereby.

18. Placing the Balls for the Croquet Stroke

(*a*) To take croquet the striker places his ball on the ground in contact with the ball roqueted however he chooses and with no other ball. Subject to (*b*) below, no other ball may be moved.

(*b*) When the striker is taking croquet from one of a group of balls in mutual contact, any one of which is a yard-line ball, all balls other than the ball actually roqueted or deemed to have been roqueted, which remains where it is, become balls in hand when the roqueted ball has been placed and are temporarily removed. If the group be a group of three balls, the striker shall place both balls in contact with the roqueted ball however he chooses provided that his striker's ball is only in contact with the roqueted ball. If the group be a group of four balls, the fourth ball shall be placed out of contact with the striker's ball and in contact with one or both of the other two balls.

(*c*) Before playing his stroke the striker may touch or steady the roqueted ball, and may further apply such pressure by hand or foot, but not by mallet, as is reasonably necessary to make it hold its position. He may not move such ball intentionally, but if he does so unintentionally he shall replace it without penalty.

19. The Croquet Stroke

(*a*) The ball, hitherto known as the roqueted ball, is in the croquet stroke known as the croqueted ball.

(*b*) The striker now makes a stroke with the balls placed as in the preceding Law and in doing so must move or shake the croqueted ball.

(*c*) The striker's turn ends if in the croquet stroke he sends off the court:
  (i) the croqueted ball; or
  (ii) the striker's ball, unless it makes a roquet or scores a hoop point in that stroke.

20. The Continuation Stroke

After the croquet stroke, the striker shall be entitled to play a continuation stroke unless (i) his turn has ended under Law 19(*c*) above; or (ii) he is otherwise entitled to take croquet.

(C) MISCELLANEOUS LAWS OF PLAY

21. Marking Direction of Aim

See Law 51(*c*).

22. Ball Moving Between Strokes

Should a ball which has finally come to rest move or make a point not due to the action of the striker, it shall be replaced immediately and the point shall not be scored.

A ball is deemed finally to have come to rest if the striker has taken his stance for the next stroke or indicated his belief that his turn has ended, or if its position has been agreed or adjudicated upon.

23. Imperfections on Surface of the Court

(a) Loose impediments (such as worm-casts, leaves and the like) may be removed.

(b) The striker must not move any ball on account of inequalities on the surface of the court unless such inequalities come into the category of special damage, examples of which are a hole on a corner spot, and unrepaired or imperfectly repaired holes or scars; but special damage does not include that which is part of the normal hazards of an indifferent Court. In cases of special damage balls may be moved, but no more than is necessary to avoid such damage and never to such a position as would be advantageous to the striker. When any ball is moved under this Law, any other ball likely to be affected by this stroke shall also be moved so as to maintain the relative position of such ball. Any ball so moved and not displaced by this stroke shall at once be replaced.

(c) *Wiping.* Any ball may be wiped at any time by the striker, subject to Law 45(d).

24. Obstacles Interfering with Stroke

If the striker find that any fixed obstacle outside the court is likely to interfere with his stroke, he may move his ball, and any other ball likely to be affected by the stroke, sufficiently to allow a free swing of the mallet. In so doing he must move his own ball along the line of aim, maintaining the relative positions of any balls so moved. Any ball so moved, and not displaced by the stroke, shall at once be replaced.

25. Local Laws

Clubs or persons controlling courts may submit to the Council for approval local laws to suit any particular need. If such local laws are approved by the appropriate Council, the play shall be in accordance therewith.

(D) LAWS GOVERNING IRREGULARITIES IN PLAY AND INTERFERENCE WITH PLAY

26. Definitions

(a) *Forestalling.* The adversary is said to forestall when he observes that the striker has committed or is about to commit an irregularity and requests him to cease play until it can be corrected or investigated. An adversary may forestall by word or gesture. After forestalling play shall cease until the matter about to be raised is settled. Should a player, through a break-down in communications, continue to play, the balls shall be replaced.

(b) *Limit of claims.* The limit of claims is the period within which a fault or an irregularity can be rectified under the Laws. Limits of claims are given in detail in the Laws concerned.

(c) *Condoning.* A fault or irregularity is said to be condoned by these Laws if it is not discovered within the limit of claims. In that event the play is deemed to have been valid.

(d) *Waiving.* A fault is said to be waived if the adversary exercises his option under Law 32(b) (i) to treat the balls as having been validly played. In this case any points made in that stroke shall be scored, but the striker's turn ends under Law 19(c).

(e) *End of game.* The game shall end when the players have quitted the court in the belief that it has ended, or, if it is a match and the players have not quitted the court, when they start the next game.

27. Playing when Not Entitled to Do So

If a player under a misapprehension makes a stroke or series of strokes when he is not entitled to play, his adversary, if he observes the error, shall immediately intervene, and in that event or in the event of the striker realizing his own mistake all such strokes are null and void and the balls shall be replaced to their proper positions. If the error is not observed by either player until the player has stopped playing and his adversary has made one further stroke, the error is condoned and all such play shall be valid, but only points in order made during such period shall be scored. (See Law 39A(a) for handicap play.)

28. Playing when Any Ball is Misplaced—General Rule

(*a*) If an adversary observes the striker about to make a stroke when any ball, including the striker's ball, which may be affected by the stroke is not properly placed he shall forestall the stroke (subject to (*b*) below). In the instances specified below this right and duty is the only remedy of the adversary and if he fails so to forestall, the stroke shall be valid subject to Law 32; but any ball improperly placed which has not been moved during the stroke shall then be properly placed. Such instances are:

   (i) Playing without first replacing any ball irregularly moved after the termination of the preceding stroke.

   (ii) Playing when the striker's ball, which should have been in the yard-line area, has been improperly brought on to the yard-line during a turn.

  (iii) Playing when a ball, other than the striker's ball, has been improperly left in the yard-line area.

  (iv) Playing the striker's ball when it is a ball in baulk otherwise than from a position on a baulk-line.

   (v) In a croquet stroke, playing when the striker's ball is not actually touching the ball from which he is attempting to take croquet.

  (vi) In a croquet stroke, playing when the striker's ball is in actual contact with a third ball.

 (vii) In any other cases except those dealt with in Law 29, following.

(*b*) *Exception to forestalling.* A player shall not forestall play when the striker is about to play with the wrong ball, even though a ball is misplaced.

29. Playing when any Ball is Misplaced—Exceptions to the General Rule

(*a*) *Taking Croquet from the Wrong Ball.* If the striker, being entitled to take croquet, takes croquet from the wrong ball, his adversary, if he observes the irregularity, shall forestall play at any time before the next stroke but one of that turn. In that event, the adversary has the option of deciding whether there should be a replay or not. If he elects there should be a replay, the striker shall place the balls in a lawful position for the croquet stroke and play shall continue accordingly. If he elects otherwise, the position of the two balls involved in the irregularity shall be interchanged and play shall continue as if croquet had been taken from the correct ball. If he fails so to forestall, the balls shall remain in play as they lie and play shall continue as if the preceding roquet had been made on the ball from which croquet was taken.

(*b*) *Taking Croquet when not Entitled to Do So*. If the striker takes croquet from a ball under the misapprehension that he has already made a roquet, his adversary, if he observes the irregularity, shall forestall play at any time before the next stroke but one of that turn, and in that event, all balls shall be replaced and the striker shall continue his turn without penalty. If the adversary fails so to forestall, play shall continue as if the striker had made a roquet on the ball from which he took croquet.

(*c*) *Failing to take Croquet when Entitled to Do So*. If the striker, who is entitled to take croquet, fails so to do, the adversary, if he observes the mistake, shall forestall play at any time before the next stroke but one of that turn, and in that event, any balls moved shall be replaced, and the striker shall take croquet. If the adversary fails so to forestall, play shall continue as if the striker, being entitled to play, had never made the preceding roquet.

(*d*) *Wrongly Removing or Failing to Remove a Ball from the Game*. If a ball which has not been pegged out is removed from the Court under the misapprehension that it has been pegged out, or if a ball which has been pegged out is left in play under the misapprehension that it has not been pegged out, all play subsequent to the error is null and void; if the error is discovered before the end of the game the balls shall be replaced; the score shall be adjusted accordingly, and in a time-limited game the lost time shall be restored. The person then entitled to play shall play.

30. Playing the Wrong Ball

(*a*) If, at the beginning of the game as defined in Law 10, the striker makes the first stroke of his turn with an adversary's ball that has not hitherto been in play, such stroke, and any subsequent strokes made with that ball during that turn before the error is discovered, shall be deemed valid, any points in order made shall be scored as if they had been made by the correct ball, and when the error is discovered the correct ball shall be substituted without penalty for the adversary's ball.

(b) Save as in (a) above, if the striker strikes a wrong ball, the turn shall end unless the error is condoned. Unless the first stroke in error was a croquet stroke, the balls shall be replaced. If the first stroke in error was a croquet stroke, all balls other than the striker's ball shall be replaced, and the striker's ball, then being in hand, shall be placed by the striker in any lawful position to take croquet. If, as a result of the balls being so placed, any ball is lying in the yard-line area, it shall be brought on to the yard-line in accordance with these laws.

(c) The error is condoned if it is not discovered before the first stroke of the adversary's next turn. In that event, the balls shall remain in play as they lie, but the only points which shall score are as follows, namely:

(i) When playing any ball in error, any points made by peeling any other ball.

(ii) When playing the striker's other ball in error, any points in order for that other ball. (See Law 39A(b) for handicap play.)

31. Definition of a Stroke and the Limits of the Striking Period

(a) The striker shall begin to strike when he swings his mallet with intent to hit the ball. But, if before he had made a stroke or committed a fault, he deliberately checks his mallet, he shall not begin to strike until once again he begins to swing his mallet with intent to hit the ball.

(b) A stroke is any movement of the mallet with intent to hit the ball, or, after the striker has begun to strike, any contact between mallet and ball which moves the ball. A stroke shall be deemed to have been made if the striker misses his ball or announces his intention of leaving it where it lies. In all the above cases he shall be deemed to have played it where it lies.

(c) The striking shall end when the striker has completed his swing and quitted his stance under control. After this period, no fault can be committed under the next Law; but the stroke includes the consequence of the striking and does not end until all the balls set in motion have come to rest or have been pegged out or sent off the court.

32. Making a Fault during the Striking

(*a*) A fault is made during the striking if the striker:

 (i) Touches the head of the mallet with the hand; or causes or attempts to cause the mallet to strike the ball by kicking or hitting the mallet;

 (ii) Rests a hand, or an arm, or the shaft of the mallet on the ground;

 (iii) Rests a hand or an arm directly connected with the stroke, or the shaft of the mallet, against any part of the leg or foot;

 (iv) Strikes his ball with any part of the mallet other than an end face of the head; an accidental mis-hit in an unhampered stroke shall not constitute a fault under this law;

 (v) Plays a stroke without first striking his ball audibly or distinctly;

 (vi) In a croquet stroke or in a continuation stroke when the balls start in contact, pushes or pulls his ball after the balls have parted contact.

 (vii) In a single ball stroke pushes or pulls his ball.

 NOTE.—*In* (*vi*) *and* (*vii*) *above a "push" or a "pull" means maintaining contact between mallet and ball for an appreciable period or any acceleration following a check of the mallet head after its initial contact with the ball.*

 (viii) Strikes his ball audibly or distinctly twice in the same stroke (double tap), or maintains contact between mallet and ball after his ball has hit another ball, except that no fault can be committed under this sub-law if the cause of the second hit or the maintenance of contact is due to the making of a roquet or to interference by a ball pegged out in that stroke.

 (ix) Moves or shakes a ball at rest by hitting a hoop or the peg with the mallet;

 (x) Strikes his ball so as to cause it to touch an upright or the peg while still in contact with the mallet (crush stroke);

  (xi) Strikes his ball, when lying in contact with an upright or the peg, otherwise than in a direction away from the upright or the peg (crush stroke);

 (xii) Touches a ball, other than his own ball, with the mallet or any part of his body or clothes or allows his own ball to touch any part of his body or clothes or to re-touch his mallet;

(xiii) When making a croquet-stroke, fails to move or shake the croqueted ball.

(*b*) *The Effect of making a Fault, including Penalty.*

  (i) Unless the fault is condoned, the striker's turn ends, no point can be scored, and in all cases, except for a fault made during a croquet stroke wherein the striker's turn would have ended under Law 19(*c*), the balls are re-placed. If during a croquet stroke the turn would have ended under Law 19(*c*) the adversary may waive any fault under this Law and treat the balls as having been validly played.

 (ii) The fault is condoned if it is not discovered before the making of the next stroke but one of that turn.

33. Interference with Balls between Strokes

If between strokes any ball which has finally come to rest, which is defined in Law 22, is moved it shall be replaced without penalty.

34. Interference with Balls during Strokes

(*a*) *Interference by the Striker after the Conclusion of the Striking but before the Conclusion of the Stroke.* If during the above period the striker interferes with a ball there shall be no penalty. If any such ball is at rest it shall be replaced. If it is moving it shall be placed where, as nearly as can be judged, it would otherwise have come to rest. But after such interference such ball cannot in that stroke make a roquet or be roqueted, score a point or cause another ball to score a point or be displaced.

(*b*) *Interference by Outside Agency during Stroke.* If a ball is interfered with by an outside agency except weather, in a way which materially affects the outcome of the stroke, that stroke shall be replayed. Otherwise, the ball shall be placed, as nearly as can be judged, where it would have come to rest, provided that no point or roquet can thereby be made. A rover ball prevented from scoring the peg by a pegged-out ball shall be placed where it would otherwise have come to rest.

(c) *Interference by Adversary during Stroke.* Any interference by an adversary shall be treated as in Law 34(b).

(d) *Interference with Ball that has made a Roquet.* A ball that has made a roquet remains in play throughout the stroke and may only be picked up or arrested in its course to save time if the state of the game will not be affected thereby.

35. Mistakes in the Score—Including Misplaced Clips

(a) Any player seeing a clip misplaced shall immediately call attention to it and it shall then be properly placed.

(b) The score shall be adjusted at all times before the end of the game.

(c) Should the striker at the end of his turn fail to place any clip correctly and in consequence thereof his adversary is led into a line of play which he would not otherwise have adopted, such adversary has the right to replace the balls where they were when he was first misled provided that this claim is made before the second stroke of the offending party's next turn. If such adversary has been misled on the first stroke of a turn he may at his option play his other ball in the replay.

(d) Further, if the striker makes any stroke or strokes in consequence of any other false information concerning the state of the game supplied by his adversary, he shall be entitled to replay as in the preceding sub-law above.

III(A). LAWS OF ADVANCED SINGLES PLAY

When play is agreed or directed to be played under the conditions of advanced singles play the laws of ordinary level singles play shall apply with the following additional law:

36. Optional Lift and Contact in Advanced Singles Play

(*a*) When the striker's ball has scored one-back or four-back for his ball during a turn, the adversary may choose, subject to (*c*) below, to begin his subsequent turn, either:

  (i) by playing as the balls lie; or

  (ii) by lifting either ball of his side even if it be in contact with one or more balls. As soon as such ball is lifted it immediately becomes in hand and shall be played by the striker from any point on either baulk-line. (See Law 5(*b*).)

(*b*) When the striker has scored one-back and four back for his ball during a turn and his partner ball has not scored one-back before that turn, the adversary may choose, subject to (*c*) below, to begin his subsequent turn, either:

  (i) as in (*a*) (i) above; or

  (ii) as in (*a*) (ii) above; or

  (iii) by lifting either ball of his side, even if it be in contact with one or more balls, placing it in contact with any ball, and taking croquet forthwith.

(*c*) A player who has previously pegged out any ball during the game is not entitled to a lift or a contact under this law.

(*d*) This law is subject to the provisions of Law 10 which states that the partner balls must be played in the third and fourth turns respectively but overrides the provision of that law which says that such balls must be played from baulk.

III(B). LAWS OF SEMI-ADVANCED SINGLES PLAY

When play is agreed or directed to be played under the conditions of semi-advanced singles play the laws of ordinary level singles play shall apply with the following additional law:

37. Optional Lift and Contact in Semi-Advanced Singles Play

The preceding Law 36 shall apply with the omission of the words "or four-back" in sub-section (*a*) thereof.

III(C). LAWS OF HANDICAP SINGLES PLAY

When play is agreed or directed to be played under conditions of handicap singles play the laws of ordinary level singles play shall apply subject to the following additions and modifications:

38. Bisques

(*a*) A bisque is an extra turn given in handicap play and can only be played by the striker with the ball with which he was playing in the preceding turn. A half-bisque is a restricted turn in which no point can be scored for any ball. If, however, the striker plays the first stroke of a non-bisque turn with an adversary's ball and the error is discovered within the limits of claims, he may elect to play a bisque or half-bisque after the balls have been replaced and in that event he may play with either of his balls.

(*b*) The number of bisques to be given shall be the difference between the respective handicaps of the players.

(*c*) A player entitled to a bisque or a series of bisques may play one or more in succession at any time of the game whatsoever and this overrides the provision of Law 10. A striker who has declared his intention to play a bisque may change his mind at any time before making the stroke. But if the striker after he has played all the strokes to which he is entitled signifies that he is not going to play a bisque either by words or by quitting the court he may not change his mind. An adversary shall not begin to play until the striker has so signified his intention.

(*d*) If the striker is entitled to play either a bisque or a half-bisque he shall be deemed to have played the bisque unless before beginning the extra turn he has announced his intention of playing the half-bisque.

(*e*) If the adversary observes the striker about to play a bisque or half-bisque before he has made all the strokes to which he is entitled he shall forestall play. If he fails so to forestall the striker shall be deemed regularly to have begun his extra turn.

(*f*) At the conclusion of a turn, the striker must give a clear indication of his intention before taking a bisque or half-bisque. If he fails to do so, but continues to play, the provisions of Law 27 shall apply. When all balls have been replaced, the striker shall have the option whether or not to take a bisque or half-bisque.

39. Pegging Out
Unless an adversary's ball has already been pegged out a player may not peg out his own ball before his partner ball has become a rover. Should he do so and remove it from the court all strokes subsequent thereto are null and void and the provisions of Law 29(*d*) shall apply.

39A. Restoration of Bisques after Irregularities in Play
(*a*) *Playing When not Entitled to Play.* If a player continues to play after running a wrong hoop, any half-bisque or bisques taken when so playing shall be restored should the error be discovered at any time before the end of the game. (See Law 27.)

(*b*) *Playing the Wrong Ball.* If the striker whilst playing the wrong ball plays a half-bisque or one or more bisques, the provisions of Law 30 shall apply, but unless the error is condoned any half-bisque or bisques taken after the first stroke in error shall be restored and play resumed accordingly. (See Law 43(*c*) for handicap doubles.)

III(D). LAWS OF DOUBLES PLAY

40. (*a*) *Introduction to the Game.* The game is played between two sides, each side consisting of two players. One player plays throughout with one ball of the side and his partner with the other. The partner of the striker is under the same obligations as the striker to avoid interference with balls. If he does so interfere accidentally the consequences are as if it had been the striker who interfered.

(*b*) *Assistance to Partner.* A player may not only advise but may assist his partner in the making of a stroke in the sense that he may set the balls for a croquet stroke and indicate the direction in which the mallet should be swung. But at the time the stroke is actually made he should stand well clear of the striker and well clear of any spot which may help the striker in gauging the strength or direction of the stroke.

(*c*) *Playing the Wrong Ball.* Law 30(*c*) shall be modified so as to exclude from scoring any point for any ball during such period of error except hoop points in order for a ball made by way of peeling.

(*d*) *Effect of Misplaced Clip.* If a side is entitled to replay as from the beginning of a turn in consequence of a misplaced clip or other misleading information, the side may elect which player shall make the replay.

41. Ordinary Level Play

Subject to the preceding Law 40, the laws of ordinary level doubles play are the laws of ordinary level singles play but where appropriate the world player shall be taken to include side and the word striker to include the partner of the striker.

42. Advanced and Semi-Advanced Play

When play is directed or agreed to be played under the conditions of advanced or semi-advanced play the laws of ordinary level doubles play shall apply with the following additional laws, namely, Laws 36 and 37, with the substitution of "Partner's ball" for "partner ball" in Law 36.

43. Handicap Play

When play is directed or agreed to be played under the conditions of handicap play, the modification of the Laws of ordinary level play to handicap play shall apply with the following further modifications:

(*a*) The number of bisques to be given shall be half the difference between the joint handicaps of the sides, a fraction above a half being counted as one bisque and a fraction under a half as a half-bisque.

(*b*) A player may not peel his partner's ball through more than four hoops. (See Law 57(*b*) for modified games.)

(*c*) When a side plays the first stroke of a non-bisque turn with a wrong ball and the error is discovered within the limit of claims, either player may elect to play a half-bisque or bisque after the balls have been replaced.

IV. CUSTOMS OF THE GAME

44. The State of the Game

Any questions as to the correct position of the balls or clips, whether a fault or irregularity has been committed, whether one ball is wired from another, which player played a ball to a particular position, whether a ball has been hit or a hoop has been run or may be run, and any such kindred matters, relate to the state of the game.

45. Refereeing

(*a*) *The Players as Joint Referees*. In the absence of a referee appointed or agreed the players act as their own joint referees, but there is no obligation on the adversary to watch the game, and, if he fails to do so, the striker is during such period the sole referee. In doubles, all players share the rights and duties of a referee and a reference to the striker includes his partner.

(*b*) *Certain Specified Duties of the Referee*. As a joint referee of the game the striker must immediately announce any fault or irregularity he believes or suspects he may have committed. Likewise, the adversary should immediately draw attention to any irregularity he observes, except as provided in Law 28(*b*), notwithstanding it may be to his disadvantage. Further similar but not exhaustive examples are that an adversary should inform the striker that he must complete his turn by playing another stroke, or deeming it to have been played, if he sees him about to leave the court under the impression that his turn has ended; in handicap play, if the striker announces his intention to play a bisque turn before his previous turn has ended, the adversary should tell the striker that he must complete such turn in a similar manner; a player should immediately call attention to a misplaced clip; a player should on request give another player any information as to the state of the game.

(*c*) *Questionable Stroke*. The striker about to play a stroke of which he suspects either the fairness or the effect may be doubtful must consult with his adversary before playing. This is known as a questionable stroke. The stroke should then be specially watched, preferably by an independent person. If no such person is available, the players must do the best they can. It is for the striker to take the initiative, but if he fails to do so the adversary should interrupt for the purpose of having the stroke specially watched.

(*d*) *Testing the Position of a Ball.* The striker in his capacity as referee should not test whether a ball has run a hoop by placing his mallet against the hoop without first consulting his adversary. Any such test should be made in conjunction with the adversary, or, if either party so desire, by an independent person if available. The same principle applies when the question is whether a ball is off the court, or may be lifted under Law 13, or moved or wiped under Law 23 if the position of replacement is critical; or whether any ball is in position to run a hoop. All such decisions made between strokes should be made jointly.

(*e*) *The Striker as the Active Referee.* The adversary should not follow the striker around the court but should allow most decisions to be made by the striker without reference to himself. This is because the striker, generally speaking, is in the better position to give the correct decision. If, however, a close decision has to be made and the adversary is in as good or better position to do this, the striker should seek confirmation of his opinion before continuing to play.

(*f*) *When the Players' Opinions Differ.* If a ball has to be replaced because of the carelessness of a player, the offending party should ordinarily defer to the opinion of the other. When the question is whether a roquet has been made on a ball or whether a ball has moved the positive opinion is generally to be preferred to the negative opinion. If there are any reliable witnesses the players should agree to consult them in order to solve differences; but no player should consult a witness without the express permission of the other player.

46. Interruption of the Striker

The adversary should not interrupt the striker except to discharge his duty as a referee.

47. Presence on Court

A player should not ordinarily remain on the court while his adversary is playing or move on to it until his turn has ended, and, in the case of handicap play, until his adversary has indicated that he does not intend to play a bisque turn. A player should indicate at the earliest opportunity whether or not he intends to take a bisque.

48. Replacing Balls

(a) Especial care must be taken in the replacement of yard-line balls, but time should not be wasted unnecessarily.

(b) In replacing a ball on the yard-line a player should do so with his back to the court.

49. Expedition in Play

(a) A player should play his strokes with reasonable despatch. In time-limited games the adversary should anticipate as far as possible with which ball he will play so that he may waste no time in approaching it at the beginning of his turn. In doubles, time should not be wasted in prolonged discussion.

(b) A player may not enquire from a referee whether one ball is wired from another unless he is claiming that he is entitled to a lift under Law 13(b) in the turn about to be played. Accordingly, a player may not circumvent this law by himself spending time in testing whether one ball is wired from another. In the interests of expedition, he must rely on an unaided ocular test.

50. Unpenalised Infringement of Laws

If there is any infringement of these Laws, including the customs of the game, the balance of the game shall be restored as best meets the justice of the case.

51. Advice and Aids

(a) No player is entitled to advice from anyone other than his partner in doubles. It must be a matter of conscience how a player acts when in receipt of unsolicited information or advice. Warning a player that he is about to run a wrong hoop or play the wrong ball constitutes advice and in tournaments players must not so warn.

(*b*) Players may not make use of technical assistance from books or notes, or artificial aids such as coins, to assist them in arranging balls for a croquet stroke.

(*c*) A mark shall not be made, either inside or outside the court, for the purpose of guiding the striker in the direction or strength of a stroke.

(*d*) No ball, whether in hand or not, shall be used as a trial ball. This includes any experiment to test the pace or imperfections of the court or the width of the hoops.

52. Tournaments

In tournaments a referee should always be called before a questionable stroke, and all disputes should be referred to a referee. If the adversary fails to call a referee before what he should have recognised as a questionable stroke, he should not appeal. He should confine himself to requesting the striker to take the initiative in calling for a referee if another such stroke is about to be played. But it may be that the adversary is of the opinion that the striker is making faults such as "pushing" or "double tapping" in an unhampered stroke; if so, he should inform the striker with a view to a referee being called to watch a stroke or temporarily to take charge of the game. The striker has no justification for taking offence when any such request is made. Players can quite legitimately differ as to what is and what is not permissible under Law 32.

53. Emergency Law

Any situation which does not appear to be covered by these Laws shall be decided as best meets the justice of the case.

V. LAWS RELATING TO MODIFIED GAMES AND COURTS

54. Modified Games

The Standard Game of 26 points may be modified as follows:

(*a*) *Game of 22 Points*. The game is started with all clips on the third hoop.

(b) *Game of* 18 *Points*. Variations:
  (i) The game is started with all clips on the fifth hoop.
  (ii) The game is started with all clips on the first hoop and the peg is the next point in order after two back.
  (iii) The standard setting is modified by removal of the two centre hoops. The game is started with all clips on the first hoop, 1-back becomes the next point in order after the fourth hoop and the peg the next point in order after 4-back.

  This variation is only for singles. The game is started with all clips on the first hoop but as soon as a player's first ball scores that point his other clip is removed to 3-back.

(c) *Game of* 14 *Points*. The game is started with all clips on the first hoop, and the peg is the next point in order after the sixth hoop.

55. Advanced Play in Modified Games

In Advanced Play the provisions of Law 36(b) (iii) shall not apply but the options allowed the adversary as set out in Law 36(a) shall apply when the striker has scored the following hoops or both of them in a turn:
  (a) *Game of* 22 *Points*. Hoops 1-back and 4-back.
  (b) *Game of* 18 *Points*. Variations:
   (i) Hoops 1-back and 4-back.
   (ii) Hoops 4 and 6.
   (iii) Hoops 4 and 2-back.
   (iv) Hoops 1-back and 4-back.
  (c) *Game of* 14 *Points*. Hoop 4.

56. Semi-Advanced Play

In semi-advanced play the adversary shall be allowed the options in Law 55 only after the striker has scored the first of the hoops listed above for the various modified games.

57. Games Played Under Handicap

(a) *Bisques*. The number of bisques to be given in a modified game is the difference between the respective handicaps in

SCHEDULE OF BISQUES

Full Game	Game of 22 Points	Game of 18 Points	Game of 14 Points	Full Game	Game of 22 Points	Game of 18 Points	Game of 14 Points
$\frac{1}{4}$	0	0	0	$10\frac{1}{4}$	$8\frac{1}{2}$	7	$5\frac{1}{2}$
$\frac{1}{2}$	$\frac{1}{2}$	$\frac{1}{2}$	$\frac{1}{2}$	$10\frac{1}{2}$	9	$7\frac{1}{2}$	$5\frac{1}{2}$
$\frac{3}{4}$	$\frac{1}{2}$	$\frac{1}{2}$	$\frac{1}{2}$	$10\frac{3}{4}$	9	$7\frac{1}{2}$	6
1	1	$\frac{1}{2}$	$\frac{1}{2}$	11	$9\frac{1}{2}$	$7\frac{1}{2}$	6
$1\frac{1}{4}$	1	1	$\frac{1}{2}$	$11\frac{1}{4}$	$9\frac{1}{2}$	8	6
$1\frac{1}{2}$	$1\frac{1}{2}$	1	1	$11\frac{1}{2}$	$9\frac{1}{2}$	8	6
$1\frac{3}{4}$	$1\frac{1}{2}$	1	1	$11\frac{3}{4}$	10	8	$6\frac{1}{2}$
2	$1\frac{1}{2}$	$1\frac{1}{2}$	1	12	10	$8\frac{1}{2}$	$6\frac{1}{2}$
$2\frac{1}{4}$	2	$1\frac{1}{2}$	1	$12\frac{1}{4}$	$10\frac{1}{2}$	$8\frac{1}{2}$	$6\frac{1}{2}$
$2\frac{1}{2}$	2	$1\frac{1}{2}$	$1\frac{1}{2}$	$12\frac{1}{2}$	$10\frac{1}{2}$	$8\frac{1}{2}$	$6\frac{1}{2}$
$2\frac{3}{4}$	$2\frac{1}{2}$	2	$1\frac{1}{2}$	$12\frac{3}{4}$	11	9	7
3	$2\frac{1}{2}$	2	$1\frac{1}{2}$	13	11	9	7
$3\frac{1}{4}$	3	$2\frac{1}{2}$	2	$13\frac{1}{4}$	11	9	7
$3\frac{1}{2}$	3	$2\frac{1}{2}$	2	$13\frac{1}{2}$	$11\frac{1}{2}$	$9\frac{1}{2}$	$7\frac{1}{2}$
$3\frac{3}{4}$	3	$2\frac{1}{2}$	2	$13\frac{3}{4}$	$11\frac{1}{2}$	$9\frac{1}{2}$	$7\frac{1}{2}$
4	$3\frac{1}{2}$	3	2	14	12	10	$7\frac{1}{2}$
$4\frac{1}{4}$	$3\frac{1}{2}$	3	$2\frac{1}{2}$	$14\frac{1}{4}$	12	10	$7\frac{1}{2}$
$4\frac{1}{2}$	4	3	$2\frac{1}{2}$	$14\frac{1}{2}$	$12\frac{1}{2}$	10	8
$4\frac{3}{4}$	4	$3\frac{1}{2}$	$2\frac{1}{2}$	$14\frac{3}{4}$	$12\frac{1}{2}$	10	8
5	4	$3\frac{1}{2}$	$2\frac{1}{2}$	15	$12\frac{1}{2}$	$10\frac{1}{2}$	8
$5\frac{1}{4}$	$4\frac{1}{2}$	$3\frac{1}{2}$	3	$15\frac{1}{4}$	13	$10\frac{1}{2}$	8
$5\frac{1}{2}$	$4\frac{1}{2}$	4	3	$15\frac{1}{2}$	13	$10\frac{1}{2}$	$8\frac{1}{2}$
$5\frac{3}{4}$	5	4	3	$15\frac{3}{4}$	$13\frac{1}{2}$	11	$8\frac{1}{2}$
6	5	4	3	16	$13\frac{1}{2}$	11	$8\frac{1}{2}$
$6\frac{1}{4}$	$5\frac{1}{2}$	$4\frac{1}{2}$	$3\frac{1}{2}$	$16\frac{1}{4}$	14	$11\frac{1}{2}$	9
$6\frac{1}{2}$	$5\frac{1}{2}$	$4\frac{1}{2}$	$3\frac{1}{2}$	$16\frac{1}{2}$	14	$11\frac{1}{2}$	9
$6\frac{3}{4}$	$5\frac{1}{2}$	$4\frac{1}{2}$	$3\frac{1}{2}$	$16\frac{3}{4}$	14	$11\frac{1}{2}$	9
7	6	5	4	17	$14\frac{1}{2}$	12	9
$7\frac{1}{4}$	6	5	4	$17\frac{1}{4}$	$14\frac{1}{2}$	12	$9\frac{1}{2}$
$7\frac{1}{2}$	$6\frac{1}{2}$	5	4	$17\frac{1}{2}$	15	12	$9\frac{1}{2}$
$7\frac{3}{4}$	$6\frac{1}{2}$	$5\frac{1}{2}$	4	$17\frac{3}{4}$	15	$12\frac{1}{2}$	$9\frac{1}{2}$
8	7	$5\frac{1}{2}$	$4\frac{1}{2}$	18	15	$12\frac{1}{2}$	$9\frac{1}{2}$
$8\frac{1}{4}$	7	$5\frac{1}{2}$	$4\frac{1}{2}$	$18\frac{1}{4}$	$15\frac{1}{2}$	$12\frac{1}{2}$	10
$8\frac{1}{2}$	7	6	$4\frac{1}{2}$	$18\frac{1}{2}$	$15\frac{1}{2}$	13	10
$8\frac{3}{4}$	$7\frac{1}{2}$	6	$4\frac{1}{2}$	$18\frac{3}{4}$	16	13	10
9	$7\frac{1}{2}$	6	5	19	16	13	10
$9\frac{1}{4}$	8	$6\frac{1}{2}$	5	$19\frac{1}{4}$	$16\frac{1}{2}$	$13\frac{1}{2}$	$10\frac{1}{2}$
$9\frac{1}{2}$	8	$6\frac{1}{2}$	5	$19\frac{1}{2}$	$16\frac{1}{2}$	$13\frac{1}{2}$	$10\frac{1}{2}$
$9\frac{3}{4}$	$8\frac{1}{2}$	7	$5\frac{1}{2}$	$19\frac{3}{4}$	$16\frac{1}{2}$	$13\frac{1}{2}$	$10\frac{1}{2}$
10	$8\frac{1}{2}$	7	$5\frac{1}{2}$	20	17	14	11

Should the difference be greater than 20 bisques, refer to the number equal to half the difference, and then double the adjusted figure.

singles, and half the difference in doubles, which is then scaled down in accordance with the Schedule on page 242.

(*b*) *Peeling Partner's Ball in Handicap Doubles.* In modified handicap doubles each player is limited to peeling his partner's ball through hoops as follows:

Games of 22 *or* 18 *Points*—3 hoops.
Game of 14 *Points*—2 hoops.

58. Modified Courts

(*a*) *The Standard Length Unit.* The standard length unit of the standard court which measures 35 yd by 28 yd is 7 yd. The corner hoops are 7 yd from their adjacent boundaries; the centre hoops each 7 yd from the peg.

(*b*) *Modified Length Units.* Should the area be too small to accommodate a standard court, a modified court may be laid out in accordance with Part I of these laws maintaining the same proportions of five length units long by four length units wide but using a smaller modified length unit.

(*c*) *Baulk-Lines.* The baulk-lines shall measure one half of the width of the Court less the width of the corner square.

(*d*) *Special Adjustments for Very Small Courts:*

   (i) *The Court.* If the available area necessitates a length unit of less than $3\frac{1}{2}$ yd, then the largest possible rectangular area (provided it is not more than twice as long as it is wide) shall be enclosed by boundaries, and the four corner hoops shall be placed $3\frac{1}{2}$ yd from the adjacent boundaries with, in the centre of the area, a fifth hoop which shall face in the same direction and also serve as the Rover hoop. The peg shall be set halfway between hoops two and three and in line with them.

   (ii) *The Yard-Line.* The distance between the boundary and the yard-line may be reduced to half a yard and the corner pegs will be adjusted accordingly.

   (iii) *Baulk-Lines.* The baulk-lines shall measure one quarter of the width of the court less the width of the corner square.

   (iv) *Standard Game for the Above Setting.* The standard game consists of 22 points. The game is started with all clips on the first hoop; but, as there is no sixth or

Penultimate hoop, the next point in order after the fifth hoop is 1 back and after 4-back the Rover hoop.

LAWS OF GOLF CROQUET

The Laws relating to Ordinary Level Play, singles and doubles, and Handicap Play apply subject to the following modifications:

1. The Course

(*a*) There is no A baulk. Balls are played into the game from B baulk.

(*b*) When 13 points are contested the first 12 points are as in Association Croquet. The 13th point is the third hoop. When 19 points are contested the hoops 1-back to the rover are contested twice before contesting the third hoop. The peg is not contested.

2. The Game

(*a*) All balls are always for the same hoop in order. The point is scored for the side whose ball first runs the hoop.

(*b*) A short game is a contest for the best of 13 points and a long game for the best of 19 points. The game ends as soon as one side has scored a majority of the points to be played. It is customary to keep the tally of the score by declaring a side to be one or more points up or down or all square as the case may be.

(*c*) Each turn consists of one stroke. The Laws relating to roquet and croquet, continuation strokes and wiring do not apply.

(*d*) The balls are played in the sequence: blue, red, black, and yellow. Therefore, if yellow is played on the first stroke, blue is played on the second stroke, and so on.

3. Running a Hoop

If the striker causes one of the balls of his side partly to run a hoop during a stroke, such ball must begin afresh to run such hoop before it can be scored by that ball in any subsequent stroke. But if an adversary cause a ball partly to run a hoop during a stroke such ball may run that hoop in a subsequent stroke. If a ball runs two loops in one stroke, it scores both hoops for its side.

4. Jump Stroke
A player may not deliberately make his ball rise from the ground.

If he does so accidentally or in ignorance of this Law, and in consequence runs a hoop for his striker's or partner's ball, the point shall not be scored. Likewise, if in consequence thereof any ball is displaced such ball may be replaced at the option of the adversary side.

5. Advancing a Ball Prematurely for the Next Point
A player must play so as to contest the hoop in order rather than seek to gain an advantage for the next hoop in order. But a player *bona fide* contesting the hoop in order by, for example, attempting to cannon another ball, may legitimately play the stroke at a strength calculated to bring his ball to rest nearer the next hoop in order.

6. Playing Out of Turn or with a Wrong Ball
If the striker plays out of turn or with a wrong ball, that stroke, and any subsequent strokes, are null and void. All balls shall be replaced; the right ball shall be played by the correct player, and the other balls shall follow in due sequence. No points made during the period of error shall be scored.

Any dispute should be settled by a referee.

7. Method of Handicapping
Handicaps shall be allotted in the 13 point game according to Association Croquet handicaps as follows:

-1 and under	0	$6\frac{1}{2}$ to 9	3
$-\frac{1}{2}$ to 2	1	10 to 12	4
$2\frac{1}{2}$ to 6	2	Over 12	5

In the longer game of 19 points the bisques received shall be increased by 50 per cent.

Notwithstanding the above provisions, special Golf Croquet handicaps may be given.

The Laws of
Eton Fives

Eton Fives

DEFINITIONS

The Court is enclosed on three sides and open at the back. The "front wall" is the wall facing the player, and the "right-hand" and "left-hand" walls are the walls on his right hand and left hand respectively.

The "step" is a shallow step dividing the court into two portions, an " upper" or "top" and a "lower" or "bottom" "court" or "step". The vertical face of the "step" does not reckon as part of the floor of the court.

The "pepper-box" is a buttress projecting from the left-hand wall. With the "step", it encloses a small square portion of the floor called "Dead Man's Hole".

The "line" is the lower angle of the ledge running across the front wall, at the height of 4 ft 6 in.

A vertical line is marked on the front wall at a distance of 3 ft 8 in from the right-hand wall.

1. The ball must in every case be hit up; i.e., it must be returned against the front wall on or above the line. Any ball which drops on the top of any of the walls or of the coping, or which hits any part of the roof or the sides of the court above the coping, or which touches the ground first outside the court, or touches any person or object outside the court before the first bound except in the case of a Blackguard (see Law 6 (b)) other than at Game Ball (see Law 11)), is out of court and counts against the striker. The sides and lower face of the coping shall be in.

2. The ball must be fairly hit with a single blow of the hand or hands or wrist, and must not touch any other part of the striker's person under penalty of losing the stroke. It must not be caught, carried, or held in any way, except to serve or to stop a ball as provided for in Law 6. A ball taken with both hands or with a cupped hand may often be technically held, in

which case the striker should declare a hold and allow the point to go against him.

Position of the Players

3. The game, is played by four persons, two against two. Thus, if A and B (with first service) play C and D, A, the server, should stand in the upper court and his side is said to be up. C should stand in the lower court ready to return the service, and his side is said to be down. B and D also stand in the lower court, B having choice of position.

Choice of First Service

4. The choice of first service shall be decided by one of the home side tossing a coin or placing the ball behind his back in one of his hands and one of the opposing side calling. The first server in each game also cuts first (see Law 6 for definition of, and rules for, the first cut) for his side after he and his partner have been sent down; thereafter the player who has the second hand of a service cuts first. If in the first game A serves first and C cuts, then in the second game C serves first and A cuts; in the third game B serves first and D cuts; in the fourth game D serves first and B cuts; and in the fifth game A again serves first and C cuts.

The Service

5. The ball when served must hit first the front wall above the line and then the right-hand wall, and must fall in the lower court. The player who is cutting need not return the first or any service until he gets one to his mind, and if he fails to return the service above the line no stroke is counted. A service which goes out of court carries no penalty and may be taken by the player making the first cut.

The First Cut

6. (a) Only the player who is cutting may return the service, and he may do so only between the first and second bounds. This return is called the "First Cut". He must return it so that it should hit either (1) first the right-hand wall and subsequently the front wall above the line; or (2) first the front wall above

the line between the right-hand wall and the vertical line marked on the front wall. In both cases the ball may afterwards hit any wall or walls and may fall anywhere in the upper or lower court.

(*b*) If the first cut is hit in such a way that it will probably fall out of court, the side which is down may, *without interference*, touch the ball so that it falls within the court, or catch it, provided that the player touching or catching the ball has one or both feet on the floor of the court, or, if he jumps for the purpose, alights on the floor of the court with the foot which first touches the ground. If the ball is caught, no stroke is counted; if only touched, one of the side which is up may, if he pleases, return the ball and neither of the opposing side may interfere with his shot; if he fails to return the ball up, no stroke is counted.

(*c*) If the first cut hits the front wall above the line but to the left of the vertical line marked on the front wall and without first touching the right-hand wall, this shot is called a "Blackguard". It may be returned before the second bound by either the server or his partner at their option, but if it is not returned above the line, no stroke is counted. The last sentence does not apply at Game Ball (see Law 11).

The Rally

7. After the service and the first cut the ball is returned alternately by either side. It may be returned by either of the partners before the first or second bound, and may or may not hit the side walls. A rally is lost to his side by the player who fails to return the ball above the line, or hits it out of court.

Lets

8. (*a*) A let may be *requested* when a player is in any way prevented from returning or impeded in his attempt to return the ball by one of the opposite side. A let may not be requested when the ball is returned above the line, whether or not it falls out of court, nor when a player is impeded by bystanders.

(*b*) A ball which would have hit the front wall above the line, but is prevented from doing so by one of the opposite side, counts as a let, unless it first strikes one of the opposite side, and thereafter the front wall above the line, in which case it counts as up; but if it first strikes one of the same side, it does not count as up, whether it goes up or not.

(*c*) If a ball after going up from a return by A or B strikes A or B before the second bound, it shall count as a let if C or D consider they could have returned it, if it had not hit A or B, except that if the ball clearly would have fallen out of court it shall count against A and B (subject to the provisions of Law 6 relating to a first cut). C or D may, however, elect to return the ball and continue the rally. If not returned up, it counts as a let. If returned above the line, a let may not be requested, whether or not it falls out of court.

(*d*) Where a ball becomes lodged on any ledge within the court before the second bound, it shall count as a let.

NOTE.—*If there is no umpire, a request for a let is generally allowed, except where this Law expressly provides that no let can be claimed.*

Scoring

9. A game is won by the side which first obtains twelve points, except as provided in Law 12. Matches generally consist of the best of five games. Only the side which is up may score points. When A is put out B takes his place. When B is out, the side is out and their opponents go up, the player who has been cutting being the first hand to go up, except as provided in Law 10. The result of each rally, except in the case of a let, is either to add one to the score of the side which is up, or to put one of them out, as the case may be.

Two Down

10. If C loses one point to the opposite side when he is cutting, he is said to be one down. If he loses a second point, he is said to be two down, and D takes his place; if D in turn loses two points, he is two down and C cuts again; and so on until both A and B are put out; provided that he who was two down first is then the first to go up; but if, through inadvertence or otherwise, he does not do so, the error cannot be corrected after service has been returned. All balls which fall in the upper

court belong to the player who is cutting. Failure to return a ball out of Dead Man's Hole does not count as one down against the player who is cutting. The player who is cutting cannot be two down at Game Ball.

Game Ball

11. When the side which is serving requires one point for game, this is called Game Ball and the following rules must be observed:

(*a*) The player serving must stand with at least one foot in the lower court, and he may not place both feet on the top step until the player who is cutting has hit the ball. If he forgets to stand thus, and serves the ball with both feet on the top step, the player who is cutting, or his partner, may try to catch the ball before it bounds. If they succeed in this, the side serving is out. If, however, they do not succeed in catching the ball, or if the player serving or his partner manage to touch the ball first, or if it hits the ground before being touched, it counts neither way. A player may remind his partner of this Law. Where the server places both feet on the top step after the first bound but before the player who is cutting has hit the ball a let may be claimed by the side cutting.

(*b*) When the ball is properly served, the player who is cutting may return the first cut against any part of the front wall above the line, with or without hitting the side walls.

(*c*) The side which is down may not touch or catch a game ball cut which is going out of Court (see Law 6 *(c)*).

Setting

12. If the score is at 10 all, the game may, at the option of the side which is cutting, be set to 5 or 3, or not at all, if 11 all, to 3 or not at all. If the game is set, Law 11 shall apply at 4 or 2 respectively. At 14 all or 12 all in the first case, or at 13 all in the second case, or at 11 all if the game is not set, the game shall be decided by "sudden death", Law 11 being observed on either side.

The Rules of
Rugby Fives

Rugby Fives

As approved by the Rugby Fives Association

DEFINITIONS

The game is played in a court enclosed by four walls. The "front" wall is distinguished by a board of wood running across it at an even height from the floor.

The wall opposite the front wall is the "back" wall, and the two adjoining walls, as the players stand facing the front wall, are respectively the "right" side wall and the "left" side wall.

The game may be played between two or four players i.e., as Singles or Doubles.

Server and Receiver. The player first hitting the ball is the "server" (who is said to be "out" or "down"), his opponent being known as the "receiver" (who is said to be "in" or "up").

"Up". The ball is said to be "up" when it is hit before the second bounce, strikes the front wall above the board, and does not leave the confines of the playing surface.

RULES OF THE SINGLES GAME

1.

At the commencement of a game a preliminary rally shall be played. The winner of this becomes the receiver, and the loser, the server.

2.

At the start of a rally the ball is thrown up so that it first strikes the front wall above the board and then one of the side walls, in such a manner as the server desires. The server may either throw up the ball for himself or request the receiver to do so. When the receiver is required to throw up the ball for the server, he shall not be required to do so in such a manner as to penalise himself in his attempt to return the service.

3.

The server may not serve unless the ball has been thrown up as described in Rule 2.

4. Service

The server shall serve in such a way that after the first bounce and before the second bounce the ball strikes first the side wall against which it has been thrown and then the front wall above the board.

5.

After the service and its return, the opponents shall alternately hit the ball, before the second bounce, on to the front wall above the board, either directly or after it has hit the side and/ or back walls. No second attempt may be made to hit a ball after it has once been touched.

6. Blackguard

A service which hits the front wall above the board without having first touched the near side wall, but remains within the confines of the playing surface of the court, is called a "blackguard". The receiver may return a blackguard provided he calls out his intention to do before striking the ball. Such decision shall be irrevocable.

The server may not intentionally stop a blackguard. (See Rule 8(*b*) and (*d*).)

When the receiver requires one point to win the game, he may not take a blackguard.

7. Scoring

The player who first scores 15 points (except as provided when the score reaches 14–14) wins the game.

Only the receiver can score points. When the receiver wins a rally, he scores one point. When the server wins a rally, he becomes receiver for the next rally.

Should each player score 14 points, the first player to reach 16 points wins the game.

8.

A rally is won by a player if:

(*a*) His opponent fails to hit the ball (except as provided under Rule 9(*d*)), or hits it after the second bounce, or hits it on to or below the board, or against the roof, or otherwise out of the confines of the playing surface, or on to the floor before hitting the front wall.

NOTE.— *When the receiver requires one point to win the game, the server is not penalised if he serves not more than twice incorrectly. The third service must be right or the server loses the point and game.*

(*b*) His opponent, being server, serves more than two consecutive untaken blackguards, or intentionally stops a blackguard.

(*c*) His opponent strike him with a ball which would not have gone "up". (See Rule 9(*a*).)

(*d*) His opponent causes the ball, after it has hit the front wall, to strike himself before it has bounced. This also applies to blackguards.

(*e*) His opponent hits the ball otherwise than with the hand or forearm.

9. Lets

A let is allowed, and the rally shall not count if:

(*a*) A player strikes his opponent with a ball which would have gone "up".

(*b*) A player causes the ball, after it has hit the front wall, to strike himself after it has bounced.

(*c*) A player is prevented by his opponent from correctly returning the ball. Should a player, though impeded, hit the ball so that it go "up" he may claim a let at once; otherwise the rally shall continue.

(*d*) The Server, when about to serve, fails to hit the ball, or changes his mind and calls out "No" before hitting the ball, even if it accidentally go "up".

10.

The umpires decision is final.

RULES OF THE DOUBLES GAME

The Rules of the Singles Game shall apply to the Doubles Game, and wherever the words "server", "receiver", "opponent" , or "player" are used in the Rules of the Singles Game, such words shall, whenever possible, be taken to include his partner in the Doubles Game. Thus, if the duration of the preliminary rally requires their participation, all four players shall take part.

1.

The receiver and his partner are known as "hands". The side winning the peliminary rally may choose whether to serve or receive and the side receiving shall have only one hand.

2.

The receiver remains "in" until his side loses a rally, whereupon his partner shall receive (except as provided for in Rule 1). When his side loses another rally, his opponents become receivers.

3.

The side that is "down" must change servers after every point scored by their opponents.

4.

If the wrong player serves or receives, the mistake must be pointed out before the start of the next rally, otherwise the rally counts; but at the next "hand", the players shall revert to their correct order.

5.

Only the receiver may return the service; either he or his partner may elect to take a blackguard. If either of them says "Yes" to a blackguard, the rally commences.

RULES OF MATCH PLAY

(*a*) For the preliminary rally (see Rule 1 of the Rules of Singles game) the receiver and server shall be decided by tossing—the winner to make his choice.

(*b*) A preliminary rally shall not be played at the beginning of the second and each subsequent game of a match and the winner of the previous game shall continue to receive. In doubles the winners shall have only one "hand".

(*c*) A new ball shall be taken before the start of each game if either side wishes it. A defective ball may be replaced at any time, if in the opinion of the umpire, a change is desirable. In selecting a replacement, the umpire shall take into account the time during which the defective ball has been in play.

(*d*) A let shall be allowed as in Rule 9(*a*), (*b*) and (*c*) only on a player's successful appeal to the umpire.

(*e*) A player shall not leave the court during a game, except with the permission of the umpire.

(*f*) A player shall not unreasonably delay between rallies. The umpire shall at once order the game to continue, if, in his opinion, such delay is occurring. If, after further warning by the umpire, a player is responsible for further delay or delays, the umpire may award the game (15 points or when appropriate 16 points) to the opponent or opponents of the defaulting player. In this event the losing side retains any points it may have scored.

(*g*) If a player, by reason of injury or ill-health, is, in the opinion of the umpire, unfit to continue a game, the umpire shall stop the game and award it to that player's opponent or opponents. Points shall be allotted as in Rule (*f*).

(*h*) In a match consisting of more than one game, not more than three minutes' interval shall be allowed between games.

The Laws of
Association Football

Association Football

1. THE FIELD OF PLAY

The Field of Play and appurtenances shall be as shown in the following plan:

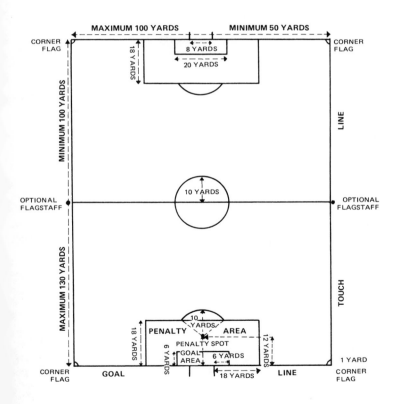

1. Dimensions

The field of play shall be rectangular, its length being not more than 130 yd nor less than 100 yd and its breadth not more than 100 yd nor less than 50 yd. (In International Matches the length shall be not more than 120 yd nor less than 110 yd and the breadth nor more than 80 yd nor less than 70 yd.) The length shall in all cases exceed the breadth.

2. Marking

The field of play shall be marked with distinctive lines, not more than 5 in in width, not by a **V**-shaped rut, in accordance with the plan, the longer boundary lines being called the touch-lines and the shorter the goal-lines. A flag on a post not less than 5 ft high and having a non-pointed top, shall be placed at each corner; a similar flag-post may be placed opposite the halfway-line on each side of the field of play, not less than 1 yd outside the touch-line. A halfway-line shall be marked out across the field of play. The centre of the field of play shall be indicated by a suitable mark and a circle with a 10 yd radius shall be marked round it.

4. The Penalty-Area

At each end of the field of play two lines shall be drawn at right angles to the goal-line, 18 yd from each goal-post. These shall extend into the field of play for a distance of 18 yd and shall be joined by a line drawn parallel with the goal-line. Each of the spaces enclosed by these lines and the goal-line shall be called a penalty-area. A suitable mark shall be made within each penalty-area, 12 yd from the mid-point of the goal-line, measured along an undrawn line at right angles thereto. These

3. The Goal-Area

At each end of the field of play two lines shall be drawn at right angles to the goal-line, 6 yd from each goal-post. These shall extend into the field of play for a distance of 6 yd and shall be joined by a line drawn parallel with the goal-line. Each of the spaces enclosed by these lines and the goal-line shall be called the goal-area.

shall be the penalty-kick marks. From each penalty-kick mark an arc of a circle, having a radius of 10 yd, shall be drawn outside the penalty-area.

5. The Corner-Area
From each corner-flag post a quarter circle, having a radius of 1 yd, shall be drawn inside the field of play.

6. The Goals
The goals shall be placed on the centre of each goal-line and shall consist of two upright posts, equidistant from the corner-flags and 8 yd apart (inside measurement), joined by a horizontal cross-bar, the lower edge of which shall be 8 ft from the ground. The width and depth of the goal-posts and the width and depth of the cross-bars shall not exceed 5 in (12 cm). The goal-posts and the cross-bars shall have the same width.

Nets may be attached to the posts, cross-bars and ground behind the goals. They should be appropriately supported and be so placed as to allow the goalkeeper ample room.

2. THE BALL
The ball shall be spherical; the outer casing shall be of leather or other approved materials. No material shall be used in its construction which might prove dangerous to the players. The circumference of the ball shall not be more than 28 in nor less than 27 in. The weight of the ball at the start of the game shall not be more than 16 oz nor less than 14 oz. The pressure shall be equal to 0.6–0.7 atmosphere, which equals 9.0–10.5 lb/sq in (= 600–700 gm/cm^2) at sea level. The ball shall not be changed during the game unless authorised by the Referee.

3. NUMBER OF PLAYERS
(1) A match shall be played by two teams, each consisting of not more than eleven players, one of whom shall be the goalkeeper.
(2) Substitutes may be used in any match played under the

rules of an official competition at F.I.F.A., Confederation or National Association level, subject to the following conditions:

(*a*) that the authority of the International Association(s) or National Association(s) concerned, has been obtained:

(*b*) that, subject to the restriction contained in the following paragraph (*c*), the rules of a competition shall state how many, if any, substitutes may be used, and

(*c*) that a team shall not be permitted to use more than two substitutes in any match.

(3) Substitutes may be used in any other match provided that the two teams concerned reach agreement on a maximum number, not exceeding five, and that the terms of such agreement are intimated to the referee, before the match. If the referee is not informed, or if the teams fail to reach agreement, no more than 2 substitutes shall be permitted.

(4) Any of the other players may change places with the goal-keeper, provided that the referee is informed before the change is made, and provided also, that the change is made during a stoppage in the game.

(5) When a goalkeeper or any other player is to be replaced by a substitute, the following conditions shall be observed:

(*a*) the referee shall be informed of the proposed substitution, before it is made;

(*b*) the substitute shall not enter the field of play until the player he is replacing has left, and then only after having received a signal from the referee.

(*c*) he shall enter the field during a stoppage in the game, and at the halfway-line.

(*d*) a player who has been replaced shall not take any further part in the game.

(*e*) a substitute shall be subject to the authority and juris-diction of the Referee whether called upon to play or not.

Punishment. (*a*) Play shall not be stopped for an infringe-ment of para. 4. The players concerned shall be cautioned immediately the ball goes out of play.

(*b*) If a substitute enters the field of play without the autho-rity of the Referee, play shall be stopped. The substitute shall be cautioned and removed from the field or sent off according to the circumstances. The game shall be restarted by the Referee dropping the ball at the place where it was when he stopped play.

(*c*) For any other infringement of this law, the player concerned shall be cautioned, and if the game is stopped by the referee, to administer the caution, it shall be restarted by an indirect free-kick, to be taken by a player of the opposing team, from the place where the ball was when play was stopped. If the free-kick is awarded to a side within its own goal-area, it may be taken from any point within that half of the goal-area in which the ball was when play was stopped.

4. PLAYERS' EQUIPMENT

A player shall not wear anything which is dangerous to another player. Footwear (boots or shoes) must conform to the following standard:

(*a*) Bars shall be made of leather or rubber and shall be transverse and flat, not less than half an inch in width and shall extend the total width of the sole and be rounded at the corners.

(*b*) Studs which are independently mounted on the sole and are replaceable shall be made of leather, rubber, aluminium, plastic or similar material and shall be solid. With the exception of that part of the stud forming the base, which shall not protrude from the sole more than one quarter of an inch, studs shall be round in plan and not less than half an inch in diameter. Where studs are tapered, the minimum diameter of any section of the stud must not be less than half an inch. Where metal seating for the screw type is used, this seating must be embedded in the sole of the footwear and any attachment screw shall be part of the stud. Other than the metal seating for the screw type of stud, no metal plates even though covered with leather or rubber shall be worn, neither studs which are threaded to allow them to be screwed on to a base screw that is fixed by nails or otherwise to the soles of footwear, nor studs which, apart from the base, have any form of protruding edge rim, or relief marking, or ornament, should be allowed.

(*c*) Studs which are moulded as an integral part of the sole and are not replaceable, shall be made of rubber, plastic, polyurethane or similar soft materials. Provided that there are no fewer than ten studs on the sole, they shall have a minimum diameter of $\frac{3}{8}$ in (10 mm). Additional supporting material to stabilise studs of soft materials, and ridges which shall not protrude more than 5 mm from the sole and moulded to strengthen it, shall be permitted provided that they are in no way dangerous to other players. In all other respects they shall conform to the general requirements of this law.

(*d*) Combined bars and studs may be worn, provided the whole conforms to the general requirements of this law. Neither bars nor studs on the soles shall project more than $\frac{3}{4}$ in. If nails are used they shall be driven in flush with the surface.

The goalkeeper shall wear colours which distinguish him from the other players and from the referee.

Punishment. For any infringement of this Law, the player at fault shall be sent off the field of play to adjust his equipment and he shall not return without first reporting to the Referee, who shall satisfy himself that the player's equipment is in order; the player shall only re-enter the game at a moment when the ball has ceased to be in play.

5. REFEREES

A Referee shall be appointed to officiate in each game. His authority and the exercise of the powers granted to him by the Laws of the Game commence as soon as he enters the field of play. His power of penalizing shall extend to offences committed when play has been temporarily suspended, or when the ball is out of play. His decision on points of fact connected with the play shall be final, so far as the result of the game is concerned.

He shall:

(*a*) Enforce the Laws.

(*b*) Refrain from penalising in cases where he is satisfied that, by doing so, he would be giving an advantage to the offending team.

(*c*) Keep a record of the game; act as time-keeper and allow the full or agreed time, adding thereto all time lost through accident or other cause.

(*d*) Have discretionary power to stop the game for any infringement of the Laws and to suspend or terminate the game whenever, by reason of the elements, interference by spectators or other cause, he deems such stoppage necessary. In such a case he shall submit a detailed report to the competent authority, within the stipulated time, and in accordance with the provisions set up by the National Association under whose jurisdiction the match was played. Reports will be deemed to be made when received in the ordinary course of post.

(*e*) From the time he enters the field of play, caution any player guilty of misconduct or ungentlemanly behaviour and, if he persists, suspend him from further participation in the game. In such cases the Referee shall send the name of the offender to the competent authority, within the stipulated time, and in accordance with the provisions set up by the National Association under whose jurisdiction the match was played. Reports will be deemed to be made when received in the ordinary course of post.

(*f*) Allow no person other than the players and Linesmen to enter the field of play without his permission.

(*g*) *Stop the game if, in his opinion, a player has been seriously injured; have the player removed as soon as possible from the field of play, and immediately resume the game. If a player is slightly injured the game shall not be stopped until the ball has ceased to be in play. A player who is able to go to the touch- or goal-line for attention of any kind, shall not be treated on the field of play.*

(*h*) Send off the field of play any player who in his opinion is guilty of violent conduct, serious foul play, or the use of foul or abusive language.

(*i*) Signal for recommencement of the game after all stoppages.

(*j*) Decide that the ball provided for a match meets with the requirements of Law 2.

6. LINESMEN

Two Linesmen shall be appointed whose duty (subject to the decision of the Referee) shall be to indicate when the ball is out of play and which side is entitled to the corner-kick, goal-kick or throw-in. They shall also assist the Referee to control the game in accordance with the Laws. In the event of undue interference or improper conduct by a Linesman, the Referee shall dispense with his services and arrange for a substitute to be appointed. (The matter shall be reported by the Referee to the competent authority.) The Linesmen should be equipped with flags by the Club on whose ground the match is played.

7. DURATION OF THE GAME

The duration of the game shall be two equal periods of 45 minutes, unless otherwise mutually agreed upon, subject to the following:

(*a*) Allowance shall be made in either period for all time lost through accident or other cause, the amount of which shall be a matter for the discretion of the Referee.

(*b*) Time shall be extended to permit of a penalty-kick being taken at or after the expiration of the normal period in either half.

At half-time the interval shall not exceed five minutes, except by the consent of the Referee.

8. THE START OF PLAY

(*a*) *At the beginning of the game* choice of ends and the kick-off shall be decided by the toss of a coin. The team winning the toss shall have the option of choice of ends or the kick-off.

The Referee having given a signal, the game shall be started by a player taking a place-kick (i.e., a kick at the ball while it is stationary on the ground in the centre of the field of play) into his opponents' half of the field of play. Every player shall be in his own half of the field and every player of the team opposing that of the kicker shall remain not less than 10 yd from the ball until it is kicked-off; it shall not be deemed in play until it has travelled the distance of its own circumference. The kicker shall not play the ball a second time until it has been played or touched by another player.

(*b*) *After a goal has been scored* the game shall be restarted in like manner by a player of the team losing the goal.

(*c*) *After half-time*; when restarting after half-time, ends shall be changed and the kick-off shall be taken by a player of the opposite team to that of the player who started the game.

Punishment. For any infringement of this Law, the kick-off shall be retaken, except in the case of the kicker playing the ball again before it has been touched or played by another player; for this offence, an indirect free-kick shall be taken by a player of the opposing team from the place where the infringement occurred, unless the offence is committed by a player in his opponents' goal-area, in which case the free-kick shall be taken from a point anywhere within that half of the goal-area in which the offence occurred. A goal shall not be scored direct from a kick-off.

(*d*) *After any other temporary suspension*; when restarting the game after a temporary suspension of play from any cause not mentioned elsewhere in these Laws, provided that immediately prior to the suspension the ball has not passed over the touch- or goal-lines, the Referee shall drop the ball at the place where it was when play was suspended and it shall be deemed in play when it has touched the ground; if, however, it goes over the touch- or goal-lines after it has been dropped by the Referee, but before it is touched by a player, the Referee shall again drop it. A player shall not play the ball until it has touched the ground. If this section of the Law is not complied with, the Referee shall again drop the ball.

9. BALL IN AND OUT OF PLAY

The ball is out of play:

(*a*) When it has wholly crossed the goal-line or touch-line, whether on the ground or in the air.

(*b*) When the game has been stopped by the Referee.

The ball is in play at all other times from the start of the match to the finish, including:

(*a*) If it rebounds from a goal-post, cross-bar or corner-flag post into the field of play.

(*b*) If it rebounds off either the Referee or Linesmen when they are in the field of play.

(*c*) In the event of a supposed infringement of the Laws, until a decision is given.

10. METHOD OF SCORING

Except as otherwise provided by these Laws, a goal is scored when the whole of the ball has passed over the goal-line, between the goal-posts and under the cross-bar, provided it has not been thrown, carried or propelled by hand or arm, by a player of the attacking side, except in the case of a goalkeeper, who is within his own penalty area.

The team scoring the greater number of goals during the game shall be the winner; if no goals or an equal number of goals are scored the game shall be termed a "draw".

11. OFF-SIDE

(1) A player is in an off-side position if he is nearer to his opponents' goal-line than the ball *unless*:

(*a*) He is in his own half of the field of play, or

(*b*) There are at least two of his opponents nearer to their own goal-line than he is.

(2) A player shall only be declared off-side and penalised for being in an off-side position, if, at the moment the ball touches, or is played by, one of his team, he is, in the opinion of the Referee

(*a*) interfering with play or with an opponent or

(*b*) seeking to gain an advantage by being in that position.

(3) A player shall not be declared off-side by the Referee

(*a*) merely because of his being in an off-side position, or

(*b*) if he receives the ball, direct, from a goal-kick, a corner-kick, a throw-in, or when it has been dropped by the Referee.

(4) If a player is declared off-side, the Referee shall award an indirect free-kick, which shall be taken by a player of the opposing team from the place where the infringement occurred, unless the offence is committed by a player in his opponents' goal-area, in which case, the free-kick shall be taken from a point anywhere within that half of the goal-area in which the offence occurred.

12. FOULS AND MISCONDUCT

A player who intentionally commits any of the following nine offences:

(*a*) Kicks or attempts to kick an opponent;

(*b*) Trips an opponent, i.e., throwing or attempting to throw him by the use of the legs or by stooping in front of or behind him;

(*c*) Jumps at an opponent;

(*d*) Charges an opponent in a violent or dangerous manner;

(*e*) Charges an opponent from behind unless the latter be obstructing;

(*f*) Strikes or attempts to strike an opponent;

(*g*) Holds an opponent;

(*h*) Pushes an opponent with his hand or any part of his arm;

(*i*) Handles the ball, i.e., carries, strikes or propels the ball with his hand or arm. (This does not apply to the goalkeeper within his own penalty-area);

shall be penalised by the award of a *direct free-kick* to be taken by the opposing side from the place where the offence occurred, unless the offence is committed by a player in his opponents' goal-area, in which case the free-kick shall be taken from a point anywhere within that half of the goal-area in which the offence occurred.

Should a player of the defending side intentionally commit one of the above nine offences within the penalty-area he shall be penalised by a *penalty-kick*.

A penalty-kick can be awarded irrespective of the position of the ball, if in play, at the time an offence within the penalty-area is committed.

A player committing any of the five following offences:

1. Playing in a manner considered by the Referee to be dangerous, e.g., attempting to kick the ball while held by the goalkeeper;

2. Charging fairly, i.e., with the shoulder, when the ball is not within playing distance of the players concerned and they are definitely not trying to play it;

3. When not playing the ball, intentionally obstructing an

opponent, i.e., running between the opponent and the ball, or interposing the body so as to form an obstacle to an opponent;

4. Charging the goalkeeper except when he:

(*a*) is holding the ball;

(*b*) is obstructing an opponent;

(*c*) has passed outside his goal-area;

5. When playing as goalkeeper, (*a*) takes more than four steps while holding, bouncing or throwing the ball in the air and catching it again without releasing it so that it is played by another player, or (*b*) indulges in tactics which, in the opinion of the Referee, are designed merely to hold up the game and thus waste time and so give an unfair advantage to his own team:

shall be penalised by the award of an *indirect free-kick* to be taken by the opposing side from the place where the infringement occurred, unless the offence is committed by a player in his opponents' goal-area, in which case the free-kick shall be taken from a point anywhere within that half of the goal-area in which the offence occurred.

A player shall be *cautioned* if:

(*a*) He enters or re-enters the field of play to join or rejoin his team after the game has commenced or leaves the field of play during the progress of the game (except through accident) without, in either case, first having received a signal from the Referee showing him that he may do so. If the Referee stops the game to administer the caution it shall be restarted by an indirect free-kick taken by a player of the opposing team from the place where the ball was when the Referee stopped the game. If the free-kick is awarded to a side within its own goal-area, it may be taken from any point within the half of the goal-area in which the ball was when play was stopped. If, however, the offending player has committed a more serious offence he shall be penalised according to that section of the Law infringed.

(*b*) He persistently infringes the Laws of the Game.

(*c*) He shows, by word or action, dissent from any decision given by the Referee.

(*d*) He is guilty of ungentlemanly conduct.

For any of these last three offences, in addition to the

caution, an *indirect free-kick* shall also be awarded to the opposing side from the place where the offence occurred, unless a more serious infringement of the Laws of the Game was committed. If the offence is committed by a player in his opponents' goal-area, a free-kick shall be taken from a point anywhere within that half of the goal-area in which the offence occurred.

A player shall be sent off the field of play if in the opinion of the Referee, he:

  (*a*) *is guilty of violent conduct, or serious foul play;*

  (*b*) *uses foul or abusive language;*

  (*c*) *persists in misconduct after having received a caution.*

If play be stopped by reason of a player being ordered from the field for an offence without a separate breach of the Law having been committed, the game shall be resumed by an *indirect free-kick* awarded to the opposing side from the place where the infringement occurred, unless the offence is committed by a player in his opponents' goal-area, in which case the free-kick shall be taken from a point anywhere within that half of the goal-area in which the offence occurred.

13. FREE-KICK

Free-kicks shall be classified under two heads:

"Direct" (from which a goal can be scored direct against the *offending side*), and "Indirect" (from which a goal cannot be scored unless the ball has been played or touched by a player other than the kicker before passing through the goal).

When a player is taking a direct or an indirect free-kick inside his own penalty-area, all of the opposing players shall be at least ten yards from the ball and shall remain outside the penalty-area until the ball has been kicked out of the area. The ball shall be in play immediately it has travelled the distance of its own circumference and is beyond the penalty-area. The goalkeeper shall not receive the ball into his hands, in order that he may thereafter kick it into play. If the ball is not kicked direct into play, beyond the penalty-area, the kick shall be retaken.

When a player is taking a direct or an indirect free-kick

outside his own penalty-area, all of the opposing players shall be at least ten yards from the ball, until it is in play, unless they are standing on their own goal-line, between the goal-posts. The ball shall be in play when it has travelled the distance of its own circumference.

If a player of the opposing side encroaches into the penalty-area, or within ten yards of the ball, as the case may be, before a free-kick is taken, the Referee shall delay the taking of the kick until the Law is complied with.

The ball must be stationary when a free-kick is taken, and the kicker shall not play the ball a second time, until it has been touched or played by another player.

Notwithstanding any other reference in these Laws to the point from which a free-kick is to be taken, any free-kick awarded to the defending side, within its own goal-area, may be taken from any point within that half of the goal-area in which the free-kick has been awarded.

Punishment. If the kicker, after taking the free-kick, plays the ball a second time before it has been touched or played by another player, an indirect free-kick shall be taken by a player of the opposing team from the spot where the infringement occurred, unless the offence is committed by a player in his opponents' goal-area, in which case the free-kick shall be taken from a point anywhere within that half of the goal-area in which the offence occurred.

14. PENALTY-KICK

A penalty-kick shall be taken from the penalty-mark and, when it is being taken, all players, with the exception of the player taking the kick, and the opposing goalkeeper, shall be within the field of play, but outside the penalty-area, and at least 10 yd from the penalty-mark. The opposing goalkeeper must stand (without moving his feet) on his own goal-line, between the goal-posts, until the ball is kicked. The player taking the kick must kick the ball forward; he shall not play the ball a second time until it has been touched or played by another player. The ball shall be deemed in play directly it is kicked, i.e., travelled the distance of its circumference, and a goal may be scored direct from such a penalty-kick. If the ball touches the goal-keeper before passing between the posts, when a penalty-kick is being taken at or after the expiration of half-time or full-time, it does not nullify a goal. If necessary, time of play shall be extended at half-time or full-time to allow a penalty-kick to be taken.

Punishment. For any infringement of this Law: (*a*) by the defending team the kick shall be retaken, if a goal has not resulted;

(*b*) by the attacking team, other than by the player taking the kick, if a goal is scored, the goal shall be disallowed and the kick retaken.

(*c*) by the player taking the penalty-kick, committed after the ball is in play, a player of the opposing team shall take an indirect free-kick from the spot where the infringement occurred.

If, in the case of paragraph (*c*), the offence is committed by the player in his opponents' goal area, the free-kick shall be taken from a point anywhere within that half of the goal-area in which the offence occurred.

15. THROW-IN

When the whole of the ball passes over a touch-line, either on the ground or in the air, it shall be thrown in from the point where it crossed the line, in any direction, by a player of the team opposite to that of the player who last touched it. The thrower at the moment of delivering the ball must face the field of play and part of each foot shall be either on the touch-line or on the ground outside the touch-line. The thrower shall use both hands and shall deliver the ball from behind and over his head. The ball shall be in play immediately it enters the field of play, but the thrower shall not again play the ball until it has been touched or played by another player. A goal shall not be scored direct from a throw-in.

Punishment. (*a*) If the ball is improperly thrown in, the throw-in shall be taken by a player of the opposing team.

(*b*) If the thrower plays the ball a second time, before it has been touched or played by another player, an indirect free-kick shall be taken by a player of the opposing team from the place where the infringement occurred, unless the offence is committed by a player in his opponents' goal-area, in which case the free-kick shall be taken from a point anywhere within that half of the goal-area in which the offence occurred.

16. GOAL-KICK

When the whole of the ball passes over the goal-line, excluding that portion between the goal-posts, either in the air or on the ground, having last been played by one of the attacking team, it shall be kicked direct into play beyond the penalty-area, from a point within that half of the goal-area nearest to where it crossed the line, by a player of the defending team. A goal-keeper shall not receive the ball into his hands from a goal-kick in order that he may thereafter kick it into play. If the ball is not kicked beyond the penalty-area, i.e., direct into play, the kick shall be re-taken. The kicker shall not play the ball a second time until it has touched or been played by another player. A goal shall not be scored direct from such a kick. Players of the team opposing that of the player taking the goal-kick shall remain outside the penalty-area until the ball has been kicked out of the penalty-area.

Punishment. If a player taking a goal-kick plays the ball a second time after it has passed beyond the penalty-area, but before it has touched or been played by another player, an indirect free-kick shall be awarded to the opposing team, to be taken from the place where the infringement occurred, unless the offence is committed by a player in his opponents' goal-area, in which case the free-kick shall be taken from a point anywhere within that half of the goal-area in which the offence occurred.

17. CORNER-KICK

When the whole of the ball passes over the goal-line, excluding that portion between the goal-posts, either in the air or on the ground, having last been played by one of the defending team, a member of the attacking team shall take a corner-kick, i.e.

the whole of the ball shall be placed within the quarter circle at the nearest corner-flag post, which must not be moved, and it shall be kicked from that position.

A goal may be scored direct from such a kick. Players of the team opposing that of the player taking the corner-kick shall not approach within 10 yd of the ball until it is in play, i.e., it has travelled the distance of its own circumference, nor shall the kicker play the ball a second time until it has been touched or played by another player.

Punishment. (*a*) If the player who takes the kick plays the ball a second time before it has been touched or played by another player, the Referee shall award an indirect free-kick to the opposing team, to be taken from the place where the infringement occurred, unless the offence is committed by a player in his opponents' goal-area, in which case the free-kick shall be taken from a point anywhere within that half of the goal-area in which the offence occurred.

(*b*) For any other infringement the kick shall be retaken.

NOTES: *Provided the principles of these Laws be maintained they may be modified in their application:*

1. *To players of school age as follows:*

(*a*) *size of playing pitch;*

(*b*) *size, weight and material of ball;*

(*c*) *width between the goal-posts and height of the cross-bar from the ground;*

(*d*) *the duration of the periods of play.*

2. *For matches played by women as follows:*

(*a*) *size, weight and material of ball;*

(*b*) *duration of the periods of play;*

(*c*) *further modifications are only permissible with the consent of the International Board.*

Laws of
Rugby Union
Football

Plan of the Field (see Law 1)

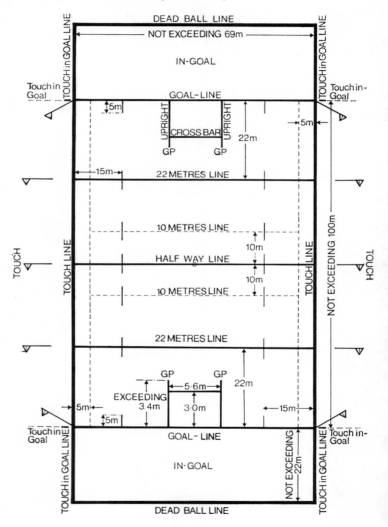

Rugby Union Football

The plan, including all words and figures thereon, is to take effect as part of these Laws.

The terms appearing on the plan are to bear their apparent meaning, and to be deemed part of the definitions as if separately included.

Notes: Length and breadth of field to be as near to dimensions indicated as possible. All areas to be rectangular.

— — — These broken lines indicate 10 m. distance from the halfway line and 5 m distance from the touch lines.

— These lines at the goal lines and intersecting the 22 m and 10 m lines and the halfway line are 15 m from the touch lines.

The lines at the goal lines extend 5 m into the field of play.

Goal dimensions: 3 m is taken from the ground to the top edge of the cross-bar, and 5.60 m inside to inside of the goal posts.

Where practicable the intersection of the dead-ball line and touch-in-goal lines should be indicated by a flag. A minimum height of 1.20 m above the ground is desirable for corner posts.

OBJECT OF THE GAME

The object of the game is that two teams of fifteen players each, observing fair play according to the Laws and a sporting spirit, should by carrying, passing, and kicking the ball score as many points as possible, the team scoring the greater number of points to be the winner of the match.

DECLARATION OF AMATEURISM

The game is an amateur game. No one is allowed to seek or to receive payment or other material reward for taking part in the game.

DEFINITIONS

The following terms have the meaning assigned to them:

Beyond or *Behind* or *In front* of any position implies "with both feet" except when unsuited to the context.

Dead means that the ball is for the time being out of play. This occurs when the Referee's whistle is blown to indicate a stoppage of play or when an attempt to convert a try is unsuccessful.

Defending team means the team in whose half of the ground the stoppage to play occurs and the opponents of the defending team are referred to as "the attacking team".

Kick. A kick is made by propelling the ball with any part of the leg or foot (except the heel) from knee to toe inclusive. If the player is holding the ball, he must propel it out of his hands or, if it is on the ground, he must propel it a visible distance.

Drop kick. A drop kick is made by letting the ball fall from the hand (or hands) to the ground and kicking it at the first rebound as it rises.

Place kick. A place kick is made by kicking the ball after it has been placed on the ground for that purpose.

Punt. A punt is made by letting the ball fall from the hand (or hands) and kicking it before it touches the ground.

Mark. The mark is the place at which a free kick or penalty is awarded.

Line through the Mark (or Place). Except where specifically stated otherwise, the words "a line through the mark" or "a line through the place" always mean a line parallel to the touch line.

Union means the controlling body under whose jurisdiction the match is played and in the case of an International Match it means the International Rugby Football Board or a Committee thereof.

Other definitions are included in and have effect as part of the Laws.

LAWS

1. Ground

The field-of-play is the area shown on the plan, bounded by, but not including, the goal lines and touch lines. The playing enclosure is the field-of-play, In-goal, and a reasonable area surrounding them.

(1) All lines shown on the Plan of the Field must be suitably marked out. The touch lines are in touch. The goal lines are In-goal. The dead-ball line is *not* In-goal. The touch-in-goal lines and corner posts are in touch-in-goal. The goal posts are to be erected in the goal lines.

(2) The game must be played on a ground of the area (maximum) shown on the plan and marked in accordance with the plan. The surface must be grass-covered or, where this is not available, clay or sand provided the surface is not of dangerous hardness.

(3) Any objection by the visiting team about the ground or the way it is marked out must be made to the referee before the first kick-off.

2. Ball

(1) The ball when new shall be oval in shape, of four panels, and of the following dimensions:

Length in line	280 to 300 mm
Circumference (end on)	760 to 790 mm
Circumference (in width)	580 to 620 mm
Weight	400 to 440 gm.

(2) The dimensions of the ball may be reduced only for younger schoolboys.

(3) Balls may be specially treated to make them resistant to mud and easier to grip. The casings need not be of leather.

3. Number of Players

(1) A match shall be played by not more than 15 players in each team.

(2) Replacement of players shall be allowed in recognised trial matches as determined by the Unions having jurisdiction over the match.

(3) In all other matches, a player may be replaced only on account of injury and subject to the following conditions:

(*a*) Not more than two players in each team may be replaced. *Exception:* In matches between teams of schoolboys or teams where all players are under the age of 19, up to six players may be replaced.

(*b*) A player who has been replaced must *NOT* resume playing in the match.

(4) (*a*) In matches in which a national representative team is playing, a player may be replaced *ONLY* when, in the opinion of a medical practitioner, the player is so injured that he should not continue playing in the match.

(*b*) For such competition and other domestic matches as a Union gives express permission, an injured player may be replaced on the advice of a medically trained person, or if a medically trained person is not present, with the approval of the referee.

(5) If the referee is advised by a Doctor or other medically trained person that a player is so injured that it would be harmful for him to continue playing the referee shall require the player to leave the playing area.

(6) Any objection by either team as regards the number of players in a team may be made to the referee at any time but the objection shall not affect any score previously obtained.

4. Players' Dress

(1) A player must not wear dangerous projections such as buckles or rings.

(2) Shoulder pads of the "harness" type must not be worn. If the referee is satisfied that a player requires protection following an injury to a shoulder, the wearing of a pad of cotton-wool, sponge rubber or similar soft material may be permitted provided the pad is attached to the body or sewn on to the jersey.

(3) Studs of a player's boots must be of leather, rubber, aluminium, or any approved plastic. They must be circular, securely fastened to the boots and of the following dimensions:

Maximum length (measured from sole)	18 mm
Minimum diameter at base	13 mm
Minimum diameter at top	10 mm
Minimum diameter of washer (if separate from stud)	20 mm

The wearing of a single stud at the toe of a boot is prohibited.

(4) The Referee has power to decide before or during the game that any part of a player's dress is dangerous. He must then order the player to remove the dangerous part and not allow him to take further part in the match until after it has been removed.

5. Toss, Time

No-side is the end of a match.

(1) Before a match begins the captains shall toss for the right to kick-off or the choice of ends.

(2) The duration of play in a match shall be such time not exceeding 80 minutes as shall be directed by the Union or, in the absence of such direction, as agreed upon by the teams or, if not agreed, as fixed by the referee. In International matches two periods of 40 minutes each shall be played.

(3) Play shall be divided into two halves. At half-time the teams shall change ends and there shall be an interval of not more than 5 minutes.

(4) A period not exceeding 1 minute shall be allowed for any other permitted delay. A longer period may be allowed only if the additional time is required for the removal of an injured player from the field-of-play.

Playing time lost as a result of any such permitted delay or of delay in taking a kick at goal shall be made up in that half of the match in which the delay occurred, subject to the power vested in the referee to declare no-side before time has expired.

6. Referee and Touch Judges

A. REFEREE

(1) There shall be a referee for every match. He shall be appointed by or under the authority of the Union or, in case no such authorised referee has been appointed, a referee may be mutually agreed upon between the teams or, failing such agreement, he shall be appointed by the home team.

(2) If the referee is unable to officiate for the whole period of a match a replacement shall be appointed either in such manner as may be directed by the Union, or in the absence of such direction, by the referee or, if he is unable to do so, by the home team.

(3) The referee shall keep the time and the score, and he must in every match apply fairly the Laws of the Game without any variation or omission, except only when the Union has authorised the application of an experimental law approved by the International Board.

(4) He must not give any instruction or advice to either team prior to the match. During the match he must not consult with anyone except only

(*a*) either or both touch judges on a point of fact relevant to their functions, or

(*b*) in regard to time.

(5) The referee is the sole judge of fact and of law. All his decisions are binding on the players. He cannot alter a decision except when given before he observes that a touch judge's flag is raised or before he has received a report related to Law 26(3) from a touch judge.

(6) The referee must carry a whistle and must blow it

(*a*) to indicate the beginning of the match, half-time, resumption of play after half-time, no-side, a score or a touchdown, and

(*b*) to stop play because of infringement or otherwise as required by the Laws.

(7) During a match no person other than the players, the referee and the touch judges may be within the playing enclosure or the field-of-play unless with the permission of the referee which shall be given only for a special and temporary purpose.

(8) (*a*) All players must respect the authority of the referee and they must not dispute his decisions. They must (except in the case of a kick-off) stop playing at once when the referee has blown his whistle.

(*b*) A player must when so requested, whether before or during the match, allow the referee to inspect his dress.

(*c*) A player must not leave the playing enclosure without the referee's permission. If a player retires during a match because of injury or otherwise, he must not resume playing in that match until the referee has given him permission.

Penalty. Infringement by a player is subject to penalty as misconduct.

B. TOUCH JUDGES

(1) There shall be two touch judges for every match. Unless touch judges have been appointed by or under the authority of the Union, it shall be the responsibility of each team to provide a touch judge.

(2) A touch judge is under the control of the referee who may instruct him as to his duties and may over-rule any of his decisions. The referee may request that an unsatisfactory touch judge be replaced and he has power to order off and report to the Union a touch judge who in his opinion is guilty of misconduct.

(3) Each touch judge shall carry a flag (or other suitable object) to signal his decisions. There shall be one touch judge on each side of the ground and he shall remain in touch except when judging a kick at goal.

(4) He must hold up his flag when the ball or a player carrying it has gone into touch and must indicate the place of throw in and which team is entitled to do so. He must also signal to the referee when the ball or a player carrying it has gone into touch-in-goal.

(5) The touch judge shall lower his flag when the ball has been thrown in except on the following occasions when he must keep it raised:

(*a*) when the player throwing in the ball puts any part of either foot in the field-of-play,

(*b*) when the ball has not been thrown in by the team entitled to do so.

It is for the referee to decide whether or not the ball has been thrown in from the correct place.

(6) In matches in which a national representative team is playing and in such domestic matches for which a Union gives express permission, and where referees recognised by the Union are appointed as touch judges, the touch judges may report incidents of foul play and misconduct under Law 26(3) to the referee for the match.

A touch judge may signal such an incident to the referee by raising his flag to a horizontal position pointing in the direction of the goalline of the offending team. The touch judge must remain in touch and continue to carry out his other functions until the next stoppage in play when the referee shall consult him regarding the incident. The referee may then take whatever action he deems appropriate and any consequent penalties shall be in accordance with Law 26(3).

(7) When a kick at goal from a try, free kick or penalty kick

is being taken both touch judges must assist the referee by signalling the result of the kick. One touch judge shall stand at or behind each of the goal posts and shall raise his flag if the ball goes over the cross bar.

7. Mode of Play

A match is started by a kick-off, after which any player who is on-side may at any time:

    (*a*) catch or pick up the ball and run with it,

    (*b*) pass, throw or knock the ball to another player,

    (*c*) kick or otherwise propel the ball,

    (*d*) tackle, push or shoulder an opponent holding the ball,

    (*e*) fall on the ball,

    (*f*) take part in scrummage, ruck, maul or line-out,

provided he does so in accordance with these Laws.

8. Advantage

The referee shall not whistle for an infringement during play which is followed by an advantage gained by the non-offending team. An advantage must be either territorial or such possession of the ball as constitutes an obvious tactical advantage. A more opportunity to gain advantage is not sufficient.

The *only* occasions when advantage does not apply are:

(*a*) when the ball or a player carrying it touches the referee (Law 9(1)).

(*b*) when the ball emerges from either end of the tunnel at a scrummage not having been played (Law 20).

(*c*) when a player is "accidentally" off-side (*Exception* (i) Law 24(A)(2)(*b*)).

9. Ball or Player Touching Referee

(1) If the ball or a player carrying it touches the referee in the field-of-play, play shall continue unless the referee considers either team has gained an advantage in which case he shall order a scrummage. The team which last played the ball shall put it in.

(2) (*a*) If the ball in a player's possession or a player carrying it touches the referee in that player's In-goal, a touch-down shall be awarded.

(*b*) If a player carrying the ball in his opponent's In-goal touches the referee before grounding the ball, a try shall be awarded at that place.

10. Kick-off

Kick-off is (a) a place kick taken from the centre of the half-way line by the team which has the right to start the match or by the opposing team on the resumption of play after the half-time interval or by the defending team after a goal has been scored, or (b) a drop kick taken at or from behind the centre of the half-way line by the defending team after an unconverted try.

(1) The ball must be kicked from the correct place; otherwise it shall be kicked off again.

(2) The ball must reach the opponents' 10 m line, unless first played by an opponent; otherwise it shall be kicked off again, or a scrummage formed at the centre, at the opponents' option. If it reaches the 10 m line and is then blown back, play shall continue.

(3) If the ball pitches in touch, touch-in-goal or over or on the dead-ball line, the opposing team may accept the kick, have the ball kicked off again, or have a scrummage formed at the centre.

(4) The *kicker's team* must be behind the ball when kicked; otherwise a scrummage shall be formed at the centre.

(5) The *opposing team* must stand on or behind the 10 m line. If they are in front of that line or if they charge before the ball has been kicked, it shall be kicked off again.

11. Method of Scoring

Try. A try is scored by first grounding the ball in the opponents' In-goal.

A try may be awarded if one would probably have been scored but for foul play by the opposing team.

Goal. A goal is scored by kicking the ball over the opponents' crossbar and between the goal posts from the field-of-play by any place kick or drop kick, except a kick-off, free kick or drop-out, without touching the ground or any player of the kicker's team.

A goal is scored if the ball has crossed the bar, even though it may have been blown backwards afterwards, and whether it has touched the cross-bar or either goal post or not.

A goal is scored if the ball has crossed the bar notwithstanding a prior offence of the opposing team.

A goal may be awarded if the ball is illegally touched by any player of the opposing team and if the referee considers that a goal would otherwise probably have been scored.

The *scoring values* are as follows:

A try	4 points
A goal scored after a try	2 points
A goal from a penalty kick	3 points
A dropped goal otherwise obtained	3 points

12. Try and Touch-down

Grounding the ball is the act of a player who

(a) while holding the ball in his hand (or hands) or arm (or arms) brings the ball in contact with the ground, or

(b) while the ball is on the ground either (i) places his hand (or hands) or arm (or arms) on it with downward pressure, or (ii) falls upon it and the ball is anywhere under the front of his body from waist to neck inclusive.

Picking up the ball from the ground is not grounding it.

A. TRY

(1) A player who is on-side scores a try when (*a*) he carries the ball into his opponents' In-goal, or (*b*) the ball is in his opponents' In-goal, and he first grounds it there.

(2) The scoring of a try includes the following cases:

(*a*) if a player carries, passes, knocks or kicks the ball into his In-goal and an opponent first grounds it,

(*b*) if, at a scrummage or ruck, a team is pushed over its goal line and before the ball has emerged it is first grounded in In-goal by an attacking player,

(*c*) if the momentum of a player, when held in possession of the ball, carries him into his opponents' In-goal and he first there grounds the ball, even though it touched the ground in the field-of-play,

(*d*) if a player first grounds the ball on his opponents' goal line or if the ball is in contact with the ground and a goal post.

(3) If a player grounds the ball in his opponents' In-goal and picks it up again, a try is scored where it was first grounded.

(4) A try may be scored by a player who is in touch or in touch-in-goal provided he is not carrying the ball.

B. PENALTY TRY

A penalty try shall be awarded between the posts if but for foul play by the defending team,

(*a*) a try would probably have been scored, or

(*b*) it would probably have been scored in a more favourable position than that where the ball was grounded.

C. TOUCH-DOWN

(1) A touch-down occurs when a player first grounds the ball in his In-goal.

(2) After a touch-down, play shall be restarted either by a drop-out or a scrummage, as provided in Law 14.

D. SCRUMMAGE AFTER GROUNDING IN CASE OF DOUBT

Where there is doubt as to which team first grounded the ball in In-goal, a scrummage shall be formed 5 m from the goal line opposite the place where the ball was grounded. The attacking team shall put in the ball.

13. Kick at Goal after a Try

(1) After a try has been scored, the scoring team has the right to take a place kick or drop kick at goal, on a line through the place where the try was scored.

If the scoring team does not take the kick, play shall be restarted by a drop kick from the centre unless time has expired.

(2) If a kick is taken:

(*a*) it must be taken without undue delay;

(*b*) any player including the kicker may place the ball;

(*c*) the *kicker's team*, except a placer, must be behind the ball when kicked;

(*d*) if the kicker kicks the ball from a placer's hands without the ball being on the ground, the kick is void;

(*e*) the *opposing team* must be behind the goal line until the kicker begins his run or offers to kick when they may charge or jump with a view to preventing a goal.

(3) Neither the kicker nor a placer shall wilfully do anything which may lead the opposing team to charge prematurely. If either does so, the charge shall not be disallowed.

Penalty. For an infringement by the *kicker's team*—the kick shall be disallowed.

For an infringement by the *opposing team*—the charge shall be disallowed. If, however, the kick has been taken successfully, the goal shall stand. If it was unsuccessful, the kicker may take another kick under the original conditions without the charge and may change the type of kick.

14. In-Goal

In-goal is the area bounded by a goal line, touch-in-goal lines and dead-ball line. It includes the goal line and goal posts but excludes touch-in-goal lines and dead-ball line.

Touch-in-goal occurs when the ball touches or crosses a touch-in-goal line or when the ball, or a player carrying it, touches a corner post, a touch-in-goal line or the ground beyond it. The flag is not part of the corner post.

Five Metres Scrummage

(1) If a player carrying the ball in In-goal is so held that he cannot ground the ball, a scrummage shall be formed 5 m from the goal line opposite the place where he was held.

The attacking team shall put in the ball.

(2) (*a*) If a defending player heels, kicks, carries, passes or knocks the ball over his goal line and it there becomes dead except where
 (i) a try is scored, or
 (ii) he wilfully knocks or throws the ball from the field-of-play into touch-in-goal or over his dead-ball line, or

(*b*) if a defending player in In-goal has his kick charged down by an attacking player after he carried the ball back from the field-of-play, or a defending player put it into In-goal and the ball is then touched down or goes into touch-in-goal or over the dead-ball line, or

(*c*) if a defending player carrying the ball in the field-of-play is forced into his In-goal and he then touches down, or (*d*) if, at a scrummage or ruck, a defending team with the ball in its possession is pushed over its goal line and before the ball has emerged first grounds it in In-goal:

a scrummage shall be formed 5 m from the goal line opposite the place where the ball or a player carrying it crossed the goal line. The attacking team shall put in the ball.

Drop-Out

(3) Except where the ball is knocked on or thrown forward or a try or goal is scored, if an attacking player kicks, carries, passes or knocks the ball and it travels into his opponents' In-goal either directly or after having touched a defender who does not wilfully attempt to stop, catch or kick it, and it is there

(*a*) grounded by a player of *either team*, or

(*b*) goes into touch-in-goal or over the dead-ball line

a drop-out shall be awarded.

Penalties

(*a*) A penalty try shall be awarded when by foul play in In-goal the defending team has prevented a try which otherwise would *probably* have been scored.

(*b*) A try shall be disallowed and a drop-out awarded, if a try would *probably not* have been gained but for foul play by the attacking team.

(*c*) For foul play in In-goal while the ball is out of play the penalty kick shall be awarded at the place where play would otherwise have restarted and, in addition, the player shall either be ordered off or cautioned that he will be sent off if he repeats the offence.

(*d*) For wilfully charging or obstructing in In-goal a player who has just kicked the ball the penalty shall be a drop-out, or, at the option of the non-offending team, a penalty kick where the ball alights as provided for an infringement of Law 26(3)(*d*).

(*e*) for other infringements in In-goal, the penalty shall be:

(i) for an offence by the *attacking team*—a drop-out,

(ii) for an offence by the *defending team*—a scrummage 5 m from the goal line opposite the place of infringement.

15. Drop-out

A drop-out is a drop kick awarded to the defending team.

(1) The drop kick must be taken from anywhere on or behind the 25 yd (22 m) line; otherwise the ball shall be dropped out again.

(2) The ball must reach the 25 yd (22 m) line; otherwise the opposing team may have it dropped out again, or have a scrummage formed at the centre of the 25 yd (22 m) line and is then blown back, play shall continue.

(3) If the ball pitches in touch, the opposing team may accept the kick, have the ball dropped out again, or have a scrummage formed at the centre of the 25 yd (22 m) line.

(4) The *kicker's team* must be behind the ball when kicked; otherwise a scrummage shall be formed at the centre of the 25 yd (22 m) line.

(5) The *opposing team* must not charge over the 25 yd (22 m) line; otherwise the ball shall be dropped out again.

16. Fair-Catch (Mark)

(*a*) *A player makes a fair-catch when being stationary with both feet on the ground on his side of his 22 m line he cleanly catches the ball direct from a kick, knock-on or throw-forward by one of his opponents and, at the same time, he exclaims "Mark".*

A fair-catch may be obtained even though the ball on its way touches a goal post or cross-bar and can be made in In-goal.

(*b*) *A free kick is awarded for a fair-catch.*

(1) The kick shall be taken by the player making the fair-catch, unless he is injured in doing so. If he is unable to take the kick within 1 minute a scrummage shall be formed at the mark. His team shall put in the ball.

(2) If the mark is in In-goal, any resultant scrummage shall be 5 m from the goal line on a line through the mark.

17. Knock-on or Throw-forward

A knock-on occurs when the ball travels forward towards the direction of his opponents' dead-ball line after a player loses possession of it, or a player propels or strikes it with his hand or arm, or it strikes a player's hand or arm.

A throw-forward occurs when a player carrying the ball throws or passes it in the direction of his opponents' dead-ball line. A throw-in from touch is not a throw-forward. If the ball is not thrown or passed forward but it bounces forward after hitting a player or the ground, it is not a throw-forward.

(1) The knock-on or throw-forward must not be *intentional*. *Penalty*. Penalty kick at the place of infringement.

(2) If the knock-on or throw-forward is *unintentional*, a scrummage shall be formed either at the place of infringement or, if it occurs at a line-out, 15 m from the touch line along the line-of-touch unless:

(*a*) a fair catch has been allowed, or

(*b*) the ball is knocked on by a player who is in the act of charging down the kick of an opponent but is not attempting to catch the ball, or

(*c*) the ball is knocked on one or more times by a player who is in the act of catching or picking it up or losing possession of it and is recovered by that player before it has touched the ground or another player.

18. Tackle

A tackle occurs when a player carrying the ball in the field-of-play is held by one or more opponents so that while he is so held he is brought to the ground or the ball comes into contact with the ground. If the ball carrier is no longer on his feet he is deemed to have been brought to the ground.

(1) A tackled player must release the ball immediately *without playing it in any other way* and get up or move away from it. He must not play or interfere with the ball in any way until he has got up on his feet.

(2) It is illegal for any player:

(*a*) to prevent a tackled player from releasing the ball, or getting up after he has released it, or

(*b*) to pull the ball from a tackled player's possession or attempt to pick up the ball before the tackled players has released it,

(*c*) while lying on the ground after a tackle to play or interfere with the ball in any way.

Nevertheless while still lying on the ground *any* player may tackle or attempt to tackle an opponent carrying the ball.

Penalty. Penalty kick at the place of infringement.

(3) If a player carrying the ball is thrown or knocked over but not tackled, he may pass the ball or get up and continue his run even though the ball has touched the ground.

(4) A try may be scored if the momentum of a player carries him into his opponents' In-goal even though he is held.

19. Lying with, on or Near the Ball

(1) A player who has not been tackled but who is lying on the ground and holding the ball must immediately pass or release the ball or roll away from it or get up on his feet.

(2) A player or players lying on the ground in close proximity to the ball must not prevent an opponent gaining possession of it.

(3) A player or players from either team must not *wilfully* fall on or over a player who is lying on the ground with the ball in his possession, or on players lying on the ground with the ball between them.

(4) A player must not fall on or over the ball emerging from a scrummage or ruck.

A player on one knee or both knees or sitting on the ground is deemed to be lying on the ground.

Penalty. Penalty kick at the place of infringement.

20. Scrummage

A scrummage, which can take place only in the field-of-play, is formed by players from each team closing up in readiness to allow the ball to be put on the ground between them.

The middle player in each front row is the hooker, and the player on either side of him are the props.

The middle line means an imaginary line on the ground directly beneath the line formed by the junction of the shoulders of the two front rows.

Forming a Scrummage

(1) A team must not wilfully delay the forming of a scrummage.

(2) Every scrummage shall be formed at the place of infringement or as near thereto as is practicable within the field-of-play. It must be stationary with the middle line parallel to the goal lines until the ball has been put in.

(3) It is dangerous play for a front row to form down some distance from its opponents and rush against them.

(4) Each front row of a scrummage shall have three players in it *at all times*. Subject to this, any number of players may form a scrummage. The head of a player in a front row shall not be next to the head of a player of the same team.

(5) While a scrummage is forming and is taking place, all players in each front row must adopt a normal stance. Both feet must be on the ground, must not be crossed and must be in the position for an effective forward shove.

Binding of Players

(6) (*a*) The players of each front row shall bind firmly and continuously while the ball is being put in and while it is in the scrummage.

(*b*) The hooker may bind either over or under the arms of his props but, in either case, he must bind firmly around their bodies at or below the level of the armpits. The props must bind the hooker similarly. The hooker must not be supported so that he is not carrying any weight on either foot.

(*c*) The outside (loose head) prop may either (i) bind his opposing (tight head) prop with his left arm inside the right arm of his opponent, or (ii) place his left hand or forearm on his left thigh. The tight head prop *must* bind his opposing loose head prop with his right arm over the top of the left shoulder of his opposing loose head prop.

(*d*) All players in a scrummage, other than those in a front row, must bind with at least one arm and hand around the body of another player of the same team.

(*e*) Any outside player other than a prop may hold an opponent with his outer arm but only to keep himself and the scrummage steady. He must not push or pull an opponent or his dress.

Putting the Ball into the Scrummage

(7) The team not responsible for the stoppage of play shall put in the ball. In the event of doubt as to responsibility, the ball shall be put in by the team which was moving forward prior to the stoppage or, if neither team was moving forward, by the defending team.

(8) The ball shall be put in without delay as soon as the two front rows have closed together. A team must put in the ball when ordered to do so and on the side first chosen.

(9) The player putting in the ball shall:

(a) stand *one* m. from the scrummage and midway between the two front rows;

(b) hold the ball with both hands midway between the two front rows at a level midway between his knee and ankle;

(c) from that position put in the ball without any delay or without feint or backward movement, i.e. with a *single* forward movement and at a quick speed straight along the middle line so that it first touches the ground immediately beyond the width of the nearer prop's shoulders.

(10) If the ball is put in and it comes out at either end of the tunnel, it shall be put in again, unless a free kick or penalty kick has been awarded. If the ball comes out otherwise than at either end of the tunnel and if a penalty kick has not been awarded play shall proceed.

Restrictions on Front Row Players

(11) All front row players must place their feet so as to allow a clear tunnel. A player must not prevent the ball from being put into the scrummage, or from touching the ground at the required place.

(12) No front row player may raise or advance a foot until the ball has touched the ground.

(13) When the ball has touched the ground, any foot of any player in either front row may be used in an attempt to gain possession of the ball, subject to the following:

Players in the front rows must not *at any time* during the scrummage:

(*a*) raise both feet off the ground at the same time, or

(*b*) wilfully adopt any position or wilfully take any action, by twisting or lowering the body or by pulling on an opponent's dress, which is likely to cause the scrummage to collapse, or

(*c*) wilfully kick the ball out of the tunnel in the direction from which it is put in.

Restrictions on Players

(14) Any player who is not in either front row must not play the ball while it is in the tunnel.

(15) A player must not:

(*a*) return the ball into the scrummage, or

(*b*) handle the ball in the scrummage except in the act of obtaining a "push over" try or touch-down, or

(*c*) pick up the ball in the scrummage by hand or legs, or

(*d*) wilfully collapse the scrummage, or

(*e*) wilfully fall or kneel in the scrummage, or

(*f*) attempt to gain possession of the ball in the scrummage with any part of the body except the foot or lower leg.

(16) The player putting in the ball and his immediate opponent must not kick the ball while it is in the scrummage.

Penalty. (*a*) for an infringement of paragraphs 2, 5, 8, 9, 11, 12 and 14, a free kick at the place of infringement; (*b*) for an infringement of paragraphs 1, 3, 4, 6, 13, 15 and 16, a penalty kick at the place of infringement.

For Off-side at Scrummage see Law 24B.

21. Ruck

A ruck, which can take place only in the field-of-play, is formed when the ball is on the ground and one or more players from each team are on their feet and in physical contact, closing around the ball between them.

(1) A player joining a ruck must bind with at least one arm around the body of a player of his team in the ruck.

(2) A player must not:

(*a*) return the ball into the ruck, or

(*b*) handle the ball in the ruck except in the act of securing a try or touch-down, or

(*c*) pick up the ball in the ruck by hand or legs, or

(*d*) wilfully collapse the ruck, or

(*e*) jump on top of other players in the ruck, or

(*f*) wilfully fall or kneel in the ruck, or

(*g*) while lying on the ground interfere in any way with the ball in or emerging from the ruck. He must do his best to roll away from it.

Penalty. Penalty kick at the place of infringement.

For Off-side at Ruck see Law 24C.

22. Maul

A maul, which can take place only in the field-of-play, is formed by one or more players from each team on their feet and in physical contact closing round a player who is carrying the ball.

A maul ends when the ball is on the ground or the ball or a player carrying it emerges from the maul or when a scrummage is ordered.

(1) A player is not in physical contact unless he is caught in or bound to the maul and not merely alongside it.

(2) A player must not jump on top of other players in the maul.

(3) When the ball in a maul becomes unplayable a scrummage shall be ordered and the team which was moving forward immediately prior to the stoppage shall put in the ball, or if neither team was moving forward, the defending team shall put it in.

Penalty. Penalty kick at the place of infringement.

For Off-side at Maul see Law 24C.

23. Touch and Line-out

A. TOUCH

(1) The ball is in touch (*a*) when it is not being carried by a player and it touches a touch line or the ground or a person or object beyond it, or (*b*) when it is being carried by a player and it or the player carrying it touches a touch line or the ground beyond it.

(2) If the ball is not in touch a player who is in touch may kick the ball or propel it with his hand but not hold it.

B. LINE-OUT

The line-of-touch is an imaginary line in the field-of-play at right angles to the touch line through the place where the ball is to be thrown in.

Formation of Line-Out

(1) A line-out is formed by at least two players from each team lining up in single lines parallel to the line-of-touch in readiness for the ball to be thrown in between them. Players who so line up are those "in the line-out", unless excluded below.

(2) Each player in the line-out must stand at least 1 m from the next player of his team in the line-out.

(3) The line-out stretches from 5 m from the touch line from which the ball is being thrown in to the position at the time the line-out begins of the furthest player in the line-out of the team throwing in the ball, but the furthest player must not be more than 15 m from that touch line.

(4) Any player of either team who is further from the touch line than the position of the "furthest player" when the line-out begins is *not* in the line-out.

(5) A clear space of 2 ft (500 mm) must be left between the two lines of players.

Throwing in the Ball

(6) When the ball is in touch the place at which it must be thrown in is as follows:

(*a*) when the ball goes into touch from a penalty kick, free kick, or from a kick within 25 yd (22 m) of the kicker's goal line, at the place where it touched or crossed the touch line;

(*b*) when the ball pitches directly into touch after having been kicked otherwise than as stated above, opposite the place from which the ball was kicked or at the place where it touched or crossed the touch line if that place be nearer to the kicker's goal line, or (*c*) on all other occasions when the ball is in touch, at the place where it touched or crossed the touch line.

In each instance the place is where the ball last crossed the touch line before being in touch.

(7) The ball must be thrown in at the line-out by an opponent of the player whom it last touched, or by whom it was carried, before being in touch. In the event of doubt as to which team should throw in the ball, the defending team shall do so.

(8) The ball must be thrown in without delay.

(9) The player must throw in the ball (*a*) at the place indicated and (*b*) so that it first touches the ground or touches or is touched by a player at least 5 m from the touch line along the line-of-touch, and (*c*) while throwing in the ball, he must not put any part of either foot in the field-of-play.

If any of the foregoing is infringed, the opposing team shall have the right, at its option, to throw in the ball or to take a scrummage.

If on the second occasion the ball is not thrown in correctly a scrummage shall be formed and the ball shall be put in by the team which threw it in on the first occasion.

(10) A *quick throw in* from touch without waiting for the players to form a line-out is permissible provided the ball that went into touch is used, it has been handled only by the players and it is thrown in correctly.

Beginning and End of Line-out

(11) The line-out begins when the ball leaves the hands of the player throwing it in.

(12) The line-out ends when (*a*) a ruck or maul is taking place and all feet of players in the ruck or maul have moved beyond the line-of-touch, or (*b*) a player carrying the ball leaves the line-out, or (*c*) the ball has been passed, knocked back or kicked from the line-out, or (*d*) the ball is thrown beyond the furthest player, or (*e*) the ball becomes unplayable.

Peeling Off

"*Peeling off*" *occurs when a player* (*or players*) *moves from his position in the line-out for the purpose of catching the ball when it has been passed or knocked back by another of his team in the line-out.*

(13) When the ball is in touch players who approach the line-of-touch must *always* be presumed to do so for the purpose of forming a line-out. Except in the peeling off movement such players must not leave the line-of-touch, or the line-out when formed, until the line-out has ended. A player must not begin to peel off until the ball has left the hand of the player throwing it in.

Exceptions. (i) At a quick throw-in, when a player may come to the line-of-touch and retire from that position without penalty.

(ii) when the furthest player in the line-out of the team throwing in the ball is less than 15 m from the touch line, to conform to the established length opposing players may retire without penalty, provided they do so without delay and to their off-side line as defined at the head of Law 24(D).

(14) In a peeling off movement a player must move parallel and close to the line-out. He must keep moving until a ruck or maul is formed and he joins it or the line-out ends.

Restrictions on Players in Line-out

(15) *Before* the ball has been thrown in and has touched the ground or has touched or been touched by a player, any player in the line-out must not: (*a*) be off-side, or (*b*) push, charge, shoulder or bind with or in any way hold another player of *either* team, or (*c*) use any other player as a support to enable him to jump for the ball, or (*d*) stand within 5 m of the touch line or prevent the ball from being thrown 5 m.

(16) *After* the ball has touched the ground or touched or been touched by a player, any player in the line-out must not (*a*) be off-side, or (*b*) hold, push, shoulder or obstruct an opponent not holding the ball, or (*c*) charge an opponent except in an attempt to tackle him or to play the ball.

(17) Except when jumping for the ball, or peeling off, each player in the line-out must remain at least 1 m from the player of his team until the ball has touched or has been touched by a player or has touched the ground.

(18) Except when jumping for the ball or peeling off, a clear

space of 500 mm (2 ft) must be left between the two lines of players until the ball has touched or has been touched by a player or has touched the ground.

(19) A player in the line-out may move into the space between the touch line and the 5 m mark only when the ball has been thrown beyond him and, if he does so, he must not move towards his goal line before the line-out ends, except in a peeling off movement.

(20) Until the line-out ends, no player may move beyond the position of the furthest player when the line-out begins except as allowed when the ball is thrown beyond that position, in accordance with the *Exception* following Law 24D (1)(*d*). If the furthest player moves towards the touch line after the ball has been thrown in, other players in the line-out are not required to follow him in order to remain on-side.

Restrictions on Players not in Line-out

(21) Players of either team who are not in the line-out may not advance from behind the line-out and take the ball from the throw-in except only (*a*) a player at a quick throw-in or (*b*) a player advancing at a long throw-in, or (*c*) a player "participating in the line-out" (as defined in Section D of Law 24) who may run into a gap in the line-out and take the ball provided he does not charge or obstruct any player in the line-out.

Penalty. (*a*) For an infringement of paragraphs (1), (2), (3), (4), (5), (8), (13), (17), (18) or (19), a free kick 15 m from the touch line along the line-of-touch.

(*b*) For an infringement of paragraphs (13), (14), (15), (16) or (20), a penalty kick 15 m from the touch line along the line-of-touch.

(*c*) For an infringement of paragraph (21) a penalty kick on the offending team's off-side line (as defined in Law 24D) opposite the place of infringement, but not less than 15 m from the touch line.

Place of Scrummage taken or ordered under this Law or as the result of any infringement in a line-out shall be formed 15 m from the touch line along the line-of-touch.

For off-side at Line-out see Law 24D.

24. Off-Side

Off-side means that a player is in a position in which he is out of the game and is liable to penalty.

In general play *the player is in an off-side position because he is in front of the ball when it has been last played by another player of his team.*

In play at scrummage, ruck, maul *or* line-out *the player is off-side because he remains or advances in front of the line or place stated in, or otherwise infringes, the relevant sections of this Law.*

A. OFF-SIDE IN GENERAL PLAY

(1) A player is in an off-side position if the ball has been kicked, or touched, or is being carried, by one of his team behind him.

(2) There is no penalty for being in an off-side position unless: (*a*) the player plays the ball or obstructs an opponent, or (*b*) he approaches or remains within 10 m of an opponent waiting to play the ball.

Where no opponent is waiting to play the ball but one arrives as the ball pitches, a player in an off-side position must not obstruct or interfere with him.

Exceptions.

(i) When an off-side player cannot avoid being touched by the ball or by a player carrying it, he is "accidentally off-side". Play should be allowed to continue unless the infringing team obtains an advantage, in which case a scrummage shall be formed at that place.

(ii) A player who receives an unintentional throw-forward is not offside.

(iii) If, because of the speed of the game, an off-side player finds himself unavoidably within 10 m of an opponent waiting to play the ball, he shall not be penalized provided he retires without delay and without interfering with the opponent.

Penalty. Penalty kick at the place of infringement, or, at the option of the non-offending team, a scrummage at the place where the ball was last played by the offending team. If the latter place is In-goal, the scrummage shall be formed 5 m from the goal line on a line through the place.

B. OFF-SIDE AT SCRUMMAGE

The term "off-side line" means a line parallel to the goal lines through the hindmost foot of the player's team in the scrummage.

While a scrummage is forming or is taking place:

(1) A player is off-side if

(*a*) he joins it from his opponents' side, or,

(*b*) he, not being in the scrummage nor the player of either team who puts the ball in the scrummage, fails to retire behind the off-side line or to his goal line whichever is the nearer, or places either foot in front of the off-side line while the ball is in the scrummage.

A player behind the ball may leave a scrummage provided he retires immediately behind the off-side line. If he wishes to rejoin the scrummage, he must do so behind the ball. He may not play the ball as it emerges between the feet of his front row if he is in front of the off-side line.

Exception. The restrictions on leaving the scrummage in front of the off-side line do not apply to a player taking part in "wheeling" a scrummage providing he immediately plays the ball.

(2) A player is off-side if he, being the player on either team who puts the ball in the scrummage, remains, or places either foot, in front of the ball while it is in the scrummage, or if he is the immediate opponent of the player putting in the ball, takes up position on the opposite side of the scrummage in front of the off-side line.

Penalty. Penalty kick at the place of infringement.

C. OFF-SIDE AT RUCK OR MAUL

The term "off-side line" means a line parallel to the goal lines through the hindmost foot of the player's team in the ruck or maul.

(1) *Ruck or maul otherwise than at line-out.*

While a ruck or maul is taking place (including one which continues after a line-out has ended), a player is off-side if he: (*a*) joins it from his opponents' side, or (*b*) joins it in front of the ball, or (*c*) does not join the ruck or maul but fails to retire behind the off-side line *without delay*, or (*e*) advances beyond the off-side line with either foot and does not join the ruck or maul, or (*d*) unbinds from the ruck or leaves the maul and does not *immediately* either rejoin it behind the ball or retire behind the off-side line.

Penalty. Penalty kick at the place of infringement.

(2) *Ruck or maul at line-out.*

The team "participating in the line-out" has the same meaning as in Section D of this Law. A player participating in the line-out is not obliged to join or remain in the ruck or maul and if he is not in the ruck or maul he continues to participate in the line-out, until it has ended.

While a line-out is in progress and a ruck or maul takes place, a player is off-side if he: (*a*) joins the ruck or maul from his opponents' side, or (*b*) joins it in front of the ball, or (*c*) being a player who is participating in the line-out and is not in the ruck or maul, does not retire to and remain at the off-side line defined in this Section.

Penalty. Penalty kick 15 m from the touch line along the line-of-touch.

(*d*) Or being a player who is not participating in the line-out, remains or advances with either foot in front of the off-side line defined in Section D of this Law.

Penalty. Penalty kick on the offending team's off-side line (as defined in Section D of this Law) opposite the place of infringement, but not less than 15 m from the touch line.

D. OFF-SIDE AT LINE-OUT

The term "participating in the line-out" refers exclusively to the following players: those players who are in the line-out, and the player who throws in the ball, and his immediate opponent who may have the option of throwing in the ball, and one other player of either team who takes up position to receive the ball if it is passed or knocked back from the line-out.

All other players are *not* participating in the line-out.

The term "off-side line" means a line 10 m behind the line-of-touch and parallel to the goal lines or, if the goal line be nearer than 10 m to the line-of-touch, the "off-side line" is the goal line.

Off-side while participating in line-out

(1) A participating player is off-side if: (*a*) *before* the ball has touched a player or the ground he wilfully remains or advances with either foot in front of the line-of-touch, unless he advances solely in the act of jumping for the ball, or (*b*) *after* the ball has touched a player or the ground, if he is not carrying the ball, he advances with either foot in front of the ball, unless he is lawfully tackling or attempting to tackle an opponent who is participating in the line-out. Such tackle or attempt to tackle must, however, start from his side of the ball.

(*c*) in a peeling off movement he fails to keep moving close to the line-out until a ruck or maul is formed and he joins it or the line-out ends, or (*d*) before the line-out ends he moves beyond the position of the furthest player.

Exception. Players of the team throwing in the ball may move beyond the position of the furthest player for a long throw-in to them. They may do so only when the ball leaves the hands of the player throwing it in and if they do so their opponents participating in the line-out may follow them. If players so move and the ball is not thrown to or beyond them they must be penalised for off-side.

Penalty. Penalty kick 15 m from the touch line along the line-of-touch.

(2) The player throwing in the ball and his immediate opponent must: (*a*) remain within 5 m of the touch line, or (*b*) retire to the off-side line, or (*c*) join the line-out after the ball has been thrown in 5 m or (*d*) move into position to receive the ball if it is passed or knocked back from the line-out provided no other player is occupying that position at that line-out.

Off-side while not participating in line-out

(3) A player who is not participating is off-side if before the line-out has ended he advances or remains with either foot in front of the off-side line.

Exception. Players of the team throwing in the ball who are not participating in the line-out may advance for a long throw-in to them beyond the line-out. They may do so only when the ball leaves the hand of the player throwing in the ball and, if they do, their opponents may advance to meet them. If players so advance for a long throw-in to them and the ball is not thrown to them they must be penalised for off-side.

Players returning to "on-side" position

(4) A player is not obliged, before throwing in the ball, to wait until players of his team have returned to or behind the line-out but such players are off-side unless they return to an on-side position *without delay*.

Penalty. Penalty kick on the offending team's off-side line opposite the place of infringement, but not less than 15 m from the touch line.

25. On-side

On-side means that a player is in the Game and not liable to penalty for off-side.

Player made on-side by action of his team

(1) Any player who is off-side in general play, *including* an off-side player who is within 10 m of an opponent waiting to play the ball and is retiring as required, becomes on-side as a result of any of the following actions of his team:

(*a*) when the off-side player has retired behind the player of his team who last kicked, touched or carried the ball, or

(*b*) when one of his team carrying the ball has run in front of him; or

(*c*) when one of his team has run in front of him after coming from the place or from behind the place where the ball was kicked. In order to put the off-side player on-side, this other player must be in the playing area. But he is not debarred from following up in touch or touch-in-goal.

Player made on-side by action of opposing team

(2) Any player who is off-side in general play, *except* an off-side player within 10 m of an opponent waiting to play the ball, becomes on-side as a result of any of the following actions: when an opponent carrying the ball has run 5 m or when an opponent kicks or passes the ball, or when an opponent *intentionally* touches the ball and does not catch or gather it.

An off-side player within 10 m of an opponent waiting to play the ball *cannot* be put on-side by *any* action of his opponents. Any *other* off-side player in general play is *always* put on-side when an opponent plays the ball.

Player retiring at scrummage, ruck, maul or line-out.

(3) A player who is in an off-side position when a scrummage, ruck, maul or line-out is forming or taking place and is retiring as required by Law 24 (Off-side) becomes on-side: when an opponent carrying the ball has run 5 m, or when an opponent has kicked the ball.

An off-side player in this situation is *not* put on-side when an opponent passes the ball.

26. Foul Play

Foul Play *is any action by a player which is contrary to the letter and spirit of the Game and includes obstruction, unfair play, misconduct, dangerous play, unsporting behaviour, retaliation and repeated infringements.*

OBSTRUCTION

(1) It is illegal for any player:

(*a*) who is running for the ball to charge or push an opponent also running for the ball, except shoulder to shoulder,

(*b*) who is in an off-side position wilfully to run or stand in front of another player of his team who is carrying the ball, thereby preventing an opponent from reaching the latter player,

(*c*) who is carrying the ball after it has come out of a scrummage, ruck, maul or line-out, to attempt to force his way through players of his team in front of him,

(*d*) who is an outside player in a scrummage or ruck, to prevent an opponent from advancing round the scrummage or ruck.

Penalty. Penalty kick at the place of infringement. A penalty try may be awarded.

UNFAIR PLAY, REPEATED INFRINGEMENTS

(2) It is illegal for any player:

(*a*) deliberately to play unfairly or wilfully infringe any Law of the Game,

(*b*) wilfully to waste time,

(*c*) wilfully to knock or throw the ball from the field-of-play into touch, touch-in-goal or over his dead-ball line.

(*d*) to infringe repeatedly any Law of the game.

Penalty. Penalty kick at the place of infringement. A penalty try may be awarded.

MISCONDUCT, DANGEROUS PLAY

(3) It is illegal for any player:

(*a*) to strike an opponent,

(*b*) wilfully to hack or kick an opponent or trip him with the foot, or to trample on an opponent lying on the ground,

(*c*) to tackle early or late or dangerously, including the action known as "a stiff arm tackle",

(*d*) who is not running for the ball wilfully to charge or obstruct an opponent who has just kicked the ball,

(*e*) to hold, push, charge, obstruct or grasp an opponent not holding the ball, except in a scrummage, ruck or maul. (Except in a scrummage or ruck, the dragging away of a player lying close to the ball is permitted. Otherwise pulling any part of the clothing of an opponent is holding.)

(*f*) in the front row of a scrummage to form down some distance from the opponents and rush against them,

(*g*) wilfully to cause a scrummage or ruck to collapse,

(*h*) while the ball is out of play to molest, obstruct or in any way interfere with an opponent or be guilty of any form of misconduct,

(*i*) to commit any misconduct on the playing area which is prejudicial to the spirit of good sportsmanship.

Penalty. A player guilty of misconduct and dangerous play shall either be ordered off or else cautioned that he will be sent off if he repeats the offence. For a similar offence after caution the player must be sent off.

In addition to a caution or ordering off, a penalty try or a penalty kick shall be awarded as follows:

(i) If the offence prevents a try which would otherwise *probably* have been scored, a penalty try shall be awarded.

(ii) The place for a penalty kick shall be: **(a)** For offences other than (*d*) and (*h*), at the place of infringement. **(b)** In the case of an infringement of (*d*) the non-offending team shall have the option of taking the kick at the place of infringement or where the ball alights, and if the ball alights in touch, the mark is 15 m from the touch line on a line parallel to the goal lines through the place where it went into touch. If the ball alights within 15 m from the touch line, the mark is 15 m from the touch line on a line parallel to the goal lines through the place where it alighted. If the ball alights in In-goal, touch-in-goal, or over or on the dead-ball line, the mark is 5 m from the goal line on a line parallel to the touch line through the place where it crossed the goal line or 15 m from the touch line, whichever is the greater. When the offence takes place in touch the "place of infringement" in the optional penalty award is 15 m from the touch line opposite to where the offence took place. If the offence takes place in touch-in-goal Law 14, Penalty (*d*) applies. (**c**) In the case of an offence against (*h*) the penalty kick may be taken at any place where the ball would next have been brought into play, if the offence had not occurred, or if that place is on the touch line, at a point 15 m from that place on a line parallel to the goal lines.

(iii) For an offence in In-goal, a penalty kick is to be awarded *only* for offences under Law 14, Penalty (*d*) and Law 26(3)(*h*).

(iv) For an offence under Law 26(3)(*h*), the penalty kick is to be taken at whichever is the place where play would restart, i.e. at the 25 yd (22 m) line (at any point the non-offending team may select), or at the centre of the half-way line, or, if a scrummage 5 m from the goal line would otherwise have been awarded, at that place or 15 m from the touch line on a line 5 m from and parallel to the goal line, whichever is the greater.

(v) For an offence which occurs outside the playing area while the ball is *still in play* and which is not otherwise covered in the foregoing, the penalty kick shall be awarded in the playing area 15 m from the touch line and opposite to where the offence took place.

(vi) For an offence reported by a Touch Judge under Law 6B(6) a penalty kick may be awarded where the offence occurred or at the place where play would restart.

Player Ordered Off

A player who is ordered off shall take no further part in the match. When a player is ordered off, the Referee shall, as soon as possible after the match, send to the Union or other disciplinary body having jurisdiction over the match, a report naming the player and describing the circumstances which necessitated the ordering off. Such report shall be considered by the Union or other disciplinary body having jurisdiction over the match who shall take such action and inflict such punishment as they see fit.

27. Penalty Kick

A penalty kick is a kick awarded to the non-offending team as stated in the Laws. It may be taken by any player of the non-offending team and by any form of kick provided that the kicker, if holding the ball, must propel it out of his hands or, if the ball is on the ground, he must propel it a visible distance from the mark. He may keep his hand on the ball while kicking it.

(1) The non-offending team has the option of taking a scrummage at the mark and shall put in the ball.

(2) When a penalty kick is taken the following shall apply:

(*a*) The kick must be taken without undue delay.

(*b*) The kick must be taken at or behind the mark, on a line through the mark, and the kicker may place the ball for a place kick.

If the place prescribed by the Laws for the award of a penalty kick is within 5 m of the opponents' goal line, the mark for the penalty kick or a scrummage taken instead of it shall be 5 m from the goal line on a line through that place.

(*c*) The kicker may kick the ball in any direction and may play the ball again without restriction except that if the kicker has indicated to the Referee that he intends to attempt a kick at goal, or has taken any action indicating such intention, he must not kick the ball in any other way. Any indication of intention is irrevocable.

(*d*) The kicker's team, except the placer for a place kick, must be behind the ball until it has been kicked.

(*e*) The opposing team must run *without delay* (and continue to do so while the kick is being taken and while the ball is being played by the kicker's team) to or behind a line parallel to the goal lines and 10 m from the mark, or to their own goal line if nearer to the mark, and there remain motionless with their hands by their sides until the kick has been taken. Retiring players will not be penalised if their failure to retire 10 m is due to the rapidity with which the kick has been taken, but they may not stop retiring and enter the game until an opponent carrying the ball has run 5 m.

(*f*) The opposing team must not prevent the kick or interfere with the kicker in any way. This applies to actions such as wilfully carrying, throwing or kicking the ball out of reach of the kicker.

Penalty. (i) For an infringement by the kicker's team—a scrummage at the mark.

(ii) For an infringement by the opposing team—a penalty kick 10 m in front of the mark or 5 m from the goal line, whichever is the nearer, on a line through the mark. Any player of the non-offending team may take the kick

28. Free Kick

A free kick is a kick awarded for a fair-catch, or to the non-offending team as stated in the Laws.

A goal shall not be scored by the kicker from a free kick unless the ball has first been played by another player.

For an infringement it may be taken by any player of the non-offending team.

It may be taken by any form of kick provided that the kicker, if holding the ball, must propel it out of his hands or, if the ball is on the ground, he must propel it a visible distance from the mark. He may keep his hand on the ball while kicking it.

(1) The team allowed or awarded a free kick has the option of taking a scrummage at the mark and shall put in the ball.

(2) When a kick is taken, it must be taken without undue delay.

(3) The kick must be taken at or behind the mark on a line through the mark and the kicker may place the ball for a place kick.

(4) If the place prescribed by the Laws for the award of a free kick is within 5 m of the opponents' goal line, the mark for the free kick, or the scrummage taken in place of it, shall be 5 m from the goal line on a line through that place.

(5) The kicker may kick the ball in any direction and he may play the ball again without restriction.

(6) The *kicker's team*, except a placer for a place kick, must be behind the ball until it has been kicked.

(7) The *opposing team* must not wilfully resort to any action which may delay the taking of a free kick. This includes actions such as wilfully carrying, throwing or kicking the ball away out of reach of the kicker.

(8) The *opposing team* must retire without delay to or behind a line parallel to the goal lines and 10 m from the mark or to their own goal line if nearer to the mark. Having so retired, players of the opposing team may charge with a view to preventing the kick, as soon as the kicker begins his run or offers to kick.

Retiring players will not be penalised if their failure to retire 10 m is due to the rapidity with which the kick has been taken, but they may not stop retiring and enter the game until an opponent carrying the ball has run 5 m.

(9) If the kicker kicks the ball from a placer's hands without the ball being on the ground, the kick is void.

(10) If having charged fairly, players of the opposing team prevent the kick from being taken, it is void.

(vi) Neither the kicker nor the placer shall wilfully do anything which may lead the opposing team to charge prematurely. If either does so, the charge shall not be disallowed.

Penalty: For an infringement by the *kicker's team* or for a void kick—a scrummage at the place of the free kick and the *opposing team* shall put in the ball.

If the mark is in In-goal, the scrummage shall be awarded 5 m from the goal line on a line through the mark.

For an infringement by the *opposing team*—a penalty kick at the mark. If the mark is in In-goal, a drop-out shall be awarded.

The Laws of
Rugby League Football

LAWS OF
RUGBY LEAGUE FOOTBALL

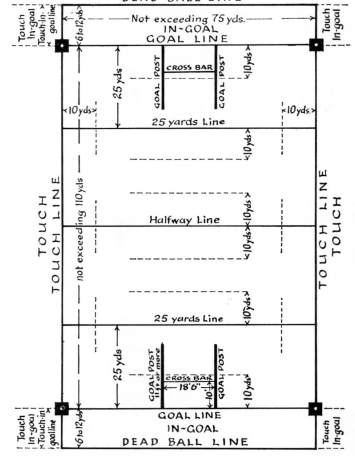

Laws of
Rugby League Football

1. THE FIELD OF PLAY

The plan (overleaf) and markings thereon and the Notes relating thereto are part of these Laws.

NOTES:

1. The Touch Lines are in Touch, the Touch-in-goal lines are in Touch-in-Goal, the Goal-Lines are in-goal and the dead-ball line is beyond in-goal.

2. ■ Indicates corner-post (see Glossary) placed at the intersection of a goal-line and touch-line. A corner-post is in touch-in-goal. Touch-Judges should ensure that corner-posts are at all times correctly positioned.

3. The goal-posts are considered to extend indefinitely upwards. It is recommended that the bottom 5 ft of each upright be padded.

└┬┘-shaped goal-posts are permissible provided the relevant dimensions are observed.

4. For adult games the dimensions should be as near maximum as possible. Minimum permissible dimensions should be laid down in the rules of the Competition in which a match is played.

5. The transverse broken lines in the Plan shall consist of marks or dots on the ground not more than 5 yd apart. It is of advantage for these broken lines to be marked across the full width of the Field.

The metric equivalents (rounded off) of the distances shown in the Plan are as follows:

75 yd	=	68 m
6 to 12 yd	=	6 to 11 m
10 yd	=	10 m
25 yd	=	22 m
110 yd	=	100 m

18 ft 6 in	=	5.50 m
10 ft	=	3.5 m
11 ft	=	4 m

II. GLOSSARY

The terms set out below shall have the meanings assigned to them:

Advantage

Allowing the advantage means allowing play to proceed if it is to the advantage of the side which has not committed an offence or infringement. The advantage must be allowed in all circumstances. (See Section XVI.)

Attacking Team

The team which at the time has a territorial advantage. If a scrum is to be formed on the halfway line the team which last touched the ball before it went out of play is the attacking team.

Back

As applied to a player means one who is not taking part in the scrum.

Ball Back

Means to form a scrum where the ball was kicked after it has entered touch on the full.

Behind

When applied to a player means, unless otherwise stated, that both feet are behind the position in question. Similarly "in front" implies "with both feet".

When applied to a position on the field-of-play, "behind" means nearer to one's own goal-line than the point in question. Similarly "in front of" means nearer to one's opponents' goal-line.

Blind-side

Means the side of the scrum or of the play-the-ball nearer to touch (*cf*. Open Side).

Charging-down

Blocking the path of the ball with hands, arm or body as it rises from an opponent's kick.

Corner Post

A post surmounted by a flag placed at the intersection of each touch-line and goal-line. The post shall be of non-rigid material and shall be not less than 4 ft (1.25 m) high. The corner-posts are in touch-in-goal.

Dead Ball

Means that the ball is out of play.

Defending Team

The team opposing the attacking team (see above).

Differential Penalty

See Section XIII.

Drop-kick

A kick whereby the ball is dropped from the hands (or hand) and is kicked immediately it rebounds from the ground.

Drop-out

Means a drop-kick from between the posts or from the centre of the "25" line when bringing the ball back into play.

Dummy

The pretence of passing or otherwise releasing the ball while still retaining possession of it.

Field-of-Play

The space bounded by, but not including, the touch-lines and goal-lines.

Forward

Means in a direction towards the opponents' goal-line. As applied to a player it means one who is at the time packing down in the scrum.

Forward Pass
A throw towards the opponents' goal-line (see Section X).

Full Time
Means the end of the game. Also referred to as No-side.

Goal
See Section VI.

Grounding the Ball
(*a*) Placing the ball on the ground with hand or hands, or

(*b*) Exerting a downward pressure on the ball with hand or arm, the ball itself being on the ground, or

(*c*) Dropping on the ball and covering it with the part of the body above the waist and below the neck, the ball itself being on the ground.

Half-time
Means the end of the first half of the game.

Heel
When a player propels the ball behind him with the sole or heel of his foot.

Hook
The act of the hooker when he strikes for the ball in the scrum.

In-Goal
See Plan (Section I).

In Possession
Means to be holding or carrying the ball.

Kick
Means imparting motion to the ball with any part of the leg (except the heel) from knee to toe inclusive.

Kick-off
See Section VIII.

Knock-on

Means to knock the ball towards the opponents' goal-line with hand or arm.

Loose Arm

An offence by the hooker if he packs with one arm loose in the scrum.

Loose Ball

When during play the ball is not held by a player and is not being scrummaged.

Loose Head

Refers to the front row forward in the scrum who is nearest to the referee.

Mark

The point at which a penalty kick is awarded.

Obstruction

The illegal act of impeding an opponent who does not have the ball.

Off-side

As applied to a player means that he is temporarily out of play and may be penalised if he joins in the game (see Section XIV).

On-side

Means that a player is not off-side.

Open-side

Means the side of the scrum or the play-the-ball further from touch (*cf.* Blind Side).

On the Full

Means the ball is kicked over a given line without first bouncing.

Pack

Refers collectively to the forwards of any one team. To pack down means to form a scrum.

Pass

A throw of the ball from one player to another.

Penalise

To award a penalty kick against an offending player.

Penalty Kick

See Section XIII.

Place Kick

To kick the ball after it has been placed on the ground for that purpose.

Playing Area

The space enclosed by the fence, or other such line of demarcation, which prevents the encroachment of spectators.

Play-the-Ball

The act of bringing the ball into play after a tackle. (See Section XI.)

Punt

A kick whereby the ball is dropped from the hand or hands and is kicked before it touches the ground.

Scrum

Or Scrummage or Scrimmage. (See Section XII.)

Strike

As applied to the foot means to attempt to secure possession of the ball, usually by heeling it, in a scrum or at a play-the-ball.

Tackle

See Section XI.

Touch-down

The grounding of the ball by a defending player in his own in-goal.

Touch-in-Goal

See Section IX.

Upright Tackle

Where the player in possession is effectively tackled without being brought to the ground (see Section XI).

III. THE BALL

1. The game shall be played with an oval air-inflated ball the outer casing of which shall be of leather or other approved material and nothing shall be used in its construction which might prove dangerous to the players.

2. The dimensions of the ball shall be:

	Desired Dimensions	*Permissible Min.*	*Permissible Max.*
Length	11 in	$10\frac{3}{4}$ in	$11\frac{1}{2}$ in
Longest circumference	29 in	$28\frac{3}{4}$ in	$29\frac{3}{4}$ in
Widest circumference	$23\frac{1}{4}$ in	23 in	24 in
Weight (clean and dry)	$14\frac{1}{2}$ oz	$13\frac{1}{2}$ oz	$15\frac{1}{2}$ oz

The metric equivalents (rounded off) of the dimensions relating to the ball are as follows:

	Desired Dimensions	*Permissible Min.*	*Permissible Max.*
Length	28 cm	27 cm	29 cm
Longest circumference	74 cm	73 cm	76 cm
Widest circumference	59 cm	58 cm	61 cm
Weight (clean and dry)	410 gm	380 gm	440 gm

3. The Referee shall blow his whistle immediately he notices that the size and shape of the ball no longer comply with the Laws of the Game.

IV. THE PLAYERS AND PLAYERS' EQUIPMENT

1. The game shall be played by two teams each consisting of not more than thirteen players.

2. Each team may replace up to two players at any time provided that the names of the substitutes are made known to the referee before the commencement of the game.

A replacement must be sanctioned by the referee and can only be effected when the ball is out of play or play is stopped because of injury.

3. The numbers displayed on the backs of the jerseys worn by the players shall normally indicate the positions occupied by the players as set out hereunder.

Backs:	No. 1.	Full-back.
	No. 2.	Right Wing-threequarter.
	No. 3.	Right Centre-threequarter.
	No. 4.	Left Centre-threequarter.
	No. 5.	Left Wing-threequarter.
	No. 6.	Stand-off-half.
	No. 7.	Scrum-half.
Forwards:	No. 8.	Front Row Prop Forward.
	No. 9.	Hooker.
	No. 10.	Front Row Forward.
	No. 11.	Second Row Forward.
	No. 12.	Second Row Forward.
	No. 13.	Loose Forward.
Substitutes:	No. 14.	Reserve back.
	No. 15.	Reserve forward.

4. (*a*) A player shall not wear anything that might prove dangerous to other players.

(*b*) A player's normal gear shall consist of a jersey of distinctive colour and/or pattern (preferably numbered—see para.

3 above), a pair of shorts, stockings of distinctive colour and/ or pattern and studded boots or shoes.

(c) Protective clothing may be worn provided it contains nothing of a rigid nature.

(d) The referee shall order a player to remove any part of his equipment which might be considered dangerous and shall not allow the player to take any further part in the game until the order is obeyed. The player shall retire from the field-of-play to remove the offending item if the start or re-start of the game would otherwise be delayed.

(e) The colours of the jerseys worn by competing teams shall be easily distinguishable and, if, in the opinion of the Referee similarity between the jerseys might affect the proper conduct of the game he may, at his discretion, order either team to change jerseys in accordance with the Rules governing the competition in which the game is played.

(f) Studs on boots or shoes shall be no less than $\frac{5}{16}$ in (8 mm) diameter at the apex and, if made of metal, shall have rounded edges.

V. MODE OF PLAY

1. The object of the game shall be to ground the ball in the opponents' in-goal to score tries and to kick the ball over the opponents' cross-bar to score goals (see Section VI).

2. The captains of the two teams shall toss for choice of ends in the presence of the referee. The team of the captain losing the toss shall kick-off to start the game.

3. Once play has started any player who is on-side or not out of play can run with the ball, kick it in any direction and throw or knock it in any direction other than towards his opponents' goal-line. (See Section X for Knock-on and Forwards Pass.)

4. A player who during play is holding the ball may be tackled by an opposing player in order to prevent him from running with the ball or from kicking or passing it to one of his own side. (See Section XI for Tackle.)

5. A player who is not holding the ball shall not be tackled or obstructed. (See Section XV.)

VI. SCORING—TRIES AND GOALS

1. A Try shall count three points. A Goal shall count two points. A Drop Goal one point.

2. The game shall be won by the side scoring the greater number of points. If both sides score equal number of points, or if both sides fail to score, then the game shall be drawn.

3. A try is scored when:

(*a*) a player first grounds the ball in his opponents' in-goal provided that he is not in touch or touch-in-goal or on or over the dead-ball line;

(*b*) opposing players simultaneously ground the ball in the in-goal area provided that the attacking player is not in touch or touch-in-goal or on or over the dead-ball line;

(*c*) a tackled player's momentum carries him into the opponents' in-goal where he grounds the ball even if the ball has first touched the ground in the field-of-play but provided that when the ball crosses the goal-line the player is not in touch or touch-in-goal or on or over the dead-ball line;

(*d*) the Referee awards a penalty try which he may do if, in his opinion, a try would have been scored but for the unfair play of the defending team. A penalty try is awarded between the goal-posts irrespective of where the offence occurred;

(*e*) an attacking player carrying the ball comes into contact with the Referee or a Touch-Judge or an encroaching spectator in the opponents' in-goal and play is thereby irregularly affected.

4. The Try is awarded:

(*a*) where grounded if scored as in 3(*a*) and 3(*b*) above;

(*b*) where it first crosses the goal-line if scored as in 3(*c*) above;

(*c*) between the posts if a penalty try;

(*d*) where contact took place if scored as in 3(*e*) above.

5. Only the referee may award a try but he may take into consideration advice given by the Touch-Judges before arriving at his decision. He shall signal that a try has been scored by pointing to where the try has been allowed.

6. A goal is scored if the whole of the ball at any time during its flight passes over the opponents' cross-bar towards the dead

ball line after being kicked by a player (and not subsequently touching the ground or being touched in flight by any other player) in any of these circumstances:

(*a*) by a place-kick after a try has been scored;

(*b*) by a place-kick or a drop-kick when a penalty kick has been awarded;

(*c*) by a drop-kick during play from any position in the field-of-play.

7. A kick at goal after a try may be taken from any point on an imaginary line drawn parallel to the touch-line in the field-of-play and through the point where the try was awarded. A kick at goal from a penalty kick may be taken from the Mark or from any point on an imaginary line drawn from the Mark towards the kicker's own goal-line and parallel to the touch-line.

8. When a kick at goal is being taken following a try, the opposing players shall stand outside the field-of-play. Players of the kicker's side must be behind the ball.

When a kick at goal is being taken from a penalty kick, the opponents shall retire to their goal-line or not less than 10 yd from the Mark. (See Section XIII.)

It is illegal to attempt to distract the attention of a player who is kicking at goal.

9. For the purpose of judging a kick-at-goal, the goal-posts are assumed to extend indefinitely upwards.

10. When a kick at goal is being taken, the Referee shall assign one Touch-Judge to each post. If a Touch-Judge is of the opinion that a goal has been scored he shall raise his flag above his head. If the kick is unsuccessful he shall wave his flag in front of him and below the waist. If there is no disagreement between the Touch-Judges their decision shall be accepted. In the event of disagreement, the Referee shall decide.

VII. TIME-KEEPING

1. The game shall normally be of 80 min duration.

At half-time there shall be an interval of 5 min but this may be extended or reduced by the referee.

2. A team shall defend one in-goal for the first half of the game and then change ends for the second half.

3. If time expires in either half when the ball is out of play or a player in possession is tackled, the referee shall immediately blow his whistle to terminate play. If the ball is in play when time expires, the referee shall terminate play when next the ball goes out of play or a player in possession is tackled but time shall be extended to allow a penalty kick or a kick at goal to be taken in which case the half is terminated when next the ball goes out of play or a tackle is effected.

4. Extra time shall be added to each half to compensate for time wasted or lost from any cause. The Referee shall be the sole judge of extra time. He shall inform the respective captains how much extra time is to be played and shall keep a written record of same except where these duties have been delegated to a timekeeper.

5. If the continuance of play endangers an injured player the Referee may stop the game. If, when the game is stopped, a player is about to play-the-ball after a tackle, then the game shall be re-commenced by that player playing-the-ball. If the injured player was in possession and is unable to resume playing or the ball is loose when play is stopped, then play is re-started with a scrum.

VIII. THE KICK-OFF AND DROP-OUT

1. The kick-off is a place-kick from the centre of the half-way line. The team which loses the toss for choice of ends kicks-off to start the first half of the game and their opponents kick-off to start the second half.

When points have been scored, the team against which the points have been scored shall kick-off to re-start the game.

2. The game is re-started with a place-kick from the centre of the "25" line if:

(*a*) an attacking player last touches the ball before it goes out of play over the dead-ball line or into touch-in-goal except after a penalty kick (see 3 below).

(*b*) an attacking player infringes in the in-goal area.

(*c*) an attacking player is tackled in the in-goal area before he grounds the ball.

The ball may be kicked in any direction and is immediately in play. Opposing players shall retire 10 yd from the "25" line and shall not advance until the ball has been kicked. Defending players shall not advance in front of the ball before it is kicked. Any deliberate offence by either side shall incur a penalty to be awarded at the centre of the "25" line.

3. If the ball goes dead after an unsuccessful penalty kick at goal the game is restarted with a drop-out by a defending player from the centre of the "25" line.

4. The game is restarted with a drop-out by a defending player from the centre of his goal-line if:

(*a*) a defending player last touches the ball before it goes over the dead-ball line or into touch-in-goal;

(*b*) a defending player accidentally infringes in the in-goal area;

(*c*) a defending player touches down in the in-goal area;

(*d*) a defending player in possession is tackled in the in-goal area;

(*e*) a defending player kicks the ball into touch on the full from his own in-goal;

(*f*) the ball or a defending player carrying the ball touches the Referee, a touch-judge, or an encroaching spectator in the in-goal area and play is thereby irregularly affected.

5. A player who kicks-off or drops-out shall be penalised if he:

(*a*) advances in front of the appropriate line before kicking the ball;

(*b*) kicks the ball on the full over the touch-line or over the dead-ball line;

(*c*) kicks the ball so that it fails to travel at least 10 yd forward in the field-of-play;

(*d*) kicks the ball other than in the prescribed manner.

6. Any other player shall be penalised if he:

(*a*) wilfully touches the ball after a kick-off or drop-out before it has travelled 10 yd forward in the field-of-play;

(*b*) runs in front of one of his own side who is kicking-off or dropping-out;

(*c*) approaches nearer than 10 yd to the line from which the kick is being taken when an opponent is kicking-off or dropping-out.

IX. TOUCH AND TOUCH-IN-GOAL

1. The ball is in touch when it or a player in contact with it touches the touch-line or the ground beyond the touch-line or any object on or outside the touch-line except when a player, tackled in the field-of-play, steps into touch as he regains his feet, in which case he shall play-the-ball in the field-of-play.

The ball is in touch if a player jumps from touch and while off the ground touches the ball. The ball is not in touch if during flight it crosses the touch-line but is knocked back by a player who is off the ground after jumping from the field-of-play.

2. The ball is in touch-in-goal when it or a player in contact with it touches the touch-in-goal line, or any object on or outside the touch-in-goal lines.

3. When a ball has entered touch or touch-in-goal, the point of entry shall be taken as the point at which the ball first crossed the touch or touch-in-goal line.

4. If the ball is kicked by or bounces off a player in a forward direction and it goes into touch on the full, a scrum is formed where contact with the ball was made (but not nearer than 10 yd to the touch-line or 5 yd to the goal-line. (See Section XII.)

5. If the ball is kicked into touch from a penalty kick the game is restarted by placing the ball on the ground 10 yd in field opposite the point of entry into touch and kicking it. (See Section XIII.)

6. Other than as outlined in paras. 4 and 5 above, the game is restarted after the ball has gone into touch by forming a scrum 10 yd in-field opposite the point of entry into touch but not nearer than 5 yd to the goal-line. (See Section XII.)

X. KNOCK-ON AND FORWARD PASS

1. A player shall be penalised if he deliberately knocks-on or passes forward.

2. If, after knocking-on accidentally, the player knocking-on kicks the ball before it touches the ground, a goal-post or a cross-bar, then play shall be allowed to proceed. Otherwise play shall stop and a scrum shall be formed.

3. To charge-down a kick is permissible and is not a knock-on.

XI. THE TACKLE AND PLAY-THE-BALL

1. A player in possession may be tackled by an opposing player or players. It is illegal to tackle or obstruct a player who is not in possession.

2. A player in possession is tackled:

(*a*) when he is held by one or more opposing players and the ball or the hand or arm holding the ball comes into contact with the ground;

(*b*) when he is held by one or more opposing players in such a manner that he can make no further progress and cannot part with the ball;

(*c*) when, being held by an opponent, the tackled player makes it evident that he has succumbed to the tackle and wishes to be released in order to play-the-ball;

(*d*) when he is lying on the ground and an opponent places a hand on him.

3. Once a player in possession has been tackled it is illegal for any player to move or try to move him from the point where the tackle is effected.

4. A player in possession shall not deliberately and unnecessarily allow himself to be tackled by voluntarily falling to the ground when not held by an opponent. If a player drops on a loose ball he shall not remain on the ground waiting to be tackled if he has time to regain his feet and continue play.

5. If a tackled player, because of his momentum, slides along the ground, the tackle is deemed to have been effected where his slide ends. (See Section VI, 3(*c*).)

6. If any doubt arises as to a tackle, the Referee should give a verbal instruction to "play on" or shout "held" as the case may be.

7. A team in possession shall be allowed five successive "play-the-balls" but if tackled a sixth time, the ball not having been

touched by an opponent during this period, play shall be re-started with a scrum. The team which was not in possession shall put the ball into this scrum and shall have the loose head.

8. A tackled player shall not intentionally part with the ball other than by bringing it into play in the prescribed manner. If, after being tackled, he accidentally loses possession, a scrum shall be formed.

9. Once a tackle has been completed, no player shall take or attempt to take the ball from the tackled player.

10. The play-the-ball shall operate as follows:

(*a*) the tackled player shall be *immediately* released and shall not be touched until the ball is in play;

(*b*) the tackled player shall *without delay* regain his feet where he was tackled, lift the ball clear of the ground, face his opponents' goal-line and drop or place the ball on the ground in front of his foremost foot;

(*c*) when the ball touches the ground it may be kicked or heeled in any direction by the foot of any player after which it is in play;

(*d*) one opponent may take up position immediately oppo-site the tackled player;

(*e*) neither the tackled player nor the player marking him shall raise a foot from the ground before the ball has been released;

(*f*) a player of each side, to be known as the acting half-back, may stand immediately and directly behind his own player taking part in the play-the-ball;

(*g*) players, other than the two taking part in the play-the-ball and the two acting half-backs, are out of play if they fail to retire 5 yd or more behind their own player taking part in the play-the-ball or to their own goal-line. Having retired 5 yd they may advance as soon as the ball has been dropped to the ground. A player who is out of play may again take part in the game when the advantage gained by not retiring has been lost.

11. The play-the-ball must be performed as quickly as possible. Any player who intentionally delays the bringing of the ball into play shall be penalised.

XII. THE SCRUM

1. A scrum is formed to restart play whenever play is not being restarted with a kick-off, a drop-out (Section VIII), a penalty kick (Section XIII) or a play-the-ball (Section XI).

2. To form a scrum not more than three forwards of either side shall interlock arms and heads and create a clear tunnel at right angles to the touch-line. The forward in the centre of a front row (i.e. the hooker) shall bind with his arms over the shoulders of the two supporting forwards. Not more than two second-row forwards on each side shall pack behind their respective front rows by interlocking arms and placing their heads in the two spaces between the hooker and his prop forwards. The loose forward of each side shall pack behind his second-row forwards by placing his head in the space between them. All forwards must pack square, i.e. their bodies and legs must be at right angles to the tunnel. Once the ball has been put in the scrum no other player can lend his weight to it.

3. No more than six players on each side shall assist in the formation of a scrum and when the ball is in the scrum no more than eight players of each side shall act as backs (i.e. the loose forward need not pack down).

4. It is permissible for the forwards to push once the scrum has been correctly formed, but if it moves an appreciable distance to the disadvantage of any one side before the ball is put in, then the Referee shall order the scrum to re-form in its original position.

5. If a scrum is ordered after a side has been tackled six successive times the attacking team shall have the Loose Head in the scrum and the defending team shall have the put-in. (This pertains to all scrummages whatever the reason for the award of a scrum.)

6. (*a*) The ball shall be put into the scrum from the Referee's side either by a downward throw from not above waist high or by rolling it along the ground. It must be put into the centre of the tunnel formed by opposing front row forwards.

(*b*) The ball shall not be put in before the scrum has been correctly formed.

(*c*) There shall be no undue delay in putting the ball into the scrum.

(*d*) The player putting it in shall not hesitate or dummy and after putting it in he shall immediately retire behind his own pack of forwards.

7. All players outside the scrum (other than the scrum-half putting the ball in) shall take up positions behind their own forwards and shall remain so until the ball has emerged correctly from the scrum.

8. When the ball is in the scrum it can only be played with the foot.

The front-row forwards shall pack with the upper portions of their bodies parallel to the ground and shall not advance their feet into the tunnel or have one foot raised before the ball is put in or strike for the ball before the hookers.

A hooker may strike for the ball with either foot but not until it first contacts the ground in the centre of the tunnel.

After the hookers have struck for the ball the other forwards in the scrum may kick or heel the ball.

No player shall wilfully collapse a scrum or wilfully have any part of him other than his feet in contact with the ground.

A player shall not wilfully delay the correct formation of a scrum.

9. To be in play, the ball must emerge from between and behind the inner feet of the second row forwards.

If the ball does not emerge correctly and the fault cannot be attributed to any one side then it should be put into the scrum once again.

10. If a scrum is ordered it shall normally be formed where the breach of Laws occurs. If such breach is within 10 yd of a touch-line or 5 yd of a goal-line the scrum shall be brought in 10 yd from the touch-line and 5 yd from the goal-line.

11. If a penalty kick is awarded relating to a scrum offence and the scrum has wandered from its original position, the Mark is where the scrum was first formed.

12. If the ball emerges correctly from the scrum it is in play even though the scrum has wheeled. Any forward can detach himself from the scrum to gather or kick the ball. Any back can

similarly play it provided he remained behind the scrum until the ball emerged.

XIII. PENALTY KICK

1. A Penalty Kick shall be awarded against any player who is guilty of misconduct (Section XV) provided that this is not to the disadvantage of the non-offending side. Unless otherwise stated, the Mark is where the offence occurs. If misconduct occurs in touch the Mark shall be 5 yd from the touch-line in the field-of-play and opposite where the offence occurred or, in the case of obstruction, where the ball next bounces in the field-of-play, or 5 yd opposite the point of entry if the ball enters touch on the full, or 5 yd from the goal-line if the ball crosses the goal-line on the full, whichever is to the greater advantage of the non-offending side. If the offence is committed by a defender in his own in-goal the Mark is taken 5 yd into the field-of-play opposite where the offence occurred.

2. A player must take a Penalty Kick by punting, drop-kicking, or place-kicking the ball from any point on or behind the Mark and equidistant from the touch-line. The ball may be kicked in any direction, after which it is in play.

3. Players of the kicker's side must be behind the ball when it is kicked.

Players of the side opposing the kicker shall retire to their own goal-line or 10 yd or more from the Mark towards their own goal-line and shall not make any attempt to interfere with or distract the attention of the kicker. They may advance after the ball has been kicked.

4. If the ball is kicked into touch without touching any other player the kicking side shall restart play by placing the ball on the ground 10 yd infield opposite the point of entry into touch and kicking it. Opposing players shall retire 10 yd from the point of entry into touch or to their own goal-line.

5. No player shall deliberately take any action which is likely to delay the taking of a Penalty Kick.

6. If the kick is not taken as stated or if a player of the kicker's side infringes, a scrum shall be formed at the Mark.

7. If a player of the side opposing the kicker infringes, another

Penalty Kick shall be awarded at the Mark or where the offence occurred, whichever is to the greater advantage to the non-offending side.

8. When the Referee penalises a player he must explain the nature of the offence.

9. Where a penalty would normally be awarded in the in-goal area for an offence by the attacking team, play shall be restarted with a place-kick from the centre of the "25" line as described in Section VIII, para. 2.

For an in-goal offence by the defending team which incurs a penalty the Mark is in the field-of-play 5 yd from the goal-line and opposite where the offence occurred except where foul play is committed on a player who scores a try, in which case the Mark shall be the centre of the line 10 yd from the goal-line. This penalty kick shall take the form of a kick at goal only and shall be taken after the attempted conversion of the try.

10. The Differential Penalty will operate for technical offences at the scrum, the non-offending side being awarded a tap penalty to be taken at the Mark. The side may elect to kick for touch and follow this with a second phase tap but may *not* kick for goal.

XIV. OFFSIDE

1. A player is offside except when he is in his own in-goal if the ball is kicked, touched or held by one of his own side behind him.

2. An offside player shall not take any part in the game or attempt in any way to influence the course of the game. He shall not encroach within 5 yd of an opponent who is waiting for the ball and shall immediately retire 5 yd from any opponent who first secures possession of the ball.

3. An offside player is placed onside if:

(*a*) an opponent moves 5 yd or more with the ball;

(*b*) an opponent touches the ball without retaining it;

(*c*) one of his own side in possession of the ball runs in front of him;

(*d*) one of his own side kicks the ball forward and takes up a position in front of him in the field-of-play;

(*e*) he retires behind the point where the ball was last touched by one of his own side.

XV. PLAYER'S MISCONDUCT

A player is guilty of misconduct if he:

(*a*) deliberately trips, kicks or strikes another player;

(*b*) unnecessarily and viciously attacks the head of an opponent when effecting a tackle;

(*c*) drops knees first on to an opponent who is on the ground;

(*d*) uses any dangerous throw when effecting a tackle;

(*e*) deliberately breaks the Laws of the Game;

(*f*) uses foul or obscene language;

(*g*) disputes a decision of the Referee or Touch-Judge;

(*h*) re-enters the field-of-play without the permission of the Rereree or a Touch-Judge having previously temporarily retired from the game;

(*i*) behaves in any way contrary to the true spirit of the game;

(*j*) Deliberately obstructs an opponent who is not in possession.

XVI. DUTIES OF REFEREE AND TOUCH-JUDGES

1. In all matches a Referee and two Touch-Judges shall be appointed or mutually agreed upon by the contesting teams.
2. The Referee shall enforce the Laws of the Game and may impose penalties for any deliberate breach of the Laws. He shall be the sole judge on matters of fact except those relating to Touch and Touch-in-Goal. (See para. 11 below.)
3. He shall record the tries and goals scored during the match.
4. He shall be the sole time-keeper except where this duty has been delegated to another person. (See Section VII.)
5. He may, at his discretion, temporarily suspend or prematurely terminate a match because of adverse weather, undue interference by spectators, misbehaviour by players, or any

other cause which, in his opinion, interferes with his control of the game.

6. He shall not allow anyone apart from the players on to the playing area without his permission.

7. In the event of misconduct by a player, the Referee shall, at his discretion, caution or dismiss the offender. He shall dismiss any player who is guilty of foul play and who has previously been cautioned.

8. The players are under the control of the Referee from the time they enter the playing area until they leave it.

9. The Referee must carry a whistle which he shall blow to commence and terminate each half of the game. Except for these occasions the blowing of the whistle shall temporarily stop the play. The Referee shall blow the whistle:

(*a*) when a try or a goal has been scored;

(*b*) when the ball has gone out of play;

(*c*) when he detects a breach of the Laws of the Game, except when to stop the play would be to the disadvantage of the non-offending team;

(*d*) when play is irregularly affected by the ball or the player carrying the ball coming into contact with the Referee, a Touch-Judge, or with any person not taking part in the match or with any object which should not normally be on the field-of-play, a scrum shall be formed at the point of contact, the defending side to put the ball in, the attacking side to have the Loose Head;

(*e*) when any irregularity, not provided for in these Laws, occurs and one team unjustifiably gains an advantage;

(*f*) when a stoppage is necessary in order to enforce the Laws or for any other reason.

10. If the Referee judges on a matter of fact, he shall not subsequently alter that judgement but he may cancel any decision made if facts of which he had no prior knowledge are reported to him by a Touch-Judge.

11. The Referee shall accept the decision of a neutral Touch-Judge relating to touch and touch-in-goal play and to kicks at goal.

12. Each Touch-Judge shall remain in touch, one on each side of, and near to, the playing area except:

(*a*) when judging kicks at goal (see Section VI), and

(*b*) when reporting a player's misconduct which has escaped the notice of the Referee.

13. Each Touch-Judge must carry a flag, triangular in shape, the longest sides being equal and not less than 12 in (30 cm) and the short side shall be not less than 9 in (23 cm). The flag must be attached by the short side to a stick, the length of which shall be not lesss than 18 in (45 cm).

14. A Touch-Judge shall indicate when and where the ball goes into touch by raising his flag and standing opposite the point of entry into touch except in the case of "ball back" (see Section IX, para. 4) when the Touch-Judge must indicate that no ground has been gained by waving his flag above his head accentuating the movements in the direction of the kicker's goal-line.

15. If the ball enters Touch-in-Goal the Touch-Judge shall wave his flag above his head and then point it towards the goal-posts if the ball last touched a defending player or towards the "25" line if it was last touched by an attacking player.

16. Touch-Judges shall assist the Referee in judging kicks at goal. (See Section VI, para. 10.)

17. When a Penalty Kick is being taken, the nearer Touch-Judge shall take up a position near the touch-line 10 yd beyond the Mark to act as a marker for the team which is required to retire. He shall wave his flag horizontally in front of him if any player fails to retire 10 yd.

18. In cases where circumstances in connection with the match are likely to be made the subject of official investigation, the Referee and Touch-Judges shall report to the investigating authority only and shall refrain from expressing criticism or comment through other channels.

Printed by permission of the R.F.L. Full notes and interpretations of these Laws, and the referee's signals, can be found in the official Rugby Football League Guide.

The Rules of
Golf

Golf

As approved by the Royal and Ancient Golf Club of St. Andrews, Scotland, and the United States Golf Association. See Note on p. *407*.

1. ETIQUETTE

Courtesy on the Course

Consideration for Other Players

In the interest of all, players should play without delay.

No player should play until the players in front are out of range.

Players searching for a ball should signal the players behind them to pass as soon as it becomes apparent that the ball will not easily be found: they should not search for five minutes before doing so.

They should not continue play until the players following them have passed and are out of range.

When the play of a hole has been completed, players should immediately leave the putting green.

Behaviour During Play

No one should move, talk or stand close to or directly behind the ball or the hole when a player is addressing the ball or making a stroke.

The player who has the honour should be allowed to play before his opponent or fellow-competitor tees his ball.

Priority on the Course

In the absence of special rules, two-ball matches should have precedence of and be entitled to pass any three- or four-ball match. A single player has no standing, and should give way to a match of any kind.

Any match playing a whole round is entitled to pass a match playing a shorter round.

If a match fails to keep its place on the course and loses more than one clear hole on the players in front, it should allow the match following to pass.

Care of the course

Holes in Bunkers

Before leaving a bunker, a player should carefully fill up and smooth over all holes and footprints made by him.

Restore Divots, Repair Ball-Marks and Damage by Spikes

Through the green, a player should ensure that any turf cut or displaced by him is replaced at once and pressed down, and that any damage to the putting green made by the ball is carefully repaired. Damage to the putting green caused by golf shoe spikes should be repaired *on completion of the hole*.

Damage to Greens—Flagsticks, Bags, etc.

Players should ensure that, when putting down bags, or the flagstick, no damage is done to the putting green, and that neither they nor their caddies damage the hole by standing close to it, in handling the flagstick or in removing the ball from the hole. The flagstick should be properly replaced in the hole before the players leave the putting green. Players should not damage the putting green by leaning on their putters, particularly when removing the ball from the hole.

Golf Carts

Local Notices regulating the movement of golf carts should be strictly observed.

Damage through Practice Swings

In taking practice swings players should avoid causing damage to the course, particularly the tees, by removing divots.

II. DEFINITIONS

1. Addressing the Ball

A player has "addressed the ball" when he has taken his stance (Definition 29) and has also grounded his club, except that in a hazard a player has addressed the ball when he has taken his stance.

2. Advice

"Advice" is any counsel or suggestion which could influence a player in determining his play, the choice of a club, or the method of making a stroke.

Information on the Rules or Local Rules is not advice.

3. Ball Deemed to Move

A ball is deemed to have "moved" if it leave its position and come to rest in any other place.

4. Ball Holed

A ball is "holed" when it lies within the circumference of the hole and all of it is below the level of the lip of the hole.

5. Ball in Play, Provisional Ball, Wrong Ball

(*a*) A ball is "in play" as soon as the player has made a stroke on the teeing ground. It remains as his ball in play until holed out, except when it is out of bounds, lost, or lifted, or another ball has been substituted under an applicable Rule or Local Rule: a ball so substituted becomes the ball in play.

(*b*) A "provisional ball" is a ball played under Rule 30 for a ball which may be lost outside a water hazard or may be out of bounds. It ceases to be a provisional ball when the Rule provides *either* that the player continue play with it as the ball in play *or* that it be abandoned.

(*c*) A "wrong ball" is any ball other than the ball in play or a provisional ball or, in stroke play, a second ball played under Rule 11-5 or under Rule 21-3(*d*).

6. Ball Lost

A ball is "lost" if:

(*a*) It be not found, or be not identified as his by the player, within five minutes after the player's side or his or their caddies have begun to search for it; *or*

(*b*) The player has put another ball into play under the Rules, even though he may not have searched for the original ball; *or*

(*c*) The player has played any stroke with a provisional ball from a point nearer the hole than the place where the original ball is likely to be, whereupon the provisional ball becomes the ball in play.

Time spent in playing a wrong ball is not counted in the five-minute period allowed for search.

7. Caddie, Forecaddie and Equipment

(*a*) A "caddie" is one who carries or handles a player's clubs during play and otherwise assists him in accordance with the Rules.

When one caddie is employed by more than one player, he is always deemed to be the caddie of the player whose ball is involved, and equipment carried by him is deemed to be that player's equipment, except when the caddie acts upon specific directions of another player, in which case he is considered to be that other player's caddie.

NOTE. *In threesome, foursome, best-ball and four-ball play, a caddie carrying for more than one player should be assigned to the members of one side.*

(*b*) A "forecaddie" is one employed by the Committee to indicate to players the position of balls on the course, and is an outside agency (Definition 22).

(*c*) "Equipment" is anything used, worn or carried by or for the player except his ball in play. Equipment includes a golf cart. If such a cart is shared by more than one player, its status under the Rules is the same as that of a caddie employed by more than one player.

8. Casual Water

"Casual water" is any temporary accumulation of water which is visible before or after the player takes his stance and which is not a hazard of itself or is not in a water hazard. Snow and ice are either "casual water" or loose impediments, at the option of the player.

9. Committee

The "Committee" is the committee in charge of the competition or, if the matter does not arise in a competition, the Committee in charge of the course.

10. Competitor

A "competitor" is a player in a stroke competition. A "fellow-competitor" is any person with whom the competitor plays. Neither is partner of the other.

In stroke play foursome and four-ball competitions, where the context so admits, the word "competitor" or "fellow-competitor" shall be held to include his partner.

11. Course

The "course" is the whole area within which play is permitted. It is the duty of the Committee to define its boundaries accurately.

12. Flagstick

The "flagstick" is a movable straight indicator provided by the Committee, with or without bunting or other material attached, centred in the hole to show its position. It shall be circular in cross-section.

13. Ground under Repair

"Ground under repair" is any portion of the course so marked by order of the Committee or so declared by its authorised representative. It includes material piled for removal and a hole made by a greenkeeper, even if not so marked. Stakes and lines defining "ground under repair" are not in such ground.

NOTE. *Grass cuttings and other material left on the course which have been abandoned and are not intended to be removed are not ground under repair unless so marked.*

14. Hazards

A "hazard" is any bunker or water hazard. Bare patches, scrapes, roads, tracks and paths are not "hazards".

(*a*) A "bunker" is an area of bare ground, often a depression, which is usually covered with sand. Grass-covered ground bordering or within a "bunker" is *not* part of the "hazard".

(*b*) A "water hazard" is any sea, lake, pond, river, ditch, surface drainage ditch or other open water course (regardless of whether or not it contains water), and anything of a similar nature.

All ground or water within the margin of a water hazard, whether or not it be covered with any growing substance, is part of the water hazard. The margin of a water hazard is deemed to extend vertically upwards.

(c) A "lateral water hazard" is a water hazard or that part of a water hazard so situated that it is not possible or is deemed by the Committee to be impracticable to drop a ball behind the water hazard and keep the spot at which the ball last crossed the hazard margin between the player and the hole.

NOTE. *Water hazards should be defined by yellow stakes or lines and lateral water hazards by red stakes or lines.*

15. Hole

The "hole" shall be $4\frac{1}{4}$ in (108 mm) in diameter and at least 4 in (100 mm) deep. If a lining be used, it shall be sunk at least 1 in (25 mm) below the putting green surface unless the nature of the soil makes it impractical to do so; its outer diameter shall not exceed $4\frac{1}{4}$ in (108 mm).

16. Honour

The side which is entitled to play first from the teeing ground is said to have the "honour".

17. Loose Impediments

The term "loose impediments" denotes natural objects not fixed or growing and not adhering to the ball, and includes stones not solidly embedded, leaves, twigs, branches and the like, dung, worms and insects and casts or heaps made by them.

Snow and ice are either casual water or loose impediments, at the option of the player.

Sand and loose soil are loose impediments on the putting green, but not elsewhere on the course.

18. Marker

A "marker" is a scorer in stroke play who is appointed by the Committee to record a competitor's score. He may be a fellow-competitor. He is not a referee.

A marker should not lift the ball or mark its position unless authorised to do so by the competitor and, unless he is a fellow-competitor, should not attend the flagstick, or stand at the hole or mark its position.

19. Observer

An "observer" is appointed by the Committee to assist a referee to decide questions of fact and to report to him any breach of a Rule or Local Rule. An observer should not attend the flagstick, stand at or mark the position of the hole, or lift the ball or mark its position.

20. Obstructions

An "obstruction" is anything artificial, whether erected, placed or left on the course, including the artificial surfaces and sides of roads and paths; but excepting:

(*a*) Objects defining out of bounds, such as walls, fences, stakes and railings;

(*b*) In water hazards, artificially surfaced banks or beds, including bridge supports when part of such a bank. Bridges and bridge supports which are not part of such a bank are obstructions;

(*c*) Any construction declared by the Committee to be an integral part of the course.

21. Out of Bounds

"Out of bounds" is ground on which play is prohibited.

When out of bounds is fixed by stakes or a fence, the out of bounds line is determined by the nearest inside points of the stakes or fence posts at ground level; the line is deemed to extend vertically upwards. When out of bounds is fixed by a line on the ground, the line itself is out of bounds.

A ball is out of bounds when all of it lies out of bounds.

22. Outside Agency

An "outside agency" is any agency not part of the match or, in stroke play, not part of a competitor's side, and includes a referee, a marker, an observer, or a forecaddie employed by the Committee. Neither wind nor water is an outside agency.

23. Partner

A "partner" is a player associated with another player on the same side.

In a threesome, foursome or a four-ball, where the context so admits, the word "player" shall be held to include his partner.

24. Penalty Stroke

A "penalty stroke" is one added to the score of a side under certain Rules. It does not affect the order of play.

25. Putting Green

The "putting green" is all ground of the hole being played which is specially prepared for putting or otherwise defined as such by the Committee.

A ball is deemed to be on the putting green when any part of it touches the putting green.

26. Referee

A "referee" is a person who has been appointed by the Committee to accompany players to decide questions of fact and of golf law. He shall act on any breach of Rule or Local Rule which he may observe or which may be reported to him by an observer (Definition 19).

In stroke play the Committee may limit a referee's duties.

A referee should not attend the flagstick, stand at or mark the position of the hole, or lift the ball or mark its position.

27. Rub of the Green

A "rub of the green" occurs when a ball in motion is stopped or deflected by any outside agency.

28. Sides and Matches

Side. A player, or two or more players who are partners.

Single. A match in which one plays against another.

Threesome. A match in which one plays against two, and each side plays one ball.

Foursome. A match in which two play against two, and each side plays one ball.

Three-ball. A match in which three play against one another, each playing his own ball.

Best-ball. A match in which one plays against the better ball of two or the best ball of three players.

Four-ball. A match in which two play their better ball against the better ball of two other players.

NOTE. *In a best-ball or four-ball match, if a partner be absent for reasons satisfactory to the Committee, the remaining member(s) of his side may represent the side.*

29. Stance

Taking the "stance" consists in a player placing his feet in position for and preparatory to making a stroke.

30. Stipulated Round

The "stipulated round" consists of playing the holes of the course in their correct sequence, unless otherwise authorised by the Committee. The number of holes in a stipulated round is eighteen unless a smaller number is authorised by the Committee.

In match play only, the Committee may, for the purpose of settling a tie, extend the stipulated round to as many holes as are required for a match to be won.

31. Stroke

A "stroke" is the forward movement of the club made with the intention of fairly striking at and moving the ball.

32. Teeing

In "teeing", the ball may be placed on the ground, on an irregularity of surface created by a player on the ground or on sand or other substance in order to raise it off the ground.

33. Teeing Ground

The "teeing ground" is the starting place for the hole to be played. It is a rectangular area two club-lengths in depth, the front and sides of which are defined by the outside limits of two tee-markers. A ball is outside the teeing ground when all of it lies outside the stipulated area.

When playing the first stroke with any ball (including a

provisional ball) from the teeing ground, the tee-markers are immovable obstructions (Definition 20).

34. Terms Used in Reckoning in Match Play

In match play, the reckoning of holes is kept by the terms: so many "holes up" or "all square" and so many "to play".

A side is "dormie" when it is as many holes up as there are holes remaining to be played.

35. Through the Green

"Through the green" is the whole area of the course except:

(*a*) Teeing ground and putting green of the hole being played;

(*b*) All hazards on the course.

36. Types of Club

There are three recognised types of golf club: an "iron" club is one with a head which usually is relatively narrow from face to back, and usually is made of steel; a "wood" club is one with a head relatively broad from face to back, and usually is made of wood, plastic or a light metal; a "putter" is a club designed primarily for use on the putting green (see Definition 25).

III. THE RULES OF PLAY

RULE 1
The Game

The Game of Golf consists in playing a ball from the teeing ground into the hole by successive strokes in accordance with the Rules.

Penalty for Breach of Rule
Match play—Loss of hole;
Stroke play—Disqualification.

RULE 2
The Club and the Ball

The Royal and Ancient Golf Club and the United States Golf

Association reserve the right to change the Rules and the inter-
pretations regulating clubs and balls at any time.

1. Legal Clubs and Balls

The player's clubs, and the balls he uses, shall conform with
Clauses 2 and 3 of this Rule.

2. Form and Make of Clubs

(*a*) *General characteristics.* The golf club shall be composed of
a shaft and a head, and all of the various parts shall be fixed so
that the club is one unit; the club shall not be designed to be
adjustable, except for weight.

NOTE. *Playing characteristics not to be changed during a*
round—Rule 2 (2b).

The club shall not be substantially different from the traditional and customary form and make, and shall conform with
the regulations governing the design of clubs approved by the
Royal and Ancient Golf Club of St Andrews.

(*b*) *Playing characteristics not to be changed.* The playing
characteristics of a club shall not be purposely changed during
a round; foreign material shall not be added to the club face at
any time.

NOTE. *Players in doubt as to the legality of clubs are advised*
to consult the Royal and Ancient Golf Club.

3. The Ball

(*a*) *Specifications.* The ball shall be designed and manufactured
to perform in general as if it were spherically symmetrical
(*consult the R. & A. if further details are required*). The weight
of the ball shall be *not greater* than 1.620 oz avoirdupois
(45.93 gm), and the size *not less* than 1.620 in (41.15 mm) in
diameter.

The velocity of the ball shall be *not greater* than 250 ft
(76.2 m) per second when measured on apparatus approved by
the Royal and Ancient Golf Club: a maximum tolerance of 2%
will be allowed. The temperature of the ball when so tested
shall be 75° F (24° C).

NOTE 1. *Under the Rules of the United States Golf Association,*
the size of the ball shall be not less than 1·680 *in* (42.67 *mm*) *in*

diameter, but in international team competitions the size of the ball shall be not less than 1.620 *in* (41.15 *mm*) *in diameter.*

NOTE 2. *In laying down the conditions under which a competition is to be played (Rule 36-1), the Committee may stipulate that the ball to be used shall be of certain specifications, provided these are within the limits prescribed by Rule 2(3a) and that it be of a size, brand and marking as detailed on the current Lists of Conforming Golf Balls issued by the Royal and Ancient Golf Club of St Andrews.*

(*b*) *Foreign material prohibited.* Foreign material shall not be applied to a ball for the purpose of changing its playing characteristics.

Penalty for Breach of Rule. Disqualification.

RULE 3
Maximum of Fourteen Clubs

1. Selection and Replacement of Clubs

The player shall start a stipulated round with not more than fourteen clubs. He is limited to the clubs so selected for that round except that, without unduly delaying play, he may:

(*a*) If he started with fewer than fourteen, add as many as will bring his total to that number.

(*b*) Replace, with any club, a club which becomes unfit for play in the normal course of play.

The addition or replacement of a club or clubs may not be made by borrowing from any other person playing on the course.

2. Side may Share Clubs

Partners may share clubs provided that the total number of clubs carried by the side does not exceed fourteen.

Penalty for Breach of Rule 3-1 or 3-2, regardless of number of wrong clubs carried. Match play—loss of one hole for each hole at which any violation occurred; maximum penalty per round: loss of two holes. The penalty shall be applied to the state of the match at the conclusion of the hole at which the violation is discovered, provided all players in the match have not left the putting green of the last hole of the match. Stroke play—

Two strokes for each hole at which any violation occurred; maximum penalty per round: four strokes.

Bogey and Par competitions—Penalties as in match play.

Stableford competitions—From total points scored for the round, deduction of two points for each hole at which any violation occurred; maximum deduction per round: four points.

NOTE. *A serious breach of this Rule should be dealt with by the Committee under Rule 1.*

3. Wrong Club Declared Out of Play

Any club carried or used in violation of this Rule shall be declared out of play by the player immediately upon discovery and thereafter shall not be used by the player during the round *under penalty of disqualification.*

RULE 4
Agreement to Waive Rules Prohibited

Players shall not agree to exclude the operation of any Rule or Local Rule or to waive any penalty incurred.

Penalty for breach of Rule. Match play—Disqualification of both sides; Stroke play—Disqualification of competitors concerned.

RULE 5
General Penalty

Except when otherwise provided for, the penalty for a breach of a Rule or Local Rule is:

Match play—Loss of hole; Stroke play—Two strokes.

RULE 6
Match Play

1. Winner of Hole

In match play the game is played by holes.

Except as otherwise provided for in the Rules, a hole is won by the side which holes its ball in the fewer strokes. In a handicap match the lower net score wins the hole.

2. Halved Hole

A hole is halved if each side holes out in the same number of strokes.

When a player has holed out and his opponent has been left with a stroke for the half, nothing that the player who has holed out can do shall deprive him of the half which he has already gained; but if the player thereafter incur any penalty, the hole is halved.

3. Winner of Match

A match (which consists of a stipulated round, unless otherwise decreed by the Committee) is won by the side which is leading by a number of holes greater than the number of holes remaining to be played.

RULE 7
Stroke Play

1. Winner

The competitor who holes the stipulated round or rounds in the fewest strokes is the winner.

2. Failure to Hole Out

If a competitor fail to hole out at any hole before he has played a stroke from the next teeing ground, or, in the case of the last hole of the round, before he has left the putting green, *he shall be disqualified. (Ball purposely moved, touched or lifted—Rules 27-1c and 35-1k.)*

RULE 8
Practice

1. During Play of Hole

During the play of a hole, a player shall not play any practice stroke.

Penalty for Breach of Rule 8-1. Match play—Loss of hole; Stroke play—Two strokes.

2. Between Holes

Between the play of two holes, a player shall not play a practice stroke from any hazard, or on or to a putting green other than that of the hole last played.

*Penalty for Breach of Rule 8-2.** Match play—Loss of hole; Stroke play—Two strokes.

* NOTE. *The penalty applies to the next hole.*

3. Stroke Play

On any day of a stroke competition or play-off, a competitor shall not practise on the competition course before a round or play-off. When a competition extends over consecutive days, practice on the competition course between rounds is prohibited.

If a competition extending over consecutive days is to be played on more than one course, practice between rounds on any competition course remaining to be played is prohibited.

NOTE. *The Committee may, at its discretion, waive or modify these prohibitions in the conditions of the competition.*

Penalty for Breach of Rule 8-3. Disqualification.

(Duty of Committee to define practice ground—Rule 36-4*b*.)

NOTE 1. *A practice swing is not a practice stroke and may be taken at any place on the course provided the player does not violate the Rules.*

NOTE 2. *Unless otherwise decided by the Committee, there is no penalty for practice on the course on any day of a match play competition.*

RULE 9
Advice (Def. 2) and Assistance

1. Giving or Asking for Advice; Receiving Assistance

(*a*) *Advice.* A player may give advice to, or ask for advice from only his partner, or either of their caddies.

(*b*) *Assistance.* In making a stroke, a player shall not seek or accept physical assistance or protection from the elements.

2. Indicating Line of Play

Except on the putting green, a player may have the line of play indicated to him by anyone, but no one shall stand on or close to the line while the stroke is being played. Any mark placed during the play of a hole by a player or with his knowledge to indicate the line shall be removed before the stroke is played.

(Indicating line of play on putting green—Rule 35-1e.)

Penalty for breach of Rule. Match play—Loss of hole; Stroke play—Two strokes.

RULE 10
Information as to Strokes Taken

1. General

The number of strokes a player has taken shall include any penalty strokes incurred.

2. Match Play

A player who has incurred a penalty shall inform his opponent as soon as possible. If he fail to do so, he shall be deemed to have given wrong information.

An opponent is entitled to ascertain from the player, during the play of a hole, the number of strokes he has taken and, after play of a hole, the number of strokes taken on the hole just completed.

If during the play of a hole the player give or be deemed to give wrong information as to the number of strokes taken, he shall incur no penalty if he correct the mistake before his opponent has played his next stroke. If after play of a hole a player give or be deemed to give wrong information as to the number of strokes taken on the hole just completed, he shall incur no penalty if he correct his mistake before any player plays from the next teeing ground or, in the case of the last hole of the match, before all players leave the putting green.

If the player fail so to correct the wrong information, *he shall lose the hole.*

3. Stroke Play

A competitor who has incurred a penalty should inform his marker as soon as possible.

RULE 11
Disputes, Decisions and Doubt as to Rights

1. Claims and Penalties

(*a*) *Match play.* In match play, if a dispute or doubt arise between the players on any point, in order that a claim may be considered it must be made before any player in the match plays from the next teeing ground, or, in the case of the last hole of the match, before all players in the match leave the putting green. No later claim shall be considered unless it is based on facts previously unknown to the player making the claim and the player making the claim had been given wrong information (Rule 10) by an opponent. In any case, however, no later claim shall be considered after the result of the match has been officially announced, unless the Committee is satisfied that the opponent knew he was giving wrong information.

(*b*) *Stroke play.* In stroke play no penalty shall be imposed after the competition is closed unless the Committee is satisfied that the competitor has knowingly returned a score for any hole lower than actually taken (Rule 38-3); no penalty shall be rescinded after the competition is closed. A competition is deemed to have closed:

In stroke play only—when the result of the competition is officially announced;

In stroke play qualifying followed by match play—when the player has teed off in his first match.

2. Referee's Decision

If a referee has been appointed by the Committee, his decision shall be final.

3. Committee's Decision

In the absence of a referee, the players shall refer any dispute to the Committee, whose decision shall be final.

If the Committee cannot come to a decision, it shall refer the dispute to the Rules of Golf Committee of the Royal and Ancient Golf Club of St Andrews, whose decision shall be final.

If the point in dispute or doubt has not been referred to the

Rules of Golf Committee, the player or players have the right to refer an agreed statement through the Secretary of the Club to the Rules of Golf Committee for an opinion as to the correctness of the decision given. The reply will be sent to the Secretary of the Club or Clubs concerned.

If play be conducted other than in accordance with the Rules of Golf, the Rules of Golf Committee will not give a decision on any question.

4. Decision by Equity

If any point in dispute be not covered by the Rules or Local Rules, the decision shall be made in accordance with equity.

5. Stroke Play: Doubt as to Procedure

In stroke play only, when during play of a hole a competitor is doubtful of his rights or procedure, he may, without penalty, play a second ball. After the doubtful situation has arisen and before taking further action, he should announce to his marker his decision to proceed under this Rule and which ball he will score with if the Rules permit.

On completing the round, the competitor must report the facts immediately to the Committee; if he fail to do so, *he shall be disqualified.* If the Rules allow the procedure selected in advance by the competitor, the score with the ball selected shall be his score for the hole. Should the competitor fail to announce in advance his procedure or selection, the ball with the higher score shall count if the Rules allow the procedure adopted for such ball.

NOTE 1. *A second ball played under Rule 11-5 is not a provisional ball under Rule 30.*

NOTE 2. *The privilege of playing a second ball does not exist in match play.*

RULE 12
The Honour (Def. 16)

1. The Honour

(*a*) *Match play.* A match begins by each side playing a ball from the first teeing ground in the order of the draw. In the absence of a draw, the option of taking the honour shall be decided by lot.

The side which wins a hole shall take the honour at the next teeing ground. If a hole has been halved, the side which had the honour at the previous teeing ground shall retain it.

(*b*) *Stroke play*. The honour shall be taken as in match play.

2. Playing out of Turn

(*a*) *Match play*. If, on the teeing ground, a player play when his opponent should have played, the opponent may immediately require the player to abandon the ball so played and to play a ball in correct order, without penalty.

(*b*) *Stroke play*. If, on the teeing ground, a competitor by mistake play out of turn, no penalty shall be incurred and the ball shall be in play.

(*c*) *Second ball from tee*. If a player play a second ball, including a provisional ball, from the tee, he should do so after the opponent or the fellow-competitor has played his first stroke. If a player play a second ball out of turn, the provisions of Clauses 2(*a*) and 2(*b*) of this Rule apply.

RULE 13
Playing Outside Teeing Ground (Def. 33)

1. Match Play

If a player, when starting a hole, play a ball from outside the teeing ground, the opponent may immediately require the player to replay the stroke, in which case the player shall tee a ball and play the stroke from within the teeing ground, without penalty.

2. Stroke Play

If a competitor, when starting a hole, play from outside the teeing ground, he shall be penalised two strokes and shall then play from within the teeing ground. Strokes played by a competitor from outside the teeing ground do not count in his score. If the competitor fail to rectify his mistake before making a stroke on the next teeing ground, or, in the case of the last hole of the round, before leaving the putting green, *he shall be disqualified*.

NOTE. *Stance — A player may take his stance outside the teeing ground to play a ball within it.*

RULE 14
Ball Falling off Tee

If a ball, when not in play, fall off a tee or be knocked off a tee by the player in addressing it, it may be re-teed without penalty, but if a stroke be made at the ball in these circumstances, whether the ball be moving or not, the stroke shall be counted but no penalty shall be incurred.

RULE 15
Order of Play in Threesome or Foursome

1. General

In a threesome or a foursome, the partners shall strike off alternately from the teeing grounds, and thereafter shall strike alternately during the play of each hole. Penalty strokes (Definition 24) do not affect the order of play.

2. Match Play

If a player play when his partner should have played, *his side shall lose the hole*.

In a match comprising more than one stipulated round, the partners shall not change the order of striking from the teeing grounds after any stipulated round.

3. Stroke Play

If the partners play a stroke or strokes in incorrect order, such stroke or strokes shall be cancelled, and *the side shall be penalised two strokes*. A ball shall then be put in play as nearly as possible at the spot from which the side first played in incorrect order. This must be done before a stroke has been played from the next teeing ground, or, in the case of the last hole of the round, before the side has left the putting green. If they fail to do so, *they shall be disqualified*. If the first ball was played from the teeing ground, a ball may be teed anywhere within the teeing ground; if from through the green or a hazard, it shall be dropped; if on the putting green, it shall be placed.

NOTE. *As in stroke play a stipulated round cannot be more than 18 holes (Def. 30) the order of play between partners may be changed for a second or subsequent round, unless the conditions of the competition provide otherwise.*

RULE 16
Ball Played as it Lies; Embedded Ball

1. General

The ball shall be played as it lies except as otherwise provided for in the Rules or Local Rules.

(Ball at rest moved by player, purposely—Rule 27-1c.)
(Ball at rest moved by player accidentally—Rule 27-1d.)
(Ball at rest moving accidentally after address—Rule 27-1f.)

2. Embedded Ball

A ball embedded in its own pitch-mark in any closely mown area through the green may be lifted and dropped, without penalty, as near as possible to the spot where it lay but not nearer the hole.

Penalty for Breach of Rule 16-2. Match play—Loss of hole. Stroke play—Two strokes.

RULE 17
Improving Lie or Stance and Influencing
Ball Prohibited

1. Improving Line of Play or Lie Prohibited

A player shall not improve, or allow to be improved, his line of play, the position or lie of his ball or the area of his intended swing by moving, bending or breaking anything fixed or growing or by removing or pressing down sand, loose soil, cut turf placed in position or other irregularities of surface except:

(*a*) As may occur in the course of fairly taking his stance;
(*b*) In making the stroke or the backward movement of his club for the stroke;

(*c*) On his teeing ground a player may create or eliminate irregularities of surface;

(*d*) In repairing damage to the putting green under Rule 35-1*c*.

The club may be grounded only lightly and must not be pressed on the ground.

Sand and loose soil on the putting green—Definition 17 and Rule 35-1b.

(Removal of obstructions—Rule 31-1.)

NOTE. *Things fixed include objects defining out of bounds.*

2. Long Grass and Bushes

If a ball lie in long grass, rushes, bushes, whins, heather or the like, only so much thereof shall be touched as will enable the player to find and identify his ball; nothing shall be done which may in any way improve its lie.

The player is not of necessity entitled to see the ball when playing a stroke.

3. Building of Stance Prohibited

A player is always entitled to place his feet firmly on the ground when taking his stance, but he is not allowed to build a stance.

4. Exerting Influence on Ball

No player or caddie shall take any action to influence the position or the movement of a ball except in accordance with the Rules.

Penalty for Breach of Rule. Match play—Loss of hole; Stroke play—Two strokes.

NOTE. *In the case of a serious breach of Rule 17-4, the Committee may impose a penalty of disqualification.*

RULE 18
Loose Impediments (Def. 17)

Any loose impediment may be removed without penalty except when both the impediment and the ball lie in or touch a hazard. When a player's ball is in motion, a loose impediment on his line of play shall not be removed.

Penalty for Breach of Rule. Match play—Loss of hole; Stroke play—Two strokes. (Finding ball in hazard—Rule 33-1*e*.) (Ball moving after loose impediment touched—Rules 27-1*e* and 35-1*b*.)

<h2 style="text-align:center">RULE 19
Striking at Ball</h2>

1. Ball to be Fairly Struck at

The ball shall be fairly struck at with the head of the club and must not be pushed, scraped or spooned.

Penalty for Breach of Rule 19-1. Match play—Loss of hole; Stroke play—Two strokes.

2. Striking Ball Twice

If the player strike the ball twice when making a stroke, he shall count the stroke and *add a penalty stroke*, making two strokes in all.

(Playing a moving ball—Rule 25.)

<h2 style="text-align:center">RULE 20
Ball Farther from the Hole Played First</h2>

1. General

When the balls are in play, the ball farther from the hole shall be played first. If the balls are equidistant from the hole, the option of playing first shall be decided by lot.

A player or a competitor incurs no penalty if a ball is moved in measuring to determine which ball is farther from the hole. A ball so moved shall be replaced.

2. Match Play

Through the green or in a hazard, if a player play when his opponent should have done so, the opponent may immediately require the player to replay the stroke. In such a case, the player shall drop a ball as near as possible to the spot from which his previous stroke was played, and play in correct order without penalty.

Exception. Three-ball, best-ball and four-ball match play. See Rule 40-1*d*.

Penalty for Breach of Rule 20-2. Loss of hole.

(Playing out of turn on putting green—Rule 35-2*b*.)

3. Stroke Play

If a competitor play out of turn, no penalty shall be incurred. The ball shall be played as it lies.

RULE 21
Playing a Wrong Ball (Def. 5) or from a Wrong Place

1. General

A player must hole out with the ball driven from the teeing ground unless a Rule or Local Rule permit him to substitute another ball.

2. Match Play

(*a*) *Wrong ball.* If a player play a stroke with a wrong ball (Def. 5) except in a hazard, *he shall lose the hole.* There is no penalty if a player play any strokes in a hazard with a wrong ball provided he then play the correct ball; the strokes so played with a wrong ball do not count in the player's score.

If the wrong ball belong to another player, its owner shall place a ball on the spot from which the wrong ball was played.

When the player and the opponent exchange balls during the play of a hole, the first to play the wrong ball other than from a hazard shall lose the hole; when this cannot be determined, the hole shall be played out with the balls exchanged.

(*b*) *Ball played from wrong place.* If a player play a stroke with a ball which has been dropped or placed under an applicable Rule but in a wrong place, *he shall lose the hole.*

Note. *For a ball played outside teeing ground, see Rule 13-1.*

3. Stroke Play

(*a*)   *Wrong ball.* If a competitor play a stroke with a wrong ball (Def. 5) except in a hazard, *he shall add two penalty strokes* to his score and shall then play the correct ball. There is no penalty if a competitor play any strokes in a hazard with a wrong ball provided he then play the correct ball. Strokes played by a competitor with a wrong ball do not count in his score.

If the wrong ball belong to another player, its owner shall place a ball on the spot from which the wrong ball was played.

(*b*) *Rectification after holing out.* If a competitor hole out with a wrong ball, he may rectify his mistake by proceeding in accordance with Clause 3(*a*) of this Rule, subject to the prescribed penalty, provided he has not made a stroke on the next teeing ground, or, in the case of the last hole of the round, has not left the putting green. *The competitor shall be disqualified* if he does not so rectify his mistake.

(*c*) *Ball played from wrong place.* If a competitor play a stroke with a ball which has been dropped or placed under an applicable Rule but in a wrong place, *he shall add two penalty strokes* to his score and play out the hole with that ball. If a serious breach of the applicable Rule is involved, *the competitor shall be disqualified* unless the breach has been rectified as provided by Rule 21-3*d*.

NOTE. *For a ball played outside teeing ground, see Rule 13-2.*

(*d*) *Rectification.* If a serious breach under the applicable Rule under Rule 21-3*c* may be involved and the competitor has not made a stroke on the next teeing ground or, in the case of the last hole of the round, has not left the putting green, the competitor may rectify any such serious breach by *adding two penalty strokes to his score*, dropping or placing a ball in accordance with the applicable Rule and playing out the hole. On completion of the round, the competitor must report the facts immediately to the Committee, which shall determine whether a serious breach of the Rule was involved and, accordingly, whether the score with the ball played under this Rule 21-3*d* shall count.

NOTE. *Penalty strokes incurred by playing the ball ruled not to count and strokes subsequently taken with that ball shall be disregarded.*

RULE 22
Lifting, Dropping and Placing

1. Lifting

A ball to be lifted under the Rules or Local Rules may be lifted by the player, his partner or another person authorised by the player. In any such case the player shall be responsible for any breach of the Rules or Local Rules.

NOTE. *A referee or observer should not lift a ball or mark its position (Defs. 19 and 26).*

2. Dropping

(*a*) *How to drop.* A ball to be dropped under the Rules or Local Rules shall be dropped by the player himself. He shall face the hole, stand erect, and drop the ball behind him over his shoulder. If a ball be dropped in any other manner and remain the ball in play (Def. 5), *the player shall incur a penalty stroke.*

If the ball touch the player before it strikes the ground, the player shall re-drop without penalty. If the ball touch the player after it strikes the ground, or if it come to rest against the player and move when he then moves, there is no penalty, and the ball shall be played as it lies.

(*b*) *Where to drop.* When a ball is to be dropped, it shall be dropped as near as possible to the spot where the ball lay, but not nearer the hole; except when a Rule permits it to be dropped elsewhere or placed. In a hazard, the ball must come to rest in that hazard; if it roll out of the hazard, it must be re-dropped, without penalty.

(*c*) *When to re-drop.* If a dropped ball roll into a hazard, on to a putting green out of bounds or more than two club-lengths from the point where it first struck the ground, or come to rest nearer the hole than its original position, it shall be re-dropped, without penalty. If the ball again roll into such a position, it shall be placed where it was last dropped, without penalty.

Penalty for breach of Rule 22-2. Match play—Loss of hole; Stroke play—Two strokes.

3. Placing

(*a*) *How and where to place.* A ball to be placed under the Rules or Local Rules shall be placed by the player or his partner. A ball to be replaced shall be replaced by the player, his partner or the person who lifted it, on the spot where the ball lay. In any such case, the player shall be responsible for any breach of the Rules or Local Rules.

(*b*) *Lie of ball to be placed or replaced altered.* If the original lie of a ball to be placed or replaced has been altered, the ball shall be placed in the nearest lie most similar to that which it originally occupied, not more than two club-lengths from the original lie and not nearer the hole.

(*c*) *Spot not determinable.* If it be impossible to determine the spot where the ball is to be placed: through the green or in a hazard the ball shall be dropped, or on the putting green it shall be placed, as near as possible to the place where it lay, but not nearer the hole.

(*d*) *Ball moving.* If a ball when placed fail to remain on the spot on which it was placed, it shall be replaced without penalty. If it still fail to remain on that spot, it shall be placed at the nearest spot not nearer the hole where it can be placed at rest.

Penalty for breach of Rule 22-3. Match play—Loss of hole; Stroke play—Two strokes.

4. Ball in Play when Dropped or Placed

A ball dropped or placed under a Rule governing the particular case is in play (Definition 5) and shall not be lifted or re-dropped or replaced except as provided in the Rules.

5. Lifting Ball Wrongly Dropped or Placed

A ball dropped or placed but not played may be lifted without penalty if:

(*a*) It was dropped or placed under a Rule governing the particular case but not in the right place or otherwise not in accordance with that Rule. The player shall then drop or place the ball in accordance with the governing Rule.

(*b*) It was dropped or placed under a Rule which does not govern the particular case. The player shall then proceed under a Rule which governs the case. However, in match play, if, before the opponent plays his next stroke, the player fails to inform him that the ball has been lifted, *the player shall lose the hole.*

NOTE. *In stroke play, in the event of a serious breach of Rule 22, see Rules 21-3c and 21-3d.*

RULE 23
Identifying or Cleaning Ball

The responsibility for playing the proper ball rests with the player. Each player should put an identification mark on his ball.

1. Identifying Ball

Except in a hazard, the player may, without penalty, lift his ball in play for the purpose of identification and replace it on the spot from which it was lifted, provided this is done in the presence of his opponent in match play or marker in stroke play. If the player lift his ball for identification in a hazard, or elsewhere other than in the presence of his opponent or marker, *he shall incur a penalty of one stroke*, and the ball shall be replaced.

(Touching grass, etc., for identification—Rule 17-2).

2. Cleaning Ball

A ball may be cleaned when lifted as follows: from an embedded lie under Rule 16-2; from an unplayable lie under Rule 29-2; for relief from an obstruction under Rule 31; from casual water, ground under repair, or otherwise under Rule 32; from a water hazard under Rule 33-2 or 33-3; on the putting green under Rule 35-1d or on a wrong putting green under Rule 35-1j; identification under Rule 23-1, but the ball may be cleaned only to the extent necessary for identification; or under a Local Rule permitting cleaning the ball.

If the player clean his ball during the play of a hole except as permitted under this Rule, *he shall incur a penalty of one stroke*, and the ball if lifted shall be replaced.

NOTE. *If a player who is required to replace a ball fail to do so, the general penalty for breach of Rule 22-3(a) will apply in addition to any other penalty incurred.*

RULE 24
Ball Interfering with Play

When the player's ball lies through the green or in a hazard, the player may have any other ball lifted if he consider that it interfere with his play. A ball so lifted shall be replaced after the player has played his stroke.

If a ball be accidentally moved in complying with this Rule, no penalty shall be incurred and the ball shall be replaced.

(Lie of ball to be placed or replaced altered—Rule 22-3*b*.)

(Putting green—Rule 35-2*a* and 3*a*.)

Penalty for breach of rule. Match play—Loss of hole; Stroke play—Two strokes.

RULE 25
A Moving Ball

1. Playing Moving Ball Prohibited

A player shall not play while his ball is moving.

Exceptions. Ball falling off tee—Rule 14.

               Striking ball twice—Rule 19-2.

               As hereunder—Rule 25-2.

When the ball only begins to move after the player has begun the stroke or the backward movement of his club for the stroke, he shall incur no penalty under this Rule, but he is not exempted from the provisions for:

Ball at rest moving after loose impediment touched—Rule 27-1*e*.

Ball at rest moved accidentally by player—Rule 27-1*d*.

Ball at rest moving accidentally after address—Rule 27-1*f*.

2. Ball Moving in Water

When a ball is in water in a water hazard, the player may, without penalty, make a stroke at it while it is moving, but he must not delay to make his stroke in order to allow the wind or current to better the position of the ball. A ball moving in water in a water hazard may be lifted if the player elect to invoke Rule 33-2 or 33-3.

Penalty for breach of Rule. Match play—Loss of hole; Stroke play—Two strokes.

RULE 26
Ball in Motion Stopped or Deflected

1. General

(*a*) *By outside agency.* If a ball in motion be accidentally stopped or deflected by any outside agency, it is a rub of the green and the ball shall be played as it lies, without penalty.

Exception. On putting green—Rule 35-1*h*.

(*b*) *Lodging in outside agency.* If a ball lodge in any moving outside agency, the player shall, through the green or in a hazard, drop a ball, or on the putting green place a ball, as near as possible to the spot where the object was when the ball lodged in it, without penalty.

2. Match Play

(*a*) *By player.* If a player's ball be stopped or deflected by himself, his partner or either of their caddies or equipment, *he shall lose the hole.*

(*b*) *By opponent accidentally.* If a player's ball be accidentally stopped or deflected by an opponent, his caddie or equipment, no penalty shall be incurred. The player may play the ball as it lies or, before another stroke is played by either side, he may cancel the stroke, place a ball on the spot where the ball previously lay and replay the stroke.

(Ball striking opponent's ball—Rule 27-2*b*.)

Exception. Ball striking person attending flagstick—Rule 34-3b.

3. Stroke Play

(*a*) *By competitor.* If a competitor's ball be stopped or deflected by himself, his partner or either of their caddies or equipment, *the competitor shall incur a penalty of two strokes.* The ball shall be played as it lies, except when it lodges in the competitor's, his partner's or either of their caddies' clothes or equipment, in which case the competitor shall, through the green or in a hazard, drop the ball, or on the putting green place the ball, as near as possible to where the article was when the ball lodged in it.

(*b*) *By fellow-competitor.* If a competitor's ball be accidentally stopped or deflected by a fellow-competitor, his caddie, ball or equipment, it is a rub of the green and the ball shall be played as it lies.

Exceptions. Ball lodging in fellow-competitor's clothes, etc.—Clause 1*b* of this Rule.

On the putting green, ball striking fellow-competitor's ball in play—Rule 35-3*c*.

Ball played from putting green stopped or deflected by fellow-competitor or his caddie—Rule 35-1*h*.

Ball striking person attending flag-stick—Rule 34-3*b*.

Penalty for breach of Rule. Match play—Loss of hole; Stroke play—Two strokes.

NOTE. *If the referee or the Committee determine that a ball has been deliberately stopped or deflected by an outside agency, including a fellow-competitor or his caddie, further procedure should be prescribed in equity under Rule 11-4. On the putting green, Rule 35-1h applies.*

RULE 27
Ball at Rest Moved (Def. 3)

1. General

(*a*) *By outside agency.* If a ball at rest be moved by any outside agency, the player shall incur no penalty and shall replace the ball before playing another stroke.

(Opponent's ball moved by player's ball—Rule 27-2*b*.)

NOTE 1. *Neither wind nor water is an outside agency.*

NOTE 2. *If the ball moved is not immediately recoverable, another ball may be substituted.*

(*b*) *During search.* During search for a ball, if it be moved by an opponent, a fellow-competitor or the equipment or caddie of either, no penalty shall be incurred. The player shall replace the ball before playing another stroke.

(*c*) *By player, purposely.* When a ball is in play, if a player, his partner or either of their caddies purposely move, touch or lift it, except as provided for in the Rules or Local Rules, *the player shall incur a penalty stroke* and the ball shall be replaced. The player may, however, without penalty, touch the ball with his club in the act of addressing it, provided the ball does not move (Def. 3). (On putting green—Rule 35-1*k*.)

(*d*) *By player, accidentally.* When a ball is in play, if a player, his partner, their equipment or either of their caddies accidentally move it, or by touching anything cause it to move (except as otherwise provided for in the Rules or Local Rules), *the player shall incur a penalty stroke.* The ball shall be replaced unless the movement of the ball occurs after the player has begun his swing and he does not discontinue his swing. (Ball accidentally moved when measuring to determine which ball farther from the hole—Rule 20-1.) (Ball accidentally moved in the process of marking—Rule 35-2*a* or 35-3*a*.)

(*e*) *Ball moving after loose impediment touched.* Through the green, if the ball move before the player has addressed it but after any loose impediment lying within a club-length of it has been touched by the player, his partner or either of their caddies, the player shall be deemed to have caused the ball to move. *The penalty shall be one stroke.* The ball shall be replaced unless the movement of the ball occurs after the player has begun his swing and he does not discontinue his swing.

(*Loose impediment on putting green*—Rule 35-1*b*.)

(*f*) *Ball moving accidentally after address.* If a ball in play move after the player has addressed it (Definition 1), he shall be deemed to have caused it to move and *shall incur a penalty stroke*, and the ball shall be played as it lies.

2. Match Play

(*a*) *By opponent.* If a player's ball be touched or moved by an opponent, his caddie or equipment (except as otherwise provided in the Rules), *the opponent shall incur a penalty stroke.* The player shall replace the ball before playing another stroke.

(*b*) *Opponent's ball moved by player's ball.* If a player's ball move an opponent's ball, no penalty shall be incurred. The opponent may either play his ball as it lies, or, before another stroke is played by either side, he may replace the ball.

If the player's ball stop on the spot formerly occupied by the opponent's ball and the opponent declare his intention to replace his ball, the player shall first play another stroke, after which the opponent shall replace his ball.

(Putting green—Rule 35-2*c*.)

(Three-ball, Best-ball and Four-ball match play—Rule 40-1*c*.)

3. Stroke Play

Ball moved by a fellow-competitor. If a competitor's ball be moved by a fellow-competitor, his caddie, ball or equipment, no penalty shall be incurred. The competitor shall replace his ball before playing another stroke.

Exception to penalty. Ball striking fellow-competitor's ball on putting green—Rule 35-3*c*.

Penalty for breach of Rule. Match play—Loss of hole;* Stroke play—Two strokes.

(Playing a wrong ball—Rule 21.)

NOTE 1. *If a player who is required to replace a ball fail to do so, the general penalty for a breach of this Rule will apply in addition to any other penalty incurred.*

NOTE 2. *If it be impossible to determine the spot on which a ball is to be placed or if a ball when placed fail to remain on the spot on which it was placed, Rule 22-3 applies.*

*NOTE 3. *In stroke play, in the event of a serious breach of Rule 27, see Rules 21-3c and 21-3d.*

RULE 28
Ball Unfit for Play

The ball may be deemed unfit for play when it is visibly cut or out of shape or so cracked, pierced or otherwise damaged as to interfere with its true flight or true roll or its normal behaviour when struck. The ball shall not be deemed unfit for play solely because mud or other material adhere to it, its surface be scratched or its paint be damaged or discoloured.

If a player has reason to believe his ball is unfit for play, the player, after he has announced his intention to proceed under this Rule to his opponent in match play or marker in stroke play, may, without penalty, lift his ball in play for the purpose of determining whether it is unfit. If the ball be so damaged as to be unfit for play, the player may substitute another ball, placing it on the spot where the original ball lay. Substitution may only be made on the hole during the play of which the damage occurred. If a ball break into pieces as a result of a stroke, a ball shall be placed where the original ball lay and the stroke shall be replayed, without penalty.

A player is not the sole judge as to whether his ball is unfit for play. If the opponent or the marker dispute a claim of unfitness, the referee, if one is present, or the Committee shall settle the matter (Rule 11-2 or 11-3).

Penalty for breach of Rule. Match play—Loss of hole; Stroke play—Two strokes.

(Ball unplayable—Rule 29-2.)

RULE 29
Ball Lost (Def. 6),
Out of Bounds (Def. 21) or Unplayable

1. Lost or Out of Bounds

(*a*) *Procedure.* If a ball be lost outside a water hazard or be out of bounds, the player shall play his next stroke as nearly as possible at the spot from which the original ball was played or moved by him, *adding a penalty stroke* to his score for the hole.

If the original stroke was played from the teeing ground, a ball may be teed anywhere within the teeing ground; if from through the green or a hazard, it shall be dropped; if on the putting green, it shall be placed.

(*Ball lost in casual water, ground under repair, etc.—Rule 32-4.*)

(*b*) *Ascertaining location.* A player has the right at any time of ascertaining whether his opponent's ball is out of bounds.

A person outside the match may point out the location of a ball for which search is being made.

(*c*) *Standing out of bounds.* A player may stand out of bounds to play a ball lying within bounds.

2. Unplayable

(*a*) *Player sole judge.* The player is the sole judge as to whether his ball is unplayable. It may be declared unplayable at any place on the course except in a water hazard (Rule 33-2, 33-3).

(*b*) *Procedure.* If the player deem his ball to be unplayable, he shall either:

(i) Play his next stroke as provided in Clause 1*a* of this Rule (stroke-and-distance penalty), or

(ii) Drop a ball, *under penalty of one stroke*, either (*a*) within two club-lengths of the point where the ball lay, but not nearer the hole, or (*b*) behind the point where the ball lay, keeping that point between himself and the hole, with no limit to how far behind that point the ball may be dropped: if the ball lay in a bunker and a player elect to play under this Clause (ii), a ball must be dropped in the bunker.

(Ball in casual water, etc.—Rule 32.)

(Ball unfit for play—Rule 28.)

Penalty for breach of Rule. Match play—Loss of hole; *Stroke play—Two strokes.

* NOTE. *In stroke play, in the event of a serious breach of Rule, see Rules 21-3c and 21-3d.*

RULE 30
Provisional Ball (Def. 5)

1. Procedure

If a ball may be lost outside a water hazard or may be out of bounds, to save time the player may play another ball provisionally as nearly as possible from the spot at which the original ball was played. If the original ball was played from the teeing ground, the provisional ball may be teed anywhere within the teeing ground; if from through the green or a hazard, it shall be dropped; if on the putting green, it shall be placed.

(*a*) The player must inform his opponent or marker that he intends to play a provisional ball, and he must play it before he or his partner goes forward to search for the original ball: if he fail to do so, and plays another ball, such ball is not a provisional ball and becomes the ball in play *under penalty of stroke and distance* (Rule 29-1); the original ball is deemed to be lost (Def. 6*b*).

(*b*) Play of a provisional ball from the teeing ground does not affect the order in which the sides play (Rule 12-2).

(*c*) A provisional ball is never an outside agency.

2. Play of a Provisional Ball

(*a*) The player may play a provisional ball until he reaches the place where the original ball is likely to be. If he play any strokes with the provisional ball from a point nearer the hole than that place, the original ball is deemed to be lost (Def. 6*c*).

(*b*) If the original ball be lost outside a water hazard or be out of bounds, the provisional ball becomes the ball in play *under penalty of stroke and distance* (Rule 29-1).

(*c*) If the original ball be neither lost outside a water hazard nor out of bounds, the player shall abandon the provisional ball and continue play with the original ball. Should he fail to do so, any further strokes played with the provisional ball shall constitute playing a wrong ball and the provisions of Rule 21 shall apply.

Penalty for breach of Rule. Match play—Loss of hole; Stroke play—Two strokes.

NOTE. *If the original ball be unplayable or lie or be lost in a water hazard, the player must proceed under Rule 29-2 or Rule 33-2 or 33-3, whichever is applicable*.

RULE 31
Obstructions (Def. 20)

1. Movable Obstruction May be Removed

Any movable obstruction may be removed. If the ball be moved in so doing, it shall be replaced on the exact spot from which it was moved, without penalty. If it be impossible to determine the spot or to replace the ball, the player shall proceed in accordance with Rule 22-3.

When a ball is in motion, an obstruction on the player's line of play other than an attended flagstick and equipment of the players shall not be removed.

2. Interference by Immovable Obstruction

(*a*) *Interference*. Interference by an immovable obstruction occurs when the ball lies in or on the obstruction, or so close to the obstruction that the obstruction interferes with the player's stance or the area of his intended swing. The fact that an immovable obstruction intervenes on the line of play is not, of itself, interference under this Rule.

(*b*) *Relief.* A player may obtain relief from interference by an immovable obstruction, without penalty, as follows:

(i) *Through the green:*

Through the green, the point nearest to where the ball lies shall be determined (without crossing over, through or under the obstruction) which (*a*) is not nearer the hole, (*b*) avoids interference as defined in Clause 2*a* of this Rule, and (*c*) is not in a hazard or on a putting green. He shall lift the ball and drop it within one club-length of the point thus determined on ground which fulfils (*a*), (*b*) and (*c*) above.

NOTE. *The prohibition against crossing over, through or under the obstruction does not apply to the artificial surfaces and sides of roads and paths or when the ball lies in or on the obstruction.*

(ii) *In a hazard:*

In a hazard, the player may lift and drop the ball in accordance with Clause (i) above, except that the ball must be dropped in the hazard.

(iii) *On the putting green:*

On the putting green, the player may lift and place the ball in the nearest position to where it lay which affords relief from interference, but not nearer the hole.

(*c*) *Re-dropping.* If a dropped ball roll into a position covered by this Rule, or nearer the hole than its original position, it shall be re-dropped without penalty. If it again roll into such a position, it shall be placed where it first struck the ground when re-dropped.

Penalty for breach of Rule. Match play—Loss of hole; Stroke play—Two strokes.

RULE 32
Casual Water (Def. 8)
Ground Under Repair (Def. 13)
Hole Made by Burrowing Animal

1. Interference

Interference by casual water, ground under repair, or a hole, cast or runway made by a burrowing animal, a reptile or a bird, occurs when a ball lies in or touches any of these conditions or when the condition interferes with the player's stance, or the area of his intended swing. If interference exists, the player may either play the ball as it lies or take relief as provided in Clause 3 of this Rule.

2. Finding Ball

If a ball lying in casual water, ground under repair or a hole, cast or runway made by a burrowing animal, a reptile or a bird is not visible, the player may probe for it. If the ball be moved in such search, no penalty shall be incurred, and the ball shall be replaced unless the player elect to proceed under Clause 3 of this Rule.

3. Relief

If the player elect to take relief, he shall proceed as follows:

(*a*) *Through the green.* Through the green, the point nearest to where the ball lies shall be determined which (*a*) is not nearer the hole, (*b*) avoids interference by the condition, and (*c*) is not in a hazard or on a putting green. The player shall lift the ball and drop it without penalty within one club-length of the point thus determined on ground which fulfils (*a*), (*b*) and (*c*) above.

(*b*) *In a hazard.* In a hazard, the player shall lift and drop the ball either:

Without penalty, in the hazard as near as possible to the spot where the ball lay, but not nearer the hole, on ground which affords maximum relief from the condition, or

Under penalty of one stroke, outside the hazard, but not nearer the hole, keeping the spot where the ball lay, between himself and the hole.

(*c*) *On the putting green.* On the putting green, or if such condition on the putting green intervene between a ball lying on the putting green and the hole, the player shall lift the ball and place it without penalty in the nearest position to where it lay which affords maximum relief from the condition, but not nearer the hole nor in a hazard.

4. Ball Lost

(*a*) *Outside a hazard.* If a ball be lost under a condition covered by this Rule, except in a hazard, the player may take relief as follows: the point nearest to where the ball last crossed the margin of the area shall be determined which (*a*) is not nearer the hole than where the ball last crossed that margin, (*b*) avoids interference by the condition, and (*c*) is not in a hazard or on a putting green. He shall drop a ball without penalty within one club-length of the point thus determined on ground which fulfils (*a*), (*b*) and (*c*) above.

(*b*) *In a hazard*. If a ball be lost in a hazard under a condition covered by this Rule, the player may drop a ball either: without penalty, in the hazard, but not nearer the hole than the spot at which the ball last crossed the margin of the area, on ground which affords maximum relief from these conditions; *or under penalty of one stroke*, outside the hazard, but not nearer the hole, keeping the spot at which the ball last crossed the margin of the hazard between himself and the hole.

In order that a ball may be treated as lost, there must be reasonable evidence to that effect.

5. Re-Dropping

If a dropped ball roll into the area from which relief was taken, or come to rest in such a position that that area still affects the player's stance, or the area of his intended swing, the ball shall be re-dropped, without penalty. If the ball again roll into such a position, it shall be placed where it first struck the ground when re-dropped.

Penalty for breach of Rule. Match play—Loss of hole; Stroke play—Two strokes.

RULE 33
Hazards (Def. 14)

1. Touching Hazard Prohibited

When a ball lies in or touches a hazard or a water hazard, nothing shall be done which may in any way improve its lie. Before making a stroke, the player shall not touch the ground in the hazard or the water with a club or otherwise, nor touch or move a loose impediment lying in or touching the hazard, nor test the condition of the hazard or of any similar hazard; subject to the following considerations:

(*a*) *Stance.* The player may place his feet firmly in taking his stance.

(*b*) *Touching fixed or growing object.* In addressing the ball or in the stroke or in the backward movement for the stroke, the club may touch any wooden or stone wall, paling or similar fixed object or any grass, bush, tree, or other growing substance (but the club may not be soled in the hazard).

(*c*) *Obstructions.* The player is entitled to relief from obstructions under the provisions of Rule 31.

(*d*) *Loose impediment outside hazard.* Any loose impediment not in or touching the hazard may be removed.

(*e*) *Finding ball.* If the ball be covered by sand, fallen leaves or the like, the player may remove as much thereof as will enable him to see the top of the ball; if the ball be moved in such removal, no penalty shall be incurred, and the ball shall be replaced.

If the ball is believed to be lying in water in a water hazard, the player may probe for it with a club or otherwise. If the ball be moved in such search, no penalty shall be incurred; the ball shall be replaced, unless the player elects to proceed under Clause 2 or 3 of this Rule.

The ball may not be lifted for identification.

(*f*) *Placing clubs in hazard.* The player may, without penalty, place his clubs in the hazard prior to making a stroke, provided nothing is done which may improve the lie of the ball or constitute testing the soil.

(*g*) *Smoothing irregularities.* There is no penalty should soil or sand in the hazard be smoothed by the player after playing a stroke, or by his caddie at any time without the authority of the player, provided nothing is done that improves the lie of the ball or assists the player in his subsequent play of the hole.

(*h*) *Casual water, ground under repair.* The player is entitled to relief from casual water, ground under repair, and otherwise as provided for in Rule 32.

(*i*) *Interference by a ball.* The player is entitled to relief from interference by another ball under the provisions of Rule 24.

2. Ball in Water Hazard

If a ball lie or be lost in a water hazard (whether the ball lie in water or not), the player may drop a ball, *under penalty of one stroke*, either:

(*a*) Behind the water hazard, keeping the spot at which the ball last crossed the margin of the water hazard between himself and the hole, and with no limit to how far behind the water hazard the ball may be dropped, or

(*b*) As near as possible to the spot from which the original ball was played; if the stroke was played from the teeing ground, the ball may be teed anywhere within the teeing ground.

NOTE. *If a ball has been played from within a water hazard and has not crossed any margin of the hazard, the player may drop a ball behind the hazard under Rule 33-2a.*

3. Ball in Lateral Water Hazard (Def. 14-c)

If a ball lie or be lost in a lateral water hazard, the player may, *under penalty of one stroke*, either:

(*a*) Play his next stroke in accordance with Clause 2*a* or 2*b* of this Rule, or

(*b*) Drop a ball outside the hazard within two club-lengths of (*i*) the point where the ball last crossed the margin of the hazard, or (*ii*) a point on the opposite margin of the hazard equidistant from the hole. The ball must be dropped and come to rest not nearer the hole than the point where the original ball last crossed the margin of the hazard.

NOTE. *If a ball has been played from within a lateral water hazard and has not crossed any margin of the hazard, the player may drop a ball outside the hazard under Rule 33-3b.*

Penalty for breach of Rule. Match play—Loss of hole;* Stroke play—Two strokes.

* NOTE 1. *In stroke play, in the event of a serious breach of Rule 33, see Rules 21-3c and 21-3d.*

NOTE 2. *It is a question of fact whether a ball lost after having been struck toward a water hazard is lost inside or outside the hazard. In order to treat the ball as lost in the hazard there must be reasonable evidence that the ball lodged therein. In the absence of such evidence the ball must be treated as a lost ball and Rule 29-1 applies.*

RULE 34
The Flagstick (Def. 12)

1. Flagstick Attended, Removed or Held Up

Before and during the stroke, the player may have the flagstick attended, removed or held up to indicate the position of the hole. This may be done only on the authority of the player before he plays his stroke.

If the flagstick be attended or removed by an opponent, a fellow-competitor or the caddie of either with the knowledge of the player and no objection is made, the player shall be deemed to have authorised it.

If a player or a caddie attend or remove the flagstick or stand near the hole while a stroke is being played, he shall be deemed to attend the flagstick until the ball comes to rest.

If the flagstick be not attended before the stroke is played, it shall not be attended or removed while the ball is in motion.

2. Unauthorised Attendance

(*a*) *Match play*. In match play, an opponent or his caddie shall not attend or remove the flagstick without the knowledge or authority of the player.

(*b*) *Stroke play*. In stroke play, if a fellow-competitor or his caddie attend or remove the flagstick without the knowledge or authority of the competitor, and if the ball strike the flagstick or the person attending it, it is a rub of the green, there is no penalty, and the ball shall be played as it lies.

Penalty for Breach of Rule 34-1 and 34-2. Match play—Loss of hole; Stroke play—Two strokes.

3. Ball Striking Flagstick or Attendant

The player's ball shall not strike either: (*a*) the flagstick when attended or removed by the player, his partner or either of their caddies, or by another person with the knowledge or authority of the player; or (*b*) the player's caddie, his partner, or his partner's caddie when attending the flagstick, or another person attending the flagstick with the knowledge or authority of the player, or equipment carried by any such person; or (*c*) the flagstick in the hole, unattended, when the ball has been played from the putting green.

Penalty for Breach of Rule 34-3. Match play—Loss of hole; Stroke play—Two strokes, and the ball shall be played as it lies.

4. Ball Resting Against Flagstick

If the ball rest against the flagstick when it is in the hole, the player shall be entitled to have the flagstick removed, and if the ball fall into the hole the player shall be deemed to have holed out at his last stroke; otherwise, the ball shall be placed on the lip of the hole, without penalty.

RULE 35
The Putting Green (Def. 25)

1. General

(*a*) *Touching line of putt*. The line of the putt must not be touched except as provided in Clauses 1*b*, 1*c* and 1*d* of this Rule, or in measuring (Rule 20-1), or in removing movable obstructions (Rule 31-3) but the player may place the club in front of the ball in addressing it without pressing anything down.

(*b*) *Loose impediments*. The player may move sand, loose soil or any loose impediments on the putting green by picking them up or brushing them aside with his hand or a club without pressing anything down. If the ball be moved, it shall be replaced without penalty.

(*c*) *Repair of hole plugs and ball marks*. The player or his partner may repair an old hole plug or damage to the putting green caused by the impact of a ball. If the player's ball lie on the putting green, it may be lifted to permit repair and shall be replaced on the spot from which it was lifted; in match play the ball must be replaced immediately if the opponent so requests.

If a ball be moved during such repair, it shall be replaced, without penalty.

(*d*) *Lifting and cleaning ball*. A ball lying on the putting green may be lifted without penalty, cleaned if desired, and replaced on the spot from which it was lifted; in match play the ball must be replaced immediately if the opponent so requests.

(*e*) *Direction for putting.* When the player's ball is on the putting green, the player's caddie, his partner or his partner's caddie may, before the stroke is played, point out a line for putting, but the line of the putt shall not be touched in front of, to the side of, or behind the hole.

While making the stroke, the player shall not allow his caddie, his partner or his partner's caddie to position himself on or close to an extension of the line of putt behind the ball.

No mark shall be placed anywhere on the putting green to indicate a line for putting.

(*f*) *Testing surface.* During the play of a hole, a player shall not test the surface of the putting green by rolling a ball or roughening or scraping the surface.

(*g*) *Other ball to be at rest.* While the player's ball is in motion after a stroke on the putting green, an opponent's or a fellow-competitor's ball shall not be played or touched.

(*h*) *Ball in motion stopped or deflected.* If a ball in motion after a stroke on the putting green be stopped or deflected by, or lodge in, any animate outside agency, the stroke shall be cancelled and the ball shall be replaced.

NOTE. *If the referee or the Committee determine that a ball has been deliberately stopped or deflected by an outside agency, including a fellow-competitor or his caddie, further procedure should be prescribed in equity under Rule 11-4.*

(*i*) *Ball overhanging hole.* When any part of the ball overhangs the edge of the hole, the owner of the ball is not allowed more than a few seconds to determine whether it is at rest. If by then the ball has not fallen into the hole, it is deemed to be at rest.

(*j*) *Ball on a wrong putting green.* If a ball lie on a putting green other than that of the hole being played the point nearest to where the ball lies shall be determined which (*a*) is not nearer the hole and (*b*) is not in a hazard or on a putting green. The player shall lift the ball and drop it without penalty within one club-length of the point thus determined on ground which fulfils (*a*) and (*b*) above.

NOTE. *Unless otherwise stipulated by the Committee, the term "a putting green other than that of the hole being played"* includes a practice putting or pitching green lying within the boundaries of the course.

(*k*) *Ball to be marked when lifted.* When a ball on the putting green is to be lifted, its position shall be marked. If the player fail so to mark the position of the ball, *the player shall incur a penalty of one stroke* and the ball shall be replaced.

(*Lifting and placing—Rule 22.*)

NOTE. *The position of a lifted ball should be marked by placing a ball-marker or other small object on the putting green, immediately behind the ball. If the marker interfere with the play, stance or stroke of another player, it should be placed one or more putterhead-lengths to one side.*

(*l*) *Standing astride or on line of putt prohibited.* The player shall not make a stroke on the putting green from a stance astride, or with either foot touching, the line of the putt or an extension of that line behind the ball. For the purpose of Rule 35-1*l* only, the line of putt does not extend beyond the hole.

Penalty for breach of Rule 35-1. Match play—Loss of hole; Stroke play—Two strokes.

2. Match Play

(*a*) *Ball interfering with play.* When the player's ball lies on the putting green, if the player consider that the opponent's ball interfere with his play, he may require that the opponent's ball be lifted. The opponent's ball shall be replaced after the player has played his stroke. If the player's ball stop on the spot formerly occupied by the lifted ball, the player shall first play another stroke before the lifted ball is replaced.

If a ball be accidentally moved in complying with this Rule, no penalty shall be incurred and the ball shall be replaced.

(*b*) *Playing out of turn.* If a player play when his opponent should have done so, the opponent may immediately require the player to replay the stroke, in which case the player shall replace his ball and play in correct order, without penalty.

(*c*) *Opponent's ball displaced.* If the player's ball knock the opponent's ball into the hole, the opponent shall be deemed to have holed out at his last stroke.

If the player's ball move the opponent's ball, the opponent may replace it, but this must be done before another stroke is played by either side. If the player's ball stop on the spot formerly occupied by the opponent's ball, and the opponent declare his intention to replace his ball, the player shall first play another stroke, after which the opponent shall replace his ball. (Three-ball, Best-ball and Four-ball match play—Rule 40-1c.)

(d) *Conceding opponent's next stroke.* When the opponent's ball had come to rest, the player may concede the opponent to have holed out with his next stroke and may remove the opponent's ball with a club or otherwise. If the player does not concede the opponent's next stroke and the opponent's ball fall into the hole, the opponent shall be deemed to have holed out with his last stroke.

If the opponent's next stroke has not been conceded, the opponent shall play without delay in correct order.

Penalty for breach of Rule 35-2. Loss of hole.

3. Stroke Play

(a) *Ball interfering with play.* When the competitor's ball lies on the putting green, if the competitor consider that a fellow-competitor's ball interfere with his play he may require that the fellow-competitor's ball be lifted or played at the fellow-competitor's option.

If a ball be accidentally moved in complying with this Rule no penalty shall be incurred and the ball shall be replaced.

NOTE. *It is recommended that the interfering ball be played, rather than lifted, unless the subsequent play of a fellow-competitor is likely to be affected.*

(b) *Ball assisting play.* If the fellow-competitor consider that his ball lying on the putting green might be of assistance to the competitor, the fellow-competitor may lift or play first, without penalty.

(c) *Ball striking fellow-competitor's ball.* When both balls lie on the putting green, if the competitor's ball strike a fellow-competitor's ball, the *competitor shall incur a penalty of two strokes* and shall play his ball as it lies. The fellow-competitor's ball shall be at once replaced.

(*d*) *Ball lifted before holed out*. For ball lifted before holed out, see Rules 27-1*c* and 35-1*k*.

RULE 36
The Committee (Def. 9)

1. Conditions

The Committee shall lay down the conditions under which a competition is to be played.

Certain special rules governing stroke play are so substantially different from those governing match play that combining the two forms of play is not practicable and is not permitted. The result of matches played and the scores returned in these circumstances shall not be accepted.

2. Order and Times of Starting

(*a*) *General*. The Committee shall arrange the order and times of starting.

(*b*) *Match play*. When a competition is played over an extended period, the Committee shall lay down the limit of time within which each round shall be completed.

When players are allowed to arrange the date of their match within these limits, the Committee should announce that the match must be played at a stated hour on the last day of the period unless the players agree to a prior date.

(*c*) *Stroke play*. Competitors shall play in couples unless the Committee authorises play by threes or fours. If there be a single competitor, the Committee shall provide him with a player who shall mark for him, or provide a marker and allow him to compete alone, or allow him to compete with another group.

3. Decision of Ties

The Committee shall announce the manner, day and time for the decision of a halved match or of a tie, whether played on level terms or under handicap. A halved match shall not be decided by stroke play. A tie in stroke play shall not be decided by a match.

4. The Course

(*a*) *New holes*. New holes should be made on the day on which a stroke competition begins, and at such other times as the Committee considers necessary, provided all competitors in a single round play with each hole cut in the same position.

(*b*) *Practice ground*. Where there is no practice ground available outside the area of a competition course, the Committee should lay down the area on which players may practise on any day of a competition, if it is practicable to do so. On any day of a stroke competition, the Committee should not normally permit practice on or to a putting green or from a hazard of the competition course.

(*c*) *Course unplayable*. If the Committee or its authorised representative consider that for any reason the course is not in a playable condition, or that there are circumstances which render the proper playing of the game impossible, it shall have the power in match and stroke play to order a temporary suspension of play, or in stroke play to declare play null and void and to cancel all scores for the round in question.

When a round is cancelled, all penalties incurred in that round are cancelled.

When play has been temporarily suspended, it shall be resumed from where it was discontinued, even though resumption occur on a subsequent day.

(Procedure in discontinuing play—Rule 37-6*b*.)

5. Modification of Penalty

The Committee has no power to waive a Rule of Golf. A penalty of disqualification, however, may, in exceptional individual cases, be waived or be modified or be imposed if the Committee consider such action warranted.

6. Defining Bounds and Margins

The Committee shall define accurately:

(*a*) The course and out of bounds.

(*b*) The margins of hazards, water hazards, and lateral water hazards.

(*c*) Ground under repair.

(*d*) Obstructions.

7. Local Rules

(*a*) *Policy.* The Committee shall make and publish Local Rules for abnormal conditions, having regard to the policy of the Governing Authority of the country concerned.

(*b*) *Waiving penalty prohibited.* A penalty imposed by a Rule of Golf shall not be waived by a Local Rule.

RULE 37
The Player

1. Conditions

The player shall be responsible for acquainting himself with the conditions under which the competition is to be played.

2. Caddie

For any breach of a Rule or Local Rule by his caddie, the player incurs the relative penalty.

The player may have only one caddie, *under penalty of disqualification.*

The player may send his own caddie forward to mark the position of any ball.

3. Forecaddie

If a forecaddie be employed by the Committee, he is an outside agency (Definition 22).

4. Handicap

Before starting in a handicap competition, the player shall ensure that his current handicap is recorded correctly on the official list, if any, for the competition and on the card issued for him by the Committee. In the case of match play or bogey, par or Stableford competitions, he shall inform himself of the holes at which strokes are given or taken.

If a player play off a higher handicap than his current one, *he shall be disqualified* from the handicap competition. If he play off a lower one, the score, or the result of the match, shall stand.

5. Time and Order of Starting

The player shall start at the time and in the order arranged by the Committee.

Penalty for breach of Rule 37-5. Disqualification.

6. Discontinuance of Play

(*a*) *When permitted.* The player shall not discontinue play on account of bad weather or for any other reason, unless:

He considers that there be danger from lightning, or

There be some other reason, such as sudden illness, which the Committee considers satisfactory.

If the player discontinue play without specific permission from the Committee, he shall report to the Committee as soon as possible.

General exception. Players discontinuing match play by agreement are not subject to disqualification unless by so doing the competition is delayed.

Penalty for breach of Rule 37-6a. Disqualification.

(*b*) *Procedure.* When play is discontinued in accordance with the Rules, it should, if feasible, be discontinued after the completion of the play of a hole. If this is not feasible, the player should lift his ball after marking the spot on which it lay; in such case he shall replace the ball on that spot when play is resumed.

Penalty for breach of Rule 37-6b. Match play—Loss of hole;* Stroke play—two strokes.

* NOTE. *In stroke play, in the event of a serious breach of Rule 37-b, see Rules 21-3c and 21-3d.*

7. Undue Delay

The player shall at all times play without undue delay. Between the completion of a hole and driving off the next tee, the player may not delay play in any way.

Penalty for breach of Rule 37-7. Match play—Loss of hole;* Stroke play—Two strokes. For repeated offence—Disqualification.

* NOTE. *If the player delay play between holes, he is delaying the play of the next hole, and the penalty applies to that hole.*

8. Refusal to Comply with Rule

If a competitor in stroke play refuse to comply with a Rule affecting the rights of another competitor, *he shall be disqualified*.

9. Artificial Devices

Except as provided for under the Rules, the player shall not use any artificial device (*a*) which might assist him in making a stroke or in his play; (*b*) for the purpose of gauging or measuring distance or conditions which might affect his play, or (*c*) which, not being part of the grip, is designed to give him artificial aid in gripping the club.

(*Exceptions to Rule 37-9c:* plain gloves and material or substance applied to the grip, such as tape, gauze or resin.)

Penalty for breach of Rule 37-9. Disqualification.

RULE 38
Scoring in Stroke Play

1. Recording Scores

The Committee shall issue for each competitor a score card containing the date and the competitor's name.

After each hole the marker should check the score with the competitor. On completion of the round the marker shall sign the card and hand it to the competitor; should more than one marker record the scores, each shall sign the part for which he is responsible.

2. Checking Scores

The competitor shall check his score for each hole, settle any doubtful points with the Committee, ensure that the marker has signed the card, countersign the card himself, and return it to the Committee as soon as possible. The competitor is solely responsible for the correctness of the score recorded for each hole.

Penalty for breach of Rule 38-2. Disqualification.

The Committee is responsible for the addition of scores and application of the handicap recorded on the card.

Exception. Four-ball stroke play—Rule 41-1*d*.

3. No Alteration of Scores

No alteration may be made on a card after the competitor has returned it to the Committee.

If the competitor return a score for any hole lower than actually played, *he shall be disqualified.*

A score higher than actually played must stand as returned.

Exception. Four-ball stroke play—Rule 41-8*a*.

RULE 39
Bogey, Par or Stableford Competitions

1. Conditions

A bogey, par or Stableford competition is a form of stroke competition in which play is against a fixed score at each hole of the stipulated round or rounds.

(*a*) The reckoning for bogey or par competitions is made as in match play. The winner is the competitor who is most successful in the aggregate of holes.

(*b*) The reckoning in Stableford competitions is made by points awarded in relation to a fixed score at each hole, as follows:

For hole done in one over fixed score	1 point
For hole done in fixed score	2 points
For hole done in one under fixed score	3 points
For hole done in two under fixed score	4 points
For hole done in three under fixed score	5 points

The winner is the competitor who scores the highest number of points.

2. Rules for Stroke Play Apply

The Rules for Stroke play shall apply with the following modifications:

(*a*) *No return at any hole.* Any hole for which a competitor makes no return shall be regarded as a loss in bogey and par competitions and as scoring no points in Stableford competitions.

(*b*) *Scoring cards.* The holes at which strokes are to be given or taken shall be indicated on the card issued by the Committee.

(*c*) *Recording scores.* In bogey and par competitions, the marker shall be responsible for marking only the gross number of strokes for each hole where the competitor makes a net score equal to or less than the fixed score. In Stableford competitions, the marker shall be responsible for marking only the gross number of strokes at each hole where the competitor's net score earns one or more points.

Note. *Maximum of 14 clubs—see Rule 3-2 and Rule 41-7.*

3. Disqualification Penalties

(*a*) *From the competition. A competitor shall be disqualified* from the competition for a breach of any of the following:

Rule 2—The Club and the Ball.

Rule 4—Agreement to Waive Rules Prohibited.

Rule 8-3—Practice before Round.

Rule 35-3*a*—Putting Green: Stroke Play, Ball Interfering with Play.

Rule 37-2—Caddie.

Rule 37-4—Handicap (playing off higher handicap than current one).

Rule 37-5—Time and Order of Starting.

Rule 37-6*a*—Discontinuance of Play.

Rule 37-7—Undue Delay (repeated offence).

Rule 37-8—Refusal to Comply with Rule.

Rule 37-9—Artificial Devices.

Rule 38-2—Checking Scores.

Rule 38-3—No Alteration of Scores, except that the competitor shall not be disqualified when a breach of this Rule does not affect the result of the hole.

(*b*) *For a hole.* In all other cases where a breach of a Rule would entail disqualification, *the competitor shall be disqualified only for the hole at which the breach occurred.*

(Modification of penalty—Rule 36-5.)

RULE 40
Three-Ball, Best-Ball and Four-Ball
Match Play

1. General

(*a*) *Rules of Golf apply.* The Rules of Golf, so far as they are not at variance with the following special Rules, shall apply to all three-ball, best-ball and four-ball matches.

(*b*) *Ball influencing play.* Any player may have any ball (except the ball about to be played) lifted if he consider that it might interfere with or be of assistance to a player or side, but this may not be done while any ball in the match is in motion.

(*c*) *Ball moved by another ball.* There is no penalty if a player's ball move any other ball in the match. The owner of the moved ball shall replace the ball.

(*d*) *Playing out of turn.* On the teeing ground, if a player play when an opponent should have played, the opponent may immediately require the player to abandon the ball so played and to play a ball in correct order without penalty. Through the green or in a hazard, a player shall incur no penalty if he play when an opponent should have done so. The stroke shall not be replayed.

On the putting green, if a player play when an opponent should have done so, the opponent may immediately require the player to replay the stroke in correct order, without penalty.

2. Three-Ball Match Play

In a three-ball match, each player is playing two distinct matches.

(*a*) *Ball stopped or deflected by an opponent accidentally.* If a player's ball be accidentally stopped or deflected by an opponent, his caddie or equipment, no penalty shall be incurred. In his match with that opponent, the player may play the ball as it lies or, before another stroke is played by either side, he may cancel the stroke, place a ball on the spot where the ball previously lay and replay the stroke. In his match with the other opponent, the occurrence shall be treated as a rub of the green (Def. 27) and the hole shall be played out with the original ball.

Exception. Ball striking person attending flagstick—Rule 34-3*b.*

(*Ball purposely stopped or deflected by opponent—Rule 17-4.*)

(*b*) *Ball at rest moved by an opponent.* If the player's ball be touched or moved by an opponent, his caddie or equipment (except as otherwise provided in the Rules), Rule 27-2*a* applies. *That opponent shall incur a penalty stroke in his match with the player*, but not in his match with the other opponent.

3. Best-Ball and Four-Ball Match Play

(*a*) *Order of play.* Balls belonging to the same side may be played in the order the side considers best.

(*b*) *Ball stopped by player's side.* If a player's ball be stopped or deflected by the player, his partner or either of their caddies or equipment, *the player is disqualified for the hole.* His partner incurs no penalty.

(*c*) *Ball stopped by opponent's side accidentally.* If a player's ball be stopped or deflected by an opponent, his caddie or equipment, no penalty shall be incurred. The player may play the ball as it lies or, before another stroke is played by either side, he may cancel the stroke, place a ball on the spot where the ball previously lay and replay the stroke.

Exception. Ball striking person attending flagstick—Rule 34-3*b.*

(*Ball purposely stopped or defected by opponent—Rule 17-4.*)

(*d*) *Wrong ball.* If a player play a stroke with a wrong ball (Def. 5) except in a hazard, *he shall be disqualified for that hole*, but the penalty shall not apply to his partner. If the wrong ball belong to another player, its owner shall place a ball on the spot from which the wrong ball was played, without penalty.

(*e*) *Partner's ball moved by player accidentally.* If a player, his partner, or either of their caddies accidentally move a ball owned by their side or by touching anything cause it to move (except as otherwise provided for in the Rules), *the owner of the ball shall incur a penalty stroke*, but the penalty shall not apply to his partner. The ball shall be replaced.

(*f*) *Ball moved by opponent's side.* If a player's ball be touched or moved by an opponent, his caddie or equipment (except as otherwise provided for in the Rules), *that opponent shall incur a penalty stroke*, but the penalty shall not apply to the other opponent. The player shall replace the ball without penalty.

(*g*) *Maximum of fourteen clubs. The side shall be penalised for a violation of* Rule 3 by either partner.

(*h*) *Disqualification penalties.—A player shall be disqualified from the match* for a breach of Rule 37-5 (Time and Order of Starting), but, in the discretion of the Committee, the penalty shall not necessarily apply to his partner (Definition 28—Note).

A side shall be disqualified for a breach of any of the following:

Rule 2—The Club and the Ball.

Rule 4—Agreement to Waive Rules Prohibited.

Rule 37-2—Caddie.

Rule 37-4—Handicap (playing off higher handicap than current one).

Rule 37-7—Undue delay (repeated offence).

Rule 37-9—Artificial Devices.

A player shall be disqualified for the hole in question and from the remainder of the match for a breach of Rule 37-6*a* (Discontinuance of Play), but the penalty shall not apply to his partner.

(Modification of penalty—Rule 36-5.)

(*i*) *Infringement assisting partner or affecting opponent.* If a player's infringement of a Rule or Local Rule might assist his partner's play or adversely affect an opponent's play, *the partner incurs the relative penalty in addition to any penalty incurred by the player.*

(*j*) *Penalty applies to player only.* In all other cases where, by the Rules or Local Rules, a player would incur a penalty, the penalty shall not apply to his partner.

(*k*) *Another form of match played concurrently.* In a best-ball or a four-ball match when another form of match is played concurrently, the above special Rules shall apply.

RULE 41
Four-Ball Stroke Play

1. Conditions

(*a*) The Rules of Golf, so far as they are not at variance with the following special Rules, shall apply to four-ball stroke play.

(*b*) In four-ball stroke play two competitors play as partners, each playing his own ball.

(*c*) The lower score of the partners is the score of the hole. If one partner fail to complete the play of a hole, there is no penalty.

(*Wrong score—Rule 41-8a.*)

(*d*) The marker is required to record at each hole only the gross score of whichever partner's score is to count. The partners are responsible for the correctness of only their gross scores for each hole. The Committee is responsible for recording the better-ball score for each hole, the addition and the application of the handicaps recorded on the card.

(*e*) Only one of the partners need be responsible for complying with Rule 38.

2. Ball Influencing Play

Any competitor may have any ball (except the ball about to be played) lifted or played, at the option of the owner, if he consider that it might interfere with or be of assistance to a competitor or side, but this may not be done while any ball in the group is in motion.

If the owner of the ball refuse to comply with this Rule when required to do so, *his side shall be disqualified.*

3. Balls to be at Rest

While the competitor's ball is in motion after a stroke on the putting green, any other ball shall not be played or touched.

4. Ball Struck by Another Ball

When the balls concerned lie on the putting green, if a competitor's ball strike any other ball *the competitor shall incur a penalty of two strokes* and shall play his ball as it lies. The other ball shall be at once replaced.

In all other cases, if a competitor's ball strike any other ball, the competitor shall play his ball as it lies. The owner of the moved ball shall replace his ball, without penalty.

5. Order of Play

Balls belonging to the same side may be played in the order the side considers best.

6. Wrong Ball

If a competitor play any strokes with a wrong ball (Def. 5) except in a hazard, *he shall add two penalty strokes* to his score for the hole and then play the correct ball Rule 21-3).

If the wrong ball belong to another player its owner shall place a ball on the spot from which the wrong ball was played without penalty.

7. Maximum of Fourteen Clubs

The side shall be penalised for a violation of Rule 3 by either partner.

8. Disqualification Penalties

(*a*) *From the competition. A competitor shall be disqualified* from the competition for a breach of any of the following, but the penalty shall not apply to his partner:

Rule 8-3—Practice before Round.

Rule 37-5—Time and Order of Starting.

A side shall be disqualified from the competition for a breach of any of the following:—

Rule 2—The Club and the Ball.

Rule 4—Agreement to Waive Rules Prohibited.

Rule 37-2—Caddie.

Rule 37-4—Handicap (playing off higher handicap than current one).

Rule 37-7—Undue Delay (repeated offence).

Rule 37-8—Refusal to Comply with Rule.

Rule 37-9—Artificial Devices.

Rule 38-2—Checking Scores.

Rule 38-3—No alteration of scores, i.e. when the recorded lower score of the partners is lower than actually played. If the recorded lower score of the partners is higher than actually played, it must stand as returned.

Rule 41-2—Ball Influencing Play, Refusal to Lift.

By both partners, at the same hole, of a Rule or Rules the

penalty for which is disqualification either from the competition or for a hole.

(*b*) *From the remainder of the competition. A competitor shall be disqualified for the hole in question and from the remainder of the competition* for a breach of Rule 37-6*a* (Discontinuance of Play), but the penalty shall not apply to his partner.

(*c*) *For the hole only.* In all other cases where a breach of a Rule would entail disqualification, *the competitor shall be disqualified only for the hole at which the breach occurred.*

(Modification of penalty—Rule 36-5.)

9. Infringement Assisting Partner

If a competitor's infringement of a Rule or Local Rule assist his partner's play, *the partner incurs the relative penalty in addition to any penalty incurred by the competitor.*

10. Penalty Applies to Competitor Only

In all other cases where, by the Rules or Local Rules, a competitor would incur a penalty, the penalty shall not apply to his partner.

NOTE. RULES OF GOLF (*The Royal and Ancient Golf Club of St Andrews*) *includes Appendices dealing in some detail with "Local Rules", "Design of Clubs and the Ball", "Markings on Clubs" and "The Rules of Amateur Status".*

The Rules of
Hockey

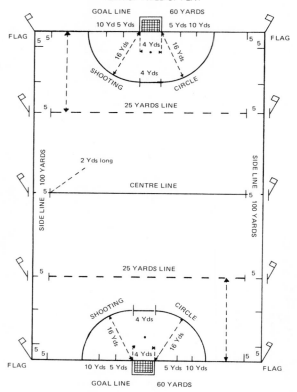

PLAN OF FIELD OF PLAY

The front of the goal-posts must be touching the outer edge of the goal-line. The circle lines and the goal-lines must be 3 in wide.

A white spot of not more than 6 in in diameter shall be marked 7 yd in front of the centre of each goal. All short indication marks must be inside the field only and shall be 12 in in length.

Hockey

Issued under the authority of the Hockey Rules Board

1. Teams and Duration of Play

(*a*) A game shall be played between two teams. Not more than eleven players of each team shall be on the field at the same time. At no time shall there be on the field more than one goalkeeper in each team.

(*b*) Each team is permitted to substitute up to two players during the game.

(*c*) No player once substituted shall be permitted on the field again, and no substitute shall be permitted for a suspended player during his suspension.

(*d*) Substitution of players may only take place with the prior permission of an umpire during any stoppage of play other than for the award of a corner, a penalty corner, or a penalty stroke. Time may be added for substitutions. If the player is also a goalkeeper, see Rules 15(*b*) and 16(*b*)(i).

(*e*) The duration of the game shall be two periods of thirty-five minutes each unless otherwise agreed before the game.

(*f*) At half-time the teams shall change ends, and the duration of the interval shall not exceed five minutes, unless otherwise agreed before the game, but it shall in no case exceed ten minutes.

(*g*) The game starts when the umpire blows his whistle for the opening bully. (See also Rule 10(*a*).)

2. Captains (see page 425 for experimental Rule 2(*a*))

The captains shall:

(*a*) Toss for the choice of ends;

(*b*) before the start of play and on any change, indicate, if necessary, to each other and to the umpires, their respective goalkeepers.

3. Umpires and Timekeepers

(*a*) There shall be two umpires to control the game and to

administer the rules. These umpires shall be the sole judges of fair and unfair play during the game.

(*b*) Unless otherwise provided, each team shall be responsible for providing one umpire.

(*c*) Each umpire shall be:

(i) primarily responsible for decisions in his own half of the field, for the whole of the game without changing ends.

(ii) solely responsible for decisions on the push-in for the full length of his nearer side-line.

(iii) solely responsible for decisions on corners, penalty corners, penalty strokes and goals in his own half and free hits in his own circle.

(*d*) The umpires shall be responsible for keeping time for the duration of the game. It shall be permissible to have a timekeeper or timekeepers. Such timekeepers shall take over only those duties of the umpires which concern the keeping of time and the indication of the end of each half.

(*e*) Umpires shall allow the full or agreed time and shall keep a written record of the goals as they are scored.

(*f*) Time shall be allowed for all enforced stoppages and, when necessary, extra time for the completion of a penalty stroke, and such time shall be added to that half in which the stoppage occurred.

(*g*) Umpires and timekeepers shall be debarred from coaching during a game and during the interval.

(*h*) Umpires shall only blow the whistle to:

(i) start and end each half of the game,

(ii) enforce a penalty or suspend the game for any other reason,

(iii) start and end a penalty stroke,

(iv) indicate, when necessary, that the ball has passed wholly outside the field of play,

(v) signal a goal,

(vi) re-start the game after a goal has been scored and after a suspension of play.

(*i*) Umpires shall satisfy themselves before the game that, as far as is practicable, Rules 4 to 9 inclusive are observed.

Umpires shall refrain from enforcing a penalty in cases where they are satisfied that by enforcing it an advantage would be given to the offending team.

4. Field of Play

(*a*) All lines used in the measurements of the field are to be 3 in. wide. The goal-lines and side-lines are part of the field of play.

(*b*) The field shall be rectangular, 100 yd long and 60 yd wide. Its boundaries shall be clearly marked out with lines in accordance with the Plan on page 410. The longer lines shall be called the side-lines and the shorter the goal-lines.

(*c*) The centre line shall be marked out, throughout its length. The 25-yd lines shall be marked with broken lines throughout their length.

(*d*) To assist in the control of the push-in, across the centre line and each 25-yd line, parallel to and 5 yd from the side-lines a mark 2 yd in length shall be made.

(*e*) A mark shall be placed inside the field of play on each side-line and parallel to the goal-line and 16 yd from its inner edge. The mark shall not exceed 12 in in length.

(*f*) For penalty corner hits, the field shall be marked inside the field of play on the goal-lines on both sides of the goal at 5 yd and 10 yd from the nearer goal-post. For corner hits the field shall be marked inside the field of play on the goal-lines, 5 yd on either side of the corner flags.

(*g*) A spot shall be marked 7 yd in front of the centre of each goal. The spot shall be of not more than 6 in diameter.

(*h*) No marks other than those shown on the Plan on page 410 are permissible on the playing surface.

(*i*) Flag posts, at least 4 ft and not more than 5 ft high, shall be placed for the whole game at each corner of the field at the centre and those at the centre shall be at least 1 yd outside the side-lines.

5. Goals, Posts, etc.

(*a*) There shall be a goal at the centre of each goal-line consisting of two perpendicular posts 4 yd (3.66 m) apart, joined together by a horizontal cross-bar 7 ft (2.14 m) from the ground (inside measurements). The front base of the goal-posts shall touch the outer edge of the goal-line. The goal-posts shall not extend upwards above the cross-bar, nor the cross-bar sideways beyond the goal-posts. The goal-posts and cross-bar shall be rectangular and shall be 2 in (5 cm) wide and not more than 3 in (8 cm) deep, and shall be painted white. Nets shall be attached firmly at intervals of not more than 6 in (15 cm) to the goal-posts and the cross-bar and shall be attached firmly to the ground behind the goal.

(*b*) A back-board 4 yd long and not exceeding 18 in (45 cm) high, shall be placed at the foot of and inside the goal-nets. Side-boards of a minimum length of 4 ft and not exceeding 18 in high shall be placed at right angles to the goal-lines. The side-boards shall be fixed to the back of the goal-posts so that the width of the goal-post is not effectively increased.

(*c*) No chocks shall be placed inside the goal to support any of the boards.

6. Shooting Circles

In front of each goal shall be drawn a line, 4 yd (3.66 m) long and 3 in (8 cm) wide, parallel to, and 16 yd (15 m) from, the goal-line. The 16 yd shall be measured from the inside front corner of the goal-posts to the outer edge of that line. This line shall be continued each way to meet the goal-lines by quarter circles having the inside front corner of the goal-posts as centres. The space enclosed by these lines, including the lines themselves, shall be called the shooting circle (hereinafter referred to as "the circle").

7. The Ball

(*a*) The cover of the ball shall be of white leather, or of any other leather painted white. It shall be sewn or it may be seamless.

(*b*) The inner portion of the ball shall be composed of cork and twine.

(*c*) The weight of the ball shall be not more than $5\frac{3}{4}$ oz (165 gm) and not less than $5\frac{1}{2}$ oz (155 gm).

(*d*) The circumference of the ball shall be not more than $9\frac{1}{4}$ in (24 cm) and not less than $8\frac{13}{16}$ in (23 cm).

(*e*) A ball of any other material or colour, but of the size and weight specified above, may be used, as agreed upon mutually before the game.

8. The Stick

(*a*) The stick shall have a flat face on its left-hand side only. The face of the stick is the whole of the flat side and that part of the handle for the whole of the length which is above the flat side.

(*b*) The head (i.e., the part below the lower end of the splice) shall be of wood. It shall not be edged with, nor have any insets or fittings of metal or any other substance, nor shall there be any sharp edges or dangerous splinters. It shall not be cut square or pointed, but shall have rounded edges.

(*c*) The total weight of the stick shall not exceed 28 oz (795 gm) for men, 23 oz (652 gm) for women, nor be less than 12 oz (340 gm), and the stick shall be of such a size (inclusive of any covering) that it can be passed through a ring with an interior diameter of 2 in (5.10 cm).

(*d*) Umpires shall forbid the use of any stick which does not comply with this Rule.

9. Players' Dress and Equipment

(*a*) Each player shall wear the dress approved by his Association or Club, unless varied to avoid confusion in a particular game. Players shall not have dangerous spikes, studs or protruding nails in footwear, or wear anything that may be dangerous to other players.

(*b*) The following equipment is permitted for use by goalkeepers only: Pads, Kickers, Gauntlet Gloves and Masks.

(*c*) Umpires shall forbid the wearing of anything which in their opinion does not comply with this Rule. (See Rule 3(i).)

Penalty. For any breach of this Rule any player concerned shall not be allowed on the field of play until such time as he has complied with this Rule.

10. The Bully (*see page 425 for experimental Rule 10*)

(*a*) A bully shall be played at the centre of the field to start the game, to re-start it after half-time and after a goal is scored. (See Rules 12 III and 18(*b*)(i).)

(*b*) To bully, a player of each team shall stand squarely facing the side-lines, each with his own goal-line on his right. The ball shall be placed on the ground between the two players. Each player shall tap with his stick first the ground between the ball and his own goal-line and then, with the flat face of his stick, his opponent's stick over the ball three times alternately, after which one of these two players shall play the ball with his stick to put it into general play.

(*c*) Until the ball is in general play, all other players shall be nearer to their own goal-line than the ball is, and shall not stand within 5 yd (4.5 m) of the ball.

(*d*) A bully in the circle shall not be played within 5 yd (4.5 m) of the goal-line.

Penalties. (i) For any breach of this Rule, the bully shall be played again.

(ii) For persistent breaches of this Rule, the umpire may award a free hit to the opposing team; or for such breaches in the circle by a defender, a penalty corner.

11. Scoring a Goal

(*a*) A goal is scored when the whole ball has passed completely over the goal-line between the goal-posts and under the cross-bar, the ball, within the circle, having been hit by, or having glanced off, the stick of an attacker except as specially provided for in Rule 15(*g*) and Rule 16. It is immaterial if the ball subsequently touch, or be played by one or more defenders. If, during the game, the goal-posts and/or the cross-bar become displaced, and the ball pass completely over the goal-line at a point which, in the umpire's opinion, be between where the goal-posts and/or under where the cross-bar, respectively, should have been, a goal is scored.

(*b*) The team scoring the greater number of goals shall be the winner.

12. Conduct of Play (*see page 426 for experimental Rules 12.I(c), 12.II(b)*)

I. A player shall not:
   (*a*) play the ball with the rounded side of his stick,
   (*b*) take part in or interfere with the game unless he has his

own stick in his hand, or change his stick for the purpose of taking part in the game under Rules 14, 15, 16, and 17 II and III.

"Own stick" means the stick with which the player began to play, or any stick that he legitimately substitutes for it.

(*c*) raise any part of his stick above his shoulder, either at the beginning or at the end of a stroke, when approaching, attempting to play, playing the ball, or stopping the ball.

(*d*) hit wildly into an opponent or play or kick the ball in such a way as to be dangerous in itself, or likely to lead to dangerous play,

(*e*) stop or deflect the ball on the ground or in the air with any part of the body *to his or his team's advantage* (save as provided for in Rule 12 II(*b*)).

(*f*) use the foot or leg to support the stick in order to resist an opponent,

(*g*) pick up, kick, throw, carry or propel the ball in any manner or direction except with the stick (but see Rule 12 II(*d*)),

(*h*) hit, hook, hold, strike at or interfere with an opponent's stick,

(*i*) charge, kick, shove, trip, strike at or personally handle an opponent or his clothing,

(*j*) obstruct by running between an opponent and the ball or interpose himself or his stick as an obstruction.

II. A player may:

(*a*) play the ball only with the flat side of his stick, which includes that part of the handle above the flat side,

(*b*) stop the ball with his hand or catch it. In the latter case the ball shall be released into play immediately,

(*c*) tackle from the left of an opponent provided that he play the ball without previous interference with the stick or person of his opponent (see Rule 12 I particularly (*h*), (*i*), (*j*),

(*d*) if he is goalkeeper, be allowed to kick the ball or stop it with any part of his body but only when the ball is inside his own circle. If in stopping a shot at goal the ball, in the umpire's opinion, merely rebound off his hand or body, no penalty shall be incurred.

III. If the ball become lodged in the pads of a goal-keeper (or in the clothing of any player or umpire) the umpire shall stop the game and restart it by a bully on the spot where the incident occurred (subject to Rule 10(*d*)). If the ball strike an umpire the game shall continue.

IV. *Misconduct. Rough or dangerous play, time-wasting or any other behaviour which in the Umpire's opinion amounts to misconduct shall not be permitted.*

Penalties.

1. *Outside the circle.*

A free hit shall be awarded to the opposing team. If the umpire be satisfied that the offence committed by any defender inside his own 25 yd (23 m) area was deliberate, he shall award a penalty corner.

2. *Inside the circle—by an attacker.*

A free hit shall be awarded to the defending team.

3. *Inside the circle—by a defender.*

A penalty corner or a penalty stroke shall be awarded to the attacking team.

4. *Inside and Outside the circle.*

(*a*) For a simultaneous breach of this Rule by two opponents, the umpire shall order a bully to be played on the spot where the breach occurred (subject to Rule 10(*d*)).

(*b*) For rough or dangerous play or misconduct, in addition to awarding the appropriate penalty, the umpire may:
  (i) warn the offending player(s) which may also be indicated by showing a green card,
  (ii) suspend him temporarily, for not less than five minutes (yellow card),
  (iii) suspend him from further participation in the game (red card).

A temporarily suspended player shall remain behind his own goal or in such other places as designated before the game, until allowed by the umpire by whom he was suspended, to resume play; when necessary changing ends at the start of the second half of the game.

13. Off-side

(*a*) A player of the same team as the striker, or pusher-in, is in an off-side position if, *at the moment when the ball is hit or pushed-in,* he be nearer to his opponents' goal-line than the ball is, unless he is in his own half of the field or there are at least two opponents nearer to their own goal-line than he is.

For the purpose of this Rule, a player of either team shall be deemed to be on the field of play even though he be outside the side-line or behind the goal-line.

(*b*) A player who is in an off-side position shall not play or attempt to play the ball or gain any advantage for his team or influence the play of an opponent.

Penalty. A free hit to the defending team.

14. Free Hit (*see page 426 for experimental Rule 14* (*b*), (*c*)

(*a*) A free hit shall be taken from the spot on which the breach occurred, except that for (i) a breach by an attacker within the circle, the free hit shall be taken either from any spot within that circle or from any spot within 16 yd (15 m) of the inner edge of the defending team's goal-line on a line drawn through the place where the breach occurred and parallel to the side-line. (ii) for a breach by an attacker outside the circle but within 16 yd of the defending team's goal-line, it shall be taken from any spot within 16 yd (15 m) of the inner edge of the defending team's goal-line on a line drawn through the place where the breach occurred and parallel to the side-line.

(*b*) The ball shall be stationary and the striker shall hit the ball, or push it along the ground.

(*c*) At the moment when a free hit is taken, no other player shall be within 5 yd (4.5 m) of the ball. If, however, in the opinion of the umpire, any player remain within 5 yd (4.5 m) of the ball, in order to gain time, he should not cause the hit to be delayed.

(*d*) If the striker hit at but miss the ball, he shall take the hit again, provided that he has not contravened Rule 12.I(*c*).

(*e*) After taking a free hit, the striker shall not approach within playing distance of the ball, until it has touched, or been played by, another player of either team.

Penalties.

1. *Inside the circle.* A penalty corner or a penalty stroke shall be awarded to the attacking team.

2. *Outside the circle.* A free hit shall be awarded to the opposing team. An umpire shall award a penalty corner for an offence by any defender in his own 25 yd area, when, in the umpire's opinion, the offence was deliberate.

15. Penalty Corner (*see page 427 for experimental Rule 15(d)* (*iii*), (*iv*)

(*a*) A player of the attacking team shall hit the ball or *push it along the ground* from a spot on the goal-line not less than 10 yd from the goal-post, on whichever side of the goal the attacking team prefers. The player concerned is not required to be wholly inside or outside the field of play when taking the corner.

(*b*) (i) At the moment when such hit or push is made, no other player shall be within 5 yd of the ball.

The rest of the attacking team shall have both sticks and feet outside the circle, in the field of play.

Not more than six of the defending team shall have both sticks and feet behind their own goal-line. The rest of the defending team shall stand beyond the centre line.

(ii) In the event of a goalkeeper being incapacitated or suspended, the Captain of the defending team shall immediately nominate another goalkeeper. This goalkeeper shall be permitted to put on, without undue delay, protective equipment if the previous goalkeeper was incapacitated, but not if he has been suspended when only a face mask and gloves may be added.

(*c*) Until the ball be hit or pushed no attacker shall enter the circle, nor shall a defender cross the goal-line or the centre line.

(*d*) No shot at goal shall be made from a penalty corner or from a deflection unless the ball first be stopped (not necessarily motionless) on the ground by an attacker or touch the stick or person of a defender.

(i) *If the ball has not previously been touched by a defender, or has not been stopped sufficiently on the ground, a flying hit, following a pass or deflection from one attacker to another, should be penalised as a breach of this Rule.*

(ii) *If the ball be stopped by the stick it need not be motionless before it is played but it must be on the ground.*

(iii) *If the hand is used to stop the ball on the ground, the ball must be stopped, motionless, and not to be moved in any direction by the hand.*

(iv) *If the hand is used to stop the ball in the air, the ball must drop perpendicularly and be motionless on the ground before a shot can be taken.*

(*e*) Having taken the penalty corner, the striker shall not approach within playing distance of the ball until it has been touched or played by another player of either team.

(*f*) If the striker of the penalty corner hit at but miss the ball, the penalty shall be taken again, provided that Rule 12.I(*c*) has not been contravened.

(*g*) No goal shall be scored directly by the player taking the penalty corner.

Penalties.

1. *For a breach of Rule* 15(*c*), *viz.:*

Attacker entering the circle or defenders crossing the goal-line or centre line too soon—the penalty corner may, at the discretion of the umpire, be taken again.

2. *For persistent breaches of Rule* 15(*c*) *by the attackers—* The umpire may award a free hit.

3. *For persistent breaches of Rule* 15(*c*) *by the defenders—* The umpire may award a penalty stroke.

4. *For any other breach of Rule* 15—A free hit shall be awarded to the defending team.

16. Penalty Stroke

(*a*) A penalty stroke shall be awarded to the opposing team if, in the opinion of the umpire:

(i) There has been an *intentional* breach of Rules 12 or 14 inside the circle, by a player of the defending team; or,

(ii) A goal would probably have been scored had an *unintentional* breach of Rule 12 inside the circle by a player of the defending team not occurred. (See also Rule 15(*c*) Penalties 3).

(*b*) (i) The penalty stroke shall be either a push, flick or scoop stroke taken from a spot 7 yd in front of the centre of the goal by a player of the attacking team and defended by the goalkeeping of the opposing team. In the event of the goalkeeper being incapacitated or suspended, the captain of the defending team shall immediately nominate another goalkeeper.

This goalkeeper shall be permitted to put on protective equipment if the previous goalkeeper was incapacitated, but not if he has been suspended. (See note 16 (*b*) (i).)

(ii) Whichever stroke is used, the ball may be raised to any height.

(iii) During the taking of a penalty stroke all the other players of both teams shall stand beyond the nearer 25-yd line.

(*c*) When taking the stroke the attacker shall stand close to the ball and shall be permitted in making the stroke to take one stride forward. The stride shall not be invalidated by reason of the rear foot moving, provided that it does not pass the front foot before the ball is moved. Dragging or lifting the rear foot is not a breach of this Rule.

He may touch the ball once only and thereafter shall not approach either the ball or the goalkeeper. The attacking player shall not take the penalty stroke until the umpire, having satisfied himself that both defender and attacker are ready, has indicated that he may do so by blowing his whistle.

(*d*) (i) The goalkeeper shall stand on the goal-line. After the player taking the stroke and the goalkeeper are in position, the goalkeeper may not leave the goal-line or move either of his feet until the ball has been played. (ii) He shall not be penalised, if, in stopping a shot at goal, the ball, in the opinion of the umpire, merely rebounds off his body or his hand. If the ball be caught and held by the goalkeeper, it shall be deemed to be at rest. (See also clause (*e*) (iii). He may not touch the ball with any part of his stick when the ball is above the height of his shoulder. The usual privileges of the goalkeeper shall be allowed to him but he shall not be allowed to delay the taking of the stroke by making unnecessary changes or modifications of clothing. (See Rule 16 (*b*) (i).)

Neither the goalkeeper nor the attacking player shall be allowed any change of dress or equipment between the award and the completion of the penalty stroke.

(iii) If any action by the striker, prior to striking the ball, induces the goalkeeper to move either of his feet or, if the striker feints at striking the ball, the stroke may be taken again.

(*e*) If, as a result of the penalty stroke:

(i) The ball passes wholly over the goal-line between the goal-posts and under the cross-bar, a goal is scored.

(ii) There is a breach of any rule by the goalkeeper which *prevents* a goal from being scored, the umpire shall award a goal, unless such breach shall have been induced by the striker as in the last paragraph of (*d*) (iii) above.

(iii) The ball should come to rest inside the circle be lodged in the goalkeeper's pads, be caught by the goalkeeper or pass outside the circle, in all cases the penalty stroke is ended. Unless a goal has been scored or awarded, the game shall be re-started by a free hit to be taken by a defender from a spot in front of the centre of the goal and 16 yd from the inner edge of that line.

(*f*) All time taken between the award of a penalty stroke and resumption of play shall be added to the time of play.

Penalties. 1 For a breach of this or any rule by an attacker, the game shall be re-started in accordance with clause (*e*) (iii) of this rule. 2 For a breach of clause (*b*) (iii) or (*d*) (i), the umpire may order the stroke to be taken again.

17. Ball Outside Field of Play (*see page 427 for experimental Rule 17*)

I. *Hit from* 16 *yd.* When the ball is sent over the goal-line by one of the attacking team, and no goal is scored, or, in the umpire's opinion, it is sent unintentionally over the goal-line by one of the defending team who is more than 25 yd from the goal-line, the game shall be re-started by a hit by one of the defending team from the spot exactly opposite the place where it crossed the goal-line and not more than 16 yd from the inner edge of that line.

Other than the striker, no player of either team shall be within 5 yd of the ball when the hit is taken.

The penalties of Rule 14 shall apply.

II. *Corner*. When the ball, in the umpire's opinion, is sent unintentionally over the goal-line by or off one of the defending team who is within his own 25 yd area, a corner shall be taken by the attacking team, unless a goal has been scored. The provision of Rule 15 shall apply to the corner, except that the player shall hit the ball, or *push it along the ground* from a spot on the goal-line or the side-line within 5 yd of the corner flag nearer to the point where the ball crossed the goal-line.

Penalties. 1, 2, 3 and 4 of Rule 15 shall apply except for 3 when the umpire may award a penalty corner for such breaches by a defender.

III. *Penalty Corner*. When the ball, in the umpire's opinion, is sent intentionally over the goal-line by a player of the defending team from any part of the field a penalty corner shall be awarded to the attacking team, unless a goal be scored.

The penalties of Rule 15 shall apply.

IV. *Push-in*.

(*a*) When the whole ball passes completely over the side-line, it, or another ball, shall be placed on the line at the spot at which it crossed the side-line. The ball shall be *pushed-in along the ground* without undue delay by a player of the team opposed to the player who last touched it in play. This player is not required to be wholly inside or outside the side-line when making his push.

(*b*) At the moment when the push-in is taken, no other player of either team shall be within 5 yd of the ball. If any player of either team be within 5 yd of the ball, the umpire may require the push to be taken again. If, however, in the umpire's opinion, any player remain within 5 yd of the ball to gain time, the push-in shall not be delayed.

(*c*) After taking a push-in the player shall not play the ball again, nor approach within playing distance of the ball until it has touched, or been played by, another player of either team.

Penalties. For any breach of the Rule:

1. By the player taking the push-in (other than for (*c*)) the push-in shall be awarded to the opposing team.

2. For (*c*) a free hit shall be awarded.

3. By any other player: the push-in shall be taken again, but for persistent breaches a free hit may be awarded to the opposing team.

18. Accidents

(*a*) If a player, or an umpire, be incapacitated, the umpire, or other umpire, shall suspend the game temporarily. In either case, if a goal be scored before the game has been suspended, it shall be allowed if, in the opinion of the umpire, it would have been scored had the accident not occurred.

(*b*) The umpire shall re-start the game as soon as possible, by:

(i) a bully (subject to Rule 10(*d*) on a spot to be chosen by the umpire in whose half of the ground the accident occurred, or (ii) the appropriate penalty when the accident was the result of a breach of the rules, or (iii) the implementation of a decision given before the game was stopped.

(*c*) If the umpire concerned cannot continue, the other umpire shall re-start the game.

EXPERIMENTAL RULES
(*effective from 1st September 1981*)

2. Captains

The captains shall:

(*a*) toss for choice of start. The winner of the toss shall have (i) the right to choose which end his team will attack in the first half, or (ii) the right to have possession of the ball at the start of the game.

The winner of the toss having made his choice, the opposing side will automatically have the second option. The team not having started the game will have possession of the ball for re-starting after half-time.

10. To Start or Re-start the Game

(*a*) To start the game, re-start it at half-time and after each goal scored, a "pass-back" shall be played at the centre of the field. The pass-back for the start of the game shall be made by a player of the team which did not make a choice of ends (see experimental Rule 2 (*a*)) after half-time and after a goal has been scored, by a player of the team against whom the goal has been awarded. The pass-back may not be directed over the centre-line.

All players of both teams other than the player making the pass-back must be in their own half of the field at a distance of at least 5 yd from the ball. Time wasting shall not be permitted.

  (*b*) (i) To re-start the game in accordance with Rule 12 III, Rule 12 Penalties 4 (*a*) or Rule 18 (*b*) (i), a bully shall be played on the spot where the incident occurred.

  (ii) To bully, as (*b*) of former Rule 10.

  (iii), (iv) As (*c*), (*d*) of former Rule 10.

Penalties: 1. For a breach of Rule 10(*a*) a free hit shall be awarded to the opposing team. 2. For a breach of Rule 10(*b*)(ii) or (iii), the bully shall be played again. 3. For persistent breaches of Rule 10(*b*) (ii) and (iii) the umpire may award a free hit to the opposing team; or, for such breaches in the circle by a defender, a corner.

12. Conduct of Play

A player shall not:

  I (*c*) raise his stick in a manner that is dangerous, intimidating or hampering to another player when approaching, attempting to play, playing or stopping the ball. A ball above the height of a player's shoulder shall not be played by any part of the stick.

(*Mandatory from 1st September 1982*)

  II (*b*) stop the ball with his hand or catch it. (For goal-keepers, see Rule 12 II(*d*).)

14. Free Hit

  (*b*) The ball shall be motionless and the striker shall push or hit it. The ball shall not be raised in such a way as to be dangerous in itself, or likely to lead to dangerous play.

  (*c*) At the moment when the free hit is taken, no player of the opposing team shall be within 5 yd of the ball. However, should the Umpire consider that a player is standing within 5 yd in order to gain time, the free hit shall not be delayed.

For a free hit awarded to the attacking team for a breach of the Rules within 5 yd of the circle, at the moment when the free hit is taken, *no player other than the striker shall be within 5 yd of the ball.*

15. Penalty Corner

(*d*) (iii), (iv) Use of hand not permitted.
(*Mandatory from 1st September 1982*)

17. Ball Outside Field of Play

The ball may be pushed in *or hit* from the side-line.

Also note that when the ball, in the Umpire's opinion, is sent unintentionally over the goal-line by or off one of the defending team who is within his own 25 yd area, a *hit* shall be taken by the attacking team, unless a goal has been scored. The player shall *hit* the ball from a spot on the goal-line within 5 yd of the corner flag nearer to the point where the ball crossed the goal-line. Other than the striker, *no player of either team shall be within 5 yd of the ball when the hit is taken.*

Penalties. 1. A free hit shall be awarded to the opposing team. 2. An Umpire shall award a penalty corner for an offence by any defender in his own 25 yd area when, in the Umpire's opinion, the offence was deliberate.

The Rules of
Ice Hockey

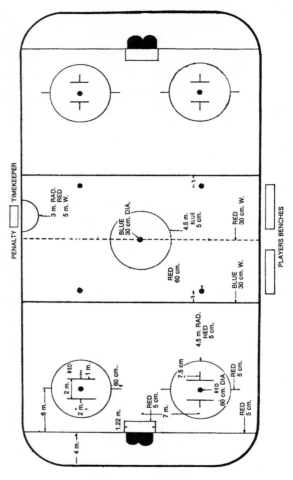

Refer to Rules 105, 106, 107 and 108.

Ice Hockey

I. THE RINK

101. Rink

The game of "Ice Hockey" shall be played on an ice surface known as a "RINK".

102. Dimensions of Rink

(*a*) The maximum size of the rink shall be 61 m long and 30 m wide with a minimum size of 56 m long and 26 m wide. The corners shall be rounded in the arc of a circle with a radius of 7 to 8.5 m.

The rink shall be surrounded by a wooden or plastic wall or fence known as the "boards" which shall extend not less than 1.15 m and not more than 1.22 m in height above the level of the ice surface.

Except for the official markings provided for in these rules, the entire playing surface and the boards shall be white in colour.

NOTE. *The above measurements must apply to the World and European Championships but for other International games and purely National games they may be varied. In enclosed rinks smoking shall be prohibited in the playing and spectator area.*

(*b*) The boards shall be constructed in such manner that the surface facing the ice shall be smooth and free of any obstruction or any object that could cause injury to players.

All doors giving access to the playing surface must swing away from the ice surface.

All protective screens and gear used to hold them in position shall be mounted on the boards on the side away from the playing surface.

NOTE. *Under this rule advertising may be placed on the boards provided specifications are approved and permission is given by the I.I.H.F. with regard to official international championships and by the National Federations with regard to national games and international games in their territory.*

103. Goals

(*a*) At a distance of 4 m from each end of the rink and in the centre of a red line 5 cm wide drawn completely across the width of the ice and continued vertically up the side of the boards, regulation goal posts and nets of approved design and materials, shall be placed in such a manner as to remain stationary during the progress of the game.

(*b*) The goal posts shall be of approved design and material, extending vertically 1.22 m above the surface of the ice and 1.83 m apart, measured from the inside of the posts. A cross bar of the same material as the goal posts shall extend from the top of one post to the top of the other.

(1) The inside measurement of the goal from the front of the goal line to the rear of the net, at its deepest point, shall not be more than 1 m or less than 60 cm.

(2) There shall be attached to the back of each goal frame a net constructed so as to keep the puck within the confines of the goal.

(*c*) The goal posts, cross bar and the exterior surface of other supporting framework for the goal shall be painted entirely in red. The surface of the base plate inside the goal and supports other than the goal posts shall be painted white.

(*d*) The red line, 5 cm wide, between the goal posts on the ice, and extended completely across the rink, shall be known as the "Goal Line".

(*e*) The goal area, enclosed by the goal line and the base of the goal, shall be painted white.

104. Goal Crease

(*a*) In front of each goal a "GOAL CREASE" area shall be marked by a red line 5 cm in width.

(*b*) The goal crease shall be laid out as follows: 30 cm from the outside of each goal post, lines 1.22 m in length and 5 cm in width shall be drawn at right angles to the goal line and the points of these lines farthest from the goal line shall be joined by another line 5 cm wide.

(*c*) The goal crease area shall include all the space outlined by the crease lines and extending vertically 1.22 m to the level of the top of the goal frame.

105. Division of Ice Surface

(*a*) The ice area between the goal lines shall be divided into three equal parts by blue lines 30 cm in width drawn completely across the surface and continued vertically up each side board.

(*b*) The portion of the ice surface in which the goal is situated shall be called the "DEFENDING ZONE" of the team defending the goal; the centre portion shall be known as the "NEUTRAL ZONE", and that portion farthest from the defended goal as the "ATTACKING ZONE". The zone line shall be considered part of the zone that the puck is in.

(*c*) There shall be a line, 30 cm in width and red in colour, marked on the ice midway between each goal line and extending completely across the rink, parallel to the goal lines and vertically up the side boards; this line shall be known as the "CENTRE LINE".

106. Centre Ice Spot and Circle

A circular blue spot, 30 cm in diameter, shall be marked on the ice in the centre of the rink; and with this spot as centre, a circle of 4.5 m radius shall be marked with a line 5 cm wide and blue in colour.

107. Face-off Spots in Neutral Zone

Two red spots 60 cm in diameter shall be marked on the ice in the neutral zone 1.5 m from each blue line and the same distance from the boards as the end zone face-off spots.

108. End Zone Face-off Spots and Circles

(*a*) In both end zones and on both sides of each goal, red face-off spots and circles shall be marked on the ice. The face-off spots shall be 60 cm in diameter and the circles shall be 5 cm wide with a radius of 4.5 m from the centre of the face-off spots. Extending from the outer edge of both sides of each face-off circle shall be two lines, 6.5 m and 6.5 m from and parallel to the goal line, 60 cm long and 5 cm wide.

On the opposite side of each end zone face-off spot, and 1.8 m and equal distance from the centre, shall be marked a "T" by a line 7.5 cm wide. The top of the "T" shall be 2 m long and parallel to the goal line. The "stem" of the "T" shall extend away from the centre of and perpendicular to the top of the "T" and be 1 m long.

(*b*) The location of the face-off spots shall be fixed in the following manner:

Establish an imaginary point 6 m directly in front of the centre of each goal. 7 m on each side of this point, parallel to and 6 m from the goal line, shall be the centre of the end zone face-off spots.

NOTE. *On open-air rinks all the lines and spots fixed in Rules* 105, 106, 107 *and* 108, *may be marked by two lines or circles in the prescribed distance.*

109. Players' Benches

(*a*) Each rink shall be provided with seats or benches for the use of players of both teams. Such seats or benches shall have accommodation for at least 14 persons of each team, and shall be placed immediately alongside the ice, in the neutral zone, as near to the centre of the rink as possible and convenient to the dressing rooms.

The players' benches should be on the same side of the playing surface opposite the penalty bench and should be separated by a substantial distance.

Where physically possible, each Players' Bench shall have two doors opening in the Neutral Zone, and all doors opening to the playing surface shall be constructed so that they swing inward.

(*b*) None but players in uniform, and not more than six team officials, shall be permitted to occupy the benches so provided.

(*c*) For the choice of players' benches, see Rule 634*b*

110. Penalty Bench

(*a*) Each rink must be provided with seats or a bench to be known as the "PENALTY BENCH". It is preferable to have separate penalty benches for each team separated from each other and substantially separated from either player's bench. The penalty bench(es) must be situated opposite the Neutral Zone.

(*b*) On the ice immediately in front of the penalty timekeeper's seat, there shall be marked a semi-circle, of 3 m in radius to be known as the "Referee's Crease".

111. Signal and Timing Devices

(*a*) Each rink shall be provided with a siren or other suitable sound device for the use of timekeepers.

(*b*) Each rink must be provided with some form of electrical clock in order that spectators, players and game officials will be accurately informed as to the time element at all stages of the game.

(*c*) Behind each goal electric lights shall be set up for the use of the Goal Judges. A red light shall signify the scoring of a goal. Where automatic lights are available, a green light will signify the end of a period, only.

NOTE. *The purpose of the green light is to enable the referee and linesmen to observe the goal and light in the same sight line and know exactly when the period ends.*

The red light shall be connected to the timing device in such a manner so that when the period has ended it will not be possible for the goal judge to put it on. However, the fact that the goal judge may not be able to put on the red light does not necessarily mean that the goal is not valid. The determining factor is whether or not the puck is completely over the goal line and in the goal before the period ends.

112. Dressing Rooms and Rink Lighting

(*a*) Each rink shall provide a suitable dressing room, equipped with sanitary toilet and shower, suitable for twenty-five persons with equipment, for the use of the visiting team.

(*b*) A separate dressing room shall be provided for the use of the referees and linesmen, which room shall be equipped with sanitary toilet and shower.

(*c*) No officer, manager, player or employee of any team may enter into an acrimonious discussion with any referee or linesmen, during or after a game and no person, except as authorised by the Federation concerned, shall be allowed to enter the referees' dressing room during the course of or immediately following a game. For any infraction of this rule the matter shall be reported by the referees to the proper authorities for further action.

(*d*) All rinks shall be sufficiently well lighted so that the players and spectators may conveniently follow play at all times.

NOTE. *If in the opinion of the referees there is not sufficient light to continue the game, the referees shall have the authority to postpone the remainder of the game or take time out pending the necessary improvement to the lights. If one team is being handicapped to a greater extent by failure of lights, and in the opinion of the referees the game should not be cancelled, they shall have the authority to alternate the teams so that each team will play the same amount of time at each end of the rink.*

II. TEAMS

201. Composition of Teams

(*a*) A team shall not have more than six players on the ice at any one time. These six players shall be designated as follows:— Goalkeeper, Right Defence, Left Defence, Centre, Right Wing and Left Wing.

(*b*) If at any time a team has more than six players on the ice, or the number to which they are entitled by reason of penalties, during the progress of play, they shall be assessed a bench minor penalty.

202. Captain of Team

(*a*) Each team shall appoint a Captain and he alone shall have the privilage of discussing with the Referee any questions relating to interpretation of rules which may arise during the progress of a game. He shall wear the letter "C" approximately 8 cm in height, in contrasting colours and in a conspicuous position on the front or sleeve of his sweater. If such a letter is not worn, the privileges under this section will not be allowed. If the captain is not available due to injury or an imposed penalty, another player who was designated on the score sheet prior to the start of the game may act as captain.

(*b*) The referee and official scorer shall be advised prior to the start of each game, the name of the captain of the team and designated substitute.

(*c*) No goalkeepers shall be entitled to the privileges of a captain.

(*d*) Only the Captain shall have the privilege of discussing with the Referee any point relating to the interpretation of rules. Any other player who comes off the bench and makes any protest or intervention with the Officials for any purpose shall be assessed a misconduct penalty in addition to a minor penalty under Rule 601 (*a*) Abuse of Officials.

A complaint about a penalty is *not* a matter "relating to the interpretation of the rules" and a minor penalty under Rule 601 (*a*) Abuse of Officials shall be imposed against any Captain or other player making such a complaint.

(*e*) No playing coach or playing manager shall be permitted to act as captain.

203. Players in Uniform

(*a*) At the beginning of each game the Manager or Coach of each team shall list the players and goalkeepers who shall be eligible to play in the game. A maximum of 18 players, plus two goalkeepers, shall be permitted.

(*b*) Each player shall wear an individual number at least 25 cm in height on the back of his sweater.

All players of each team shall be dressed uniformly in colour of their helmet, sweaters, pants and stockings. Any player not complying with this provision shall not be permitted to participate in the game.

(*c*) A list of names and numbers of all eligible players and goalkeepers shall be handed to the Referee or Official Scorer before the game, and no change shall be permitted in the list or addition thereto shall be permitted after the commencement of the game.

(*d*) Each team shall be allowed one goalkeeper on the ice at one time. The goalkeeper may be removed and another "player" substituted. Such substitute shall not be permitted the privileges of the goalkeeper.

(*e*) Each team shall have on its bench, or on a chair immediately beside the bench, a substitute goalkeeper who shall at all times be fully dressed and equipped ready to play.

The substitute goalkeeper may enter the game at any time following a stoppage of play, but no warm-up shall be permitted (see Rule 205).

(*f*) Except when both goalkeepers are incapacitated, no player on the playing roster in that game shall be permitted to wear the equipment of the goalkeeper.

(*g*) In all games when, in the opinion of the Referee, the colours of the competing teams are so much alike that there is the possibility of a miscall by the Referee or Linesman, it is the responsibility of the home team to change its sweaters if the Referee so orders.

204. Starting Line-up

(*a*) Prior to the start of the game, at the request of the referee, the manager or coach of the visiting team is required to name the starting line-up to the referee or official scorer; and at any time, at the request of the referee, must place a playing line-up on the ice and promptly commence play.

NOTE. *If in competitions the name of the home team has not been established, the competing teams will decide who is to be the home team by mutual agreement, that is, by the flip of a coin or some similar method.*

(*b*) Prior to the start of the game, the manager or coach of the home team, having been advised by the official scorer or the referee of the names of the starting line-up of the visiting team, shall name the starting line-up of the home team, which information shall be conveyed by the official scorer or the referee to the coach of the visiting team.

(*c*) No change in the starting line-up of either team, as given to the referee or official scorer, or in the playing line-up on the ice, shall be made until the game is actually in progress.

(*d*) Following the stoppage of play, the visiting team shall promptly place a line-up on the ice ready for play and no substitution shall be made from that time until play has been resumed. The home team may then make any desired substitution which does not result in the delay of the game.

205. Change of Players

(*a*) Players may be changed at any time from the players' bench, provided that the player or players leaving the ice shall be at the players' bench and out of play before any change is made.

A goalkeeper may be changed for another player at any time under the conditions set out in this section.

(*b*) If in the last two minutes of the game a Bench Minor penalty is imposed for deliberate illegal substitution (too many men on the ice) a penalty shot shall be awarded against the offending team. The Bench Minor will not be served.

(*c*) A player serving a penalty on the penalty bench, who is to be changed after his penalty has been served, must proceed at once by way of the ice and be at the players' bench before any change can be made.

For violation of this rule a Bench Minor penalty shall be imposed.

(*d*) When a substitution for the goalkeeper has been made during a stoppage of play, the goalkeeper who left the game may not re-enter the game until the first stoppage of play thereafter. There shall be no warm-up for any substitute goalkeeper.

For a violation of this rule a minor penalty shall be assessed.

206. Injured Players

(*a*) When a player, other than a goalkeeper, is injured or compelled to leave the ice during a game, he may retire from the game and be replaced by a substitute, but play must continue without the teams leaving the ice.

(*b*) If a goalkeeper sustains an injury, or for any other reason has to leave the ice, he shall immediately be replaced by the spare goalkeeper.

If both goalkeepers of the team are incapacitated and unable to play, the team shall have ten minutes to prepare and dress another player in uniform to act as the goalkeeper. In this case neither of the two regular goalkeepers may return to that game.

(*c*) If a penalised player has been injured, he may proceed to the dressing room without the necessity of taking a seat on the penalty bench but it is necessary to place a substitute for him on the penalty bench.

NOTE. *In the case where it is obvious that a player has sustained a serious injury the referee may stop play immediately.*

III. EQUIPMENT

301. Sticks

(*a*) The sticks shall be made of wood or other material approved by the I.I.H.F. and must not have any projections.

(*b*) Sticks shall not exceed 147 cm from the heel to the end of the shaft and 32 cm from the heel to the end of the blade.

The blade of the stick shall not be less than 5 cm nor greater than 7.5 cm in width, except in the case of the goalkeeper's stick. The curvature of the blade of the stick shall be restricted in such a way that the distance of a perpendicular line measured from a straight line drawn between the heel and the end of the blade to the point of maximum curvature shall not exceed 1.5 cm.

(*c*) The blade of the goalkeeper's stick shall not exceed 9 cm in width at any point except the heel, where it shall not exceed 11.5 cm and the wide portion of the shaft shall not exceed 71 cm from the heel.

(*d*) A Minor penalty shall be imposed on any player or goalkeeper who uses a stick which does not conform to the provisions of this rule.

302. Skates

(*a*) All skates (except goalkeepers') shall be equipped with safety heel tips.

(*b*) The use of speed skates or fancy skates or any skates so designed that they may cause injury is prohibited.

303. Goalkeeper's Equipment

(*a*) With the exception of skates and stick, all the equipment worn by the goalkeeper must be constructed solely for the purpose of protection of the head or body, and must not include any garment or contrivance which would give the goalkeeper undue assistance in keeping goal.

NOTE. *Cages on gloves and abdominal aprons extending down the front of the thighs on the outside of the pants are prohibited. A "cage" shall mean any lacing or webbing or other material in the goalkeeper's glove joining the thumb and index fingers which is in excess of the minimum necessary to fill the gap when the goalkeeper's thumb and forefinger in the glove are fully extended and spread, and includes any pocket or pouch effect produced by excess lacing or webbing or other material between the thumb and forefinger when fully extended. Protective padding attached to the back or forming part of goalkeeper's gloves shall not exceed 20.3 cm in width nor 40.6 cm in length at any point.*

(*b*) The leg guards worn by goalkeepers shall not exceed 25 cm in extreme width when on the legs of the goalkeeper. No further expansion than one-tenth (2.5 cm) shall be permitted for any leg guards used by goalkeepers.

(*c*) A Minor penalty shall be imposed on a goalkeeper guilty of using or wearing illegal equipment.

304. Protective Equipment

(*a*) All protective equipment, except gloves, headgear or goalkeeper's leg guards, must be worn *entirely* under the uniform. For violation of this rule, after one warning by the referee, a Minor penalty shall be imposed on the offending player.

(*b*) All players including goalkeepers must wear a hockey headgear, with chin strap properly fastened.

(*c*) All goalkeepers must wear goalkeeper's face masks.

(*d*) Face masks may be worn provided they are not dangerous to other players. Full face masks shall be worn in all I.I.H.F. sanctioned games and 18 and under-18 tournaments.

NOTE. *National Federations are authorised, at their discretion, to make the wearing of approved headgear compulsory for Referees and Linesmen.*

305. Dangerous Equipment

The use of pads or protectors made of metal or any other material likely to cause injury to a player is prohibited.

NOTE. *Football helmets with face protector or mask arrangement or baseball masks are not permitted to be worn by any player. Face and mouth guards permitted, provided they are not dangerous to other players.*

306. Puck.

The puck shall be made of vulcanized rubber or other approved material, 2.54 cm thick and 7.62 cm in diameter, and shall be approved by the I.I.H.F. The puck shall weigh not less than 5.5 oz (156 gm) or more than 6 oz (170 gm).

IV. PENALTIES

401. Penalties

Penalties shall be in actual playing time and shall be divided into the following classes:

(1) Minor Penalties.
(2) Bench Minor Penalties.
(3) Major Penalties.
(4) Misconduct Penalties.
(5) Match Penalties.
(6) Penalty Shot.

NOTE. *When play is not actually in progress and an offence is committed by any player, the same penalty shall apply as though play was actually in progress.*

When penalties are imposed after the conclusion of any game and until the players have left the ice, such penalties shall be reported to the proper authorities by the referees on the official game report.

In cases where any rule states that the manager or coach shall designate a player to serve any penalty and the manager or coach refuses to name a player, the referee shall have the authority to name any player of the offending team that he desires to serve the penalty.

402. Minor Penalties

(*a*) For a "Minor" penalty, any player, except a goalkeeper, shall be ruled off the ice for two minutes, during which time no substitute shall be permitted.

(*b*) A "Bench Minor" penalty involves the removal from the ice of one player of the team against which the penalty is imposed for a period of two minutes. Any player bar goalkeeper may be designated to serve the penalty by the manager or coach through the playing captain and such player shall take his place on the penalty bench promptly and serve the penalty as if it was a Minor penalty imposed upon him.

(*c*) If while a team is "short handed" by one or more Minor or Bench Minor penalties the opposing team scores a goal, one of such penalties shall automatically terminate.

NOTE. *"Short handed" means that the team must be below the numerical strength of its opponents on the ice at the time the goal is scored. When the minor penalties of two players of the same team terminate at the same time, the captain of that team shall designate to the referee which of such players will return to the ice first and the referee will instruct the penalty timekeeper accordingly. When a player receives a Major penalty and a Minor penalty at the same time, the Major penalty shall be served first by the penalised player.*

403. Major Penalties

(*a*) For the first "Major" penalty in any one game except to the goalkeeper, the offender shall be ruled off the ice for five minutes, during which time no substitute shall be permitted.

(*b*) For the second "Major" penalty in the same game to the same player, he shall be ruled off the ice for the balance of the playing time, but a substitute shall be permitted after five minutes have elapsed. (Major penalty plus a Misconduct penalty.)

404. Misconduct Penalty

(*a*) "Misconduct" penalties to all players, except goalkeepers, involve removal from the game for a period of ten minutes each. A substitute player is permitted to replace immediately a player serving a Misconduct penalty. A player whose Misconduct penalty has expired shall remain in the penalty box until the next stoppage of play.

(*b*) A Game Misconduct penalty involves removal for the balance of the game and the offender shall be ordered to the dressing room for the remainder of the game, but a substitute shall be permitted immediately.

NOTE. *A Game Misconduct penalty does not incur automatic suspension, except for that game, but such penalties shall be reported by the Referee to the proper authorities concerned immediately following the game who shall have the power to increase the suspension period.*

(*c*) A "Gross Misconduct" penalty involves the suspension of a player or team official for the balance of the game. Any player or team official incurring it shall be suspended from participating in any further games until his case has been dealt with by the proper authorities.

405. Match Penalties

(*a*) A "Match" penalty involves the suspension of a player for the balance of the game and the offender shall be ordered to the dressing room immediately. Ten minutes shall be charged against the offending player.

(*b*) Any player incurring a Match penalty shall not be permitted to take part in any further games until his case has been dealt with by the proper authorities concerned as soon as possible.

406. Penalty Shot

(*a*) Any infraction of the rules which calls for a "Penalty Shot" shall be taken as follows: the puck shall be placed on the centre face-off spot, midway between the side boards, and the player designated by the team captain of the non-offending team will, at the instruction of the referee, play the puck from there and shall, without interruption, attempt to score on the goalkeeper.

(*b*) The goalkeeper must remain in his goal crease until the player taking the penalty shot has touched the puck, and in the event of violation of this rule or any foul committed by the goalkeeper, the Referee shall allow the shot to be completed, and if the shot fails, he shall permit it to be retaken. The goalkeeper must then attempt to stop the puck or player in any legal manner. If he should throw his stick at the puck carrier, a goal shall be awarded (see Rule 635).

(*c*) In cases where a penalty shot has been awarded under:

Rule 608*c*, deliberately displacing the goal during a break-away, or Rule 617*c*, hooking from behind, or Rule 619*e*, interference, or Rule 623*i*, illegal entry into the game, or Rule 635*a*, throwing stick, or Rule 638*b*, tripping from behind ... the Referee shall designate the player who has been fouled as the penalty-taker.

Where the penalty shot has been awarded under:

Rule 205*b*, deliberate illegal substitution with two minutes or less remaining in the game, or Rule 608*c*, displacing the goal in the last two minutes, or Rule 611*c*, falling on the puck in the crease, or Rule 614*d*, picking up the puck from the crease ... the penalty shot shall be taken by a player selected by the Captain of the non-offending team from the players on the ice at the time the foul was committed.

(*d*) Should the player to whom the penalty shot has been awarded, himself commit a foul in connection with the same play or circumstances, either before or after the penalty shot has been awarded, he shall first take the penalty shot before being sent to the penalty bench to serve the penalty except when such a penalty is for a Game Misconduct, Gross Misconduct or Match penalty in which case the opposing Captain shall select a player from those on the ice when the offence was committed.

(*e*) While the penalty shot is being taken, players of both teams must withdraw, behind the centre red line.

(*f*) If, while the penalty shot is being taken any player of the opposing team shall by some action interfere with or distract the player taking the shot, thus causing the shot to fail, a second attempt shall be permitted and the referee shall impose a Misconduct penalty on the player so interfering or distracting.

(*g*) If a goal is scored from a penalty shot, the puck shall be faced at centre ice in the usual way. If a goal is not scored, the puck shall be faced at either end face-off spots in the zone in which the penalty shot has been tried.

407. Goalkeeper's Penalties

(*a*) No goalkeeper shall be sent to the penalty bench for an offence which incurs a Minor, Major or Misconduct penalty; instead such penalty shall be served by *any player of his team who was on the ice when the offence was committed.*

(*b*) Should a goalkeeper incur a second Major penalty in the same game, he shall also receive a Game Misconduct penalty.

(*c*) Should a goalkeeper incur a Game Misconduct penalty, he shall be replaced by the substitute goalkeeper or by a member of his team, who shall be permitted ten minutes to dress in the goalkeeper's full equipment.

(*d*) As in (*c*) should a goalkeeper incur a Match penalty but any additional penalties as specifically called for by the individual rules covering Match penalties will apply and the offending team shall be penalised accordingly. Such additional penalty shall be served by another member of the team on the ice at the time the offence was committed.

(*e*) A Minor penalty shall be imposed on a goalkeeper who leaves his crease during an altercation.

(*f*) If a goalkeeper participates in the play in any manner when he is beyond the centre red line, he shall be assessed a Minor penalty.

408. Delayed Penalties

(*a*) If a third player of any team is penalised while two other players of the same team are serving penalties, the penalty time of the third player shall not commence until the penalty time of one of the two players already penalised shall have ended. Nevertheless the third player penalised must at once proceed to the penalty bench, but may be replaced on the ice by a substitute until such time as the penalty time of the penalised player shall commence.

(*b*) When any team shall have three players serving penalties at the same time and because of the Delayed Penalty Rule, a substitute is on the ice, none of the three penalised players on the penalty bench may return to the ice until the play has been stopped. When play has been stopped the player(s) whose full penalty has expired may return to the ice.

(*c*) In the case of delayed penalties, the referee shall instruct the penalty timekeeper that penalised players whose penalties have expired shall only be allowed to return to the ice when there is a stoppage of play.

(*d*) When a Major and a Minor penalty are imposed at the same time against different players of the same team, the penalty timekeeper shall record the Minor penalty as being the first penalty imposed.

409. Calling of Penalties

(*a*) Should an infraction of the rules which would call for a penalty be committed by a player of the side in possession of the puck, the referee shall immediately stop play and give the penalty to the offending player.

(*b*) Should an infraction of the rules which would call for a penalty be committed by a player of the team not in possession of the puck, the Referee shall signify the calling of a penalty by raising his arm and on completion of the play by the team in possession, will immediately blow his whistle and give the penalty to the offending player.

NOTE. *If after the Referee has signalled a penalty but before the whistle has been blown the puck shall enter the goal of the non-offending side by the action of any member of the non-offending team the goal shall be allowed and the penalty shall be imposed in the normal manner.*

If when a team is "short handed" by reason of one or more Minor or Bench Minor penalties the Referee signals a further Minor penalty against the short handed team and a goal is scored by the non-offending side before the whistle is blown then the goal shall be allowed, and the delayed penalty shall not be assessed.

(*c*) If any other fouls are committed on the same play or after the referee has stopped play, the offending players shall be penalised. If the same player commits one or more fouls on the same play or following stoppage of play he shall be penalized for all fouls and serve his penalties consecutively.

V. OFFICIALS

501. Appointment of Officials

(*a*) For all International matches there shall be appointed one Referee and two Linesmen, one Game Timekeeper, one Penalty Timekeeper, one Official Scorer and two Goal Judges for each game.

National Federations have the authority to use the Two Referee system in games which are completely under their jurisdiction.

502. Referee

(*a*) The Referee shall have general supervision of the game, and shall have full control of all game officials and players during the game, including stoppages; and in case of any dispute, his decision shall be final. The Referee shall remain on the ice at the conclusion of each period until all players have proceeded to their dressing rooms.

(*b*) All Referees and Linesmen shall be garbed in black trousers and official sweaters. They shall be equipped with approved whistles and metal tape measures with minimum length of 2 m.

(*c*) The Referee shall order the teams on the ice at the appointed time for the beginning of a game, and at the commencement of each period. If for any reason there be more than fifteen minutes' delay in the commencement of the game or any undue delay in resuming play after the fifteen-minute interval between periods, the Referee shall state in his report to the proper authorities the cause of the delay, and the team or teams which were at fault.

(*d*) The Referee may, at his own discretion, measure any equipment. The Referee shall check or measure the equipment worn by any player when requested to do so by the Captain of either team.

(*e*) The Referee shall, before starting the game, see that the appointed Game Timekeeper, Penalty Timekeeper, Official Scorer and Goal Judges are in their respective places, and satisfy himself that the timing and signalling equipment are in order.

(*f*) It shall be his duty to impose such penalties as are prescribed by the rules for infractions thereof, and to give the final decision in matters of disputed goals. The Referee, in matters of disputed goals, may consult with the Linesmen or Goal Judge before making his decision.

(*g*) The Referee shall announce to the Official Scorer or Penalty Timekeeper all goals and assists legally scored, as well as penalties, and for what infractions such penalties are imposed.

The Referee shall cause to be announced over the public address system the reason for not allowing a goal whenever the goal signal light is turned on in the course of play. This shall be done at the first stoppage of play regardless of any standard signal given by the Referee when the goal signal light was put on in error.

The Referee shall report to the Official Scorer the name or number of the goal scorer and any players entitled to assists.

The infraction of the rules for which each penalty has been imposed will be announced correctly, as reported by the Referee, over the public address system. Where players of both teams are penalised on the same play, the penalty to the visiting player will be announced first.

(*h*) The Referee shall see to it that players of opposing teams are separated on the penalty bench to prevent feuding.

(*i*) Should a Referee accidentally leave the ice or receive an injury which incapacitates him from discharging his duties while play is in progress, the game shall be stopped immediately by the linesman, unless one of the teams has the puck in a scoring position, in which case the play shall be allowed to be completed. If it is obvious that the injury sustained is of a serious nature, play shall be stopped immediately.

(*j*) If, through misadventure or sickness, the Referee or Linesmen appointed are prevented from appearing, the team leaders of the two teams shall agree on a Referee and Linesmen. If they are unable to agree, the Proper Authorities shall appoint the officials.

(*k*) If the regularly appointed officials appear during the progress of the game, they shall at once replace the temporary officials.

(*l*) Should a Linesman appointed be unable to act at the last minute or through sickness or accident be unable to finish the game, the Referee shall have the power to appoint a replacement, if he deems it necessary.

(*m*) If, owing to illness or accident, the Referee is unable to continue to officiate, one of the Linesmen shall perform such duties of the Referee during the balance of the game, the Linesman to be selected by the Referee, or, if necessary, by the team leaders of the competing teams.

(*n*) The Referee shall secure, from the Official Scorer, the Game Report immediately following each game. He shall sign and check this report and return same to the Official Scorer.

(*o*) The Referee is required to report on the Official Game Report all Game Misconducts, Gross Misconducts, and Match penalties immediately following the game involved giving full details to the Proper Authorities concerned.

503. Linesman

(*a*) The duty of the Linesman is to determine any infractions of the rules concerning:

Off-side—Rule 625 Off-side

Off-side Pass—Rule 626 Passes

Icing—Rule 618 Icing the Puck

He shall stop the play when the puck:

—goes out of the playing area—Rule 627(*a*), Puck Out of Bounds or Unplayable;

—when it is interfered with by any ineligible person—Rule 620, Interference by Spectators;

—when it is struck with the stick above the height of the shoulder—Rule 615(*d*), High Sticks;

—when the goal post has been displaced from its normal position—Rule 608, Delaying the Game.

He shall stop the play:

—for off-sides occurring on face-off circles—Rule 610, Face-Offs;

—when there has been a premature substitution for a goal-keeper—Rule 205, Change of Players;

—for injured player(s)—Rule 206, Injured players;

—interference by spectators—Rule 620, Interference by Spectators.

(*b*) He shall conduct the face-off at all times, except at the start of the game, at the beginning of each period and after a goal has been scored.

The Referee may call upon a linesman to conduct a face-off at any time.

(*c*) He shall, when requested to do so by the Referee, give his version of any incident that may have taken place during the playing of the game.

(*d*) He shall not stop play to impose any penalty except for violations of:

—too many men on the ice—Rule 201(*b*) Composition of Teams.

—articles thrown on the ice from vicinity of the players' or penalty bench—Rule 601(*b*); Abuse of Officials and other Misconduct;

—stick thrown onto the ice from the players' or penalty bench—Rule 605, Broken Stick;

and he shall report such violations to the Referee who shall impose a Bench Minor penalty against the offending team.

He shall report immediately to the Referee his version of the circumstances with respect to deliberately displacing the goal post from its normal position—Rule 608, Delaying the Game.

He shall report immediately to the Referee his version of any infraction of the rules constituting a bench minor penalty, a major or match foul, or misconduct, game misconduct or gross misconduct penalty.

504. Two Referees

(*a*) The Referees shall have general supervision of the game, and shall have full control of all game officials and players during the game, including stoppages; and in case of any dispute, their decision shall be final. The Referees shall remain on the ice at the conclusion of each period until all players have proceeded to their dressing rooms.

(*b*) All Referees shall be garbed in black trousers and official sweaters.

They shall be equipped with approved whistles and metal tape measures with minimum length of 2 m.

(*c*) The Referees shall order the teams on the ice at the appointed time for the beginning of a game, and at the commencement of each period. If, for any reason, there be more than fifteen minutes' delay in the commencement of the game or any undue delay in resuming play after the 15-minute intervals between periods, the Referees shall state in their report to the proper authorities the cause of the delay, and the team or teams which were at fault.

(*d*) The Referees may, at their own discretion, measure any equipment. The Referee shall check or measure the equipment worn by any player when requested to do so by the Captain of either team.

(*e*) The Referees shall, before starting the game, see that the appointed Game Timekeeper, Penalty Timekeeper, Official

Scorer and Goal Judges are in their respective places, and satisfy themselves that the timing and signalling equipment are in order.

(*f*) It shall be their duty to impose such penalties as are prescribed by the rules for infractions thereof, to stop play for any other infraction of the rules, and to give the final decision in matters of disputed goals. The Referees may, in matters of disputed goals, consult with the Goal Judge before making a decision.

(*g*) The Referees shall announce to the Official Scorer or Penalty Timekeeper all goals and assists legally scored as well as penalties, and for what infractions such penalties are imposed.

The Referees shall cause to be announced over the public address system the reason for not allowing a goal whenever the goal signal is turned on in the course of play. This shall be done at the first stoppage of play regardless of any standard signal given by the Referees when the goal signal light was put on in error.

The Referees shall report to the Official Scorer the name or number of the goal scorer and any players entitled to assists.

(*h*) The Referees shall see to it that players of opposing teams are separated on the penalty bench to prevent feuding.

(*i*) Should a Referee accidentally leave the ice or receive an injury which incapacitates him from discharging his duties while play is in progress the game shall be stopped immediately by the other Referee, unless one of the teams has the puck in a scoring position, in which case the play shall be allowed to be completed. If it is obvious that the injury sustained is of a serious nature, play shall be stopped immediately.

(*j*) If, through misadventure or sickness, both Referees appointed are prevented from appearing, the team leaders of the two clubs shall agree on Referees.

If they are unable to agree, the Proper Authorities shall appoint the Officials.

(*k*) If the regularly appointed Officials appear during the progress of the game, they shall at once replace the temporary officials.

(*l*) Should one of the appointed Referees be unable to act at the last minute or through sickness or accident be unable to finish the game, the other Referee shall have the power to appoint a replacement, if he deems it necessary.

(*m*) The Referees shall secure from the Official Scorer the Game Report immediately following each game. They shall sign and check this report and return it to the Official Scorer.

(*n*) The Referees are required to report on the Official Game Report all Game Misconducts, Gross Misconducts and Match penalties immediately following the game involved, giving full details to the Proper Authorities concerned.

505. Goal Judges

(*a*) There shall be one Goal Judge behind each goal. They shall not be permitted to be members of either competing team, nor shall they be replaced during the progress of the game, unless after the commencement of the game it becomes apparent that either goal judge, on account of partisanship or any other cause, is guilty of giving unjust decisions. In such cases the referee(s) may replace him.

(*b*) They shall be stationed behind the goals during the progress of play, in properly screened cages, so that there can be no interference with their activities and they shall not change ends at any time during the game.

(*c*) The goal judge shall decide if the puck has passed between the goal posts and completely over the goal line and give the appropriate signal.

The Referee shall give the final decision on a disputed goal. He may consult with the Goal Judge or the Linesmen before making his decision.

506. Penalty Timekeeper

The Penalty Timekeeper shall keep the time served by each penalised player during the game. He shall, upon request, give information to the penalised player as to the unfinished time of his penalty; also he shall advise the Referee(s) when the same player has received his second Major Misconduct penalty.

507. Official Scorer

(*a*) The Official Scorer shall keep, on the official form provided, a correct record of the goals scored, by whom scored, and to whom assists if any are to be credited. He shall also keep a correct record of all penalties imposed by the referee(s), stating the names and numbers of the penalised players, the length of each penalty and the infraction for which the penalty was given.

(*b*) The official scorer, upon the completion of each game, shall sign the official game report, have it signed by each referee, after which he shall forward the report to the proper authority concerned by the quickest possible means.

Also, see Rules 203 and 204.

508. Game Timekeeper

(*a*) The Game Timekeeper shall record the time of the starting and finishing of each game and all actual playing time during the game.

(*b*) The game timekeeper shall signal the referee(s) for the commencement of the game, for the start of the second and third periods and any overtime period or periods. He shall allow fifteen minutes intermission between each period after which the referee(s) shall start play. He shall also signal by ringing a gong, siren or by blowing a whistle, the ending of each period, any overtime period or periods and the ending of the game. This applies in rinks that are not provided with an automatic gong or siren, or if the automatic gong or siren should fail to operate.

(*c*) Where a public address system is used, the game timekeeper shall announce when only *one minute* of actual playing time remains in the first and second period, and *two minutes* remain in the third period and overtime.

(*d*) In the event of any dispute regarding time, the referee's decision shall be final.

VI. PLAYING RULES

601. Abuse of Officials and Other Misconduct

(*a*) Any player who challenges or disputes the rulings of any official during the game shall be assessed a Minor penalty for unsportsmanlike conduct. For persistence, a Misconduct penalty and then a Game Misconduct penalty would follow.

(*b*) If any player is guilty of any one of the following, his team shall be assessed a Bench Minor penalty: (1) for not proceeding immediately to the dressing room or penalty bench when so ordered by the Referee; (2) for using obscene, profane or abusive language to any person, or using the name of any official coupled with any such remarks while off the playing surface; (3) for throwing anything on to the ice from the players' or penalty bench during the game or a stoppage; (4) for interfering in any manner while off the playing surface, with a game official, including the Referee, Linesman, Timekeepers or Goal Judges in the performance of their duties.

(*c*) Any player who is guilty of any one of the following shall be assessed a Misconduct penalty: (1) for using obscene, profane or abusive language to any person on the ice or anywhere in the rink, except in the immediate vicinity of the players' bench (see (*b*) 2); (2) for intentionally knocking or shooting the puck out of reach of an official who is retrieving it; (3) for deliberately throwing any equipment, except the stick (see Rule 635*c*) out of the playing area; (4) for banging the board with his stick or any other instrument; (5) for failing to proceed immediately to the penalty bench after a fight or other altercation in which he has been involved and for which he is penalised; (6) after a warning by the Referee, for persisting in any course of conduct designed to incite an opponent into incurring a penalty; (7) for entering or remaining in the Referee's crease while the Referee is consulting with any game official, except for the purpose of taking his place on the penalty bench.

(*d*) A player will incur a Misconduct or Game Misconduct penalty for: (1) touching or holding with his stick or hands, tripping or body checking a game official; (2) throwing a stick out of the rink; (3) continuing or attempting to continue a fight or altercation after he has been ordered to stop.

(*e*) Any player shall be assessed a Game Misconduct if he is guilty of: (1) persisting in any course of conduct for which he has previously been assessed a Misconduct penalty; (2) using obscene gestures on the ice or anywhere in the rink before, during or after the game.

(*f*) Any player guilty of (1) any manner of behaviour which makes a travesty of, interferes with or is detrimental to the conducting of the game, or (2) attempts to injure or deliberately injure a game official, shall be assessed a Gross Misconduct penalty.

(*g*), (*h*) and (*i*) Team officials are also liable to penalties for various types of misbehaviour.

602. Adjustment of Equipment

(*a*) Play shall not be stopped nor the game delayed for the adjustment of any equipment.

(*b*) The onus of maintaining equipment in proper condition shall be upon the player. If adjustments are required, the player shall retire from the ice and play shall continue.

(*c*) No delay shall be permitted for the repair or adjustment of goalkeeper's equipment. He shall retire from the ice, his place taken by the substitute goalkeeper who will be permitted no warm-up.

(*d*) For an infraction of this rule, a Minor Penalty shall be imposed.

603. Attempt to Injure or Deliberate Injury

(*a*) A Match penalty shall be imposed on any player who deliberately attempts to injure or injures an opponent.

(*b*) A Gross Misconduct penalty shall be imposed on any player who attempts to injure or deliberately injures a team official.

604. Board Checking (Boarding)

A Minor or Major penalty, at the discretion of the referee based upon the violence of the impact with the boards, shall be imposed on any player who body-checks, cross-checks, elbows, charges or trips an opponent in such a manner that causes the opponent to be thrown violently into the boards.

605. Broken Stick

(*a*) A player without a stick may participate in the game. A player whose stick is broken may participate in the game provided he drops the broken portions. A Minor penalty shall be imposed for an infraction of this rule.

(b) A goalkeeper may continue to play with a broken stick until stoppage of play or until he is legally provided with a stick.

(c) A player whose stick is broken may not receive a stick thrown on the ice from any part of the rink.

A goalkeeper may receive a stick from a team-mate without proceeding to his players' bench (d) but shall incur a Minor penalty if he goes to the players' bench.

606. Charging

(a) A Minor or Major penalty shall be imposed on any player who runs or jumps into or charges an opponent.

(b) A Major penalty shall be imposed on any player who charges a goalkeeper while the goalkeeper is within his crease.

607. Cross-checking

(a) A Minor or Major penalty at the discretion of the referee shall be imposed on any player who cross-checks an opponent.

(b) A Major penalty shall be imposed on any player who injures an opponent as the result of a cross-check.

NOTE. *"Cross-check" means a check delivered with both hands on the stick and no part of the stick on the ice.*

608. Delaying the Game

(a) A Minor penalty shall be imposed on any player who deliberately shoots or bats with his hand or stick or throws the puck outside the playing area during or after a stoppage of play.

(b) A Minor penalty shall be imposed on any player who by any action deliberately upsets or knocks a goal from its position.

(c) A Bench Minor penalty shall be imposed on a team which, in the opinion of the referee, is deliberately delaying the game in any manner.

609. Elbowing and Kneeing

(a) A Minor or Major penalty at the discretion of the referee shall be imposed on any player who uses his elbow or knee to foul an opponent.

(*b*) Injury caused to an opponent by elbowing or kneeing shall incur a Major penalty.

610. Face-offs

(*a*) The puck shall be "faced" by the referee or linesman dropping the puck on the ice between the sticks of the players "facing". Players taking the face-off will stand squarely facing their opponents' end of the rink with their feet beside one another and parallel to the side of the rink approximately one-stick length from the face-off spot and with the full blade of their sticks on the ice. No other player shall be allowed to enter the face-off circle or come within 4.5 m of the players "facing" the puck and must stand "on-side" on all face-offs. The sticks of both players facing off shall have the full blade on the ice and be entirely clear of the spot or place where the puck is to be dropped.

If a violation of this sub-section of this rule occurs, the referee or linesman shall stop the play and conduct another face-off *unless* the non-offending team gained possession of the puck.

(*b*) If, after being warned, either player fails to take his proper position for the face-off, the referee or linesman shall be entitled to face-off the puck notwithstanding.

(*c*) In the conduct of any face-off anywhere on the playing surface, no player facing-off shall make physical contact with his opponent's body with his own body or stick, except in the course of playing the puck after the face-off has been completed. For violation of this rule a Minor penalty or penalties shall be imposed on the player(s) whose action(s) caused the physical contact.

(*d*) If a player facing-off fails to take his proper position immediately when directed by the referee or linesman, the referee or linesman may order him replaced for that face-off by any player on the ice.

(*e*) If a second violation of this rule occurs at the same face-off, by a player of the same team, the referee shall impose a Minor penalty on the player who commits the second offence.

(*f*) When an infringement of a rule has been committed or a stoppage of play has been caused by any player of the attacking team in their attacking zone, the ensuing face-off shall take place in the neutral zone at the nearest face-off spot.

NOTE. *This includes stoppage of play caused by a player of the attacking side shooting the puck on to the back of the defending team's goal net without any opposition from the defending team.*

(*g*) When an infringement of any rule has been committed by the players of both teams, the ensuing face-off shall be at the place where stoppage occurred, unless stated otherwise in the rules.

(*h*) When a stoppage of play has been caused by a defending player in his defending zone, the face-off shall take place where the stoppage occurred, unless otherwise stated in the rules.

(*i*) When a stoppage of play occurs between the end face-off spots and the nearest end of the rink, the face-off shall be at the nearest end face-off spot, unless otherwise stated in the rules.

(*j*) No face-off shall be made within 6 m of the goal or closer to the side-boards than the end-zone and neutral zone face-off spots.

(*k*) When a goal is illegally scored as the result of the puck being deflected *directly* off an official the face-off shall be at the end face-off spot in the defending zone.

(*l*) When play is stopped for any reason not specifically covered in the official rules, the face-off shall be where stoppage occurred.

(*m*) The whistle shall not be blown by the official to start play. Playing time shall start from the instant the puck is faced-off.

611. Falling on the Puck

(*a*) A Minor penalty shall be imposed on any player, except a goalkeeper, who deliberately falls on or gathers the puck into his body.

(*b*) A Minor penalty shall be imposed on a goalkeeper who deliberately falls on or gathers the puck into his body or who holds or places the puck against any part of the goal or against the boards when the puck is behind the goal line and when the goalkeeper's body is entirely outside the boundaries of his own crease area.

(*c*) No defending player, except the goalkeeper, shall be permitted to fall on the puck or hold it or gather it into his body or hands when it is within the goal crease. For such an infringement, play shall immediately be stopped and a penalty shot imposed against the offending team.

612. Fisticuffs

(*a*) A Match penalty shall be imposed on any player who starts fisticuffs.

(*b*) If the attacked player fights back a Major penalty shall be imposed. However, at the discretion of the referee, a Double Minor, Major or Match penalty may be imposed, if such player continues the altercation.

(*c*) A Minor or Double Minor penalty may be imposed on any player deemed guilty of unnecessary roughness.

(*d*) A Game Misconduct penalty shall be imposed on any player or players involved in fisticuffs off the playing surface. If one player is on the ice and one is off the ice, both shall be considered "on the ice" for the application of this rule.

(*e*) Any player who is the first to intervene in an altercation then in progress will incur a Game Misconduct penalty.

613. Goal and Assists

(*a*) A goal shall be scored when the puck shall have been put between the goal posts by the stick of a player of the attacking team, from in front and below the cross bar and entirely across the goal line.

(*b*) A goal shall be scored if the puck is put into the goal in any manner by a player of the defending team. The player of the attacking team who last played the puck shall be credited with the goal, but no assist shall be given.

(*c*) If an attacking player kicks the puck and it is deflected into the goal by a defending player except the goalkeeper, the goal shall be allowed. The player who kicked the puck shall be credited with the goal, but no assist shall be given.

(*d*) If the puck shall have been deflected into the goal from the shot of an attacking player by striking the stick or any part of the person or skates of another attacking player, the goal shall be allowed. The player from whom the puck was deflected shall be credited with the goal. The goal shall *not* be allowed if the puck shall have been kicked, thrown or otherwise deliberately directed into the goal by any means other than a stick.

(*e*) A goal shall not be allowed if the puck has been deflected directly into goal off an official.

(*f*) Should a player propel the puck into the goal crease of the opposing team and the puck should become loose and available to another attacking player, a goal scored on this play shall be legal.

(*g*) Unless the puck is in the goal crease area, a player of the attacking side may not stand on the goal crease line or in the goal crease or hold his stick in that area, and if the puck should enter the goal while such condition prevails (except as in (*h*) of this rule) a goal shall not be allowed, and the puck shall be faced in the neutral zone at the face-off spot nearest the attacking zone of the offending team.

(*h*) If a player of the attacking side has been physically interfered with by the action of any defending player so as to cause him to be in the goal crease, and the puck should enter the goal while he is still there, the "goal" shall be allowed—unless, the Referee deems he had sufficient time to get out of the crease but stayed there of his own accord.

(*i*) Any goal scored, other than as covered by the official rules, shall not be allowed.

(*j*) A goal shall be credited in the scoring records to a player who shall have propelled the puck into the opponents' goal. Each goal shall count one point in the scoring records.

(*k*) When a player scores a goal an assist shall be credited to the player or players taking part in the play immediately preceding the goal, but not more than two assists shall be given on any one goal. Each assist so credited shall count one point in the scoring records.

614. Handling the Puck with Hands

(*a*) A player, except the goalkeeper, shall not close his hand on the puck.

(*b*) No goalkeeper shall be permitted to hold the puck in his hands for longer than 3 seconds or in any manner which, in the Referee's opinion causes a stoppage of play; throw the puck forward towards his opponents' goal which is first played by a team mate; deliberately drop the puck into his pads.

(c) For violation of this rule he shall be assessed a Minor penalty.

(d) A Minor penalty shall be imposed on a defending player (except a goalkeeper) who picks up the puck off the ice with his hand. However if the puck was in the goal crease at the time of the violation a penalty shot shall be awarded to the opposing team.

(e) A player shall be permitted to stop or bat a puck in the air with his open hand, or push it along the ice with his hand and the play shall not be stopped, unless in the opinion of the referee he has deliberately directed the puck to a team mate, in which case play shall be stopped and the face-off shall be at the spot where the offence occurred. If this violation is committed by an attacking player in his attacking zone the face-off shall be at the nearest neutral zone face-off spot.

615. High Sticks

(a) The carrying of sticks above the normal height of the shoulders is prohibited, and a Minor penalty may be imposed on any player violating this rule, at the discretion of the referee.

(b) A goal scored from a stick so carried shall not be allowed, except by a player of the defending team.

(c) When a player carries or holds any part of his stick above the height of his shoulder so that injury to the face or head of any opponent results, the referee shall have no alternative but to impose a Major penalty on the offending player.

(d) Batting the puck above the normal height of the shoulders with the stick is prohibited and when it occurs play shall be stopped and a face-off conducted at the spot where the offence occurred unless:

(1) the puck is batted to an opponent in which case the play shall continue, or
(2) a player of the defending side shall bat the puck into his own goal in which case the goal shall be allowed, or
(3) the offence was committed by an attacking player in his attacking zone, in which case the face-off shall be at the nearest neutral zone face-off spot.

616. Holding an Opponent

A Minor penalty shall be imposed on any player who holds an opponent with his hands or stick or in any other manner.

617. Hooking

(*a*) A Minor penalty shall be imposed on a player who impedes or seeks to impede the progress of an opponent by "hooking" with his stick.

(*b*) A Major penalty shall be imposed on any player who injures an opponent by "hooking".

618. Icing the Puck

(*a*) For the purpose of this rule the centre line will divide the ice into halves. Should any player of a team shoot, bat or deflect the puck from his own half beyond the goal line of the opposing team, and it is first touched by a defending player other than the goalkeeper, play shall be stopped and the puck faced off at the end face-off spot of the offending team nearest to where they last touched the puck, unless on the play the puck shall have entered the net of the opposing team, in which case the goal shall be allowed.

(*b*) If a player of the team shooting the puck, who is "onside" and eligible to play it, is the first to touch it, the play shall continue and icing shall not be called.

(*c*) If the puck was so shot by a player of a side below the numerical strength of the opposing team, play shall continue and icing shall not be called.

(*d*) If, however, from a face-off, the puck shall go beyond the goal line at the other end of the ice, it shall not be considered a violation of the rule.

(*e*) If, in the opinion of the Linesman, a player of the opposing team excepting the goalkeeper is able to play the puck before it passes his goal line, but has not done so, icing shall not be called, and play shall continue.

If, in the opinion of the Referee, the defending side intentionally abstains from playing the puck promptly when in a position to do so, he shall stop play and order a face-off on the end-zone face-off spot nearest the defenders' goal.

(*f*) If the puck shall touch any part of a player of the opposing side or his skates or stick, or if it passes through any part of the goal crease before it shall have reached his goal line, or shall have touched the goalkeeper, or his skates or stick, before or after crossing that line it shall not be considered as "icing the puck" and play shall continue.

(*g*) If the referee or linesman shall have erred in calling an "icing infraction, the puck shall be faced on the centre ice face-off spot.

619. Interference

(*a*) A Minor penalty shall be imposed on a player who interferes with or impedes the progress of an opponent who is not in possession of the puck, or who deliberately knocks a stick out of an opponent's hands or who prevents an opponent who has dropped his stick or any other piece of equipment from regaining possession of it, or who knocks or shoots any abandoned or broken stick or other debris towards an opposing puck carrier to distract him (see also Rule 635*a*).

NOTE. *The last player to touch the puck—by body, stick or skates—other than the goalkeeper—shall be considered the player in possession. In interpreting this rule the referee should make sure which of the players is the one creating the interference—often it is the action and movement of the attacking player which causes the interference since the defending players are entitled to "stand their ground" or "shadow" the attacking players. Players of the side in possession shall not be allowed to "run" deliberate interference for the puck carrier.*

(*b*) A Minor penalty shall be imposed on any player on the players' bench or on the penalty bench who by means of his stick or his body interferes with the movements of the puck or any opponent on the ice.

(*c*) A Minor penalty shall be imposed on any player who by means of his stick or body interferes with or impedes the movements of a goalkeeper who is within his goal crease area, unless the puck is in the goal crease.

NOTE. *By* actual contact *is meant that the goalkeeper is touched by the attacking players' stick or body.*

(*d*) If, when the goalkeeper has been removed from the ice, any member of his team (including himself) not legally on the ice, including any team official, interferes by any means with the movements of the puck or an opposing player, the Referee shall immediately award a goal to the non-offending team.

(*e*) When a player in control of the puck on the opponents' side of the centre red line, and having no opponent to pass other than the goalkeeper, is interfered with by a stick or part thereof or any other object thrown or shot by any member of the defending team, including the team official, a penalty shot shall be awarded to the non-offending side.

620. Interference by Spectators

(*a*) In the event of a player being held or interfered with by a spectator the referee shall stop play, unless the team of the player being interfered with is in possession of the puck and in a scoring position at this time, when play shall be allowed to be completed before stoppage. In either case the face-off shall be where stoppage took place.

(*b*) Any player who physically interferes with a spectator shall, at the Referee's discretion, be assessed a Gross Misconduct penalty and reported to the authorities.

(*c*) In the event that objects are thrown on the ice which interfere with the progress of play, the referee shall stop play and when play is resumed the face-off shall be where stoppage took place.

621. Kicking a Player

A Match penalty shall be imposed on any player who kicks or attempts to kick an opponent.

622. Kicking the Puck

Kicking the puck shall be permitted in all zones but a goal may not be scored direct by the kick of an attacking player. If a puck so kicked is deflected into the goal by any player of the defending team, except the goalkeeper, the goal will be allowed.

623. Leaving the Players' or Penalty Bench

(*a*) No player may leave the players' or penalty bench at any time during an altercation. Substitutions made prior to the altercation shall be permitted provided the players so substituting do not enter the altercation.

(*b*) The first player to leave the players' or penalty bench during an altercation shall be assessed a Double Minor penalty and a Game Misconduct. If players of both teams leave their respective benches at the same time, the first identifiable player of each team shall be penalised under this rule.

(*c*) Any other player(s) (those not penalised under (*b*) above) who leave the players' bench during an altercation shall be assessed a Misconduct penalty up to a maximum of five Misconducts per team.

(*d*) Any player(s) (other than in (*b*) above) who leaves the players' bench and incurs a Minor, Major or Misconduct for his actions shall be automatically assessed a Game Misconduct.

(*e*) Except at the end of each period or on expiration of a penalty, no player may leave the penalty bench at any time.

(*f*) A penalised player who leaves the penalty bench before his penalty time has expired shall be assessed a Minor penalty (except for *g* below) to be served at the expiration of his previous penalty. If the violation occurred during a stoppage of play and an altercation was taking place, he shall also be assessed a Game Misconduct in addition to the Minor.

If the player is penalised under (*b*) he shall not be assessed any penalties under the first two instances of (*f*).

(*g*) If a player leaves the penalty bench before his penalty is fully served, the Penalty Timekeeper shall note the time and advise the Referee at the first stoppage of play. If the player returned to the ice prematurely because of an error of the timekeeper, he shall not be assessed an additional penalty but must serve the amount of time remaining in his penalty when he restarted the game.

(*h*) If a player shall illegally enter the game from his own players' bench or from the penalty bench by his own or the official's error, any goal scored by his own team while he is illegally on the ice shall be disallowed, but all penalties imposed against either team shall be served as regular penalties.

(*i*) If a player of an attacking team in possession of the puck shall be in such a position as to have no opposition between him and the opposing goalkeeper and while in such a position he shall be interfered with by a player of the opposing team who shall have illegally entered the game, the referee shall award a penalty shot against the offending team.

(*k*) Any team official who goes on the ice during any period without permission of the Referee shall be assessed a Game Misconduct.

624. Molesting Officials

(*a*) Any player who touches or holds a referee, linesman or any game official shall receive a Misconduct, Game Misconduct or Gross Misconduct penalty at the discretion of the referee.

(*b*) Any team official who holds or strikes an official shall be assessed a Gross Misconduct penalty.

625. Off-sides

(*a*) Players of an attacking team may not precede the puck into the attacking zone.

(*b*) For a violation of this rule, play shall be stopped and a face-off conducted.

If the puck was carried over the blue line at the time of the violation, the face-off shall take place at the nearest neutral zone face-off spot to where the puck crossed the line. If the puck was passed or shot over the blue line, the face-off shall be where the shot or pass originated.

(*c*) The position of the player's skates and not that of his stick shall be the determining factor in all instances in deciding an "off-side". A player is "off-side" when both skates are completely over the blue line into his attacking zone.

NOTE. *It should be noted that while the position of the players' skates is what determines whether a player is off-side, nevertheless the question of an off-side never arises until the puck has completely crossed the line into the attacking zone at which the decision is to be made.*

(*d*) If, however, notwithstanding the fact that a member of the attacking team shall have preceded the puck into the attacking zone, the puck is intercepted by a defender at or near the blue line, and is carried or passed by the defenders into the neutral zone, the "off-side" shall be waived.

(*e*) If a player legally carries or passes the puck back into his own defending zone while a player of the opposing team is in that zone, the "off-side" shall be waived.

(f) If, in the opinion of the Linesman, an intentional off-side play has been made, the puck shall be faced at the end face-off spot in the defending zone of the offending team.

626. Passes

(a) The puck may be passed by any player to a player of the same team within any one of the three zones into which the ice is divided, but may not be passed by a player from his defensive zone to a player of the same team who is on the opposite side of the centre red line unless the puck preceded the receiving player across the centre line.

(b) For a violation of this rule, play shall be stopped and the face-off shall be at the spot from which the pass originated or the nearest face-off location.

(c) Should the puck, having been passed, contact any part of the body, stick or skate of a player between the passing players' defensive zone and the centre red line, it shall nullify any violation of this rule.

(d) If the Linesman errs in calling an off-side pass infraction the puck shall be faced-off at the centre face-off spot.

627. Puck Out of Bounds or Unplayable

(a) When the puck goes outside the playing surface or strikes obstacles above the playing surface, except the boards, glass or netting, the face-off shall be where it last touched a player, his stick or skates, except when otherwise stated in the rules.

(b) When the puck becomes lodged in the netting on the outside of either goal and is not playable, or if it is frozen against the goal between opposing players intentionally or otherwise, the referee shall stop the play and the face-off shall be at either end face-off spots in that zone. If, in the opinion of the referee, an attacking player is responsible for the stoppage, the face-off shall be at the nearest face-off spot in the neutral zone.

(c) A Minor penalty shall be imposed on a goalkeeper who deliberately drops the puck on to the goal netting to cause a stoppage of play.

(*d*) If the puck comes to rest on top of the board surrounds, it shall be considered to be in play and may be played legally by hand or stick.

628. Puck Must be Kept in Motion

(*a*) The puck must be kept in motion at all times.

(*b*) Except to carry the puck behind its goal once, a team in possession of the puck in its defending zone shall always advance the puck towards the opposing goal, except when it shall be prevented from doing so by players of the opposing team. For the first infraction of this rule play shall be stopped and the face-off shall be at either end face-off spots adjacent to the goal of the team causing the stoppage, and the referee shall warn the captain of the offending team of the reason for the face-off. For a second violation by any player of the same team in the same period, a Minor Penalty shall be imposed on the player responsible.

(*c*) A Minor penalty shall be imposed on any player who holds the puck against or moves alongside the boards or in any manner holds the puck against any part of the goal, unless he is being checked by an opponent.

(*d*) A player outside his defence shall not pass or carry the puck backward into his own defence zone for the purpose of delaying the game.

(*e*) For violation of this rule the face-off shall be at either end face-off spot in the defending zone of the offending team.

629. Puck Out of Sight and Illegal Puck

(*a*) Should a scramble take place or a player accidentally fall on the puck, and the puck be out of sight of the referee, play shall immediately be stopped and the face-off shall be at the spot where play was stopped, unless otherwise stated in the rules.

(*b*) If at any time while play is in progress, a puck, other than the one legally in play, shall appear on the playing surface, the play shall not be stopped, but shall continue with the legal puck until the play then in progress is completed.

630. Puck Striking Officials

Play shall not be stopped if the puck touches a referee or linesman anywhere on the rink, regardless of whether a team is short-handed or not, except when the puck has entered the goal in which case a face-off shall take place at the nearest end zone face-off spot.

631. Refusing to Start Play

(*a*) If, when both teams are on the ice, one team for any reason, shall refuse to play when ordered to do so by the Referee, he shall warn the Captain and allow the team so refusing thirty seconds within which to begin the game or resume play. If, at the end of that time the team shall still refuse to play, the Referee shall impose a Bench Minor penalty on the offending team, and the case shall be reported to the proper authorities for further action.

Should there be a recurrence of the same incident, the Referee shall have no alternative but to declare that the game is forfeited to the non-offending team, and the case shall be reported to the proper authorities for further action.

(*b*) If a team, when ordered to do so by the referee, through its captain, manager or coach, fails to go on the ice and start play within two minutes, the game shall be forfeited to the opposing team and the case shall be reported to the Federation concerned for further action.

632. Slashing

(*a*) A Minor or Major penalty, at the discretion of the referee, shall be imposed on any player who impedes or seeks to impede the progress of an opponent by "slashing" with his stick.

(*b*) A Major penalty shall be imposed on any player who injures an opponent by "slashing".

NOTE. *Referees should penalise for "slashing" any player who swings his stick at any opposing player (whether in or out of range) without actually striking him or where a player on a pretext of playing the puck makes a wild swing at the puck with the object of scaring an opponent.*

(*c*) Any player who swings his stick at another player in

the course of any altercation shall be subject to a Major or Match penalty.

633. Spearing or Butt-ending

(*a*) A minor or major penalty shall be imposed on a player who spears, attempts to spear, butt-ends, or attempts to butt-end, an opponent. When a penalty is imposed for butt-ending or spearing, the offending player shall also receive an automatic misconduct penalty.

NOTE 1. *"Spearing" shall mean stabbing an opponent with the point of the stick blade whether or not the stick is being carried with one or both hands.* 2. *"Attempt to Spear" shall include all cases where a spearing gesture is made, regardless of whether or not contact is made.* 3. *"Attempt to butt-end" shall include all cases where a butt-end gesture is made, regardless of whether or not actual contact is made.*

(*b*) If an injury results from spearing or butt-ending, a match penalty shall be imposed.

634. Start of Game and Periods

(*a*) The game shall be started and resumed at the commencement of each period by a face-off in the centre of the rink.

(*b*) Home teams shall have the choice of goals to defend at the start of the game, except where both players' benches are on the same side of the rink. Then the home team shall start the game, defending the goal nearest to their bench.

635 Throwing a Stick

(*a*) When any player or team official of the defending team, deliberately throws or shoots a stick, or any article, at the puck in his defending zone the referee shall allow the play to be completed and if a goal is *not* scored a penalty shot shall be awarded to the attacking team the shot to be taken by the player designated by the Referee as the one who was fouled.

If, however, the goal being unattended and the attacking player having no defending player to pass and with a chance to score on an "open goal", a stick or any other object be thrown or shot by any member of the defending team, thereby preventing a shot, a goal shall be awarded to the attackers.

(*b*) A Major penalty shall be imposed on any player who throws his stick or any article, in any zone, except when such act has been penalised by the award of a Penalty Shot, the awarding of a goal or when a goal is scored on the play by the non-offending team.

(*c*) A Misconduct or Game Misconduct penalty shall be imposed on any player who throws a stick or any article outside the playing area, unless a penalty was imposed under 635*a* or *b* above. If the offence is committed in protest of an official's decision, a Minor penalty under Rule 607*a*, plus a Game Misconduct shall be assessed to the offending player.

NOTE. *When a player discards the broken portions of a stick by tossing them to the side of the rink (not over the boards) in such a way as not to interfere with the play or opposing players, no penalty shall be imposed.*

636. Time of Match

(*a*) Three twenty-minute periods of actual playing time, with a rest intermission between each period, will be the time allowed for each game. Play shall be resumed promptly after each intermission fifteen minutes from the completion of play in the preceding period. In games played in outside or uncovered rinks, teams shall change ends midway through the third or overtime period. Goalkeepers shall not be permitted to go to the players' bench, except to be replaced—violation of this rule brings a Minor penalty.

(*b*) The team scoring the greatest number of goals during the three twenty-minute periods shall be the winner and shall be credited with two points in the standings.

(*c*) In the intervals between periods, the ice surface shall be flooded, unless mutually agreed otherwise by the competing teams.

(*d*) If any unusual delay occurs within five minutes of the end of the first or second periods, the Referee may order the next regular intermission to be taken immediately and the balance of play with the teams defending the same goals, after which the teams will change ends and resume play of the ensuing period without delay.

637. Tied Game

Generally if, at the end of the three regular twenty-minute periods, the score of both teams shall be equal the game shall be called a "tie" with the points being shared equally between the two teams. This rule is subject to any Regulation of the I.I.H.F. or a National Federation.

638. Tripping

(*a*) A Minor penalty shall be imposed on any player who shall place his stick, knee, foot, arm, hand or elbow in such a manner as to cause his opponent to trip or fall.

NOTE. *If, in the opinion of the referee, a player is unquestionably hook-checking the puck and thereby obtains possession of it, no penalty shall be imposed, even though the puck carrier should fall.*

(*b*) When a player in control of the puck in the attacking zone (with no defending player to pass other than the goal-keeper) is tripped or otherwise fouled from behind and thus prevented from having a clear shot on the goal, a penalty shot shall be awarded to the non-offending team. Nevertheless the referee shall not stop play until the attacking team shall have lost control of the puck to the defending team.

By "control of the puck" shall be meant the act of propelling the puck with the stick. If, while it is being propelled, the puck shall touch the person, stick or skate of another player or should hit a goal post or shall go free, the player shall be deemed no longer in control.

(*c*) If, when the opposing goalkeeper has been removed from the ice, a player in control of the puck is tripped or otherwise fouled with no opposition between him and the opposing goal, thus preventing a reasonable scoring opportunity, the Referee shall immediately stop the play and award a goal to the attacking team.

These rules are copyright by the International Ice Hockey Federation (Ligue internationale de Hockey sur Glace). Some are here abbreviated for reasons of space.

The Rules of
Women's Lacrosse

POSITIONS IN THE FIELD
(as played in Great Britain)

| Goal |

1st Home   *Point*
2nd Home   *Cover Point*
3rd Home   *3rd Man*

Right Defence   *Left Defence*
Left Attack   Right Attack

Centre
Centre

Right Attack   *Left Attack*
Left Defence   Right Defence

3rd Man   *3rd Home*
Cover Point   *2nd Home*
Point   *1st Home*

| Goal |

This positioning is not compulsory

Women's Lacrosse

I. THE CROSSE

The crosse shall not exceed 1.22 m (4 ft) nor be less than 0.92 m (3 ft) in length; 0.23 m (9 in) in width and 7 cm (2.75 in) in depth. The maximum weight shall be 567 gm (20 oz). "Depth" is that of the guard/leader and the wood.

II. THE BALL

The ball shall be rubber; not less than 0.200 m ($7\frac{3}{4}$ in) nor more than 0.203 m (8 in) in circumference. It shall weigh not less than 135 gm (4.75 oz) nor more than 149 gm (5.25 oz). It shall have a bounce of not less than 1.3 m (4.3 ft) nor more than 1.4 m (4.6 ft) when dropped from 2.5 m (8.2 ft) on to concrete at a temperature of approximately 68° F (20° C).

III. THE GROUND

The ground has no measured boundaries (a minimum area of 110 × 60 m (120 × 70 yd) is desirable). The goals shall be 92 m (100 yd) apart, measured from goal line to goal line. There shall be a circle of 9 m (10 yd) radius in the centre of the field; through the centre of this shall be a line 3 m (3.3 yd) in length parallel to the goal lines. The boundaries shall be decided before the match by the Captains and the Umpire (see VI(c)). The lines marking the centre and goal circles shall be considered part of those areas.

IV. THE GOALS

Each goal shall consist of two perpendicular, wood or metal posts or pipes, 1.83 m (6 ft) high and 1.83 m apart, joined at the top by a cross-bar 1.83 m from the ground (inside measurement). The goal posts shall not extend upwards beyond the cross-bar, nor the cross-bar sideways beyond the goal posts.

The posts and cross-bar shall be painted white and be 0.05 m (2 in) square. A line called the goal line shall be drawn from post to post, continuous with them and of the same width. The netting, not more that 0.04 m (1½ in) mesh, shall be attached to the posts and cross-bar, and to a point on the ground 1.83 m behind the centre of the goal line; it shall be firmly pegged down.

The Goal Circle

The goal circle shall be a circle radius 2.6 m (8½ ft) from the centre of the goal line.

V. THE TEAMS

Twelve players shall constitute a full team, one of whom shall act as Captain.

VI. CAPTAINS

The Captains shall:
  (*a*) Toss for choice of ends.
  (*b*) Agree upon the playing time with the Umpire.
  (*c*) Agree upon the boundaries with the Umpire.
  (*d*) Be informed of the responsibilities of each Umpire (Rule XX).
  (*e*) Designate Umpires if there are no Umpires.
  (*f*) Indicate a substitute for an injured player.
  (*g*) Confer with the Umpires if the weather conditions make the continuation of play questionable.

VII. FOOTWEAR AND PROTECTIVE CLOTHING

  (*a*) Players shall wear composition or rubber soled shoes or boots. No spikes shall be allowed. Plastic, leather or rubber studs/cleats may be worn.
  (*b*) No protective clothing other than close fitting gloves shall be worn, except by the goal-keeper who may wear leg pads,

a body pad, a face mask, a protective hat and close fitting gloves.

VIII. DURATION OF PLAY

The playing time shall be 50 minutes (or such time as shall be agreed upon by the Captains). At half-time, which may not exceed ten minutes, the players shall change ends. Time out, which may not exceed five minutes, is taken for a stoppage that occurs due to accident or injury.

If weather conditions make play dangerous, the Umpire, after consultation with the Captains, may suspend the game, which shall be considered legal and complete if 80% of the playing time has elapsed.

IX. SUBSTITUTES

Substitution only takes place when an accident or injury occurs which, *in the opinion of the Umpire*, prevents a player from taking further part in the game. After substitution has taken place an injured player may not take any further part in the game. If the player is incapacitated for longer than 5 min the game is re-started without her. She may only return with the Umpire's permission and if no substitute has taken her place.

X. START OF THE GAME

(*a*) The game shall be started, and re-started after every goal and after half-time, by a draw on the centre line. All the other players' feet must be outside the centre circle "ready, draw".

The Draw

(*b*) The opposing centres shall stand with one foot toeing the centre line. The crosses shall be held in the air, above hip level, wood to wood, angle to collar, parallel to the centre line and back to back, so that the players' sticks are between the ball and the goals they are defending. The ball shall be placed between the sticks by the Umpire. On the words "Ready, draw" from the Umpire, the two opponents shall immediately draw their crosses up and away from one another.

The flight of the ball shall attain a height higher than the heads of the players taking the draw. After one warning for an illegal draw the opponent is awarded a free position. A throw is awarded after one warning if both players draw illegally. For the free position the offending centre is placed 4 m (4.4 yd) away at an angle of 45° to the centre line on goal side.

XI. SCORING

The side scoring the greater number of goals shall be the winner. In the event of the scores being equal the result is a draw (tie). A goal shall be scored by the whole ball passing completely over the goal line between the goal posts and under the cross-bar from in front, having been propelled by the crosse of an attacking player, or the crosse or person of a defending player.

A goal shall not be scored when:

(*a*) The ball is put through the goal by a non-player.

(*b*) The ball comes off the *person* of an attacking player.

(*c*) The ball enters the goal after the whistle has been blown.

(*d*) The player shooting has followed through over the circle with any part of herself or her crosse, or any other attacking player has entered the circle.

(*e*) The goal-keeper whilst within the circle is interfered with in any way by an attacking player.

(*f*) The Centre/Field Umpire has deemed the shot to be dangerous.

XII. STAND

The ball is dead when the Umpire blows her whistle, and no player shall move, unless directed by the Umpire, until the game has been re-started. The Umpire shall direct any player who moves to return to her original position.

XIII. OUT OF BOUNDS

Should the ball be thrown out of bounds, the Umpire shall blow her whistle and the players must "stand".

(*a*) When one player is nearest the ball: the nearest player takes the ball in her crosse from the place where the ball went out, stands 4 m (4.4 yd) inside the agreed boundary and on the word "play" the game proceeds. Each player concerned maintains her position relative to other players. (For agreed boundaries, see Rule 6(*c*).) Play must not be resumed within 8 m (8.8 yd) of the goal circle.

(*b*) When two opposing players are equally near the ball: a throw is taken.

XIV. THE THROW

The two players shall stand at least 1 m apart, and each shall be nearer the goal she is defending and facing in towards the game. The Umpire shall stand between 4 and 8 m from the two players, and on the word "play" shall throw the ball with a short, high throw, so that the players take it as they move in towards the game.

No player may be within 4 m of the players taking the throw.

A throw is taken when:

(*a*) the ball goes into the goal off a non-player.

(*b*) the ball goes out of bounds (Rule 13(*b*)).

(*c*) there is an incident unrelated to the ball and players are equidistant from the ball (Rule 15).

(*d*) a ball lodges in clothing or crosse (Rule 16(*a*)).

(*e*) two players foul simultaneously (Rule 19).

(*f*) the game is re-started after an accident, unless the accident has been caused by a foul.

(*g*) the game is stopped for any reason not previously mentioned.

XV. ACCIDENT, INTERFERENCE OR ANY OTHER INCIDENT UNRELATED TO THE BALL

If the game has to be stopped due to any accident unrelated to the ball at the time the whistle was blown, the game should be re-started by the ball being given to the player who was in possession, or nearest to it, at the time play was stopped. If two players are equidistant from the ball a throw is taken.

XVI. BALL LODGED IN CLOTHING OR CROSSE

Should the ball become lodged:

(*a*) In the clothing of a player, a throw shall be taken.

(*b*) In the crosse, the crosse must be struck on the ground and the ball dislodged immediately, otherwise a throw is taken where the player caught the ball.

(*c*) In the goal netting or in the clothing or pads of the goal-keeper while she is within the goal circle: she removes the ball, places it in her crosse and proceeds with the game.

XVII. DEFENDING WITHIN THE GOAL CIRCLE

(*a*) Only one player, either the goal-keeper or the person deputising for her, may be in the goal circle at one time. No other player may enter or have a part of her body or stick over the goal circle at any time.

The goal-keeper or anyone who deputises for her, whilst within the circle,

    (i) Must place the ball in her stick immediately and "clear" within 10 seconds,

   (ii) May stop the ball with her hand and/or body as well as her crosse. If she catches the ball with her hand she must put the ball in her crosse and proceed with the game,

  (iii) May remove a ball lodged in her clothing or pads, place it in her crosse and proceed with the game,

  (iv) May reach out with her stick and bring the ball into the goal circle provided no part of her body is grounded outside the circle.

(*b*) When the goal-keeper is outside the goal she loses her privileges. When outside the circle with the ball she must not step back into it with the ball.

(*c*) Any ball resting on the goal circle line is the goal-keeper's.

XVIII. FOULS

Field Fouls. A player shall not:

(*a*) Roughly or recklessly check another's crosse.

(*b*) Make a large swing with the head of the crosse when trying to tackle.

(*c*) (i) Detain an opponent at any time by pressing against her body *or stick* with an arm, leg, body or crosse.

(ii) Suddenly move into an opponent's patch causing unavoidable contact.

(*d*) Check/tackle an opponent's crosse when she is trying to get possession of the ball.

(*e*) Charge, shoulder barge, or back into an opponent, or push with the hand.

(*f*) Push her opponent off a ground ball or guard a ground ball with her foot or crosse.

(*g*) Guard her crosse with her arm. The free hand may not be used to ward off an opponent, with or without contact.

(*h*) Trip an opponent accidentally or intentionally.

(*i*) Touch the ball with her hand, except as in Rules 16(*c*), 17(ii) and 17(iii).

(*j*) Allow any part of her body, deliberately or otherwise, to impede, accelerate or change the direction of the ball to her own team's advantage.

(*k*) Propel the ball in a dangerous or uncontrolled manner at any time. Any ball propelled from close quarters straight at a player must be ruled dangerous.

(*l*) Shoot dangerously. A shot is dangerous if:

(i) the shot is directed at the goal-keeper's head or neck unless she moves into the path of the ball; (ii) the shot is uncontrolled even if it misses the goal; (iii) it is a hard rising underarm shot; (iv) the shot is directed with unnecessary force.

(*m*) Throw her crosse in any circumstances.

(*n*) Take part in the game if she is not holding her crosse.

(*o*) Draw illegally. Illegal draws occur: (i) when one player draws too soon; (ii) if no attempt is made to draw up and away (Rule 10); (iii) when the ball does not go above the heads of both centres.

(*p*) Guard the goal by positioning herself with at least one other team mate so as to obstruct shooting spaces.

Goal Circle Fouls

A field player must not: enter or have any part of her body or crosse in the circle at any time, unless she is deputising for the goal-keeper.

The goal-keeper or her deputy must not:

(*a*) when inside the circle, continue to hold the ball in her crosse, but must pass at once;

(*b*) when any part of her is grounded outside the circle, draw the ball into her circle;

(*c*) when outside the circle with the ball, step back into the circle until she no longer has the ball.

The centre/field Umpire may overrule any decision made by a goal Umpire. She may also arrange that the goal Umpires call field fouls and make boundary decisions in a clearly defined area around the goals.

XIX. PENALTY

The penalty for a foul shall be a "free position". In the event of two players fouling simultaneously, a throw is taken. The offending player is placed 4 m (4.4 yd) from the player taking the free position, in the direction from which she approached before committing the foul. The goal-keeper's free position is taken from within the goal circle unless she has been fouled when outside the circle.

Free Position. The players shall "stand". The Umpire shall indicate where the player taking the free position is to stand; no player may be nearer than 4 m to this player. If anyone be within this distance she must move to a position indicated by the Umpire. The player awarded the "free position" shall then take the ball in her crosse, and on the word "play" the game shall proceed, i.e., the player with the ball may at once shoot, pass or run with the ball. The "free position" shall not be within 8 m of the goal circle, except in the case of the goal-keeper who may be in the goal circle, and this shall be measured in any direction at the discretion of the Umpire, according to the nature of the foul. Should the foul have prevented an almost certain goal, the Umpire shall order any player or players from between such "free position" and the goal.

XX. UMPIRES

(*a*) *Centre/Field Umpire*. The duties of the Centre/Field Umpire shall be to enforce the rules, keep time and record the score. It is advisable to appoint separate time-keepers and scorers in representative matches. Her decisions shall be final and without appeal. The final decision on each goal shall be given by this Umpire. Before the match she shall see that the ground, goals, ball, crosses, clothing, including footwear are in accordance with the rules.

(*b*) *Goal Umpires*. There shall be one at each goal. She shall stand approx. 4 m from the goal to umpire the rules concerning the goal circle. She shall keep to the same goal throughout the match. In the event of the ball entering the goal without infringement of the rules concerning the goal circle (11(*a*)–(*e*)) the goal umpire raises her flag, until the centre umpire whistles to award the goal which she does unless she considers the shot to be dangerous (11(*f*), 18(*l*)). Should there be any infringement of the rules relating to the circle she shall whistle twice to stop the game.

(*c*) *Advantage/held whistle*. If a player retains possession of the ball even though her crosse has been held, the umpire should indicate that she has seen the foul by saying "advantage X". Any Umpire need not enforce a rule when this would penalise the non-offending team.

(*d*) *Rough or dangerous play*, *misconduct or unsportsmanlike behaviour*. In addition to awarding a free position, the Umpires may also warn the offending player and then may, on further offence, suspend her from participation in the game.

APPENDIX

There are likely to be rule changes after the World Tournament. Main areas of discussion will include:

1. Tackling around the sphere (imaginary area 7 in) surrounding the head.

2. Two categories of fouls: major (e.g. dangerous tackle), minor (e.g. propelling the ball with the body), with different penalties for each category.

3. Using a "shooting lane" as a path to goal as defined by two lines extending from the ball to the inside of the two goal posts. This line is the determinant for the foul obstruction of shooting space.

4. Possible use of arm signals for such as goal, free position, time out, re-draw, empty stick check, etc.

5. Extra markings (1 ft long) on the field 8 and 12 m from the goal circle to help players judge the correct distances.

6. Substitution other than for injury.

The Laws of
Men's Lacrosse

Men's Lacrosse

INTRODUCTION

The Laws of Lacrosse (hereinafter referred to as the "Laws") are authorised by the English Lacrosse Union as the only Code for the playing of Men's Lacrosse in all games under its auspices or under the auspices of affiliated Associations, Unions, Clubs or Bodies, after 1st September, 1980.

The ultimate interpretation of the Laws shall be the sole prerogative of the Council of the English Lacrosse Union.

The Laws have been formulated in such a way as to give as much clarity as possible and to give a means of fairly quick reference to any particular point. Thus the basic Law is expounded first and this is followed, in many cases, by explanatory notes. These notes are part of the Laws and possess the same authority.

A.—THE EQUIPMENT

1. The Crosse

(a) The crosse shall be of entirely non-metallic construction except for the handle, which shall be of an approved design. This includes materials used for any repairs.

(b) The crosse shall be between 40 in and 72 in (1.0 and 1.8 m) overall length. The head of the crosse shall measure (inside) between 4 in and 10 in (102–254 mm) except for that used by the designated goal-keeper which may measure up to 15 in (381 mm) inside width.

(c) A string shall be brought through a hole at the side of and near the end of the final turn of the stick, where appropriate, and then over the end. It shall be fastened to the leader in such a way as to prevent the point of the stick catching on clothing or an opponent's crosse. The strings shall be so designed that the ball is always free in the crosse.

(d) Any repair or modification to a crosse shall be carried out in such a way that no unfair advantage is conveyed to the user and that no injury could be caused to any player.

NOTE. *No net shall sag to the extent that a ball placed therein can be completely seen below the frame when the crosse is held in a horizontal plane. This ruling shall not apply to the goal-keeper's crosse.*

2. The Ball

The ball shall be white, orange or yellow rubber and between $7\frac{3}{4}$ and 8 in (197–208 mm) in circumference, between 5 and $5\frac{1}{2}$ oz (142–156 g) in weight and when dropped from a height of 72 in (1.8 m) upon a hard wood floor, shall bounce 45 to 49 in (1.1–1.2 m).

3. Boots

Boots or shoes shall be of non-metallic construction except for the studs, but shall have no sharp edges or points which may injure other players.

NOTE. *This Law forbids, inter alia, the use of boots or shoes containing nails and leather studs in any form.*

4. Protective Clothing and Equipment

(*a*) Headgear shall be of the approved lacrosse pattern and style and shall not have any sharp points which might injure other players.

(*b*) No protective clothing or gear shall be worn above the waist apart from approved headgear, arm guards, gauntlet gloves and, in the case of a goal-keeper, the normal pad for the front of the body.

NOTE. *This Law forbids, inter alia, the wearing of any protection capable of producing a sharp edge or point which may injure other players. However, shoulder protection manufactured from lightweight foam may be worn.*

(*c*) No protective gear or clothing shall be worn on the legs apart from (i) shin guards and (ii) the normal goal-keeper's padding on his thighs.

NOTE. *Goal-keepers may wear track-suit trousers if the referee deems the conditions sufficiently inclement.*

(*d*) No protective gear or clothing, other than headgear and gloves, shall be visible.

(*e*) The normal dress, in addition to that mentioned in these

Laws, shall be the team's registered jersey or shirt, shorts and stockings.

(*f*) Each player shall have a separate and distinctive number on the front and on the back of his shirt or jersey. Arabic numerals shall be used and these shall not be less than $5\frac{1}{2}$ in (14 cm) high on the front and 8 in (20.3 cm) high on the back, and shall be in a colour contrasting with that of the shirt or jersey. No player shall change his number during the game.

5. The Goalposts

A goal shall consist of two vertical posts, placed with their inner sides 6 ft (1.8 m) apart, with a cross-bar fixed rigidly across the top of these posts, joining them, but not protruding at its ends. The vertical distance between the lower surface of the cross-bar and the ground shall be 6 ft (1.8 m).

NOTE 1. *The vertical posts (known as "goal-posts") may be sunk in suitable sockets in the ground or they may be stood upon the ground by means of suitable angle-brackets and stays, protruding directly behind each post and clamped securely to the ground. All the additional fixtures shall be contained inside the goal-net.*

NOTE 2. *The vertical posts and cross-bar shall be of wood or an approved metal or alloy and each shall be of not more than 3 in (7.6 cm) square or equivalent circular cross-section. The material used and the shape shall be such as to prevent injury resulting from collision with them.*

6. The Goal-Nets

(*a*) Netting of not more than $1\frac{1}{2}$ in (3.8 cm) mesh shall be used.

(*b*) The netting shall be attached to the posts and cross-bar by means of string or twine in such a way that it will be impossible for a lacrosse ball to pass between the edge of the net and the post or cross-bar in any reasonable circumstances.

(*c*) A suitable bracket shall be attached near the top of each vertical post, and projected directly behind, so that the net fastened to the cross-bar shall be supported to form a flat "roof" of netting stretching between 9 and 12 in (22.9–30.5 cm) behind the back face of the cross-bar.

(*d*) The net shall be designed so that from the rear edge of this "roof" and from each vertical post it shall run to an apex on the ground 6 ft (1.8 m) behind the goal-line (defined in Law B, Section 2(*b*)) measured perpendicularly to this line.

(*e*) The bottom edge of the net shall be securely pegged to the ground in such a way that it makes straight lines between the apex and each post (or the rear of each bracket, if there be any) and that it is impossible for a lacrosse ball to pass between the edge of the net and the ground in any reasonable circumstances.

B.—THE PLAYING FIELD

The Playing Field

The playing field shall be, wherever possible, a rectangular field, 110 yd (100 m) long and 60 yd (55 m) wide. The boundaries of the field shall be marked with white lines.

NOTE. *Any doubts as to the boundaries of the field of play shall be decided and agreed upon by the referee and the captains before the commencement of the match.*

The Centre Line

An extra heavy white line shall be marked through the centre of the field perpendicular to the side lines. This line shall be known as the centre line and the mid-point of this line shall be marked and known as the centre spot.

The Boundary Lines

The boundary lines on each side of the field shall be designated side lines and those at each end shall be designated end or back lines. Flag markers shall be placed at the four corners of the field and at end of the centre line opposite to the gate.

The Gate

The gate is on one side of the field indicated by flags 6½ ft (2 m) either side of the halfway line through which all players must both leave and re-enter the field on all send-off penalties.

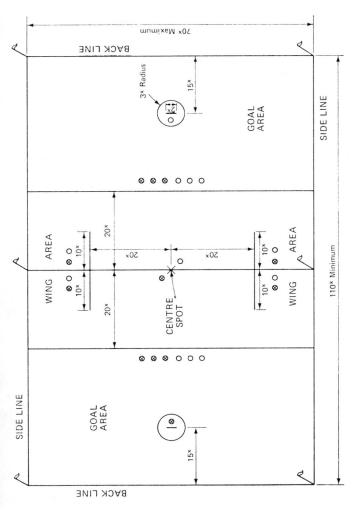

FIELD MARKINGS

493

Penalty Box

The penalty box is the area of the field immediately through the gate controlled by the offside official.

Goal Areas

In each half of the field a line shall be marked from side line to side line 20 yd (18 m) from the centre line. The areas between these lines and the back lines are called goal areas.

Wing Areas

Lines parallel to the side lines shall be marked on each side of the field 20 yd (18 m) from the centre spot and extending 10 yd (9 m) on each side of the centre line. The areas between the extremities of these lines and the side lines shall be designated wing areas.

Goal Lines

A goal line shall be marked between the two vertical posts comprising each goal and shall be the same thickness as the posts. The goal-lines shall be parallel to each other, 40 yd (36 m) from the centre line and centred between the side lines.

Goal Creases

A goal crease shall encircle each goal and shall be drawn with the centre of the goal-line as its centre, so that it encloses a space, known as the goal crease, of 3 yd (2.75 m) radius.

NOTE. *See plan of ground markings on page 493.*

C.—THE PLAYERS AND OFFICIALS

1. The Teams

(*a*) Ten players shall constitute a full team, and a match shall be played between two teams.

(*b*) Each team shall play under a playing Captain. The Captain shall be the sole representative of his team in any matter concerning the playing of the game, or in any matter arising from it. No player other than the appointed Captain shall speak to, nor approach, nor appeal to the Referee in any way. Should the Captain not be available at any time, a nominated

Deputy shall act for him to deal promptly with any matter which is normally the responsibility of the Captain.

(*c*) Should an accident or injury occur to any player which, in the opinion of the Referee, incapacitates him from playing, the opposing Captain shall withdraw one of his players from the game for the period during which the injured player stays off the field.

NOTE 1. *Neither of the two players leaving the field shall return without the other except where four or more players shall be off the field as the result of injury two uninjured players of opposing teams may pair off and return to the field after a period of five minutes or earlier if in the opinion of the Referee there is no possibility of one of the injured players participating further in the match.*

NOTE 2. *Should a player leave the field for any reason other than that stated above, the opposing Captain shall not be obliged to send off one of his players.*

NOTE 3. *See Law F.11 regarding the return of players to the field.*

(*d*) No substitute players shall be permitted to play in any circumstances other than as may be authorised from time to time for representative matches.

(*e*) The goal-keeper shall be the player who acts as goal-keeper at the commencement of the game, unless any change has been made and notified by the Captain to the Referee or unless the designated goal-keeper is sent off for a foul, when he may leave his stick only with a fellow player.

2. The Referee

(*a*) A Referee or Referees, one of whom shall be designated the senior, shall be appointed before the match and his/their authority shall commence on arrival at the ground and terminate at a reasonable time after the end of the match. During this period, his/their authority shall apply to all players including any suspended players (irrespective of the period of suspension), offside, goal or boundary officials, coaches, trainers or any other official connected with the teams.

(*b*) His duty shall be to control the match in accordance with the Laws, and to enforce them with absolute impartiality.

(*c*) His decisions shall be final. Should either side refuse to conform with his decisions concerning any matter whatsoever, or refuse to continue the match, then he shall declare them to be the losers, whatever the score may be at the time.

(*d*) Before the match commences, he shall check that the goals, nets, balls and ground markings are in accordance with the Laws and he shall ensure that any defects are rectified.

(*e*) He shall ensure that all equipment and clothing used or worn by the players is in accordance with the Laws. He shall not permit any player to use equipment or wear clothing which is not in accordance with the Laws.

(*f*) He shall be responsible for keeping the time and for starting and stopping the game at the scheduled times.

(*g*) He shall keep a record of the score and be responsible for declaring the final score to the two Captains.

(*h*) He may consult another appointed official on any matter if he so desires, but he shall not be bound by the opinion of the latter.

(*i*) He shall start and stop play with a clearly audible whistle.

(*j*) If a defending player commits a foul against an attacking player and the ball is in the attacking half of the field, and an attack player has possession of the ball at the time this foul occurs and in the opinion of the Referee, a scoring play is imminent, and the act of fouling does not cause the player in possession of the ball to lose it, the Referee must drop a signal flag and withhold his whistle until such time as the scoring play has been completed. This shall be considered to have been completed when the attacking team has lost control of the ball, has clearly lost the opportunity of scoring a goal on the original play, or has taken a shot or the ball has been passed more than once behind the goal and forward again. The slow whistle technique shall be used whether the foul is committed against the man in possession of the ball or some other member of the attacking team.

When the whistle is finally blown, the Referee shall impose the necessary time penalty on the offending player.

In all cases where a penalty has been called in the offended team's offensive half of the field, the ball shall be put back into play by the closest player of the team awarded the ball at the point on the field where the ball was when play was suspended, the only exception being where the ball is within a 20 yd radius of the goal. In this case the ball shall (1) be given to the nearest player to the ball when play was suspended, and then (2) this player shall be moved to a position laterally across the field 20 yd from the goal.

NOTES. *A pass is a movement of the ball caused by a player in control throwing or bouncing a ball to a team mate.*

During a slow whistle situation a shot remains a shot until:

1. It is clearly obvious a goal will not be scored.

2. No added impetus is given to the ball by any member of the attacking team.

3. When possession is gained by any member of the defensive team.

4. After hitting goal-keeper, or post or posts, the ball shall be declared dead as soon as it is touched by any player of either team other than the defending goal-keeper or an official.

When a penalty occurs in the offended team's defensive half of the field, where a penalty time is to be served, the ball shall be awarded to any player of the offended team on the halfway line.

(*k*) Should the Referee award any penalties to any players, he must inform the offending player and the official of the nature of the offence and the duration of the time penalty. He should endeavour to notify them by both verbal means and the Standard International penalty signals.

3. The Offside Officials

(*a*) An Offside Official may be appointed before the match, and in the event of a single Referee officiating, shall be so appointed and his authority shall last for the duration of actual playing time.

(*b*) An Official shall not give advice to nor receive advice from anyone except the Referee during the course of the match, nor shall anyone distract an Official's attention.

(*c*) The Official shall stand outside the side boundary line at the centre line.

(*d*) If an Official considers a team or teams to be offside (see Law D.8) he shall sound an audible warning and when the

Referee has stopped play he shall advise the Referee as to the team(s) and player(s) offside.

(*e*) Should the Referee suspend a player(s) from the field for any offence, then the Official shall time the penalty whatever the length as directed by the Referee and return the player(s) to the field upon the expiry of the penalty time. The timing of the penalty will only begin when the offending player reaches the penalty box or the game is re-started, whichever is the later.

(*f*) The Official and/or the Referee shall keep a record of the name and number of any player sent off for personal fouls. The Official may wish to delegate this duty to an assistant.

NOTE. *Should any player incur five or more personal fouls in any one game, then he shall be reported to the Referees Association, where records of these send-offs will be kept.*

(*g*) Where an Official makes a mistake which would result in a team or player being penalised he shall promptly correct the mistake. If a goal is scored during the mistake and it is brought to the attention of the Referee before the next face-off then the Referee must allow or disallow the goal depending upon the circumstances.

NOTE. *The Official's horn or whistle in itself never stops the game; only the Referee's whistle when appropriate, can stop the game. On hearing the horn the Referee will operate the slow whistle.*

D.—PRINCIPLES OF THE GAME

1. Duration

(*a*) The playing time shall consist of four periods of 20 minutes each.

(*b*) The teams shall change ends after each period.

(*c*) There shall be an interval of not more than ten minutes at half-time and not more than one minute shall be allowed for the change of ends at quarter and three-quarter time.

NOTE 1. *The interval may be eliminated by agreement between the Captains, provided the Referee approves.*

NOTE 2. *The Referee shall allow extra time at the end of each period to compensate for any time lost due to injuries during that period.*

2. How to "Face"

(a) A "face" shall take place between two players, one from each team.

(b) The players shall stand facing each other in such a way that the one whose team is defending the goal nearest to which the "face" is ordered shall have his back to his goal.

(c) Each player must have both hands on the handle, and not touching any strings, of his own crosse; the frame of the crosses must be approx. 1 in apart; both gloved hands must be on the ground and at least 18 in (45.8 cm) apart at the beginning of the "face"; the feet shall not touch the crosse; both hands and feet must be to the left of the throat of the crosse. The Referee shall place the ball between the backs and in the centre of the lower frames of the crosses, but not touching the ground.

(d) All other players shall be at least 10 yd (9 m) away from the ball.

NOTE. *Should any player offend against this Law in any way, then the Referee shall normally award a Free Position (Law E, Section 3) to the opposing team, to be taken at the point where the foul took place.*

(e) When the players are in position, the Referee shall start play with a clearly audible whistle.

(f) The two players shall immediately attempt to direct the course of the ball by a movement of their crosses in any manner they desire.

(g) In no circumstances shall the ball be faced closer to the goal than 20 yd (18 m) in any direction unless a face-off is required directly behind a goal. In that situation the ball shall be placed 20 ft (6 m) from the back line. At no time shall a ball be faced closer than 20 ft (6 m) from a boundary line.

3. Commencement of the Game

(a) The Referee shall toss a coin on the field of play. The Captain calling correctly shall have choice of which goal his team will attack during the first period.

NOTE. *Once his decision has been notified to the opposing Captain, it may not be changed.*

(b) One player from each team shall prepare to "face".

(*c*) The "face" shall take place at the Centre spot.

(*d*) Each team shall confine 4 players including the goal-keeper within the Goal area of the goal it is defending and 3 players within the Goal area of the goal it is attacking.

(*e*) Each team shall have one player within each Wing area.

(*f*) The Referee shall then order the "face".

(*g*) When the whistle sounds to start play, the players in the Wing areas shall be released to play the ball together with the two players "facing". All other players shall remain confined to their allocated Goal areas until any player of either team has gained possession of the ball or the ball goes out of bounds or the ball enters either Goal area.

NOTES. (i) *A player shall be considered in possession of the ball when he is in control of it and could perform any of the normal functions of play such as carrying, cradling, passing or shooting.*

(ii) *Possession shall be signalled by the Referee shouting "Possession" and raising his right hand vertically above his head.*

(iii) *Should any player offend against this law then the Referee shall normally award possession to the Centre of the opposing team, to be taken from the Centre spot. The Centres shall be the two players who last faced.*

(iv) *If a team is one or more players short of a full team it shall be exempt from confining its players in the Goal area it is defending and the Wing areas to the extent that it is short of players and may select how it shall exercise this exemption, but the Goal area it is attacking shall contain three players.*

4. Scoring

A goal shall be scored by the team attacking a particular goal when the ball enters that goal through the front, provided that it was not last propelled nor deflected by the foot or leg of a player belonging to that attacking team, and that it has not last touched anyone who is not a player. This shall apply even though the ball touch a post or cross-bar upon entering the goal.

NOTE 1. *The ball shall not be considered to have entered the goal until it has passed over the edge of the goal line (or its vertical projection) furthest from the centre-spot. Thus, a goal shall not be scored if the ball hits any part of the vertical posts or the cross-bar and rebounds into the field of play.*

NOTE 2. *Should the ball enter the goal by any means after "Dead-ball" has been whistled, then no goal shall be scored.*

5. The Result

The Referee shall declare the team which has scored the greatest number of goals to be the winners. If both teams have scored the same number of goals, then he shall declare the result to be a draw.

NOTE. *There shall be one exception as stated in Law C, Section 2(c).*

6. "Dead-ball"

(*a*) The ball shall automatically become "Dead-ball" whenever the Referee blows his whistle to stop play.

(*b*) The Referee shall whistle "Dead-ball" whenever:

(i) a period of play ends;

(ii) the ball enters a goal by any means;

(iii) a player with the ball in his possession touches with any part of his body or crosse the ground on or beyond a boundary line, a loose ball touches the ground on or beyond a boundary line or when it touches anything on or beyond a boundary line.

(iv) an offence against any of these Laws has been committed (except in so far as the Referee applies Law C, Section 2(*j*));

(v) an accident or injury occurs which is obviously serious, demanding immediate attention. (If the accident or injury is obviously not serious, the Referee shall endeavour not to stop the game whilst, by doing so, he might convey an advantage or disadvantage to either side, but he shall whistle at the first opportunity);

(vi) the ball lodges in any place inaccessible to a crosse or in the goal-netting, or in the clothing or face mask of a player;

NOTE. *Should the ball become caught in the player's crosse, the Referee shall count 1001, 1002, 1003, 1004, and if at the end of these 4 sec the ball has not been dislodged, the Referee shall stop play and the ball faced between the player in whose crosse the ball was caught and his nearest opponent. In the event that the ball shall become caught in a player's kit or equipment other than his stick, play shall be suspended immediately and the ball faced between him and his nearest opponent.*

In neither of these situations shall this general rule apply to a designated goal-keeper when he is within his goal crease area. In that event he shall be awarded possession on the back line.

(vii) the goalposts and/or cross-bar move or fall down or are accidently moved or knocked down.

7. Re-starting Play after an Interruption

The paragraphs in this Law correspond with the Sections in Law D, Section 6(*b*).

(*a*) *At the commencement of each period.* The Referee shall order a "face" at the centre-spot as described in Law D, Section 3.

(*b*) *After the ball has entered a goal.*

 (i) If a goal has been scored, then the Referee shall order a "face" at the centre-spot, as described in Law D, Section 3.

(ii) If the ball has entered a goal after last touching the foot or leg of a player attacking that goal or after last touching anyone who is not a player, then the goal-keeper defending that goal shall be awarded possession on the back line.

(*c*) *After the ball has passed over or touched a boundary line* (*see Law D, 6(b)(iii)*).

Subject to the exception of Law F, 10, the ball shall be awarded at the point where it is declared out of bounds by the Referee to the nearest player of the team opposing that of the player who last touched it, except in the case of a shot or deflected shot when the ball shall be awarded to the nearest player to the ball when it crosses a boundary line.

The player awarded possession shall, immediately the Referee whistles to re-start play, run with or pass the ball as he may choose to do so. No other player shall be nearer than 3 yd (2.75 m) to the player awarded possession. If players of opposing teams are equidistant from the ball when it crosses a boundary line following a shot or deflected shot, the Referee shall order a "face" 20 ft (6 m) within the field of play from the point where the ball crossed the boundary line.

NOTE. *A deflected shot remains a shot until the ball comes to rest on the field of play, a team gains possession of the ball, the ball goes out of bounds, or a player deliberately causes the ball to go out of bounds.*

(*d*) *After an offence against a Law has been committed.* The Referee shall order such penalty as he deems suitable and re-start the game accordingly (see also Law E, 7(*c*)).

(*e*) *After an accident or injury.* Unless any penalty be involved, the Referee shall, at his discretion, (i) order a "face" to take place either at the spot where the accident or injury occurred, or at the spot where play was actually stopped (subject to Law D, 2(*g*)), or from the point where the ball crossed the boundary line. (ii) Shall direct such other means of re-starting play as he considers appropriate.

(*f*) *After the goals have fallen or been accidentally knocked down, displaced, etc.* The Referee shall ensure that the goals are correctly in position and then re-start with the team in possession at the spot where the ball was when "Dead-ball" was whistled, unless any penalty be involved (Law D, 2(*g*)).

(*g*) *After the game has been stopped for any reason not mentioned in these Laws.* The Referee shall normally order a "face" to take place at the spot where the ball was when it became "Dead-ball" (subject to Law D, 2(*g*)), but he shall be empowered to direct that it shall take place at such other place and by such persons as he shall deem more suitable to the conditions, or to direct such other means of re-starting play as he considers apt and fair.

8. Offside Rule

A team shall be deemed to be offside when:

  (i) It has less than three men in its attack half of the field.
  (ii) It has less than four men in its defence half of the field.

NOTE. *When a team is reduced to less than 7 players it shall maintain 3 players in its attack half and its remaining players in its defence half of the field.*

E. — PENALTIES

1. General

The award of penalties shall be entirely at the discretion of the Referee, who shall award them impartially, dependent upon the play.

2. Classification of Offences

Penalties awarded by the Referee may be classified into three different categories, i.e. Technical Fouls, Personal Fouls and Expulsion Fouls.

(*a*) *Technical Fouls.* The penalty for these shall be suspension from the game for 30 sec, if the opposition had possession of the ball when the offence took place, or simply loss of possession if the offending team had possession or neither team had possession of the ball when the offence was committed.

(*b*) *Personal Fouls.* The penalty for these shall be suspension from the game for from 1 to 3 min (depending on the Referee's diagnosis of the severity and intention of the violation) and the ball shall be awarded to the offended team or faced if the foul occurs prior to the start of the game or a period or after the whistle has blown denoting the scoring of a goal or at the end of a period.

(*c*) *Expulsion Fouls.* The penalty for these shall be suspension for the remainder of the game. In such cases possession shall be given to the offended team, or faced if the foul occurs prior to the start of the game or period or after the whistle has blown denoting the scoring of a goal or at the end of a period.

Player committing five personal fouls. In any game where substitutes are allowed, any player who commits five personal fouls shall be expelled from the remainder of the game. In any game where substitutes are not allowed, any player who commits five personal fouls shall be reported to the Referees' Association.

NOTE. *Any player who has been sent off for a direct expulsion foul, no matter the reason, shall be reported to the Disciplinary Committee. Further action may be taken.*

3. Possession

(*a*) Unless these Laws state otherwise, possession shall normally be taken from the place where the event which led to the penalty occurred.

(*b*) No player shall be within 3 yd (2.75 m) of the player to whom possession has been awarded.

(*c*) The player to whom possession has been awarded shall take the ball in his crosse and may proceed to pass or run with the ball as he may choose to do so, only when the Referee orders play to proceed.

NOTE. *Should any player offend against this Law, then the Referee shall order the possession to be forfeited, and shall order a face to take place at the spot where the original possession should have taken place, but no nearer than 20 yd (18 m) from the goal.*

(*d*) In no circumstances shall possession be awarded closer than 20 yd (18 m) from the goal except when possession is awarded on back line behind goal.

(*e*) Should a foul result in the sending off of a player, possession shall be awarded at the halfway line if the offence took place in the offended player's defence half of the field, or at the position the play was stopped after a "slow whistle" situation in the attack half of the field.

4. Suspension from the Field of Play

(*a*) The Referee must suspend the offending player/s for the period outlined for the offence, but depending on the fouls severity when awarding personal fouls.

(*b*) The period of suspension shall be announced by the Referee to the offending player/s and the Official when the penalty is awarded.

(*c*) Should a goal-keeper commit a technical or personal foul of a non-violent or non-abusive nature, a defence player will serve the penalty time incurred to reduce the chance of injury to an inadequately protected deputy.

NOTE. *Before the commencement of the game the Captain*

shall nominate to the Referee the defence man to serve the goal-keeper's penalty time. For disciplinary purposes such penalties will not be credited to the defence player but to the goal-keeper.

(*d*) If the suspension be awarded for an offence which has resulted in an injury to a player, causing him to leave the field of play, another player in addition to the suspended player shall be withdrawn by his Captain in order to comply with Law C, Section 1(*c*).

(*e*) Players are reminded that should any player receive a direct expulsion foul, he shall be referred to the disciplinary committee immediately. After the game the Referee shall immediately and in writing fully report the facts of any suspension exceeding 5 minutes to the Secretary of the Referees' Committee of the Regional Association in whose area the game was played, and the Secretary shall immediately refer the case to that Association's Disciplinary Committee for attention.

The Referee shall immediately and in writing briefly report any player who receives five or more personal fouls to the Secretary of the Referees' Committee of the Regional Association to which the offending player's Club is affiliated and that Secretary shall keep a record of all such send-offs and any player who accumulates three such reports in any period of 12 calendar months shall receive an automatic two-match suspension. This will normally take effect for the two matches immediately following the match in which the third send-off occurred and notification shall be given to the player's Club by the Secretary of the Referees' Committee.

5. Penalties for Offside

(*a*) (i) When a team is offside and in possession of the ball, it shall lose possession to its opponents and the offending player(s) shall be placed onside.

(ii) When a team is offside and the ball is loose, possession shall be awarded to the opposing team and the offending player(s) shall be placed onside.

(iii) When a team is offside and its opponents have possession of the ball, the offending player(s) shall be suspended from the field of play for 30 sec and the offending team shall be placed onside.

(iv) When both teams are offside and one team has possession of the ball, the players shall be placed onside and play resumed with the team in possession of the ball retaining possession, the single exception being provided in paragraph (viii) hereof.

(v) When both teams are offside and the ball is loose, the players shall be placed onside and the Referee shall order a "face" between the players of opposing teams nearest to the ball when play was suspended.

(vi) If the attacking team is offside at the time a goal is scored, the goal shall not count and the Referee shall award a Free Position to the defending goalkeeper, to be taken from the centre of his goal-line.

(vii) If the defending team is offside when a goal is scored then the goal shall count and no penalty shall be inflicted on the offending team.

(viii) If both teams are offside when a goal is scored, the goal shall not count and the Referee shall order a "face" to be taken 20 ft (6 m) from the back line directly behind the goal, between players of each team.

(*b*) A player who has invoked a penalty for an offside offence, for which he is sent off the field by the Referee, shall leave the field at the gate and shall report at once to the Official who shall time the 30 sec penalty and order the player to return to the game through the gate upon the expiration of the penalty time.

NOTE. *The penalty time will only begin when the offending player reaches the penalty box or the game is re-started, whichever is later, and shall be interrupted only by the termination of a playing period or if the Referee should call his own time-out.*

(*c*) When a penalty for offside has been called, play shall be re-started by a player of the team offended against who is nearest to the ball when play was suspended. The only exception being when the ball is awarded to the attacking team within 20 yd of the goal, in which case play is re-started from a position 10 yd from goal, laterally across the field (also see Law D, 7(*d*)).

F.—THE GENERAL CONDUCT OF THE GAME

1. The Game

The game shall be played in a gentlemanly and sporting spirit, with no deliberate offences. The players shall at all times conform with the Laws freely and without question.

2. Playing the Ball

No player shall play the ball with a free hand (except as provided for the goal-keeper in Law F, Section 3).

NOTE. *Should a player offend against this Law, the Referee shall normally award a Technical foul.*

3. The Goal-keeper

Whilst defending his goal, being within the goal-crease, the goal-keeper may deflect the ball or block it in any manner with his body, including his hand, or crosse, but he may not catch it nor throw it with his hand.

NOTE. *Should the goal-keeper offend against this Law, the Referee shall normally award a Technical foul.*

4. The Goals

A player shall not deliberately move the goalposts and/or cross-bar or net.

NOTE 1. *Should a player defending a particular goal offend against this Law then a Technical foul shall normally be awarded to the attacking team.*

NOTE 2. *Should a player attacking a particular goal offend against this Law at that particular goal, then possession shall be given to the defending goal-keeper to be taken from the back line. If the ball has entered the goal prior to the Referee suspending play, then the score shall not count.*

5. The Goal-Crease

(*a*) An attacking player shall not, whether he has the ball in his possession or not:
  (i) enter his opponent's goal-crease area at any time when the ball is in his opponent's half of the field.

(ii) interfere with his opponent's goal-keeper whilst the latter is within his own goal-crease area. This does not prevent an attacking player from reaching within the goal-crease area to play a loose ball provided he does not interfere with the goal-keeper or step inside that area nor allow any part of his body to touch that area, neither does it prevent an attacking player from checking a goal-keeper or legally contesting possession of a ball outside the crease area, whether or not the goal-keeper be within that area.

NOTE. *Mere contact between the cross of the attacking player and the goal-keeper is not interference but checking the goal-keeper's crosse is interference.*

(*b*) A defending player with the ball in his possession may not enter the goal-crease area.

(*c*) No defending player, including the goal-keeper, with the ball in his possession, may remain within the goal-crease area for more than four seconds (counted as 1001, 1002, 1003, 1004). He may not re-enter the goal-crease area until he has parted with the ball nor play the ball again within the goal-crease area until it has been played by another player of either side.

NOTE 1. *A player is considered to be within the goal-crease area when any part of his body is touching the ground on or within the line marking that area.*

NOTE 2. *The Referee shall normally award possession to goal-keeper on the back line should any of his opponents offend against this Law. If the ball has entered the goal immediately before the Referee has signalled the offence, the score shall not count.*

NOTE 3. *Should a defender offend against this Law, the Referee shall award possession to the opponent nearest to the offending player. Play shall re-start from a point on the defenders' back boundary line, directly behind the goal.*

6. Charging and Checking

(*a*) *Charging.* A player may not charge an opponent in any way except to use a shoulder to shoulder charge against an opponent with whom he is engaged or is about to be engaged in a ground scuffle.

NOTE. *A shoulder-charge shall be considered to be made by a player using his shoulder only against another player's shoulder.*

(b) *Body-checking.* A player may "body-check" an opponent who is in possession of, or about to receive, or has just parted with, the ball.

NOTE. *A "body-check" shall be considered to be the placing of the body in the way of, and facing, an approaching opponent, so that the latter is simply impeded. The checking player's crosse must not be used to assist in any way, except for the purpose of checking the opponent's crosse as described in the next Section (c).*

(c) *Stick-checking.* A player may check an opponent's crosse providing that the opponent is in possession of the ball, or about to receive it, or is in the act of parting with it.

NOTE. *A "stick-check" shall be considered to be the striking with the crosse of an opponent's crosse in order to prevent him catching the ball, or to cause the ball to fall out of his crosse.*

(d) *Reckless and Dangerous Checking.* There shall be no reckless or dangerous checking.

NOTE. *Reckless and dangerous checking shall be considered to include, inter alia, unnecessary violence or slashing; the following through with a check so that the opponent is struck after the latter has moved his crosse; any action which might be dangerous to the body of an opponent,* whether his crosse be struck or not.

(e) *Striking the Head.* Any strike on the head or headgear by the crosse of an opponent is an offence.

NOTE. *For the purpose of this Law, mere contact is not a "strike". The contact must be a definite blow and not merely a brush.*

7. Obstruction.

A player shall not hold or trip an opponent; nor push him with his hand or crosse; nor grasp, hold or kick an opponent's crosse with hand(s), arm(s), leg(s) or feet; nor kneel, crouch, lie down or drop in front of an opponent; nor stand on or lie on the ball; nor in any way impede or obstruct an opponent's progress, except by means of a body-check.

NOTE. *The movement of an offensive player into the line of*

*a defence man, so as to cause interference once the move on goal
has commenced is illegal.*

8. Unfair Uses of the Crosse

(*a*) A player shall not throw his crosse under any circumstances.

(*b*) A player shall not touch the ball, nor body-check an
opponent, nor take any part in the game, unless he is gripping
his crosse with at least one hand.

(*c*) A player shall not strike an opponent with his crosse nor
hold his crosse out so that another player might run on to it,
nor wave his crosse in front of an opponent.

9. Misuse of the Boundaries

A player shall not deliberately throw, kick or otherwise propel
the ball, or run with the ball in his possession on to or over a
boundary line.

10. Stalling

If a team, whilst in possession of the ball, fails to play in a
reasonably progressive manner the Referee, after a verbal
warning of "Play On", shall penalise that team by loss of
possession of the ball. Possession shall be awarded to the opposing team from a point where the ball was at the time of the
infringement, but no nearer than 20 yd (18 m) to the goal of the
offending team.

NOTE 1. *Such conduct on the part of a player or team shall be
known as "Stalling", which is detrimental to the image and spirit
of the game.*

NOTE 2. *This rule shall not apply when possession is retained
in the offensive goal area.*

NOTE 3. *This rule applies whether a team is at full numerical
strength or otherwise.*

11. Players Leaving and Returning to the Field

Any player who leaves the field of play on the Referee's orders
must leave through the gate, and any player returning to the
game after his time penalty has expired must also re-enter

through the gate, except after a goal has been scored or at the end of a period.

12. Re-starting Game

A player shall not re-start game until the Referee has ordered play to re-start.

NOTE. *Should a player offend against this Law, then the Referee shall order change of possession.*

13. Definition of Penalties

(*a*) *Technical Fouls* are those of a less serious nature and the normal penalty is either loss of possession or 30 sec penalty if the opposition have possession. The scoring of a goal against a team having one or more players serving technical penalty time shall release those players but not for personal fouls.

The following is a list of these Technical Offences:

    (i) Obstruction, Law F.7
    (ii) Illegal block, Law F.7
    (iii) Holding, Law F.7
    (iv) Withholding the ball from play, Law F.7
    (v) Touching the ball with the hand, Law F.2
    (vi) Unfair uses of the crosse, Law F.8
    (vii) Infringement of the crease rules, Law F.5
    (viii) Infringement of rules at the face-off, Law D.2
    (ix) Misuse of the boundaries, Law F.9
    (x) Stalling, Law F.10
    (xi) Leaving and entering the field, without passing through the gate, Law F.11
    (xii) Offside rules, Law E.7

(*b*) *Personal Fouls* are those of a more serious nature. The following is a list of these Personal Fouls:

    (i) Illegal body-check Law F.6(*a*)
    (ii) Poke checking within the line of the body, Law F.6(*d*)
    (iii) Cross check or square check, Law F.6(*b*)
    (iv) Slashing, Law F.6(*b*)
    (v) Illegal checking, Law F.6(*c*)
    (vi) Head check, Law F.6(*e*)
    (vii) Tripping, Law F.7
    (viii) Unnecessary roughness, Law F.1

    (ix) Illegal equipment, Law A.1

    (x) Threatening, profane or obscene language and behaviour, Law F.1

(*c*) *Expulsion Fouls*

(i) The act of deliberately striking or attempting to strike an opponent, non-playing member of an opponent's squad, coach or anyone controlling the play of the game, with the hand, crosse, ball or otherwise may result in an expulsion foul.

(ii) Refusal to accept the Referee's authority or the use of foul or abusive language may result in an expulsion foul.

The Rules of
Netball

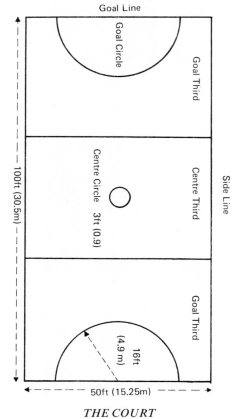

THE COURT

All lines are part of the court and shall not be more than 2 in (50 mm) wide.

Netball

THE GAME

Netball is an International Sport. It is played by two teams of seven players and is based on throwing and catching. Goals are scored from within a defined area by throwing the ball into a ring attached to a 10 ft (3.05 m) high post.

I. ORGANISATION OF THE GAME

1. Equipment

(1) COURT

    (i) The court shall have a firm surface and shall be 100 ft (30.5 m) long and 50 ft (15.25 m) wide. The longer sides shall be called side lines and the shorter sides goallines. (See Diagram.)

    (ii) The court shall be divided into three equal parts, a centre third and two goal thirds, by two transverse lines drawn parallel to the goal lines.

    (iii) A semi-circle with a radius of 16 ft (4.9 m) and with its centre at the mid-point of the goal line, shall be drawn in each goal third. This shall be called the goal circle.

    (iv) A circle 3 ft (0.9 m) in diameter shall mark the centre of the court. This shall be called the centre circle.

    (v) All lines are part of the court, and shall not be more than 2 in (50 mm) wide.

(2) GOALPOSTS

    (i) A goal post 10 ft (3.05 m) high shall be placed at the mid-point of each goal line. A metal ring 15 in (380 mm) in diameter shall project horizontally 6 in (150 mm) from the top of the post, the attachment to allow 6 in (150 mm) between the post and the near side of the ring. The ring shall be of tubular steel and $\frac{5}{8}$ in (15 mm) in diameter. It shall be fitted with a net open at both ends.

    (ii) The post may be inserted in a socket in the ground or

may be supported by a metal base which shall not project on the court.

(3) BALL

The ball shall be a netball, an Association football size 5, and shall measure between 27 and 28 in (660–690 mm) in circumference, and weigh between 14 and 16 oz (400–450 g). The ball may be of leather, rubber or similar material.

(4) PLAYERS

   (i) Shoes or boots may be worn. They shall be of light weight material. Spiked soles are not allowed.

  (ii) Registered playing uniform which shall include initials of playing positions, shall be worn at all times. Playing initials shall be worn both front and back above the waist and shall be 8 in (20 cm) high.

 (iii) No item of jewellery, except a wedding ring, shall be worn. If a wedding ring is worn, it shall be taped.

 (iv) Fingernails shall be cut short.

2. Officials

All Umpires, Official Scorers and Official Time-keepers at International matches shall be women. An Umpire shall wear a costume distinct from that of the players and preferably white or cream in colour. She shall wear suitable shoes.

(1) UMPIRES

There shall be two Umpires who shall have control of the game and give decisions. They shall umpire according to the rules and decide on any matter not covered by the rules.

The Umpire's whistle shall start and stop the game. The decisions of the Umpires shall be final and shall be given without appeal.

Each Umpire shall:

   (i) control and give decisions only in her half of the court unless appealed to by the other Umpire for a decision in her half and be ready for such an appeal at all times. For this purpose the length of the court is divided in half across the centre from side line to side line;

  (ii) give decisions for the Throw In for the whole of one side line and one goal line and shall restart the game after all goals scored in her half of the court;

(iii) umpire in the same half of the court throughout the match;

(iv) keep outside the court except when it is necessary to enter it to secure a clear view of play, or to give a Throw Up, or to indicate the point from which a penalty must be taken. If the ball strikes an Umpire during play, or if an Umpire interferes with the movements of the players, play does not cease unless one team has been unduly penalised, in which case a Free Pass is given to that team;

(v) keep moving along the side line and behind the goal line to see play in the goal circle;

(vi) refrain from blowing the whistle to penalise an infringement when by so doing she would place the non-offending team at a disadvantage;

(vii) not criticise or coach any team while a competition match is in progress.

(2) SCORERS

There shall be two Scorers who shall:

(i) keep a written record of the score together with a record of the Centre Passes;

(ii) record each goal as it is scored unless notified to the contrary by the Umpire. This constitutes the official score of the game;

(iii) keep a record of all unsuccessful shots;

(iv) call the Centre Pass if appealed to by the Umpire.

(3) TIMEKEEPER

The Timekeeper shall take the time when the game is started by the Umpire's whistle, and shall signal the end of each quarter or half to the Umpire. On instruction by the Umpire, she shall add additional time to the quarter or half in which a stoppage has occurred.

3. Duration of Game

(i) The game shall consist of four quarters of 15 min. each, with an interval of 3 min. between the first-second and third-fourth quarters and with a maximum of 10 min. at half-time. The mean time as requested by the respective teams shall determine the length of the interval at half-time. Teams shall change ends each quarter.

(ii) Where any one team plays two or more matches in one day, or where time is limited, the game shall consist of two halves of 20 min. each with a maximum 5 min. interval at half-time. The mean time as requested by the respective teams shall determine the length of the interval at half-time. Teams shall change ends at half-time.

(iii) Time lost for an accident or any other cause must be noted and added to that quarter of the game. In no case shall extra time be allowed except to take a penalty pass or shot.

(iv) In certain climatic conditions the duration of the game shall be determined by the countries concerned.

4. The Team

A team shall consist of seven players; the game is designed for single sex competition:

Goal Shooter—G.S.; Goal Attack—G.A.; Wing Attack—W.A.; Wing Defence—W.D.; Goal Defence—G.D.; Goal-keeper—G.K.; Centre—C.

No team may take the court with fewer than five players.

5. Captains

The Captains shall:

(1) Toss for choice of goal or first Centre Pass; and notify the Umpires of the result.

(2) During an interval or after stoppage for injury or illness notify the Umpires and the opposing Captain if they wish to change the position of players.

Penalty for (ii).

A free pass the first time a player enters an area which is offside in relation to her previous playing area. This pass shall be taken:

(i) from the place in the offside area where the infringement occurred.

    (ii) by a player allowed in that area.

    (iii) after time be allowed for the Captain of the non-offending team to be given the opportunity to re-arrange playing positions of her team.

(3) Be permitted to approach an Umpire during an interval or after the game for clarification of any rule.

6. Injuries and Illness

When a player is injured or ill or is unable to continue as a result of any other emergency, a stoppage of up to 5 min. is allowed to decide whether the injured or sick player is fit to continue play. The decision shall be left to the team's Officials.

7. Substitutes

A substitute is allowed only in the event of injury or illness. If a substitute is played the injured or sick player may take no further part in the match.

8. Late Arrivals

(1) No player, arriving after play has started, is allowed to replace a player who has filled the position of the latecomer.

(2) Late arrivals may not enter the game while play is in progress, but after notifying the Umpires and the opposing Captain may take the court:

    (i) After a goal has been scored. In this case the player must play in a position left vacant in her team.

    (ii) After a stoppage for injury or illness;

    (iii) Immediately following an interval.

II. PLAYING AREAS

1. Playing Areas

(1) The playing area for each player is listed below:

Goal Shooter	1,	2		
Goal Attack	1,	2,	3	
Wing Attack		2,	3	
Centre		2,	3,	4
Wing Defence			3,	4
Goal Defence			3,	4,	5
Goal Keeper				4,	5

Lines bounding each area are included as part of that area. (See Diagram.)

(2) Positions of players may be changed only:

 (i) during an interval;

 (ii) after stoppage caused by an injury or illness.

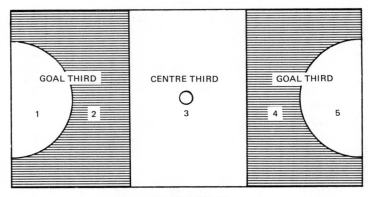

PLAYING AREAS

Diagram of Playing Areas

2. Offside

(1) A player with or without the ball shall be offside if she enters any area other than her playing area.

A player is considered to have entered an offside area if any part of her touches the ground beyond the line bounding her playing area. She may reach over and take the ball from her offside area, provided that she does not touch the ground in that area.

Penalty. A free pass to the opposing team.

(2) *Simultaneous offside.* When any two opposing players go offside at the same moment:

 (i) if neither makes any contact with the ball, they are not penalised;

 (ii) if one of them is in possession of the ball or touches it, a throw-up is given in their own area of play;

   (iii) if both of them are in possession of the ball or touch it, a throw-up is given in their own area of play;

   (iv) if they are from adjoining playing areas, a throw-up is given in the centre third, between two players allowed in that area.

3. Out of Court

(1) The ball is out when:

   (i) it touches the ground outside the court;

   (ii) it touches an object or person in contact with the ground outside the court;

   (iii) it is held by a player in contact with the ground outside the court.

A ball which hits any part of the goal-post and rebounds into play is not out of court.

(2) A player in contact with the ball is out of court when:

   (i) she touches the ground outside the boundary line;

   (ii) she touches any object or person outside the boundary line.

(3) A player having no contact with the ball may stand out of court; but before playing the ball she must re-enter the court and have no contact with the ground out of the court.

Penalty for Out of Court: A Throw In to the opposing team.

(4) If the ball is caught simultaneously by two opposing players one of whom is out of court, a Throw Up is given between these two players opposite to the point where the player was out of court.

III. CONDUCT OF THE GAME

1. Positioning of Players for Start of Play

(1) The Centre in possession of the ball shall stand wholly inside the Centre Circle.

(2) The opposing Centre shall be in the Centre Third, and free to move.

(3) All other players shall be in the Goal Third which is part of their playing area and free to move, but none of these players

is allowed into the Centre Third until the whistle has been blown to start the game.

Penalty: Free Pass to the opposing team.

2. Start of Play

(1) (i) The Umpire shall blow her whistle to start and restart play.

    (ii) Play shall be started and restarted after each goal is scored, and after each interval by a Centre Pass taken alternately by the two Centres throughout the game.

If, at a Centre Pass, the ball is still in the Centre's hands when the Umpire's whistle is blown to signal the end of the quarter or half, the Centre is deemed not to have taken the pass, and that team will therefore take the pass after the interval.

(2) (i) When the whistle is blown the Centre in possession of the ball shall throw it within 3 seconds and shall obey the Footwork Rule.

    (ii) The Centre Pass shall be caught or touched by any other player who is standing or who lands within the Centre Third. A player who lands with her first foot, or on both feet simultaneously wholly within the Centre Third is deemed to have received the ball in that third. Her subsequent throw shall be considered to have been made from the Centre Third. A player who lands on both feet simultaneously with one foot wholly within the Centre Third and the other wholly within the Goal Third is deemed to have received the ball in the Goal Third.

    (iii) If a member of the team taking the Centre Pass catches the ball in the Goal Third without it having touched it in the Centre Third, a Free Pass shall be awarded to the opposing team, to be taken in the Goal Third close to the point where the ball crossed the line.

    (iv) If a member of the opposing team touches or catches the ball in the Centre Third, or receives the Centre Pass in the Goal Third, play shall continue.

    (v) If the ball from the Centre Pass goes untouched over the Side Line bounding the Centre Third, a Throw In is awarded to the opposing team.

3. Playing the Ball

(1) A player may:

- (i) catch the ball with one or both hands,
- (ii) gain or regain control of the ball if it rebounds from the goalpost,
- (iii) bat or bounce to another player a ball that comes within her reach without first having possession of it,
- (iv) having tipped the ball in an uncontrolled manner into the air once or more than once, either catch the ball or direct it to another player.
- (v) having batted the ball once, or bounced the ball once, either catch the ball or direct it to another player,
- (vi) roll the ball to gain possession.

(2) A player may not:

- (i) deliberately kick the ball (a ball which is thrown and accidently hits the leg of a player is not deemed to be a kick),
- (ii) strike the ball with a fist,
- (iii) deliberately throw her body on the ball to get it,
- (iv) attempt to gain possession or throw the ball while lying, sitting or kneeling on the ground. A player who falls while holding the ball must regain her footing and throw the ball within three seconds of receiving the ball.
- (v) use the goalpost as a support in recovering a ball going out of court or as a means of regaining balance, or in any other way for any other purpose.

(3) *When a player has caught or held the ball she must* play it or shoot for goal within 3 seconds.

To play the ball she may:

- (i) throw it in any manner and in any direction to another player,
- (ii) bounce it with one or both hands in any direction to another player.

(4) *When a player has caught or held the ball she may not*:

- (i) roll the ball to another player,
- (ii) throw the ball and play it before it has been touched by another player,
- (iii) toss the ball into the air and replay it,

(iv) drop the ball and replay it,
(v) bounce the ball and replay it.
(5) (i) At the moment the ball is passed there must be room on the court, for a third player to move between *the hands* of the thrower and those of the receiver.
(ii) The ball may not be thrown over a complete third without being touched by a player who is standing or who lands in that third. A player who lands with her first foot wholly within the correct third is deemed to have received the ball in that third. Her subsequent throw shall be considered to have been made from that third. A player who lands on both feet simultaneously with one foot wholly within the correct third, and the other in the incorrect third shall be penalised.

Penalty: A Free Pass to the opposing team where the infringement occurred. For throwing over a third the ball is taken just beyond the second line that the ball has crossed, except when the ball thrown from the Centre Third passes out of court over the Goal Line when the penalty shall be a Throw In by the opposing team.

4. Footwork

(1) A player may receive the ball with one foot grounded, or jump to catch and land on one foot and then:
(i) step with the other foot in any direction, lift the landing foot and throw or shoot before this foot is regrounded;
(ii) step with the other foot in any direction any number of times, pivoting on the landing foot. She may lift the pivoting foot, but must throw or shoot before she regrounds it;
(iii) jump from the landing foot on to the other foot and jump again but must throw the ball or shoot before regrounding either foot;
(iv) step with the other foot and jump but must throw the ball or shoot before regrounding either foot.

(2) A player may receive the ball while both feet are grounded, or jump to catch and land on both feet simultaneously and then:

   (i) step with either foot in any direction, lift the other foot and throw or shoot before this foot is re-grounded;

  (ii) step with either foot in any direction any number of times pivoting on the other. She may lift the pivoting foot but must throw or shoot before she regrounds it;

(iii) jump from both feet, but must throw or shoot before regrounding either foot;

(iv) step with either foot and jump but must throw the ball or shoot before regrounding either foot.

(3) A player in possession of the ball may not:

  (i) drag or slide the landing foot along the ground;

  (ii) hop on either foot.

Penalty: A Free Pass to the opposing team.

5. Scoring a Goal

(1) A goal is scored when the ball is thrown or batted over and completely through the ring by Goal Shooter or Goal Attack from any point within the Goal Circle including the lines bounding the Circle.

  (i) If another player throws the ball through the ring no goal is scored and play continues.

  (ii) If a defending player deflects a shot for goal and the ball then passes over and completely through the ring the goal is scored.

(iii) Goal Shooter or Goal Attack may shoot for goal or pass if the ball is won at a Throw Up in the Goal Circle.

(iv) If the whistle for an interval or "time" is blown before the ball has passed completely through the ring, the goal is not scored.

  (v) If the whistle for an interval or "time is blown *after* a Penalty pass or shot has been awarded to Goal Shooter or Goal Attack in the Goal Circle, it shall be taken or completed.

(2) In taking a shot for goal a player shall:

  (i) have no contact with the ground outside the Goal Circle either during the catching of the ball or whilst she is holding it. She does not make the contact with the ground if she leans on the ball, but if this happens behind the Goal Line, the ball is considered to be out of court,

(ii) shoot within 3 sec. of catching or holding the ball,

(iii) obey the Footwork Rule.

Penalty: A Free Pass to the opposing team.

(3) If a defending player causes the goalpost to move so as to interfere with the shot at goal, a Penalty pass or shot shall be awarded to the opposing team who may pass or shoot. The penalty shall be taken from near where the offender was standing.

IV. PENALTIES

The penalties awarded for the breaking of the rules are:

1. The Free Pass
2. The Penalty Pass or Shot
3. The Throw In
4. The Throw Up

General Rules for the taking of penalties are as follows:

(1) A penalty for an infringement on court is taken where the infringement occurred except as provided for under Penalty for contact and obstruction.

(2) The Umpire indicates the correct place.

(3) The penalties, with the exception of the Throw Up, are awarded to a team. Providing she is allowed in the area where the penalty is awarded, any member of the opposing team may take the penalty.

(4) The player taking the penalty must throw the ball within 3 seconds after she has taken up her position at the correct place and is in possession of the ball.

(5) In the taking of a Free Pass, Penalty pass or shot or Throw In, the Footwork Rule applies as though the foot placed at the point indicated were equivalent to the landing foot in a one foot landing, or to receiving the ball with one foot grounded.

(6) If the player taking a Free Pass, or Penalty pass or shot, infringes (2)–(5) above, a Free Pass is awarded to the opposing team. In the case of an infringement by a player taking a Throw In, the opposing team is awarded the Throw In.

1. *Free Pass*

(1) A Free Pass is awarded for infringements of the rules on the court with the exception of the Rules of Contact and Obstruction, and simultaneous offences by two opposing players.

(2) When a Free Pass is awarded, the ball may be thrown by any player in the opposing team allowed in the area, but the ball may not be thrown over a complete third of the court without being touched or caught by a player in that third.

2. *Penalty Pass*

(1) A Penalty Pass is awarded for infringement of the Rules of Contact and Obstruction.

(2) When a Goal Shooter or Goal Attack is contacted or obstructed within the Goal Circle by any member of the opposing team, the player who takes the penalty may make either a pass or a shot for goal.

(3) If a player is penalised for Contact or Obstruction, she must stand beside and away from the thrower taking the penalty. She must make no movement to take part in the play until the ball has left the thrower's hands.

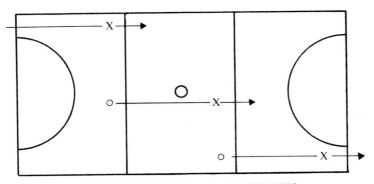

DIAGRAM OF THROWING OVER COMPLETED THIRD.

Arrow shows flight of ball.
X where the free pass is taken—just inside the second line that the ball has crossed

(4) An attempt to intercept the pass or shot may be made by any opposing player allowed in the area, other than the offender, but if the player, in making her attempt contacts or obstructs the thrower during the taking of the pass or shot, it shall be retaken with the original and the second offender each standing beside and away from the thrower taking no part in the play until the ball has left the thrower's hands.

(5) When two members of a team simultaneously contact or obstruct a member of the opposing team, each offender shall stand beside and away from the thrower, taking no part in the play until the ball has left the thrower's hands.

3. *Throw In*

(1) When it goes out of court, the ball shall be put into play by a member of the team opposing either: (i) the player who last had contact with the ball, *or* (ii) the player who received it with any part of her touching the ground outside the court.

The player throwing the ball in shall:

   (i) stand outside the court and place one foot as close as possible to the line without touching or standing on it at the point where the Umpire indicates that the ball has crossed the line;
  (ii) wait for the Umpire to say "play" when all other players are on court;
 (iii) throw within 3 seconds after the Umpire has called "play";
  (iv) not enter the court until the ball has left her hands;
   (v) throw into the nearest third of the court from behind the goal-lines, or the nearest or adjacent third from behind the sidelines;
  (vi) throw only from behind the line bounding her own playing area. If using the footwork rule the player must remain behind this area until she has released the ball.

Penalties for Infringements at the Throw In

   (i) By the thrower—a Throw In is awarded to the opposing team, except under (v).
  (ii) By a member of the opposing team who contacts, ob-

structs or intimidates on the court—a Penalty Pass is awarded on the court, where the infringement occurred.

If the ball is sent out of court simultaneously by two players in opposing teams, or the Umpire cannot decide who touched the ball last, there shall be a Throw Up, opposite the point where the ball went out.

When the ball from a Throw In goes out of court without being touched, a Throw In shall be taken by the opposing team from behind the point where the ball last went out.

4. *Throw Up*

(1) A throw-up puts the ball into play when:
  (i) opposing players gain simultaneous possession of the ball with either or both hands,
  (ii) opposing players simultaneously knock the ball out of court,
  (iii) opposing players are involved and the Umpire is unable to determine the last player to touch the ball before it goes out of court.
  (iv) opposing players are simultaneously offside, one in possession of, or touching the ball,
  (v) opposing players make simultaneous contact which interferes with play,
  (vi) after an accident, the Umpires are unable to determine who had the ball, or the ball was on the ground when play stopped.

(2) The Throw Up is taken on court between two players concerned as near as possible to the place where the incident occurred, unless boundaries of playing area prevent this, e.g.:
  (i) where the incident involves two opposing players across a line dividing areas one of which is comon to both players, the Throw Up is given between those two players in the common area,
  (ii) where the incident involves two opposing players from adjoining playing areas across a transverse line and no area is common to both, the Throw Up is given in the Centre Third between any two opposing players allowed in that area,
  (iii) where two opposing players simultaneously knock the

ball out of court over a line bounding an area which is not common to both, the Throw Up is given between any two opposing players allowed in that area, on court opposite the point where the ball crossed the line.

(3) The two players shall stand facing each other and their own goal ends with arms straight and hands to sides, but feet in any position. There shall be a distance of 3 ft (0.9 m) between the nearer foot to one player and that of her opponent. They shall not move in any way until the whistle is blown.

(4) The Umpire flicks the ball vertically not more than 2 ft (600 mm) into the air from a point midway between the players, and below the shoulder level of the shorter player's normal standing position. The whistle is blown as the ball is released. If one player moves too soon, a Free Pass is awarded to the opposing team.

(5) The ball may be caught or it may be batted in any direction except directly at the opposing player. All other players may stand or move anywhere within their playing area.

(6) Within the Goal Circle, a Goal Shooter or Goal Attack may attempt to shoot for goal or pass if she succeeds in gaining possession of the ball from the Throw Up.

V. CONTACT AND OBSTRUCTION

Penalty. For both Contact and Obstruction:
- (i) The penalty shall be taken from where the infringer was standing except where this puts the non-offending team at a disadvantage, when the penalty shall be taken where the contacted or obstructed player was standing.
- (ii) The infringer must stand beside the thrower and take no part in the play until the ball has left the player's hands. If the infringer moves before the ball has left the thrower's hands the penalty shall be retaken unless the pass or shot is successful.
- (iii) Any player allowed in the area may take the penalty.

1. Personal Contact

(1) No player shall come into personal contact with an opponent *in such a manner as to interfere with her play either accidentally or deliberately.*

(i) By her own effort to get free she shall not:
  (*a*) push her opponent in any way,
  (*b*) trip or knock her opponent in any way.
(ii) By her own effort to contact the ball she shall not throw her body against an opponent or rush into her.
(iii) By her effort to defend, she shall not:
  (*a*) keep her elbow against an opponent,
  (*b*) hold an opponent; this includes feeling her to keep near her,
  (*c*) push an opponent,
  (*d*) charge an opponent; that is, when jumping throw her body against a player.
(iv) Whether attempting to get free, or to defend, a player is responsible for any personal contact:
  (*a*) if she takes a position so near an opponent that contact is inevitable,
  (*b*) if she moves so quickly into a moving opponent's path that contact cannot be avoided.
(v) A player shall not contact another on any other occasion or in any other way in such a manner as to interfere with her play.

2. Contact with the Ball

(i) A player while holding the ball shall not touch or push an opposing player with it in such a manner as to interfere with her play.
(ii) A player shall not place a hand or hands on, or remove from her possession the ball held by an opposing player either accidentally or deliberately.
(iii) Where (i) and (ii) occur simultaneously a Throw Up is given between those two players.

3. Obstruction

(1) Defending a player in possession of the ball.

Any effort to defend a player with the ball from a distance closer than 3 ft (0.9 m) is obstruction. This distance is measured on the ground as follows:

(i) if the attacker's landing, grounded or pivoting foot

remains on the ground, the distance is measured from that foot to the nearer foot of the defender;

(ii) if the landing, grounded, or pivoting foot is lifted, the distance is measured from the spot on the ground from which the foot was lifted, to the nearer foot of the defender;

(iii) if a player jumps to catch the ball, lands on both feet simultaneously and remains grounded on both feet, the distance is measured from whichever is the nearer foot to the nearer foot of the defender.

(2) Intercepting a Throw.

A defender may attempt to intercept a ball if the distance on the ground is not less than 3 ft (0.9 m) from the attacker as specified in this rule. If, however, the attacker moves towards the defender, the defender may attempt to intercept from her original position.

(3) Obstruction of a player in possession of the ball.

(i) If, when attempting to intercept, a defender steps towards the attacker, she is obstructing if she places a foot within 3 ft (0.9 m) of the point specified in this rule.

(ii) A defender may attempt to intercept by jumping from the point specified in this rule. If she lands within 3 ft (0.9 m) of the player in possession of the ball, and her body interferes with the throwing motion, she is obstructing.

(4) Obstruction of a player not in possession of the ball.

A player is obstructing if within a distance of 3 ft (0.9 m) (measured on the ground) from an opponent without the ball:

(i) the arms are outstretched to defend that opponent, or

(ii) any movements are employed which take the arms away from the body other than those movements involved with natural body balance. The arms may be outstretched to intercept a pass.

(5) Obstruction by intimidation.

When a player with or without the ball intimidates an opponent, she is obstructing.

VI. GENERAL

1. Stoppages

(i) After stoppages for injury or illness or for any other cause, the game is continued from the spot where the ball was when play was stopped.

(ii) Time lost must be added to that quarter or half.

(iii) If the accident is due to Personal Contact or Obstruction the infringement is penalised where it occurred and play continues.

(iv) If the Umpire is unable to say who was in possession of the ball when play stopped, a Throw Up is given between any two opposing players allowed in that area, as near as possible to the spot where the ball was when play ceased.

2. Discipline

The breaking of rules and/or the employment of any action not covered by the wording of the rules, in a manner contrary to the spirit of the game, is not permitted.

This includes the breaking of rules between the scoring of a goal and the restart of play, between a ball going out of court and the Throw In, between the award and taking of a Free Pass, or a Penalty pass or shot.

An Umpire may order a player to leave the court, but only when she is sure that the ordinary penalty is insufficient, and, except in extreme cases, only after a warning. (She may stand a player off the court for a specified part of the game: until the next goal is scored; until the next interval; for the rest of the game.)

When a player is suspended, a substitute may not take her place.

In the event of a Centre being suspended that team may move *one* player only to allow play to continue.

Copyright by the All England Netball Association.

The Laws of
Real Tennis and Rackets

The Laws of Real Tennis

1. Definitions

In these laws the following words have the following meanings:

Back Walls. The walls between the floor and the penthouse adjoining the main wall.

Bandeau. The strip of wall immediately below a penthouse, usually made of the same material as the penthouse.

Better. One chase is better than another if it is made on the same side of the court and further from the net (Rule 9). In marking chases, better means that the ball makes a chase
  (a) further from the net than the line mentioned, and
  (b) nearer to that line than to any other yard or gallery line (Rule 9b).

Bisque. One stroke in a set conceded to an opponent (Rule 22).

Chase. A chase is made whenever the ball falls in the hazard court, or anywhere on the service side, or enters a gallery, except the winning gallery (Rule 9).

  ... *attacking a*—When a chase is being played for, the opponent of the player who made the chase is said to be attacking the chase (Rules 11 and 12).

  ... *calling a*—The marker calls a chase when he states the chase that is to be played for.

  ... *defending a*—When a chase is being played for, the player who made the chase is said to be defending the chase (Rules 11 and 12).

  ... *lines*—The lines marked on the floor to enable the marker to mark chases are called chase lines or chases (Rule 8).

  ... *marking a*—The marker marks a chase when that chase is made.

  ... *off*—See rule 12b.

  ... *the line*—See Line, Chase the.

Court. The enclosure in which the game is played. The court is divided into two sides, the service side and the hazard side (*q.v.*).

Dead. A ball is said to be dead when it ceases to be in play.

Dedans. The opening at the back of the service side.

Double. If the ball falls before it is struck it is a double.

Drop. A ball is said to drop when, after passing the net, it first touches the floor, or enters an opening without having previously touched the floor.

Enter a Gallery or an Opening. See Opening, Entering an.

Fall. A ball is said to fall when, after having dropped, it touches the floor again, or enters an opening.

Fault Line. The line on the floor nearest the grille and extending from the service line to the grille wall.

Gallery. An opening below the penthouse opposite to the main wall.

The starting galleries are named as follows, starting from the net:

(*a*) on the service side, the line, the first gallery, the door, the second gallery, the last gallery;

(*b*) on the hazard side, the line, the first gallery, the door, the second gallery, the winning gallery.

Gallery Post. The post between two galleries is considered to be part of the gallery nearer the net.

The part of the gallery net that is attached to and surrounds a gallery post is part of that post.

Good Return. See Return.

Grille. The opening in the grille wall.

Grille Wall. The back wall on the hazard side.

Half-Court Line. The line that bisects the floor, between the main wall and the side wall.

Hazard Chase or Hazard Side Chase. A chase made on the hazard side of the court.

Hazard Court. The floor on the hazard side from the net up to, but not including, the service line.

Hazard Side. The side of the court on the left of the net when facing the main wall.

In Play. A ball served is in play until—

(*a*) the service becomes a fault, or

(*b*) either player fails to make a good return.

Ledge. The horizontal surface of a wall that forms an opening.

Line, Chase the, is chase at the line of the net.

On the floor it is the area between the net and worse than the first gallery.

The line gallery is that between the net post and the post next to it.

Main Wall. The wall that has no penthouse.

Net Post. The post supporting the net under the penthouse.

Nick. The junction of the wall and the floor, or a return when the ball, as it drops or falls, touches the wall and floor simultaneously.

Opening. Any gallery or winning opening.

Opening, Entering an. A ball enters an opening when a good return or service—

- (*a*) touches the post (see Gallery Post), net, or tray or that opening, or
- (*b*) touches anything lying in that opening (if an article is lying in an opening any part of it, even outside, is considered to be in that opening), or
- (*c*) comes to rest in or on the ledge of that opening, or
- (*d*) in the case of the grille, touches the woodwork at the back of the framing of the grille.

Out of Court. A ball is out of court if it touches any part of

- (*a*) the walls above the area prepared for play, or
- (*b*) the roof or roof beams or girders, or passes over any of these beams or girders, or
- (*c*) the lighting equipment.

Passing the Net. The ball passes the net when it crosses it between the net post and the main wall, or when it crosses the line bisecting the side penthouse.

Rest. A stroke or series of strokes, commencing when the ball is served and terminating when the ball is dead.

Return, or Return of the Ball in Play. The return of the ball is good if—

- (*a*) it is struck before it falls, and
- (*b*) it is struck so that it passes the net without having previously touched the floor or anything lying on the floor, or the net post, or without having entered an opening, and
- (*c*) it has not touched the player or anything he wears or carries except his racket in the act of striking the ball, and
- (*d*) it does not go out of court, and
- (*e*) it is struck definitely and only once, and

(*f*) it is not on the side of the net opposed to the player when he strikes it, and

(*g*) in courts where there is a wing net between the net post and the net, it does not touch the wing net before crossing the net.

Except that such a return is not good if—

(*h*) the player touches the net before striking the ball or

(*i*) the player touches the net after the ball and before the ball is dead, or

(*j*) the ball, after passing the net, comes back and drops on the side from which it was played (even if it touches the net before so dropping the return is not good).

Service. The method of starting a rest.

Service Court. The part of the floor on the hazard side that lies between the side wall, the grille wall, the fault line and the service line (including those two lines).

Service Line or Winning Gallery Line. The line which is nearest and parallel to the grille wall.

Service Penthouse. That part of the side penthouse which is on the hazard side of the court including the line that bisects the side penthouse.

Service Side. The side of the court on the right of the net when facing the main wall.

Service Wall. The wall above the side penthouse.

Side Penthouse. The penthouse above the galleries, up to its junction with the other penthouses.

Side Wall. The wall below the side penthouse.

Striker. The player who last struck the ball.

Striker-Out. The player who is to take the service.

Tray. The inner part of the bottom of an opening behind the ledge, usually made of wood.

Uneven Odds. When points given and/or received are not the same in each game, and/or when one or more bisques or half-bisques are given.

Winning Gallery. The last gallery on the hazard side.

Winning Openings. The dedans, the grille, and the winning gallery.

Worse. One chase is worse than another if it is made on the same side of the court and nearer to the net (Rule 9).

In marking chases, worse means that the ball makes a chase

(*a*) nearer to the net than the line mentioned, and

(*b*) nearer to that line than to any other yard or gallery line (Rule 9b).

2. Net

The height of the net above the level of the floor shall be—

(*a*) at the centre, 3 ft, and

(*b*) at the main wall and below the edge of the penthouse, 5 ft.

3. Balls

The balls shall be not less than $2\frac{7}{16}$ in and not more than $2\frac{9}{16}$ in in diameter.

They shall not be less than $2\frac{1}{2}$ oz and not more than $2\frac{3}{4}$ oz in weight.

4. Rackets

There are no restrictions as to the shape or size of rackets.

5. Sides

(*a*) The choice of sides at the beginning of a match is decided by spin of a racket.

(*b*) Subsequently the players change sides only when two chases have been scored or when one player is at 40 or advantage and one chase has been scored.

(*c*) If the players change sides before they should have done so, or do not change sides when they should, any strokes so played on the wrong side shall be scored and play shall continue as if no mistake had been made, except that any chase scored (Rule 10) in excess of the proper number shall be annulled if the mistake is discovered before that chase has been played for (Rule 11).

6. Service

The service is always given by the player who is on the service side.

A service is good if it is not a fault.

A service is a fault:

(a) if the server stands on or beyond the second gallery line, or

(b) if the server misses the ball or does not definitely strike it or strikes it more than once, or

(c) if the ball served, before touching the side penthouse, touches anything except the service wall (if the ball touches the edge of the penthouse before touching anything else it is a fault), or

(d) if the ball served does not touch the service penthouse (if the ball, after striking the service wall, in dropping touches the edge of the service penthouse, it is considered to have touched the penthouse), or

(e) if the ball served goes out of court, or

(f) if the ball served strikes the main wall before dropping, or

(g) if the ball served drops anywhere except in the service court or in the winning gallery.

A service that has become a fault may not be returned but one that would otherwise become a fault may be volleyed.

If striker-out is not ready for a service and does not attempt to take it, a let (Rule 17) shall be allowed.

8. Chase Lines, How Marked

Chase lines are marked on the floor as follows:

Service Side—

Half-a-yard,

One yard,

One and two,

Two,

and so on up to six, then

Half-a-yard worse than six,

The last gallery,

Half-a-yard worse than the last gallery,

A yard worse then the last gallery,

The second gallery,

The door, and

The first gallery.

Hazard Side. The same as on the service side, except that all chases between two and the second gallery are omitted and the last or winning gallery line is called the service line.

9. Chases, How Made

(*a*) When the ball enters a gallery (except the winning gallery) or falls on the floor (unless it falls in the service court) it makes a chase at the gallery it enters or at the line on which it falls.

(*b*) When it falls between two lines it makes a chase better or worse than the yard line or the gallery line nearest to the spot where it fell, except that—

(1) it makes chase better than half a yard when it so falls, and

(2) when it falls better or worse than the line "a yard worse than the last gallery" the chase is called "nearly a yard" or "more than a yard worse than the last gallery", and

(3) when it falls nearer to the net than to the first gallery line it makes chase the line, and

(4) when it drops or falls in the net on the side opposed to the striker or drops on the side opposed to the striker and then falls on the side from which it was struck it makes chase the line on the side opposed to the striker, and

(5) when it drops or falls on another ball on the floor it makes a chase as if it had fallen where that other ball was lying.

10. Chase, How and When Scored

(*a*) When no chase is being played for, a chase is scored when made in accordance with Rule 9.

(*b*) When a chase is scored, the score in strokes is unaltered.

11. Chases, When Played For

When two chases have been scored, or when one player is at 40 or advantage and one chase has been scored, the players change sides and the chase or chases in the order in which they were made are immediately played for.

A chase is played for once only, unless there is a let (Rule 17).

12. Chases, How Won or Lost

When a chase is being played for,

(*a*) the player attacking the chase loses it if—
    (1) he serves two consecutive faults, or
    (2) he does not make a good return, or
    (3) he makes a chase worse than the one being played for;

(*b*) it is a chase off when the player attacking the chase makes a chase equal to the one being played for;
(when it is chase off the chase is annulled and the score is unaltered).

(*c*) the player attacking the chase wins it if—
    (1) his opponent serves two consecutive faults, or
    (2) his opponent does not make a good return (unless the player attacking the chase makes a chase worse than or equal to the one being played for, in which case paragraph (*a*) or (*b*) of this rule applies) or
    (3) he makes a chase better than the one being played for.

13. Errors Regarding Chases

(*a*) Either player may appeal regarding the marking of a chase (Rule 18*a*).

(*b*) If the chase to be played for is wrongly called by the marker, the server may appeal before delivering the service, and the striker-out before attempting to take it.

If there is no such appeal, the chase played for shall be that called by the marker immediately before the service is delivered, notwithstanding that this may be different from that marked when the chase was scored.

(*c*) If there has been any misunderstanding as to what chase the marker called, the rest as played shall stand or a let (Rule 17) may be allowed, whichever the marker (or referee if appealed to) considers equitable in view of all the circumstances.

(*d*) If, through any mistake, at the end of the game there is a chase that has been scored and not played for, that chase is annulled.

(*e*) If the players change sides when too few or too many chases have been made, see rule 5.

14. Strokes, How Won

A player wins a stroke—
- (*a*) if he wins a chase (Rule 12*c*), or
- (*b*) if his opponent loses a chase (Rule 12*a*), or
- (*c*) if a return or a good service played by him enters a winning opening or falls on the service line or between the service line and grille wall or
- (*d*) if when no chase is being played for and provided that no chase is made his opponent does not make a good return, or
- (*e*) if his opponent serves two consecutive faults (Rule 6).

15. Strokes and Games, How Scored

In each game, when either player wins his first stroke his score is called 15; when he wins his second stroke, 30; when he wins his third stroke, 40; and when he wins his fourth stroke, he wins the game, except as below.

When both players have won three strokes, the score is called deuce, and it is called advantage to the player who then wins the next stroke.

If the player who is at advantage wins the next stroke, he wins the game; if he loses it, the score is again called deuce, and so on until the player who is at advantage wins a stroke and the game.

16. Sets, How Won

The player who first wins 6 games in a set wins it except that advantage sets are played—
- (*a*) if uneven odds are given and/or received, or
- (*b*) if the players agree.

In advantage sets, if the score is 5 games all, the set continues until either player has won two games more than his opponent.

17. Let

In the case of a let—
- (*a*) the rest to which it refers counts for nothing, and
- (*b*) if a chase was being played for, it is then played for again, and
- (*c*) if there was a previous fault, it is not annulled.

18. Referee

(*a*) Either player may appeal to the referee (whose decision is final) about any point subject to the following:

(1) the server shall not, after delivering a service, appeal about any point prior to that service, and

(2) the striker-out shall not, after attempting to take a service, appeal about any point prior to that service.

(*b*) When the marker calls "not up" or in any way indicates that a rest has terminated, the ball is dead.

If the referee's decision is that the rest should not then have been terminated, a let (Rule 17) shall be allowed.

(*c*) In all cases of doubt the referee may—

(1) ask the opinion of one or more spectators who were in a better position to see, or

(2) allow a let (Rule 17), or

(3) accept the marker's decision.

(*d*) The referee may appoint someone, in a better position to judge the hazard side, to assist him in appeals as to where the ball dropped or fell on the hazard side.

(*e*) The referee shall not, without an appeal, correct any decisions of the marker but he should—

(1) see that the players change sides at the right time and

(2) correct errors in the calling of the score or of chases when such calls are not in accordance with the decision given when the stroke or chase was scored.

19. Marker

(*a*) In the absence of an appeal, the marker's decision is final.

(*b*) In cases of doubt the marker may appeal to the referee, or, if there is no referee, to one or more spectators.

(*c*) A fault-caller may be appointed to assist the marker.

If either the marker or the fault-caller calls fault, the service (subject to appeal) is a fault.

If the call of fault is reversed on appeal, that fault is annulled.

20. Three or Four-handed Games (also called Doubles)

(*a*) Before commencing each set the players on the service side select the partner who is to serve. He is then the server and striker-out for his side throughout that game and for alternate games throughout the set, his partner serving and striking out in the other games.

Similarly the players on the hazard side then decide who is to be striker-out and server.

(*b*) A return of service is not good if made by striker-out's partner, unless the ball served has dropped in the service court between the half-court line and the fault line (including those two lines).

(*c*) Apart from the above, the laws for Singles apply to Doubles and a player and his partner are in all cases subject to the same laws as a player in Singles.

HANDICAPS

21. Half Odds

(*a*) When half odds are given, one stroke less than the full odds is given in the first and every odd game of the set, and the full odds are given in every game (*e.g.*, $\frac{1}{2}$–30 means 15 in the first, third, etc., game and 30 in the second, fourth, etc., game).

(*b*) When half odds are owed, the full odds are owed in the odd games and one stroke less in the even games.

22. Bisque

The player receiving the bisque may take it to win one stroke in each set at any time subject to the following:

   (*a*) he may not take it during a rest, and
   (*b*) if server, he may not take it after serving one fault, and
   (*c*) if he takes it to win or to defend a chase, he may not do so before the time comes to change sides. Then, if there is only one chase, he may take it and need not change sides, or he may take it after changing sides but, after he has passed the net, he may not go back again.

If there are two chases the players must change sides before he takes it to win or to defend either of them.

23. Half-bisque

The player receiving a half-bisque may take it—

   (*a*) to call chase-off and so to annul a chase about to be played for, or (*b*) to annul a fault served by him, or

(*c*) to add a second fault to one served by his opponent, or

(*d*) the handicapper may give a half-bisque as being one bisque in every alternate set, in which case the bisque must be taken in the odd sets.

Apart from (*b*) the conditions regarding taking a bisque (Rule 22) apply equally to a half-bisque.

24. Cramped Odds

Unless specifically stated the limiting conditions of cramped odds do not apply to service.

Cramped odds may be such as are fixed by the handicapper but the more usual forms are as follows:

(*a*) *Bar the Openings*. The giver of the odds loses a stroke whenever a ball returned by him enters an opening.

(*b*) *Bar the Winning Openings*. The giver of the odds loses a stroke whenever a ball returned by him enters the dedans, the grille, or the winning gallery.

(*c*) *Chase*. When a player gives a specified chase this applies only to a chase on the service side.

Any chase made by the giver of the odds worse than the one specified loses him a stroke.

Any chase made by the receiver of the odds worse than the one specified is considered equal to the one specified.

(*d*) *Half-Court*. The players shall agree or the handicapper decide to which half-court, on each side of the net, the giver of the odds shall play. He loses a stroke if a ball returned by him drops in the other half-court or in an opening or in half the dedans in the other half-court.

A ball that drops on the half-court line does not lose him a stroke.

After the ball has dropped the ordinary rules apply.

(*e*) *Round Services*. The striker-out may refuse to take any service that does not touch the grille penthouse. If he attempts to take such a service that service becomes good if not otherwise a fault.

A service otherwise good, that does not touch the service penthouse, is not counted a fault.

(*f*) *Touch No Side Walls*. The giver of the odds loses a stroke if a ball in play returned by him touches the side wall, the service wall, or the main wall, or enters a gallery.

(*g*) *Touch No Walls.* The giver of the odds loses a stroke whenever a ball in play returned by him touches any wall, or enters an opening.

A ball that falls in a nick is not considered to have touched the wall.

A penthouse is not a wall.

A bandeau is part of a wall.

The above odds are also given in the form that the ball must drop before touching a wall, etc., but after dropping it may touch them without penalty. In this form it is usually called "Touch no walls full pitch".

DIRECTIONS TO THE MARKER

It is the duty of the marker—

to see that the net is at the correct height and that it remains correct;

to call faults;

to call the strokes when won or when asked to do so;

to mark the chases when scored;

to direct the players to change sides;

to call the chase or chases as the players change sides and to call each chase before it is played for but not otherwise to repeat the chases;

when there is a referee not to call "not up" in doubtful cases but to allow the rest to be finished;

not to call "play" in the course of a rest;

to remove balls lying on the floor;

to keep the ball troughs replenished.

GLOSSARY OF TENNIS TERMS

(*See also the definitions contained in Rule 1 of the Laws*)

Advantage. See rule 15.
Advantage Set. See rule 16.
All the Walls, also called Touch No Walls, see rule 24 (*g*).

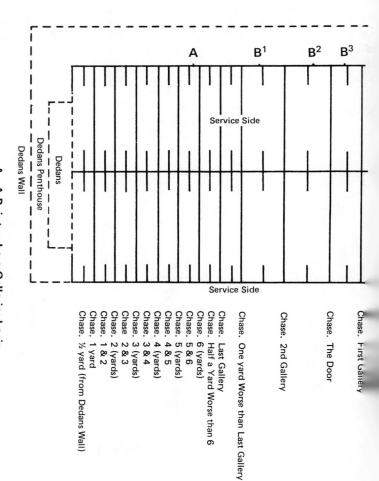

A   A Points where Galleries begin

B¹ to B³ Gallery Posts

Dedans Wall

Dedans Penthouse

Dedans

Service Side

Service Side

A

B¹

B²

B³

Chase. First Gallery

Chase. The Door

Chase. 2nd Gallery

Chase. One yard Worse than Last Gallery

Chase. Last Gallery
Chase. Half a Yard Worse than 6
Chase. 6 (yards)
Chase. 5 & 6
Chase. 5 (yards)
Chase. 4 & 5
Chase. 4 (yards)
Chase. 3 & 4
Chase. 3 (yards)
Chase. 2 & 3
Chase. 2 (yards)
Chase. 1 & 2
Chase. 1 yard
Chase. ½ yard (from Dedans Wall)

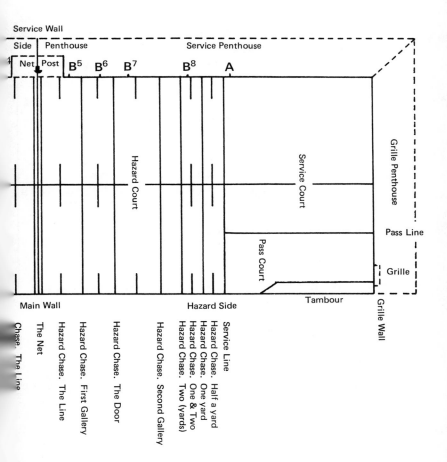

Service Wall

Side | Penthouse | Service Penthouse

Net | Post | B⁵ | B⁶ | B⁷ | B⁸ | A

Hazard Court

Service Court

Grille Penthouse

Pass Line

Grille

Main Wall | Hazard Side | Tambour | Grille Wall

Pass Court

Chase. The Line

The Net

Hazard Chase. The Line

Hazard Chase. First Gallery

Hazard Chase. The Door

Hazard Chase. Second Gallery

Hazard Chase. Two (yards)

Hazard Chase. One & Two

Hazard Chase. One yard

Hazard Chase. Half a yard

Service Line

Attack. See rule 1. Chase, attacking a.

Back Wall. See rule 1.

Bandeau. See rule 1.

Bar the Openings. See rule 24 (*a*).

Bar the Winning Openings. See rule 24 (*b*).

Batteries. The portions of wall between the openings and the floor.

Better. See rules 1 and 9.

Bisque. See rules 1 and 22.

Boast. A return that is struck against the main wall (presumably derived from *Bosse*). Originally the word appears to have been used only when it was intended that the ball should enter the dedans, but it is now used more widely to include returns struck against walls other than the main wall.

Boasted Force. A boast that drops in a winning opening. The term is usually employed only for a force to the dedans.

Chase. See rule 1.

Coup de Brèche. A straight force that drops in the dedans near to one of its outer edges.

Coup de Cabasse. A return that drops in the dedans after first striking the wall between the last gallery and the dedans wall (called after a French professional of that name who played this difficult stroke).

Coups de Chandelle. A lofted return that drops or (more usually) falls in the dedans.

Coup d'Orléans. A return that is struck against the service wall and drops in the dedans direct (called after Philippe Egalité, Duc d'Orleans, who invented or practised this stroke).

Coup de Temps. The stroke usually attempted off the back wall when the ball is too near to the wall and floor for an ordinary return to be made. The stroke is commenced before the ball reaches the wall so that immediately it leaves it the stroke can be completed with the minimum amount of further movement and acceleration of the racket.

Court. See rule 1.

Cramped Odds. Handicaps that prohibit certain strokes or services. See rule 24.

Dead. See rule 1.

Dedans. See rule 1.

Defend. See rule 1. Chase, defending a.

Deuce. See rule 15.

Door. See rules 1 (Gallery) and 8.

Double. See rule 1.

Doubles. See rule 20.

Drop. See rule 1.

Drop Service. A high service, delivered from near the main wall, that should drop near to the grille wall.

Du Tout. The score of a player who requires one stroke to win the set (cf. game-ball).

Enter a Gallery or an Opening. See rule 1.

Fall. See rule 1.

Fault. See rule 6.

Fault-Caller. See rule 19 (*c*).

Fifteen. See rule 15.

First Gallery. See rules 1 (Gallery) and 8.

First Stroke. The return of the service.

Fly Net. Not used in modern courts. In some old courts there was a fly net high up in each of the four corners. A ball striking the fly net was not out of court.

Force. A stroke that drops into an opening, usually a winning opening. The term is not used for a slow lofted return.

Forty. See rule 15. Originally this score was 45, but was subsequently called 40 for the sake of brevity.

Four-handed Game. See rule 20.

Gallery. See rule 1.

Gallery Lines. Chase lines that correspond to galleries (see rules 8 and 9 (*a*)).

Gallery Net. The net attached to a gallery post to separate a gallery from the one next to it.

Gallery Post. See rule 1.

Game. See rule 15.

Giraffe Service. A high underhand service delivered from near the side penthouse. (After dropping on the service penthouse the ball should drop on the floor near to the fault line and to the grille wall.)

Good Return. See rule 1 (Return).

Good Service. See rule 6.

Grille. See rule 1.

Grille Penthouse. The Penthouse above the grille wall.

Grille Wall. See rule 1.

Half a yard. See rule 8.

Half-Bisque. See rule 23.

Half Court. See rule 1.

Half Odds. See rule 21.

Hazard Chase. See rule 1.

Hazard Court. See rule 1.

Hazard Side. See rule 1.

Joues. The inner vertical walls of the dedans, grille, winning gallery and last gallery. A ball in touching a joue is not thereby deemed to have entered an opening (see rule 1).

Last Gallery. See rules 1 (Gallery) and 8.

Ledge. See rule 1.

Let. See rule 17.

Line. The cord that supports the net.

Line, Chase the. See rule 1.

Love. The score of a player who has not yet won a stroke in the game or a game in the set in question.

Love Game. A game won by a player in which his opponent does not score a stroke.

Love Set. A set won by a player by winning six successive games, or in the case of an advantage set, seven successive games.

Lune. A winning opening that was found in some old courts. There was no standard size, shape or position for lunes, but they were usually placed above the dedans and grille penthouses.

Net Post. See rule 1.

Nick. See rule 1.

Odds. Any form of handicap is called odds. See rules 21 to 24.

Opening. Entering an. See rule 1.

Out of Court. See rule 1.

Pass. See rule 7.

Pass Court. See rule 1.

Pass Line. See rule 1.

Passing the Net. See rule 1.

Penthouse is the sloping roof of the dedans, galleries and grille, extending along three sides of the court.

Piqué Service. The server stands near to the main wall and to the 2nd gallery line. He serves overhead on to the service penthouse and as near as possible to the service line. After striking the service wall the ball should drop near to the grille wall and the fault line.

Play Line. The line painted on the walls to mark the upper limits of the area prepared for play (see rule 1, Out of Court).

Post. See Net Post and Gallery Post, rule 1.

Railroad Service. An overhead service delivered by the server standing near the wall between the last gallery and the dedans wall. (The ball may touch the penthouse once or more times. On leaving the penthouse the ball, unless volleyed, should strike the grille wall with a twist on it that brings it back towards the side wall. A less common form of railroad service has the opposite twist on the ball so that it tends to go in the direction of the tambour after dropping.)

Referee. See rule 18.

Rest. See rule 1.

Rough. The side of the racket on which the knots are.

Second Gallery. See rules 1 (Gallery) and 8.

Service. See rule 1.

Service Court. See rule 1.

Service Line. See rule 1.

Service Penthouse. See rule 1.

Service Side. See rule 1.

Service Wall. See rule 1.

Set. See rule 16. A match is won by the player who wins an agreed number of sets. Each set is a separate unit and no game won in one set has any effect on another set. The method of scoring by sets appears to have been adopted in the 16th century. Prior to that games only were scored. At first 2 games won a set. At later periods, 3, 4, 6 and 8 game sets were usual.

Side Penthouse. See rule 1.

Side Wall. See rule 1.

Side Wall Service. Delivered from near the side penthouse. The ball usually touches the service wall before the service penthouse but need not do so. The twist on it should be such that it clings to the grille wall after dropping.

Smooth. The side of the racket on which is the gut with no knots.

Striker. See rule 1.

Striker-Out. See rule 1.

Stroke. See rules 14 and 15.

Tambour. The projection on the main wall near the grille. The whole of the projection should be called the tambour though the term is more commonly applied only to that part of it that is at an angle to the main wall.

Thirty. See rule 15.

Three-handed Game. See rule 20.

Touch No Walls. See rule 24 (*g*).

Touch No Side Walls. See rule 24 (*f*).

Twist Service. An underhand service delivered from near the side penthouse. The ball does not usually touch the service wall. The twist on it should be that, after striking the grille wall, it comes back towards the side wall.

Tray. See rule 1.

Uneven Odds. See rule 1.

Wing Net. A net put up in some courts for the protection of the marker in front of the net or post and attached to the underside of the service penthouse.

Winning Gallery. See rule 1.

Winning Openings. See rule 1.

Worse. See rule 1.

Yard. See rule 8.

Revised by the Tennis and Rackets Association, 1966.

THE LAWS OF RACKETS

The Single Game

1. The game is 15 up, that is, the player who first scores 15 aces wins the game excepting that:

(*a*) On the score being called 13 all for the first time in any game, hand-out may, before the next service has been delivered, set the game to 5; or to 3, i.e., the player winning 5 (or 3) aces first wins the game;

(*b*) similarly at 14 all hand-out may set the game to 3.

Note. *When hand-in requires one more ace to win the game, the Marker shall call his score "Game Ball".*

2. When the player fails to serve, or to return the ball, in accordance with the Rules of the game, his opponent wins the stroke. A stroke won by hand-in scores an ace. A stroke won by hand-out makes him hand-in.

3. The ball after being served, whether the service is good or not, is in play until it is a Double, or until after being properly returned it has failed to hit the front wall above the board, or until it has touched a player, or until it has gone out of court.

4. The right to serve first in a rubber shall be decided by the spin of a racket.

5. At the beginning of each game and of each hand the server may serve from either box, but after scoring an ace he shall then serve from the other, and so on alternately as long as he remains hand-in, or until the end of the game.

If the server serves from the wrong box there shall be no penalty and the service shall count as if served from the right box, except that the hand-out may, if he does not attempt to take the service, demand that it be served from the other box.

6. The hand-in serves his hand-out and loses the stroke

    (*a*) If the ball is served on to or below the board, or out of court, or against any part of the court before the front wall;

    (*b*) If he fails to strike the ball, or strikes the ball more than once;

    (*c*) If he serves two consecutive faults.

Note. *The ball is Out of Court when it touches the front, sides or back of the Court above the area prepared for play, or when it touches, or passes over, cross bars or other part of the roof or electric light fittings of the court.*

7. A service is a fault (except as provided by Rule 6)

    (*a*) If the player fails to stand with one foot at least on the floor within, and not touching, the one surrounding the Service Box (called a foot fault);

    (*b*) If the ball is served on to, or below, the Cut Line (called the Cut);

    (*c*) If the ball served touches the floor on its first bounce on, or in front of, the Short Line (called a Short);

(*d*) If the ball served touches the floor, on its first bounce, in the wrong court, or on the Half Court Line. (The wrong court is the Left for a service from the Left-Hand Box, and Right from the Right-Hand Box.)

8. Hand-out may take a fault. If he attempts to do so, the service thereupon becomes good.

9. A player wins a stroke
    (*a*) Under Rule 6;
    (*b*) If his opponent fails to make a good return of the ball in play;
    (*c*) If the ball in play touches his opponent, or anything he wears or carries (other than his racket when in the act of striking), except
        (i) as is otherwise provided by Rules 11, 12 and 14;
        (ii) in the case of a fault which hand-out does not attempt to take.

10. A return is good if the striker returns the ball above the board without previously touching the floor, or the back wall, or any part of the striker's body or clothing, and before it has become a Double, and if he does not hit the ball twice, or out of court.

11. If the ball, after being struck and before reaching the front wall, hits the striker's opponent or his racket, or anything he wears or carries, a Let on appeal shall be allowed, if the return would have been good. If the return would not have been good the striker shall lose the stroke.

NOTE. *Play shall cease even if the ball goes up.*

12. Notwithstanding anything contained in these Rules, a Let *may* be allowed, on appeal by either player, in the following circumstances—
    (*a*) If the player is prevented from obtaining a fair view of the ball, or from reaching the ball, or from striking at the ball;
    (*b*) If, owing to the position of the striker, his opponent is unable to avoid being touched by the ball;
    (*c*) If the ball in play touches any other ball in the court;
    (*d*) If the player refrains from hitting the ball owing to a reasonable fear of injuring his opponent;

(*e*) If the player in the act of striking touches his opponent.

NOTE. *No Let shall be allowed:*

(i) *In respect of any stroke, which a player attempts to make, unless, in making the stroke, he touches an opponent;*

(ii) *Unless the striker could have made a good return.*

13. An appeal may be made against any decision to the Marker provided that with regard to service, the following Rules shall apply:

(*a*) A Let shall be allowed, if the hand-out is not ready and does not attempt to take the service;

(*b*) No appeal shall be made with respect to foot faults;

(*c*) When hand-out attempts to take a first serve no appeal shall be made, but when he does not attempt to take it (i) if he appeals against the marker's call of play and the appeal is allowed the service becomes a fault and (ii) if the server appeals against a call of fault and the marker's decision is reversed, a let shall be allowed.

(*d*) When the marker calls fault to a second serve, hand-out shall not attempt to take it.

If the marker's decision is reversed on appeal a Let shall be allowed.

(*e*) When the marker calls play to a second service hand-out may appeal even though he has taken it. If the appeal is allowed, hand-out becomes hand-in.

14. If the player strikes at and misses a ball, he may make further attempts to return it, but the following provisions shall apply:

(*a*) Notwithstanding that the ball accidentally touches his opponent the player shall lose the stroke, unless he could have made a good return;

(*b*) If the ball touches his opponent, a Let may be allowed, if the player could have made a good return.

In all other respects the Rules shall apply as if the player had not struck at the ball.

15. If in the course of play the Marker calls "not up" or "out", the rally shall cease from that moment. If the Marker's decision is reversed on appeal, a Let shall be allowed.

16. If a Let be allowed, the service or rally shall not count, and the server shall serve again from the same service box. A Let shall not annul a previous fault.

17. After the first service is delivered, play shall be continuous, so far as is practical, providing that at any time play may be suspended, owing to bad light, or other circumstances beyond the control of the players, for such period as the Referee shall decide.

In the event of play being suspended for the day, the match shall start afresh, unless both players agree to the contrary.

18. After the delivery of a service, no appeal shall be made for anything that occurred before that service was delivered.

19. A new ball may only be claimed by a player when he is out of hand, but not between the delivery of the first and second service. The server may appeal to the Referee who may condemn the ball if he considers it unfit for play. If only one ball has been used throughout a game, there shall be a new ball to begin the next game.

20. If the Referee is unable to decide an appeal, he may allow a Let.

21. The Referee has power to order
   (*a*) A player, who has left the court, to play on;
   (*b*) A player to leave the court for any reason whatsoever, and may award the rubber to his opponent.

22. The Referee shall call foot faults, or must appoint a deputy.

23. Each player must get out of the way as much as possible. After making a stroke he must do all he can to:
   (*a*) Give his opponent a good view of the ball;
   (*b*) Avoid interfering with him in getting to, and striking at the ball;
   (*c*) Leave him, as far as the striker's position allows him, free to play the ball to any part of the front wall, or to either side wall near the front wall.

When a player fails to do any of these things, the Referee may on appeal allow a Let, or a stroke to his opponent, if in his opinion such is a fair decision considering all the circumstances, and in accordance with what would probably have happened had there been no such interference.

24. There may be a Referee and two Umpires, who shall decide all appeals.

If the Umpires are unanimous, the Referee shall give their decision; otherwise he shall give his own. In the absence of Umpires, the Referee shall decide all appeals.

In the absence of a Referee, the Marker shall act as Referee.

The Referee or Umpires shall give no decision unless an appeal is made, except for the purpose of preventing an accident, or correcting a mistake in the score.

The Four-Handed Game

1. The Rules of the Single Game shall apply to the Double Game and wherever the words server, hand-in, hand-out, striker, opponent or player are used in the Rules of the Single Game, such words (wherever applicable) shall be taken to include his partner in the Double Game.

2. Only one of a pair shall serve in the first hand of a game.

3. The order of serving may be changed at the beginning of any game. The player, however, who is serving when a game is won, must continue to serve in the following game, but need not serve first thereafter in that game.

4. If the player, who should serve second, serves first, hand-out may object, provided that he does so before an ace has been scored or an attempt has been made to take the first service. If no such objection is made, the server shall finish his hand and his partner shall then serve, but in subsequent hands the pair shall revert to their original order.

5. If in any hand a player serves again, after he has ceased to be hand-in, no aces so scored shall be counted, provided that the mistake is discovered before either of his opponents has served.

6. If a player does not serve when he should do so and one of his opponents serves instead, the player loses his right of service, unless it is claimed before he, or his partner, has attempted to take a service, or before an ace has been scored.

7. On each side one player shall receive the service served to the right court and one to the left. This order of receiving the service may only be changed the first time the side is hand-out in any game.

8. Hand-in scores an ace, if the player in the right court strikes a service to the left court, and vice versa.

9. While the service is being delivered, the player who is to take the service may stand where he pleases. His partner shall stand behind the server. The server's partner shall stand near the back wall, and in the court into which the service is not being delivered.

NOTE. *In these Rules the expression:*

Board means: The Board across the lower part of the front wall.

Court means: The whole building in which the game is played, the back of the Court is divided by a Half Court Line into two halves, called the Right (or Fore-Hand) Court, and the Left (or Backhand) Court.

Cut Line or Service Line means: The line drawn on the front wall.

Double means: The ball after it has touched the floor a second time.

Half-Court Line means: The line on the floor, drawn from the Short Line to the Back Wall.

Hand-in means: The player who serves.

Hand-out means: The player who receives the service.

To Serve means: To start the ball in play by striking at it with a racket.

Service Box means: The small squares on each side of the Court from which the service is delivered.

Short Line means: The line drawn across the floor parallel to the front wall.

Striker means: The player whose turn it is to play after the ball in play has hit the front wall.

Drawn up by Major Spens, 1890. Revised by the Tennis, Rackets and Fives Association, 1911. Revised by the Tennis and Rackets Association, 1923, 1950, 1966 and 1980.

The Rules of
Rounders

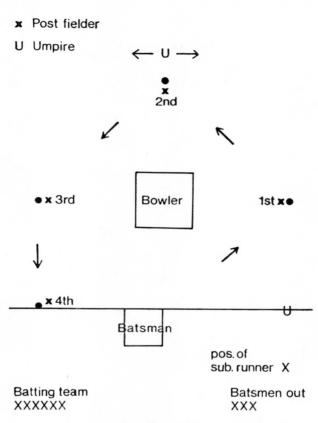

x Post fielder

U Umpire

←— U —→

●
x
2nd

● **x** 3rd | Bowler | 1st **x** ●

● **x** 4th

| Batsman |

pos. of
sub. runner X

Batting team   Batsmen out
XXXXXX   XXX

Diagram of Pitch showing suggested positions of Umpires,
Post Fielders and Batsmen.

Rounders

I. THE PITCH

(*a*) *Running Track*
The running track shall be the area used by the batsman when running, as shown in the diagram facing.

(*b*) *Bowling Square*
The bowling area shall be 2.5 m square. All lines shall be considered as part of the square.

(*c*) *Batting Square*
The batting area shall be 2 m square. The front line shall be parallel with and 7.5 m away from the front line of the bowling square. All lines shall be considered as part of the square.

(*d*) *Forward Area and Backward Area*
    (i) The front line of the batting square shall be extended in both directions by solid lines measuring at least 12 m in length.
   (ii) This line and the area in front of it and the imaginary continuation of it, shall be called the "Forward Area".
  (iii) The area behind this line and the imaginary continuation of it, shall be called the "Backward Area".
  (iv) At least 5 m behind the backward forward area line, and 9 m either side of the front right-hand corner of the batting square, lines shall be drawn to mark the positions for waiting batsmen and batsmen out.

II. EQUIPMENT

All equipment should be manufactured for the purpose and approved by the N.R.A.

(*a*) *Posts*
Each of the four posts shall be vertical and 1.2 m above the ground. The four posts shall be supported in a base and not fixed in the ground.

(*b*) *The Ball*

The ball shall weigh a minimum of 70 gm and a maximum of 85 gm and shall measure approximately 19 cm in circumference.

(*c*) *The Bat*

The bat shall be round, and shall not measure more than 17 cm round the thickest part, nor more than 46 cm in length; it shall weigh not more than 370 gm.

(*d*) *Clothing*

Spiked footwear is prohibited.

III. TEAMS

(*a*) *The Game*

The game shall be played between two teams each consisting of 9 players, viz. bowler, backstop, first post, second post, third post, fourth post, three deep fielders (these positions are given as a suggestion and not as a rule).

(*b*) *Substitutes*

One player may be substituted from two substitutes nominated prior to the match. At any dead ball situation the substitute may take the field provided that the Umpires and the other team are first informed. In a mixed team the substitute shall be of the same sex as the player leaving the field

IV. INNINGS

(*a*) An innings shall start at the time the first ball is bowled, after the Umpire has called play, and terminate when all the batsmen shall be declared out.

(*b*) The captains shall toss a coin for the choice of innings.

(*c*) A team shall keep the same batting order throughout an innings.

(*d*) A match shall consist of two innings.

(*e*) A team leading by five or more rounders in the first innings shall have the option of requiring the other team to follow on.

VI. BATTING

A batsman:

(*a*) while waiting for his turn to bat shall be in the backward area, well away from the 4th post and batting square; suggested position shown on the Diagram.

(*b*) shall have only one good ball bowled to him;

(*c*) shall stand with both feet within the square until the ball has left the bowler's hand, and shall not cross the front or back line until he has hit the ball or it has passed him;

(*d*) may, at his own discretion, take a no-ball and score in the usual way: he shall have been considered to have taken the ball if he made contact with or passed first post;

(*e*) must run to the first post after having hit, attempted to hit, or let pass the first good ball delivered by the bowler;

(*f*) who hits a ball so that it pitches in the backward area shall have made a "Backward hit". (This does not refer to balls that drop in the forward area and go afterwards behind);

(*g*) shall be entitled, if he is the only man left in on entering the square:

    (i) to have the option of 3 good balls but shall forfeit the right to any remaining balls if he is caught or takes the ball. (He shall be considered to have taken the ball if he has made contact with or passed first post.) He can then be put out in any of the usual ways or when the ball has been bounced in the batting square.

    (ii) to a rest of one minute after each rounder he may score.

VI. PROCEDURE OF GAME

Whilst waiting at a post a member of the batting team shall have the advantage of running on if a no-ball is bowled and not taken by the batsman. He can, at his discretion, continue to run round the track in the normal way. Similarly a runner need not run on for every ball bowled unless the next batsman immediately behind him is obliged to run. More than one batsman may be put out between the delivery of consecutive balls.

A bowler can leave his square to field the ball and can be

changed only after the delivery of a good ball. During the change the ball is dead.

A dummy throw or bowl is not allowed. A player losing contact through this dummy ball will be allowed to return to his original position.

VII. RUNNING ROUND THE TRACK

A batsman:

(*a*) shall round the track (carrying his bat) to reach 4th post, having passed outside or halted at the previous posts in the order 1st, 2nd and 3rd. On reaching 4th post he shall rejoin the waiting batsmen.

Penalty. The Umpire shall declare the player out if he runs deliberately inside a post. (When trying to make contact with a post, a batsman who goes inside the post owing to obstruction by a fielder is not out.)

(*b*) shall not wait between posts.

Penalty. The Umpire shall order him to continue to the next post.

(*c*) stopping (even temporarily) within reach of a post shall make and maintain contact with it using his hand or bat, except that he may run on whenever the bowler is not in possession of the ball and is in his square.

Penalty. (1) If he does not make contact the Umpire shall order him to do so, and if he does not shall declare him out.

(2) If he loses contact or runs at any time when the bowler has the ball and is in his square (except an overrun—see 7(*d*))or unless ordered to do so by an Umpire (see 7(*e*)) or during the bowler's action but before he releases the ball, the Umpire shall declare him out.

(*d*) shall *continue* his run to the next post if he is between posts when the bowler becomes in possession of the ball and in his square, but may not run past the post.

Penalty. The Umpire shall order the player back to the post he passed.

(*e*) may not remain at the same post as another batsman.

Penalty. The Umpire shall order the player who batted first to run on and he may be put out in the usual ways.

(*f*) when completing the track, shall not overtake any batsman who is running ahead.

Penalty. The Umpire shall declare the batsman who overtakes to be out.

(*g*) shall not run beyond the first post after a backward hit until the ball returns or has been returned to the forward area.

Penalty. The Umpire shall order him back to the first post.

(*h*) must touch 4th post with his hand or bat.

Penalty. The Umpire shall declare him out if 4th post is touched with the ball by the fielding side provided that another ball has not been bowled.

(*i*) shall not return to a post unless he is ordered to do so by the Umpire, or unless in the Umpire's opinion he has over-run a post.

Penalty. The Umpire shall order him on to the next post and he may be put out in the usual ways. A batsman may return to 4th post to make contact before the next ball is bowled.

VIII. OBSTRUCTION

Fielding side

A fielder shall be considered to have obstructed if he impedes, in any way, a batsman during his hitting action or when he is travelling in a direct path between posts or is attempting to make contact, whether or not the fielder is holding the ball. He shall also be considered to have obstructed if he verbally misleads the other team.

Penalty. The Umpire shall award half a rounder to the batting team and the batsman shall be allowed to make contact with the post to which he is running.

Batting side

(*a*) While waiting to bat shall stand in the backward area out of the way of backstop and 4th post fielders.

Penalty. The Umpire shall award half a rounder to the fielding side, in the event of obstruction.

(*b*) A batsman shall be considered to have obstructed if he:
impedes the player who is fielding the ball by deviating from the running track;

(ii) intentionally deflects the course of the ball;

(iii) verbally misleads the other team.

Penalty. The Umpire shall declare the batsman out.

Whilst running round the track within the Rules, a batsman shall have the right of way.

IX. SCORING

The Winning Team

The team scoring the greater number of rounders shall win the game.

If a batsman stops within reach of a post, the fielders may prevent him from scoring by touching the next post with the ball (see 9(*b*) (iii)). This does not prevent the batsman from continuing his run.

One Rounder

(*a*) One rounder only may be scored from any one hit. In the case of a no-ball which is hit and caught, the batsman may still score in the usual way. See Rule 10*(b)*.

(*b*) One rounder shall be scored if, after having hit the ball, the batsman succeeds in running round the track and touching the 4th post, or from 1st post when the ball returns or has been returned by a fielder to the forward area after a backward hit, provided that:

(i) he has not overtaken any other batsman; see Rule 7 *(f)*.

(ii) the bowler has not delivered another ball;

(iii) if he has stopped at a post, the post *immediately ahead* has not been touched by a fielder with the hand holding the ball.

Half a Rounder

Half a rounder shall be scored by the batsman if he completes the track fulfilling the same conditions as for one rounder but without hitting the ball.

A Penalty Half Rounder

A penalty half rounder shall be awarded to the batting team when:

(*a*) the bowler delivers three consecutive no-balls to the same batsman; or

(*b*) a fielder obstructs a batsman. See Rule 8, Obstruction.

A penalty half rounder shall be awarded to the fielding team when waiting batsmen obstruct the fielders. See Rule 8, Obstruction.

One Rounder and Penalty Half Rounders

It should be noted that one rounder may be scored with the addition of the award:

(*a*) one penalty half rounder if the ball that is hit is the third consecutive no-ball;

(*b*) one penalty half rounder if the batsman is obstructed;

(*c*) two penalty half rounders if the ball that is hit is the third consecutive no-ball and the batsman is obstructed.

X. BATSMEN OUT

(*a*) A Batsman shall be declared out on a good ball:

(i) if the ball be caught from bat or hand;

(ii) if his foot projects over the front or back line of the batting square before he has hit the ball or it has passed him;

(iii) if he runs to the inside of a post, unless prevented from reaching it by an obstructing fielder (see Penalty, Rule 7 (*a*));

(vi) if a fielder touches the post immediately ahead with the ball or with the hand which holds the ball, *while the batsman is running to that post*;

(v) if, after having hit, attempted to hit, or missed a ball, a fielder touches him with the hand holding the ball whilst he is still in the batting square or running round the track and not in contact with a post;

(vi) if he obstructs a fielder or intentionally deflects the course of the ball; see Rule 8, Obstruction;

(vii) if he overtakes another batsman;

(viii) if he loses contact or runs at any time when the bowler has the ball and is in his square (except an over-run— see 7(*d*)) or unless ordered to do so by an Umpire (see

7(*e*)) or during the bowler's action but before he releases the ball;

(ix) if after having been ordered to make contact with a
post a batsman has not done so.

(*b*) Rule 10(*a*) shall apply to a No-ball excepting Section (i).
Sections (iv) and (v) shall apply only after the batsman has left
the first post.

(*c*) Side Out. Where there is no batsman awaiting his turn to
bat, all the batsmen on the running track can be put out
simultaneously, by the ball being thrown full pitch or placed
by any fielder into the batting square before any one of them
has reached 4th post.

XI. NO-BALL

Decisions on height and direction are based on the position of
the batsman when the bowler releases the ball.

A no-ball is one that:

(*a*) is not delivered with a continuous and smooth underarm
action (this does not prevent spin).

(*b*) is bowled when the bowler fails to keep both feet within
the square until the ball is released (the lines of the square are
considered to be part of the square and the bowler should be
penalised *only* when any part of his foot projects over the line).

(*c*) is on the non-hitting side of the batsman or wide when it
reaches the batsman.

(*d*) is higher than the top of the head or lower than the knee
when it reaches the batsman.

(*e*) would hit the batsman.

(*f*) hits the ground on the way to the batsman.

UMPIRES

There shall be two Umpires, the Batsman's Umpire, who shall
stand on a level with the batsman in the batting square and in
a position to see the first post without turning his head, and the
Bowler's Umpire, who shall stand in such a position that he
can see all the infringements of rules for which he is responsible.

This may necessitate a change of position to facilitate his view of a left-handed batsman.

The Umpire's decisions on any aspect of the game shall be final but they should appeal to each other on any point that is doubtful.

Players may also appeal.

The Umpires should both keep a record of the score.

The Umpires should exchange positions after the first innings of both sides have been completed.

The Umpire has the right to order a player off the pitch for unsportsmanlike conduct, with no substitution being possible.

Duties of Batsman's Umpire

(i) Call "Rounder" or "Half Rounder" and give the score of both sides, after a rounder or half rounder is scored or awarded.

(ii) Call "No Ball" for balls that are not delivered with a continuous and smooth underarm action or for any balls that are too high or too low.

(iii) Call "No Ball" if the bowler puts his foot over the front line of the bowling square. See Rule 11 (b).

(iv) Give decisions concerning the batting square, 1st and 4th posts, backward hits and all catches.

Duties of Bowler's Umpire

(i) Call "Play" at beginning of each innings.

(ii) Call "No Ball" for wides, for balls straight at or on the non-hitting side of the batsman.

(iii) Give decisions concerning 2nd and 3rd posts.

(iv) Call "No Ball" if the bowler projects his foot over the back or side lines of the bowling square. See Rule 11 (b).

A SIMPLE METHOD OF MARKING
A ROUNDERS PITCH

The Pitch

The simplest way of marking the pitch is by using lengths of string. Put a peg into the ground where the right-hand front corner of the batting square is to be, and directly opposite that

Plan for marking pitch

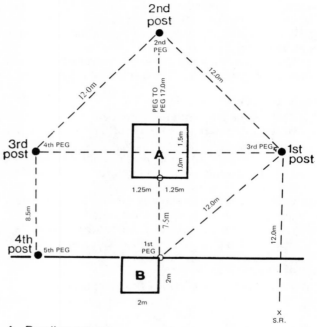

A – Bowling square

B – Batting square

Darker lines are compulsory markings

another peg at a distance of 17 m. This gives the position of the second post.

Take a length of string measuring 24 m and tie a knot in the centre (each half 12 m). Tie one end of the string to each peg and carry the centre knot out to the right until the string is taut. At the knot put in another peg. This gives the position of the first post. Then carry the centre knot to the left, pull the string taut, put in a peg. This gives the position of the third post.

Take a length of string 17 m long with a centre knot (each half 8.5 m) and tie one end to the peg at third post and the other to the peg first put in at the corner of the batting square. Carry the knot to the left. This gives the position of the fourth post.

The Bowling Square (2.5 m by 2.5 m)

To locate the centre of the front line of the square, stretch the 17 m string from the first peg to the second post, then measure a distance of 7.5 m along the string. The front line of the bowling square can then be marked, 1.25 m either side of the string and parallel to the front line of the batting square. The other three sides of the square can then be marked. It will be found that if the string is stretched between the first and third posts it cuts the side lines of the square one m from the front line.

The Batting Square (2 m by 2 m)

The front line is made by marking a line extending 2 m from the first peg towards and in a direct line with fourth post and parallel to the front line of the bowling square. The remaining three sides of the square can then be marked.

The front line of the batting square is extended in both directions for at least 12 m by solid lines.

The Rules of
Squash Rackets

Squash Rackets

Approved by the International Squash Rackets Federation (I.S.R.F.) to be effective from 1 May 1980. These Rules refer to the game of Squash Rackets in respect of the game as played on courts, the specifications for which were first determined by The Squash Rackets Association (Great Britain). Amended September *1977*.

THE SINGLES GAME

1. The Game, How Played

The game of Squash Rackets is played between two players with standard rackets, with balls officially approved by I.S.R.F. and in a rectangular court of standard dimensions, enclosed on all four sides.

2. The Score

A match shall consist of the best of three or five games at the option of the promoters of the competition. Each game is 9 points up: that is to say, the player who first wins 9 points wins the game, except that, on the score being called 8-all for the first time, hand-out may choose, before the next service is delivered, to continue the game to 10, in which case the player who first scores two more points wins the game. Hand-out must in either case clearly indicate his choice to the marker, if any, and to his opponent.

Note to Referees

If hand-out does not make clear his choice before the next service, the referee shall stop play, and require him to do so.

3. Points, How Scored

Points can only be scored by hand-in. When a player fails to serve or to make a good return in accordance with the rules, his opponent wins the stroke. When hand-in wins a stroke, he scores a point: when hand-out wins a stroke, he becomes hand-in.

4. The Service

(*a*) The right to serve first is decided by the spin of a racket. Thereafter the server continues to serve until he loses a stroke, when his opponent becomes the server, and so on throughout the match.

(*b*) At the beginning of each game and of each hand, the server may serve from either box, but after scoring a point he shall then serve from the other and so on alternately as long as he scores points and remains hand-in. However, if he serves a fault which is not taken, or a rally ends in a let, he shall serve again from the same box. If the server serves from the wrong box there shall be no penalty and the service shall count as if served from the correct box, except that hand-out may, if he does not attempt to take the service, demand that it be served from the other box.

(*c*) The ball before being struck shall be dropped or thrown in the air and shall not touch the walls or floor. The ball shall be served direct on to the front wall between the cut line and out-of-court line, so that on its return, unless volleyed, it would fall to the floor within the back quarter of the court opposite to the server's box. Should a player, having dropped or thrown the ball in the air, make no attempt to strike it, it may be dropped or thrown again without penalty. A player with the use of only one arm may utilise his racket to project the ball into the air.

(*d*) A service is good which is not a fault or which does not result in the server serving his hand-out in accordance with Rule 4(*f*). If the server serves one fault, he shall serve again. Hand-out may take a fault, and if he attempts to do so, the service becomes good and the ball continues in play.

(*e*) A service is a fault:

(i) If at the time of striking the ball the server fails to have at least one foot in contact with the floor within the service box, and no part of that foot touching the line surrounding the service box (called a foot-fault);

(ii) If the ball is served on to or below the cut line;

(iii) If the ball first touches the floor on or outside the short or half court lines delimiting the back quarter of the court required in Rule 4(*c*);

(iv) Any combination of faults in the one service counts only as one fault;

(*f*) The server serves his hand out and loses the stroke:

(i) If he serves two consecutive faults, excluding any that have been taken by hand-out, when the ensuing rally has ended in a let.

(ii) If the ball touches the walls or floor before being struck, or if he fails to strike the ball, or strikes it more than once.

(iii) If the ball is served on to, or below, the board, or out, or against any part of the court before the front wall.

(iv) If the ball, before it has bounced twice on the floor or has been struck by the opponent, touches the server or anything he wears or carries.

5. The Play

After a good service has been delivered, the players return the ball alternately until one or other fails to make a good return or the ball otherwise ceases to be in play in accordance with the rules.

6. Good Return

A return is good if the ball, before it has bounced twice upon the floor, is returned by the striker on to the front wall above the board without touching the floor or any part of the striker's body or clothing, provided the ball is not hit twice or out.

Note to Referees
It shall not be considered a good return if the ball touches the board before or after it hits the front wall.

7. Let

A let is an undecided stroke and the service or rally in respect of which a let is allowed shall not count and the server shall serve again from the same box. A let shall not annul a previous fault.

Note to Referees
This last sentence applies only to a second or subsequent service after a fault has not been taken.

8. Strokes, How Won

A player wins a stroke:

(*a*) Under Rule 4(*f*);

(*b*) If his opponent fails to make a good return of the ball in play;

(*c*) If the ball in play touches his opponent or anything he wears or carries, except as is otherwise provided by Rules 9, 10 and 13(*a*)(i).

(*d*) If a stroke is awarded by the referee as provided for in the Rules.

9. Hitting an Opponent with the Ball

If an otherwise good return of the ball has been made, but before reaching the front wall it hits the striker's opponent or his racket or anything he wears or carries, then:

(*a*) If the ball would have made a good return and would have struck the front wall without first touching any other wall, the striker shall win the stroke, except that, if the striker shall have followed the ball round and so turned, or shall have allowed the ball to pass behind his body, in either case taking the ball on the forehand in the backhand side of the court or vice versa, a let shall be allowed;

(*b*) If the ball would otherwise have made a good return, a let shall be allowed, unless, in the referee's opinion, a winning stroke has been intercepted, then the striker shall win the stroke.

(*c*) If the ball would not have made a good return, the striker shall lose the stroke.

The ball shall cease to be in play, even if it subsequently goes up.

10. Further Attempts to Hit the Ball

If the striker strikes at and misses the ball, he may make further attempts to return it. If after being missed, the ball touches his opponent or his racket or anything he wears or carries, then:

(*a*) If the striker would otherwise have made a good return, a let shall be allowed;

(*b*) If the striker could not have made a good return, he loses the stroke.

If any such further attempt is successful, but the ball before reaching the front wall hits the striker's opponent or his racket or anything he wears or carries, a let shall be allowed in all circumstances.

11. Appeals

(*a*) An appeal may be made against any decision of the marker, except for (*b*) (i) below.

> (*b*) (i) No appeal shall be made in respect of the marker's call of "foot-fault" or "fault" to the first service;
>
> (ii) If the marker calls "foot-fault" or "fault" to the second service, the server may appeal and, if the decision is reversed, a let shall be allowed.
>
> (iii) If the marker allows the second service, hand-out may appeal, either immediately or at the end of the rally if he has played the ball, and if the decision is reversed, hand-in becomes hand-out.
>
> (iv) If the marker does not call "foot-fault" or "fault" to the first service, hand-out may appeal that the service was a foot-fault or fault, provided he makes no attempt to play the ball. If the marker does not call "out", "down" or "not up" to the first service, hand-out may appeal, either immediately or at the end of the rally, if he has played the ball. In either case if the appeal is disallowed, hand-out shall lose the stroke.

(*c*) An appeal under Rule 6 shall be made at the end of the rally.

(*d*) In all cases where a let is desired, an appeal shall be made to the referee with the words "Let, please". Play shall thereupon cease until the referee has given his decision.

(*e*) No appeal may be made after the delivery of a service for anything that occurred before that service was delivered.

12. Fair View, Freedom to Play the Ball and Interference

(*a*) After playing a ball a player must make every effort to get out of his opponent's way. That is:

> (i) A player must make every effort to give his opponent a fair view of the ball, so that he may sight it adequately for the purpose of playing it.

(ii) A player must make every effort not to interfere with, or crowd, his opponent in the latter's attempt to get to, or play, the ball.

(iii) A player must make every effort to allow his opponent, as far as the latter's position permits, freedom to play the ball directly to the front wall or side walls near the front wall.

(*b*) If any such form of interference has occurred and, in the opinion of the referee, the player has not made every effort to avoid causing it, the referee shall on appeal, or stopping play without waiting for an appeal, award the stroke to his opponent.

(*c*) However, if interference has occurred, but in the opinion of the referee the player has made every effort to avoid causing it, the referee shall on appeal, or stopping play without waiting for an appeal, award a let, except that if his opponent is prevented from making a winning return by such interference or by distraction from the player, the referee shall award the stroke to the opponent.

(*d*) When, in the opinion of the referee, a player refrains from playing the ball, which, if played, would clearly and undoubtedly have won the rally under the terms of Rule 9(*a*) or (*b*), he shall be awarded the stroke.

(*e*) If either the striker or non-striker makes unnecessary physical contact with his opponent the referee may stop play and award a stroke accordingly.

Note to Referees
(i) The practice of impeding an opponent in his efforts to play the ball by crowding or obscuring his view is highly detrimental to the game. Unnecessary physical contact is also detrimental as well as being dangerous. Referees should have no hesitation in enforcing paragraphs (*b*) and (*e*) above.

(ii) The words "interfere with" in (*a*) (ii) above must be interpreted to include the case of a player's having to wait for an excessive swing of his opponent's racket.

13. Let, When Allowed

Notwithstanding anything contained in these rules and provided always that the striker could have made a good return:

(*a*) A let may be allowed:

  (i) If, owing to the position of the striker, his opponent is unable to avoid being touched by the ball before the return is made.

Note to Referees

      This rule shall be construed to include the cases of the striker whose position in front of his opponent makes it impossible for the latter to see the ball or who shapes as if to play the ball and changes his mind at the last moment, preferring to take the ball off the back wall, the ball in either case hitting the opponent who is between the striker and the back wall. This is not, however, to be taken as conflicting in any way with the referee's duties under Rule 12.

  (ii) If the ball in play touches any article lying in the court;

 (iii) If the striker refrains from hitting the ball owing to a reasonable fear of injuring his opponent;

 (iv) If the striker in the act of playing the ball, touches his opponent;

  (v) If the referee is asked to decide an appeal and is unable to do so;

 (vi) If a player drops his racket, calls out or in any other way distracts the attention of his opponent and the referee considers such occurrence to have caused his opponent to lose the stroke.

(*b*) A let shall be allowed:

  (i) If hand-out is not ready and does not attempt to take the service;

 (ii) If a ball breaks during play;

 (iii) If an otherwise good return has been made, but the ball goes out of court on its first bounce;

 (iv) As provided for by Rules 9, 10, 11(*b*)(ii), 18 and 19.

(*c*) No let shall be allowed if the player makes an attempt to play the ball, except as provided for under Rules 10, 13(*a*)(iv) and (*b*)(ii) and (iii).

(*d*) Unless an appeal is made by one of the players, no let shall be allowed except where these rules definitely provide for a let, namely Rules 9(*a*) and (*b*), 10, 12, 13(*b*)(ii) and (iii).

14. New Ball

At any time when the ball is not in actual play a new ball may be substituted by mutual consent of the players or on appeal by either player at the discretion of the referee.

15. Knock-up

(*a*) The referee shall allow on the court of play a period not exceeding five minutes to the two players together, for the purpose of knocking-up, or in the event of the players electing to knock-up separately, the referee shall allow the first player a period of three and a half minutes and to his opponent two and a half minutes, immediately preceding the start of play. In the event of a separate knock-up, the choice of knocking-up first shall be decided by the spin of a racket. The referee shall allow a further period for the players to warm the ball up if the match is being resumed after a considerable delay.

(*b*) Where a new ball has been substituted under Rule 13(*b*) (ii) or 14, the referee shall allow the ball to be knocked-up to playing condition. Play shall resume on the direction of the referee, or prior mutual consent of the players.

(*c*) Between games the ball shall remain on the floor of the court in view and knocking-up shall not be permitted except by mutual consent of the players.

16. Play in a Match to be Continuous

After the first service is delivered, play shall be continuous so far as is practical, provided that:

(*a*) At any time play may be suspended owing to bad light or other circumstances beyond the control of the players, for such period as the referee shall decide. In the event of play being suspended for the day, the match shall start afresh, unless both players agree to the contrary.

(*b*) The referee shall award a game to the opponent of any player, who, in his opinion persists, after due warning, in delaying the play in order to recover his strength or wind, or for any other reason.

(*c*) An interval of one minute shall be permitted between games and of two minutes between the fourth and fifth games of a five-game match. A player may leave the court during such intervals, but shall be ready to resume play at the end of the stated time. When ten seconds of the interval permitted between games are left, the marker shall call "Ten seconds" to warn the players to be ready to resume play. Should either player fail to do so when required by the referee, a game may be awarded to his opponent.

(*d*) In the event of an injury, the referee may require a player to continue play or concede the match, except where the injury is contributed to by his opponent, or where it was caused by dangerous play on the part of the opponent. In the former case, the referee may allow time for the injured player to receive attention and recover, and in the latter, the injured player shall be awarded the match under Rule 19(*d*)(ii).

(*e*) In the event of a ball breaking, a new ball may be knocked-up, as provided for in Rule 15(*b*).

Notes to Referees

(i) In allowing time for a player to receive attention and recover, the referee should ensure that there is no conflict with the obligation of a player to comply with Rule 16(*b*), that is, that the effects of the injury are not exaggerated and used as an excuse to recover strength and wind.

(ii) The referee should not interpret the words "contributed to by his opponent" to include the situation where the injury to the player is a result of that player occupying an unnecessarily close position to his opponent.

(iii) The practice of serving faults deliberately in order to obtain an additional period of rest is contrary to the spirit of the game and Rule 16(*b*). When the referee is satisfied that a player is doing so, he shall, after warning him in terms of Rule 16(*b*), award the game to his opponent.

17. Control of a Match

A match is normally controlled by a referee, assisted by a marker. One person may be appointed to carry out the functions of both referee and marker. When a decision has been made by a referee, he shall announce it to the players and the marker shall repeat it with the subsequent score.

Up to one hour before the commencement of a match either player may request a referee and marker other than appointed, and this request may be considered and a substitute appointed. Players are not permitted to request any such change after the commencement of a match, unless both agree to do so. In either case the decision as to whether an official is to be replaced or not must remain in the hands of the tournament referee, where applicable.

18. Duties of Marker

(*a*) The marker calls the play and the score, with the server's score first. He shall call "Fault", "Foot-Fault", "Out", "Down" or "Not up" as appropriate.

(*b*) If in the course of play the marker calls "Not up", "Out" or "Down" or in the case of a second service "Fault" or "Foot Fault" then the rally shall cease.

(*c*) If the marker's decision is reversed on appeal, a let shall be allowed, except as provided for in Rules 11(*b*)(iii) and (iv) and 19(*b*)(iv) and (v).

(*d*) Any service or return shall be considered good unless otherwise called.

(*e*) After the server has served a fault, which has not been taken, the marker shall repeat the score and add the words "One fault", before the server serves again. This call should be repeated should subsequent rallies end in a let, until the point is finally decided.

(*f*) When no referee is appointed, the marker shall exercise all the powers of the referee.

(*g*) If the marker is unsighted or uncertain, he shall call on the referee to make the relevant decision; if the latter is unable to do so, a let shall be allowed.

19. Duties of Referee

(*a*) The referee shall award lets and strokes and make decisions where called for by the rules, and shall decide all appeals, including those against the marker's calls and decisions. The decision of the referee shall be final.

(*b*) He shall in no way intervene in the marker's calling except:

  (i) Upon appeal by one of the players.

 (ii) As provided for in Rule 12.

(iii) When it is evident that the score has been incorrectly called, in which case he should draw the marker's attention to the fact.

(iv) When the marker has failed to call the ball "Not up", "Out" or "Down" and on appeal he rules that such was in fact the case, the stroke should be awarded accordingly.

 (v) When the marker has called "Not up", "Out" or "Down" and on appeal he rules that this was not the case, a let shall be allowed except that if in the referee's opinion, the marker's call had interrupted an undoubted winning return, he shall award the stroke accordingly.

(vi) In exceptional circumstances, when he is absolutely convinced that the marker has made an obvious error in stopping play or allowing play to continue, he shall immediately rule accordingly.

(*c*) The referee is responsible that all times laid down in the rules are strictly adhered to.

(*d*) In exceptional cases, the referee may order:

  (i) A player, who has left the court, to play on.

 (ii) A player to leave the court and to award the match to the opponent.

(iii) A match to be awarded to a player whose opponent fails to be present in court within ten minutes of the advertised time of play.

(iv) Play to be stopped in order to warn that the conduct of one or both of the players is leading to an infringement of the rules. A referee should avail himself of this rule as early as possible when either player is showing a tendency to break the provisions of Rule 12.

(*e*) If after a warning a player continues to contravene Rule 15(*c*) the referee shall award a game to the opponent.

APPENDIX I
DEFINITIONS

Board or Tin. The expression denoting a band, the top edge of which is 0.48 m (19 in) from the floor across the lower part of the front wall above which the ball must be returned before the stroke is good.

Cut Line. A line upon the front wall, the top edge of which is 1.829 m (6 ft) above the floor and extending the full width of the court.

Down. The expression used to indicate that a ball has been struck against the tin or board.

Game Ball. The state of the game when the server requires one point to win is said to be "Game Ball".

Half-Court Line. A line set out upon the floor parallel to the side walls, dividing the back half of the court into two equal parts.

Hand-in. The player who serves.

Hand-out. The player who receives the service, also the expression used to indicate that Hand-in has become Hand-out.

Hand. The period from the time when a player becomes Hand-in until he becomes Hand-out.

Match Ball. The state of the match when the server requires one point to win is said to be "Match Ball".

Not-up. The expression used to denote that a ball has not been served or returned above the board in accordance with the rules.

Out. The ball is out when it touches the front, sides or back of the court above the area prepared for play or passes over any cross bars or other part of the roof of the court. The lines delimiting such area, the lighting equipment and the roof are out.

Point. A point is won by the player who is Hand-in and who wins a stroke.

Quarter Court. One part of the back half of the court which has been divided into two equal parts by the half-court line.

Service Box or Box. A delimited area in each quarter court from within which Hand-in serves.

Short Line. A line set out upon the floor parallel to and 5.486 m (18 ft) from the front wall and extending the full width of the court.

Striker. The player whose turn it is to play after the ball has hit the front wall.

Stroke. A stroke is won by the player whose opponent fails to serve or make a good return in accordance with the rules.

Stop. Expression used by the referee to stop play.

Time. Expression used by the referee to start play.

APPENDIX II
DIMENSIONS OF A SINGLES COURT

Length	32 ft (9.75 m)
Breadth	21 ft (6.40 m)
Height to upper edge of cut line on front wall	6 ft (1.83 m)
Height to lower edge of front-wall line	15 ft (4.57 m)
Height to lower edge of back-wall line	7 ft (2.13 m)
Distance to further edge of short line from front wall	18 ft (5.49 m)
Height to upper edge of board from ground	19 in (0.48 m)
Thickness of board (flat or rounded at top)	$\frac{1}{2}$ to 1 in (12.5 to 25 mm)

Height of side-wall line: The diagonal line joining the front-wall line and the back-wall line.

The service boxes shall be entirely enclosed on three sides within the court by lines, the short line forming the side nearest to the front wall, the side wall bounding the fourth side.

The internal dimensions of the service boxes shall be 5 ft 3 in (1.60 m).

All dimensions in the court shall be measured, where practicable, from the junction of the floor and front wall.

All lines marking the boundaries of the court shall be 2 in (50 mm) in width.

The width of other lines shall not exceed 2 in (50 mm). All lines shall be coloured red.

In respect of the outer boundary lines on the walls, it is suggested that the plaster should be so shaped as to produce a concave channel along such lines.

APPENDIX III
DIMENSIONS OF A RACKET

1. The overall length shall not exceed 27 in (685 mm). The internal stringing area shall not exceed $8\frac{1}{2}$ in (215 mm) in length by $7\frac{1}{4}$ in (184 mm) in breadth and the framework of the head shall measure not more than $\frac{9}{16}$ in (14 mm) across the face by $\frac{13}{16}$ in (20 mm) deep.

2. The framework of the head shall be of wood or such other material as may from time to time be approved by the I.S.R.F. The handle shaft shall be made of wood, cane, metal or glass fibre. The grip and foundation may be made of any suitable material.

APPENDIX IV
SPECIFICATION FOR
SQUASH RACKET BALLS

The ball must conform to the following:

1. It must weigh not less than 23.3 gm and not more than 24.6 gm (approx. 360–380 grn).

2. Its diameter must not be less than 39.5 mm and not more than 41.5 mm (approx. 1.56–1.63 in).

3. It must have a surface finish which guarantees continuing correct rebound.

4. It must be of a type specifically approved for championship play by the International Squash Rackets Federation.

5. Compression specification: (i) the ball is mounted in an apparatus and a load of 0.5 kgm is applied which deforms the ball slightly. Subsequent deformation in the test procedure is measured from this datum. (ii) an additional load of 2.4 kgm is applied and this deforms the ball further. The deformation from the datum position is recorded. (iii) the deformation obtained in (ii) should be between 3 and 7 mm for balls of playing properties acceptable to the I.S.R.F.

APPENDIX V
CONSTRUCTION OF A COURT
(International Championship Standard)

Apply to the Squash Rackets Association, Francis House, Francis St., London SW1P 1DE for details.

APPENDIX VI
COLOUR OF PLAYERS' CLOTHING

For all events under control of the I.S.R.F., players are required to wear white and/or light matching pastel clothing during the course of play. A coloured trim with a maximum width of 50 mm (2 in) is permissible. Shoes should be predominantly white with only 20% of colour trim inclusive of sole, which must be non-marking. The maximum area permissible for advertising is 50 mm² (2 sq. in). Member Countries of the I.S.R.F. may have a limited discretion to allow advertising of a greater size to be worn for any other events under their control. The referee's decision on compliance with this Rule shall be final.

NOTE. *Footwear is deemed clothing for this Rule.*

The Rules of
Tennis

PLAN OF THE COURTS
(See Rules 1 and 32)

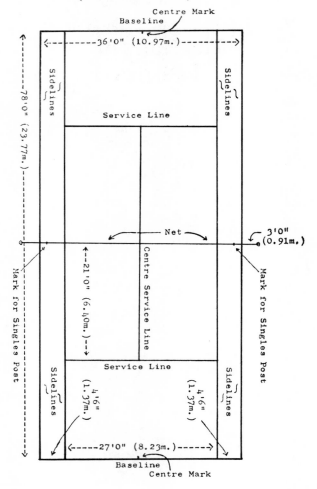

Tennis

THE SINGLES GAME

1. The Court shall be a rectangle, 78 ft (23.77 m) long and 27 ft (8.23 m) wide. It shall be divided across the middle by a net, suspended from a cord or metal cable of a maximum diameter of one-third of an inch (0.8 cm), the ends of which shall be attached to, or pass over, the tops of two posts, which shall be not more than 6 in (15 cm) square or 6 in (15 cm) in diameter. The centres of the posts shall be 3 ft (0.91 m) outside the court on each side and the height of the posts shall be such that the top of the cord or metal cable shall be 3 ft 6 in (1.07 m) above the ground.

When a combined doubles (see Rule 35) and singles court with a doubles net is used for singles, the net must be supported to a height of 3 ft 6 in (1.07 m) by means of two posts, called "singles sticks", which shall be not more than 3 in (7.5 cm) square or 3 in (7.5 cm) in diameter. The centres of the singles sticks shall be 3 ft (0.91 m) outside the singles court on each side. The net shall be extended fully so that it fills completely the space between the two posts and shall be of sufficiently small mesh to prevent the ball passing through. The height of the net shall be 3 ft (0.91 m) at the centre, where it shall be held down taut by a strap not more than 2 in (5 cm) wide and completely white in colour. There shall be a band covering the cord or metal cable and the top of the net of not less than 2 in (5 cm) nor more than $2\frac{1}{2}$ in (6.3 cm) in depth on each side and completely white in colour. There shall be no advertisement on the net, strap, band or singles sticks. The lines bounding the ends and sides of the Court shall respectively be called the Base-lines and the Side-lines. On each side of the net, at a distance of 21 ft (6.40 m) from it and parallel with it, shall be drawn the Service-lines. The space on each side of the net between the service-line and the side-lines shall be divided into two equal parts called the service-courts by the centre service-line, which must be 2 in (5 cm) in width, drawn half-way between, and parallel with, the side-lines. Each base-line shall be bisected by an imaginary continuation of the centre service-line to a line 4 in (10 cm) in length and 2 in (5 cm) in width called the centre mark drawn inside the Court, at right angles to and in contact with such base-lines. All other lines shall be not less than 1 in (2.5 cm) nor more than 2 in (5 cm) in width, except the base-line, which may be 4 in (10 cm) in width, and all measurements shall be made to the outside of the lines.

If banners are placed at the back of the court, they may not contain white or yellow or any other light colour.

NOTE. *In the case of the International Tennis Championship (Davis Cup) or other Official Championships of the International Federation, there shall be a space behind each base-line of not less than 21 ft (6.4 m) and at the sides of not less than 12 ft (3.66 m).*

2. The permanent fixtures of the Court shall include not only the net, posts, singles sticks, cord or metal cable, strap and band, but also, where there are any such, the back and side stops, the stands, fixed or movable seats and chairs round the Court, and their occupants, all other fixtures around and above the Court, and the Umpire, Net-cord Judge, Foot-fault Judge, Linesmen and Ball Boys when in their respective places.

NOTE. *For the purpose of this Rule, the word "Umpire" comprehends the Umpire, the persons entitled to a seat on the Court, and all those persons designated to assist the Umpire in the conduct of a* match.

3. The ball shall have a uniform outer surface and shall be white or yellow in colour. If there are any seams they shall be stitchless. The ball shall be more than $2\frac{1}{2}$ in (6.35 cm) and less than $2\frac{5}{8}$ in (6.67 cm) in diameter, and more than 2 oz (56.7 gm) and less than $2\frac{1}{16}$ oz (58.5 gm) in weight. The ball shall have a bound of more than 53 in (135 cm) and less than 58 in (147 cm) when dropped 100 in (254 cm) upon a concrete base. The ball shall have a forward deformation of more than 0.22 in (0.56 cm) and less than 0.29 in (0.74 cm) and a return deformation of more than 0.35 in (0.89 cm) and less than 0.425 in (1.08 cm) at 18 lb (8.165 kg) load. The two deformation figures shall be the averages of three individual readings along three axes of the

ball and no two individual readings shall differ by more than 0.03 in (0.08 cm) in each case.

4. *The Racket.* Rackets failing to comply with the following specifications are not approved for play under the Rules of Tennis.

(a) The hitting surface of the racket shall consist of a pattern of crossed strings connected to a frame and alternately interlaced or bonded where they cross; and the stringing pattern shall be generally uniform, and in particular not less dense in the centre than in any other area.

(b) The frame of the racket shall not exceed 32 in (81.28 cm) in overall length, including the handle, and $12\frac{1}{2}$ in (31.75 cm) in overall width. The strung surface shall not exceed $15\frac{1}{2}$ in (39.37 cm) in overall length, and $11\frac{1}{2}$ in (29.21 cm) in overall width.

(c) The frame, including the handle and the strings: *(i)* shall be free of attached objects and protrusions, other than those utilised solely and specifically to limit or prevent wear and tear or vibration, or to distribute weight, and which are reasonable in size and placement for such purposes; and *(ii)* shall be free of any device which makes it possible for a player to change materially the shape of the racket.

The International Tennis Federation shall rule on the question of whether any racket or prototype complies with the above specifications or is otherwise approved, or not approved, for play. Such ruling may be undertaken on its own initiative, or upon application by any party with a bona fide interest therein, including any player, equipment manufacturer or National Association or members thereof. Such rulings and applications shall be made in accordance with the applicable Review and Hearing Procedures of the I.T.F., copies of which may be obtained from the office of the Secretary.

5. The players shall stand on opposite sides of the net; the player who first delivers the ball shall be called the Server, and the other the Receiver.

6. The choice of ends and the right to be Server or Receiver in the first game shall be decided by toss. The player winning the toss may choose or require his opponent to choose:

(a) The right to be server or Receiver, in which case the other player shall choose the end; or

(b) The end, in which case the other player shall choose the right to be Server or Receiver.

7. The service shall be delivered in the following manner. Immediately before commencing to serve, the Server shall stand with both feet at rest behind (i.e. further from the net than) the base-line, and within the imaginary continuations of the centre-mark and side-line. The Server shall then project the ball by hand into the air in any direction and before it hits the ground strike it with his racket, and the delivery shall be deemed to have been completed at the moment of the impact of the racket and ball. A player with the use of only one arm may utilize his racket for the projection.

8. The Server shall throughout the delivery of the service:

(a) Not change his position by walking or running.

(b) Not touch, with either foot, any area other than that behind the base-line within the imaginary extension of the centre mark and side-line.

NOTE. *The following interpretation of Rule 8 was approved by the International Federation on 9th July, 1958: (a) The Server shall not, by slight movements of the feet which do not materially affect the location originally taken up by him, be deemed "to change his position by walking or running". (b) The word "foot" means the extremity of the leg below the ankle.*

9. *(a)* In delivering the service, the Server shall stand alternately behind the right and left Courts, beginning from the right in every game. If service from a wrong half of the court occurs and is undetected, all play resulting from such wrong service or services shall stand, but the inaccuracy of station shall be corrected immediately it is discovered.

(b) The ball served shall pass over the net and hit the ground within the Service Court which is diagonally opposite, or upon any line bounding such Court, before the Receiver returns it.

10. The service is a fault:

(a) If the Server commit any breach of Rules 7, 8 or 9;

(b) If he miss the ball in attempting to strike it;

(c) If the ball served touch a permanent fixture (other than the net, strap or band) before it hits the ground.

11. After a fault (if it be the first fault) the Server shall serve again from behind the same half of the Court from which he

served that fault, unless the service was from the wrong half, when, in accordance with Rule 9, the Server shall be entitled to one service only from behind the other half. A fault may not be claimed after the next service has been delivered.

12. The Server shall not serve until the Receiver is ready. If the latter attempt to return the service, he shall be deemed ready. If, however, the Receiver signify that he is not ready, he may not claim a fault because the ball does not hit the ground within the limits fixed for the service.

13. In all cases where a let has to be called under the rules, or to provide for an interruption to play, it shall have the following interpretations:

(a) When called solely in respect of a service that one service only shall be replayed.

(b) When called under any other circumstance, the point shall be replayed.

14. The service is a let:

(a) If the ball served touch the net, strap or band, and is otherwise good, or, after touching the net, strap or band, touch the Receiver or anything which he wears or carries before hitting the ground.

(b) If a service or fault be delivered when the Receiver is not ready (see Rule 12). In case of a let, that particular service shall not count, and the Server shall serve again, but a service let does not annul a previous fault.

15. At the end of the first game the Receiver shall become Server, and the Server Receiver; and so on alternately in all the subsequent games of a match. If a player serve out of turn, the player who ought to have served shall serve as soon as the mistake is discovered, but all points scored before such discovery shall be reckoned. If a game shall have been completed before such discovery, the order of service remains as altered. A fault served before such discovery shall not be reckoned.

16. The players shall change ends at the end of the first, third and every subsequent alternate game of each set, and at the end of each set unless the total number of games in such set be even, in which case the change is not made until the end of the first game of the next set.

If a mistake is made and the correct sequence is not followed the players must take up their correct station as soon as the discovery is made and follow their original sequence.

17. A ball is in play from the moment at which it is delivered in service. Unless a fault or a let be called it remains in play until the point is decided.

18. The Server wins the point:

(a) If the ball served, not being a let under Rule 14, touch the Receiver or anything which he wears or carries, before it hits the ground;

(b) If the Receiver otherwise loses the point as provided by Rule 20.

19. The Receiver wins the point:

(a) If the Server serve two consecutive faults;

(b) If the Server otherwise lose the point as provided by Rule 20.

20. A player loses the point if:

(a) He fail, before the ball in play has hit the ground twice consecutively, to return it directly over the net (except as provided in Rule 24 *(a)* or *(c)*); or

(b) He return the ball in play so that it hits the ground, a permanent fixture, or other object, outside any of the lines which bound his opponent's Court (except as provided in Rule 24 *(a)* and *(c)*); or

(c) He volley the ball and fail to make a good return even when standing outside the Court; or

(d) He touch or strike the ball in play with his racket more than once in making a stroke; or

(e) He or his racket (in his hand or otherwise) or anything which he wears or carries touch the net, post, singles sticks, cord or metal cable, strap or band, or the ground within his opponent's Court at any time while the ball is in play; or

(f) He volley the ball before it passed the net; or

(g) The ball in play touch him or anything that he wears or carries, except his racket in his hand or hands; or

(h) He throws his racket at and hits the ball.

(i) He deliberately and materially changes the shape of his racket during the playing of the point.

21. If a player commits any act either deliberate or involuntary which, in the opinion of the Umpire, hinders his opponent

in making a stroke, the Umpire shall in the first case award the point to the opponent, and in the second case order the point to be replayed.

22. A ball falling on a line is regarded as falling in the Court bounded by that line.

23. If the ball in play touch a permanent fixture (other than the net, posts, singles sticks, cord or metal cable, strap or band) after it has hit the ground, the player who struck it wins the point; if before it hits the ground his opponent wins the point.

24. It is a good return:

(a) If the ball touch the net, posts, singles sticks, cord or metal cable, strap or band, provided that it passes over any of them and hits the ground within the Court; or

(b) If the ball, served or returned, hit the ground within the proper Court and rebound or be blown back over the net, and the player whose turn it is to strike reach over the net and play the ball, provided that neither he nor any part of his clothes or racket touch the net, posts, singles sticks, cord or metal cable, strap or band or the ground within his opponent's Court, and that the stroke be otherwise good; or

(c) If the ball be returned outside the post, or singles stick, either above or below the level of the top of the net, even though it touch the post or singles stick, provided that it hits the ground within the proper Court; or

(d) If a player's racket pass over the net after he has returned the ball, provided the ball pass the net before being played and be properly returned; or

(e) If a player succeed in returning the ball, served or in play, which strikes a ball lying in the Court.

NOTE TO RULE 24. *In a singles match, if, for the sake of convenience, a doubles Court be equipped with singles sticks for the purpose of a singles game, then the doubles posts and those portions of the net, cord or metal cable and band outside such singles sticks shall at all times be permanent fixtures, and are not regarded as posts or parts of the net of a singles game.*

A return that passes under the net cord between the singles stick and adjacent doubles post without touching either net cord, net or doubles post and falls within the area of play, is a good return.

25. In case a player is hindered in making a stroke by anything not within his control, except a permanent fixture of the Court, or except as provided for in Rule 21, a let shall be called.

26. If a player wins his first point, the score is called 15 for that player; on winning his second point, the score is called 30 for that player; on winning his third point, the score is called 40 for that player, and the fourth point won by a player is scored game for that player except as below:

If both players have won three points, the score is called deuce; and the next point won by a player is scored advantage for that player. If the same player win the next point, he wins the game; if the other player wins the next point the score is again called deuce; and so on, until a player wins the two points immediately following the score at deuce, when the game is scored for that player.

27. *(a)* A player (or players) who first wins six games wins a set; except that he must win by a margin of two games over his opponent and where necessary a set shall be extended until this margin be achieved.

(*b*) See Appendix: (Tie-break)

28. The maximum number of sets in a match shall be five, or, where women take part, 3.

29. Except where otherwise stated, every reference in these Rules to the masculine includes the feminine gender.

30. In matches where an Umpire is appointed, his decision shall be final; but where a Referee is appointed, an appeal shall lie to him from the decision of an Umpire on a question of law, and in all such cases the decision of the Referee shall be final. In matches where assistants to the Umpire are appointed (linesmen, net-cord judges, foot fault judges) their decisions shall be final on questions of fact except that if in the opinion of an Umpire a clear mistake has been made he shall have the right to change the decision of an assistant or order a let to be played. When such an assistant is unable to give a decision he shall indicate this immediately to the Umpire who shall give a decision. When an Umpire is unable to give a decision on a question of fact he shall order a let to be played. In Davis Cup matches or other team competitions where a Referee is on

Court, any decision can be changed by the Referee, who may also authorise an Umpire to order a let to be played.

The Referee, in his discretion, may at any time postpone a match on account of darkness or the condition of the ground or the weather. In any case of postponement the previous score and previous occupancy of Courts shall hold good, unless the Referee and the players unanimously agree otherwise.

31. Play shall be continuous from the first service till the match be concluded.

(*a*) Notwithstanding the above, after the third set, or when women take part, the second set, either player is entitled to a rest, which shall not exceed 10 minutes, or in countries situated between Latitude 15 degrees North and Latitude 15 degrees South, 45 minutes, and furthermore when necessitated by circumstances not within the control of the players, the Umpire may suspend play for such a period as he may consider necessary.

If play be suspended and be not resumed until a later day the rest may be taken only after the third set (or when women take part the second set) of play on such later day, completion of an unfinished set being counted as one set.

If play be suspended and not resumed until 10 minutes have elapsed in the same day the rest may be taken only after three consecutive sets have been played without interruption (or when women take part two sets), completion of an unfinished set being counted as one set.

Any nation is at liberty to modify this provision or omit it from its regulations governing tournaments, matches or competitions held in its own country, other than the International Tennis Championships (Davis Cup and Federation Cup).

(*b*) Play shall never be suspended, delayed or interfered with for the purpose of enabling a player to recover his strength or his breath.

(*c*) A maximum of 30 seconds shall elapse from the moment the ball goes out of play at the end of one point to the time the ball is struck for the next point, except that when changing ends a maximum of one minute thirty seconds shall elapse from the moment the ball goes out of play at the end of the game to the time the ball is struck for the first point of the next game.

The Umpire shall use his discretion when there is interference which makes it impossible for the server to serve within that time.

These provisions shall be strictly construed. The Umpire shall be the sole judge of any suspension, delay or interference, and after giving due warning he may disqualify the offender.

NOTE. *A Tournament Committee has discretion to decide the time allowed for a warm-up period prior to a match. It is recommended that this does not exceed five minutes.*

32. During the playing of a match in a team competition, a player may receive coaching from a captain who is sitting on the court only when he changes ends at the end of a game, but not when he changes ends during a tie-break game. A player may not receive coaching during the playing of any other match. The provisions of this rule must be strictly construed. After due warning an offending player may be disqualified.

33. In cases where balls are changed after an agreed number of games, if the balls are not changed in the correct sequence the mistake shall be corrected when the player, or pair in the case of doubles, who should have served with the new balls is next due to serve.

THE DOUBLES GAME

34. The above Rules shall apply to the Doubles Game except as below.

35. For the Doubles Game, the Court shall be 36 ft (10.97 m) in width, i.e. $4\frac{1}{2}$ ft (1.37 m) wider on each side than the Court for the Singles Game, and those portions of the singles side-lines which lie between the two service-lines shall be called the service side-lines. In other respects, the Court shall be similar to that described in Rule 1, but the portions of the singles side-lines between the base-line and service-line on each side of the net may be omitted if desired.

36. The order of serving shall be decided at the beginning of each set as follows:

The pair who have to serve in the first game of each set shall decide which partner shall do so and the opposing pair shall decide similarly for the second game. The partner of the player who served in the first game shall serve in the third; the partner of the player who served in the second game shall serve in the fourth, and so on in the same order in all the subsequent games of a set.

37. The order of receiving the service shall be decided at the beginning of each set as follows:

The pair who have to receive the service in the first game shall decide which partner shall receive the first service, and that partner shall continue to receive the first service in every odd game throughout that set. The opposing pair shall likewise decide which partner shall receive the first service in the second game and that partner shall continue to receive the first service in every even game throughout that set. Partners shall receive the service alternately throughout each game.

38. If a partner serve out of his turn, the partner who ought to have served shall serve as soon as the mistake is discovered, but all points scored, and any faults served before such discovery, shall be reckoned. If a game shall have been completed before such discovery, the order of service remains as altered.

39. If during a game the order of receiving the service is changed by the receivers it shall remain as altered until the end of the game in which the mistake is discovered, but the partners shall resume their original order of receiving in the next game of that set in which they are receivers of the service.

40. The service is a fault as provided for by Rule 10, or if the ball touch the Server's partner or anything which he wears or carries; but if the ball served touch the partner of the Receiver, or anything which he wears or carries, not being a let under Rule 14(*a*) before it hits the ground, the server wins the point.

41. The ball shall be struck alternately by one or other player of the opposing pairs, and if a player touches the ball in play with his racket in contravention of this Rule, his opponents win the point.

APPENDIX

I.T.F. Approved Tie-Break Scoring System

27. (*b*) The tie-break system of scoring may be adopted as an alternative to the advantage set system in paragraph (*a*) of

this Rule provided the decision is announced in advance of the match.

In this case, the following Rules shall be effective:

The tie-break shall operate when the score reaches six games all in any set except in the third or fifth set of a three-set or five-set match respectively, when an ordinary advantage set shall be played, unless otherwise decided and announced in advance of the match.

Procedure

The following system shall be used in a tie-break game:

Singles

(i) A player who first wins seven points shall win the game and the set provided he leads by a margin of two points. If the score reaches six points all, the game shall be extended until this margin has been achieved. Numerical scoring shall be used throughout the tie-break game.

(ii) The player whose turn it is to serve shall be the server for the first point. His opponent shall be the server for the second and third points and thereafter each player shall serve alternately for two consecutive points until the winner of the game and set has been decided.

(iii) From the first point, each service shall be delivered alternately from the right and left courts, beginning from the right court.

(iv) Players shall change ends after every six points and at the conclusion of the tie-break game.

(v) The tie-break game shall count as one game for the ball change, except that, if the balls are due to be changed at the beginning of the tie-break, the change shall be delayed until the second game of the following set.

Doubles

In doubles, the procedure for singles shall apply. The player whose turn it is to serve shall be the server for the first point. Thereafter each player shall serve in rotation for two points, in the same order as previously in that set, until the winners of the game and set have been decided.

Rotation of Service
The player (or pair in the case of doubles) who served first in the tie-break game shall receive service in the first game of the following set.

These Rules are officially approved by the International Tennis Federation.

The Laws of
Table Tennis

Table Tennis

As adopted by the International Table Tennis Federation and approved by the
English Table Tennis Association

1. The Table

1.1 The upper surface of the table, known as the "playing
surface", shall be rectangular, 2.74 m long and 1.525 m wide,
and shall lie in an horizontal plane 76 cm above the floor.

1.2 The playing surface shall be considered to include the
top edges of the table, but not the sides of the table top below
the edges.

1.3 The playing surface may be of any material and shall
yield a uniform bounce of 22–25 cm when a standard ball is
dropped on to it from a height of 30.5 cm.

1.4 The playing surface shall be uniformly dark coloured
and matt, with a white line 2 cm wide along each edge.

1.4.1 The lines along the 2.74 m edges shall be "side lines".

1.4.2 The lines along the 1.525 m edges shall be "end lines".

1.5 The playing surface shall be divided into two "courts"
of equal size by a vertical net running parallel with the end
lines, and shall be continuous over the whole area of each
court.

1.6 For doubles,

1.6.1 each court shall be divided into two equal "half courts"
by a white line 3 mm wide, known as the "centre line", running
parallel with the side lines;

1.6.2 the centre line shall be regarded as part of the server's
right half court and of the receiver's right half court.

2. The Net

2.1 The net shall be suspended by a cord attached at each
end to an upright post 15.25 cm high, the outside limits of the
post being 15.25 cm outside the side line.

2.2 The net and its suspension, shall be 1.83 m long.

2.3 Its top, along its whole length, shall be 152.5 mm above
the playing surface.

2.4 The bottom of the net, along its whole length, shall be

close to the playing surface and the ends of the net shall be close to the supporting posts.

3. The Ball

3.1 The ball shall be spherical, not less than 37.2 mm nor more than 38.2 mm in diameter.

3.2 The ball shall weigh not less than 2.40 gm nor more than 2.53 gm.

3.3 The ball shall be made of celluloid or similar plastics and shall be white or yellow, and matt.

4. The Racket

4.1 The racket may be of any size, shape or weight.

4.2 The blade shall be of wood, continuous, of even thickness, flat and rigid.

4.2.1 The blade shall be considered as being of wood provided that at least 85% of the blade by thickness is of natural wood and that no single adhesive layer is thicker than 7.5% of the total thickness or 0.35 mm., whichever is the smaller.

4.2.2 An adhesive layer in the blade may include reinforcement with fibrous material such as carbon fibre, glass fibre or compressed paper.

4.3 The visible surface of each side of the blade, whether used for striking the ball or not, shall be uniformly dark coloured and matt; and trimming round the edge of the blade shall be matt, and no part of it shall be white or brightly reflecting.

4.4 A side of the blade used for striking the ball may be completely uncovered or covered over the whole of the striking surface with one of the permitted covering materials, each layer of covering being of uniform thickness.

4.5 An uncovered side of the blade used for striking the ball shall be either naturally dark coloured or shall be darkened in such a way as not to alter the frictional characteristics of the surface—for example, by staining and not by painting.

4.6 The covering material for a side of the blade used for striking the ball may be either ordinary "pimpled rubber" with pimples outwards, having a total thickness including adhesive of not more than 2 mm or "sandwich rubber", with pimples inwards or outwards, having a total thickness including adhesive of not more than 4 mm.

4.6.1 "Pimpled rubber" is a layer of non-cellular rubber, natural or synthetic, with pimples evenly distributed over its surface at a density of not less than 10 sq cm and not more than 50 sq cm.

4.6.2 "Sandwich rubber" is a layer of cellular rubber surfaced with a layer of pimpled rubber, the total thickness of the pimpled rubber being not more than 2 mm.

4.6.3 The part of the blade nearest the handle and gripped by the fingers may be covered with any material for convenience of grip and is to be regarded as part of the handle.

4.6.4 Slight deviations from uniformity of colour or continuity of covering due to fading, wear or accidental damage, may be ignored provided they do not significantly change the characteristics of the surface.,

4.7 A side of the blade not intended for striking the ball may be painted or covered with any material, but if a player strikes the ball in play with a side of the blade whose surface does not comply with the requirements of 4.4–4.6 he shall lose a point.

4.8 Before using a racket for the first time in a match a player shall, if so requested, show both sides of the blade to his opponent.

5. Definitions

5.1 A "rally" is the period during which the ball is in play.

5.2 A "let" is a rally the result of which is not scored.

5.3 A "point" is a rally the result of which is scored.

5.4 The "racket hand" is the hand carrying the racket.

5.5 The "free hand" is the hand not carrying the racket.

5.6 To "strike" is to touch with the racket, carried in the racket hand, or the racket hand below the wrist.

5.7 To "volley" is to strike the ball in play when it has not yet touched the playing surface on one side of the net since last being struck from the other side.

5.8 A player "obstructs" the ball if he, or anything he wears or carries, touches it in play before it has passed over the end line or side line of his court not having touched his court since last being struck by his opponent.

5.9 The "server" is the player due to strike the ball first in a rally.

5.10 The "receiver" is the player to strike the ball second in a rally.

5.11 The "umpire" is the person appointed to decide the result of each rally.

5.12 Anything that a player "wears or carries" includes anything that he was wearing or carrying at the start of the rally.

5.13 The ball shall be regarded as passing "over or around" the net if it passes under or outside the projection of the net and its supports outside the table.

6. A Good Service

6.1 Service shall begin with the ball resting on the palm of the free hand, which shall be stationary, open and flat, with the fingers together and the thumb free.

6.2 The free hand, while in contact with the ball in service, shall at all times be above the level of the playing surface.

6.3 The server shall then project the ball upwards, by hand only and without imparting spin, so that it rises from the palm of the hand within 45 degrees of the vertical.

6.4 As the ball is then descending from the height of its trajectory, the server shall strike it so that it touches first his own court and then, passing directly over or around the net, touches the receiver's court.

6.4.1 In doubles, the points of contact of the ball with the playing surface shall be the server's right half-court or centre line and then the receiver's right half-court or centre line.

6.4.2 If, in attempting to serve, a player fails to strike the ball while it is in play, he shall lose a point.

6.5 At the moment of impact of the racket on the ball in service, the ball shall be behind the end line of the server's court or an imaginary extension thereof.

6.6 It is the responsibility of the player to serve so that the umpire can see that he complies with the requirements of a good service.

6.6.1 Except when an assistant umpire has been appointed to act as service judge, the umpire because his view is obstructed by the server or his partner or for any other reason, has an element of doubt about the correctness of a player's service he may, on the first occasion in a match, interrupt play and warn the server without awarding a point.

6.6.2 On any subsequent occasion in the same match on which the same player's service is of doubtful correctness he shall not be given the benefit of any doubt but shall lose a point.

6.6.3 Where, however, there is a clear failure to comply with the requirements for a good service no warning should be given and a point should be awarded against the server on the first as on any other occasion.

6.7 Exceptionally, strict observance of the prescribed method of service may be waived where the umpire is notified, before play begins that compliance is prevented by physical disability.

7. A Good Return

7.1 The ball, having been served or returned in play, shall be struck so that it passes directly over or around the net and touches the opponent's court:

7.1.2 if the ball, having been served or returned in play, bounces back over the net it may be struck so that it touches directly the opponent's court;

7.1.1 if the ball, in passing over or around the net, touches the net or its supports, it shall be considered to have passed directly.

8. The Order of Play

8.1 In singles, the server shall first make a good service, the receiver shall then make a good return and, thereafter, server and receiver alternately shall each make a good return.

8.2 In doubles, the server shall first make a good service, the receiver shall then make a good return, the partner of the server shall then make a good return, the partner of the receiver shall then make a good return and, thereafter, each player alternately in that sequence shall make a good return.

9. In Play

9.1 The ball is in play from the last moment at which it is

stationary on the palm of the server's free hand before being projected in service until:

9.1.1 it has, except in service, touched the playing surface twice in succession without having been struck intermediately;

9.1.2 it has touched any person or object other than the net, it supports, the playing surface, the racket held in the hand or the racket hand below the wrist;

9.1.3 the rally has otherwise been decided as a let or a point.

10. A Let

10.1 The rally shall be a let:

10.1.1 if the ball served, in passing over or around the net, touches it or its supports, provided the service is otherwise good or is volleyed or obstructed by the receiver or his partner.

10.1.2 if a service is delivered when the receiver or his partner is not ready, except that a player may not be considered unready if he or his partner attempts to strike the ball;

10.1.3 if, owing to a disturbance outside his control, a player fails to make a good service or a good return or otherwise infringes a Law:

10.1.4 if it is interrupted for correction of an error in playing order or ends;

10.1.5 if it is interrupted for introduction of the Expedite System;

10.1.6 if it is interrupted for warning a player for a service of doubtful correctness.

10.1.7 if the conditions of play are disturbed in a way likely to affect the outcome of the rally.

11. A Point

11.1 Unless the rally is a let, a player shall lose a point:

11.1.1 if he fails to make a good service;

11.1.2 if he fails to make a good return;

11.1.3 if he volleys or obstructs the ball except as provided in 10.1.1;

11.1.4 if he strikes the ball twice successively;

11.1.5 if he strikes the ball with a side of the racket blade having an illegal surface;

11.1.6 if he, or anything he wears or carries, moves the playing surface while the ball is in play;

11.1.7 if his free hand touches the playing surface while the ball is in play;

11.1.8 if he, or anything he wears or carries, touches the net or its supports while the ball is in play;

11.1.9 if, in doubles, he strikes the ball out of the sequence established by the server and receiver;

11.1.10 if, under the Expedite System, his service and twelve successive good returns of the serving player or pair are all followed by good returns of the receiving player or pair.

12. A Game

12.1 A game shall be won by the player or pair first scoring 21 points except that, where both players or pairs have scored 20 points, the game shall be won by the player or pair first scoring subsequently 2 points more than the opposing player or pair.

13. A Match

13.1 A match shall consist of one game, the best of three games or the best of five games.

13.2 Play shall be continuous throughout a match, except that any player shall be entitled to claim an interval of not more than five minutes between the third and fourth games of a match and of not more than one minute between any other successive games of a match.

14. The Choice of Ends and Service

14.1 The choice of ends and the right to serve or receive first in a match shall be decided by lot.

14.2 The winner toss may:

14.2.1 choose to serve or receive first, when the loser shall have the choice of ends:

14.2.2 choose an end, when the loser shall have the right to choose to serve or receive first;

14.2.3 require the loser to make the first choice.

14.3 In doubles, the pair who have the right to serve first in any game shall decide which partner shall do so.

14.3.1 In the first game of a match, the opposing pair shall then decide which partner will receive first.

14.3.2 In subsequent games of the match, the first receiver will be established automatically to correspond with the choice of server.

15. The Order of Servicing and Receiving

15.1 In singles, after five points the receiver shall become the server, and so on, until the end of the game, or the score 20–20, or the introduction of the Expedite System.

15.2 In doubles:

15.2.1 the first five services shall be delivered by the selected partner of the pair who have the right to serve and shall be received by the appropriate partner of the opposing pair;

15.2.2 the second five services shall be delivered by the receiver of the first five services and shall be received by the partner of the first server;

15.2.3 the third five services shall be delivered by the partner of the first server and shall be received by the partner of the first receiver;

15.2.4 the fourth five services shall be delivered by the partner of the first receiver and shall be received by the first server;

15.2.5 the fifth five services shall be delivered and received as the first five, and so on, until the end of the game.

15.3 From the score 20–20, or under the Expedite System, the sequence of serving and receiving shall be the same, but each player shall deliver only one service in turn until the end of the game.

15.4 The player or pair who served first in a game shall receive first in the immediately subsequent game, and so on, until the end of the match.

15.5 In each game of a doubles match, the initial order of receiving shall be opposite to that in the immediately preceding game.

15.6 In the last possible game of a doubles match, the receiving pair shall change the order of receiving when first either pair reaches the score 10.

16. The Change of Ends

16.1 The player or pair who started at one end in a game shall start at the other end in the immediately subsequent game, and so on, until the end of the match.

16.2 In the last possible game of a match, the players or pairs shall change ends when first either player or pair reaches the score 10.

17. Out of Order of Ends, Serving or Receiving

17.1 If, by mistake, the players have not changed ends when ends should have been changed, play shall be interrupted as soon as the error is discovered and shall resume with the players at the ends at which they should be at the score that has been reached, according to the sequence established at the beginning of the match.

17.2 If, by mistake, a player serves or receives out of his turn, play shall be interrupted and shall continue with that player serving or receiving who, according to the sequence established at the beginning of the match, should be server or receiver respectively at the score that has been reached.

17.3 In any circumstances, all points scored before the discovery of an error shall be reckoned.

18. The Expedite System

18.1 If a game is unfinished after fifteen minutes of play, the game shall be interrupted and the rest of that game, and the remaining games of the match, shall be played under the Expedite System.

18.1.1 If the ball is in play when the game is interrupted, play shall restart with service by the player who served in the rally that was interrupted.

18.1.2 If the ball was not in play when the game was interrupted, play shall restart with service by the player who received in the immediately preceding rally.

18.2 Thereafter each player shall serve for one point in turn, as provided in 15.3, and if the service and twelve successive good returns of the serving player or pair are all followed by good returns of the receiving player or pair, the server shall lose a point.

18.3 The Expedite System may be introduced at any earlier time, from the beginning of the match up to the end of fifteen minutes of play in any game, at the request of both players or pairs.

The Rules of
Volleyball

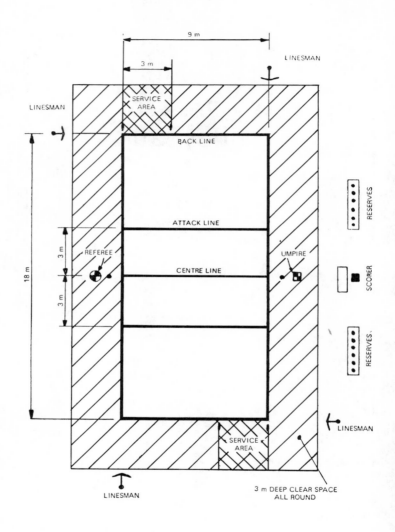

Volleyball

I. FACILITIES, PLAYING AREA AND EQUIPMENT

RULE 1

Playing Area and Lines

1. The playing area shall be 59 ft (18 m) long by 29 ft 6 in (9 m) wide, free from all obstructions up to a height of 23 ft (7 m) measured from the ground.

2. The court shall be bounded by lines 2 in (5 cm) wide, which shall be drawn at least 6 ft 6 in (2 m) from all obstructions. These lines are included in the playing area.

3. A line (the centre line) 2 in (5 cm) wide, drawn beneath the net, divides the court into two equal halves, and is limited by the side lines.

4. In each half of the court, a line of 29 ft 6 in (9 m) by 2 in (5 cm) parallel to the centre line, is drawn 10 ft (3 m) from it, the width of which is included in the 10 ft. This is known as the attack line. The attack area, as marked out by the centre line and the attack line, extends indefinitely beyond the side lines.

5. Two lines 6 in (15 cm) long and 2 in (5 cm) wide, drawn 8 in (20 cm) behind and perpendicular to the end line, mark the service area of each court. One line is an extension of the right-hand side line and the other 10 ft (3 m) to the left of it. The service area shall have a minimum depth of 6 ft 6 in (2 m).

6. The temperature shall not be below 50°F (10°C).

RULE 2
The Net

1. The net shall be 3 ft 3 in (1 m) deep and 32 ft (9.50 m) long. It shall be made of 4 in (10 cm) square mesh. A double thickness of white canvas 2 in (5 cm) wide shall be sewn along the top of the net. A flexible cable shall be stretched through the canvas and the lower edge of the net.

2. The height of the net measured in the centre shall be 7 ft

$11\frac{5}{8}$ in (2.43 m) for men and 7 ft $4\frac{1}{8}$ in (2.24 m) for women. The two ends of the net must be an equal height from the ground and cannot exceed the regulation height by more than $\frac{3}{4}$ in (2 cm).

3. Two tapes of 2 in (5 cm) wide white material, 3 ft 3 in (1 m) long, shall be fastened near each side of the net vertical to the side lines and the centre line.

Coinciding with the outside edges of the tapes two flexible antennae shall be fastened to the net at a distance of 9 m from each other. These two antennae shall be 6 ft (1.80 m) long with a diameter of approximately $\frac{3}{8}$ in (10 mm) and be made of fibreglass or similar material and shall extend 32 in (80 cm) above the top of the net. The antennae shall be of contrasting colours, alternating in sections 4 in (10 cm) long.

4. The posts supporting the net must be at least 20 in (50 cm) from the side lines and shall not interfere with the duties of the referee or the umpire. The side markers and the antennae are considered as part of the net.

RULE 3
The Ball

The ball shall be spherical, made of a supple leather case with the bladder made of rubber or similar material. The ball shall be uniform in colour; indoors this colour shall be light.

Circumference: 26 to 26.8 in (66 to 67 cm).

Weight: 9 to 10 oz (270 to 280 gm).

II. THE PLAYERS

RULE 4
Rights and Duties of Players

1. All players must know the rules of the game and abide by them.

2. During the game, a player may address the referee only through the team captain.

Only the playing team captain may address the referee and shall be the spokesman for his players. He may also address the umpire but only on matters concerning the umpire's duties.

3. *Conduct of Players, Substitutes and Coaches.* The following acts are punishable:

(*a*) Speaking persistently to officials about their decisions.

(*b*) Making uncivil remarks to officials.

(*c*) Acting in an uncivil manner with a view to influencing the decisions of officials.

(*d*) Making uncivil or personal remarks or actions to opponents.

(*e*) The deliberate coaching during the game of a player or team by anyone outside the court area.

(*f*) Leaving the court during a stoppage of play (except between sets) without permission of the referee.

(*g*) At the instant of contact with the ball, particularly during service reception, clapping, shouting or taking any action, the purpose of which is to distract the referee in his judgement concerning the handling of the ball.

4. *Penalties.*

(i) For a minor offence (e.g. talking to opponents, spectators or officials, shouting, or intentionally delaying the game)—a *warning* (yellow card).

In the case of a second offence, the player shall receive a *personal warning* (noted on the score sheet) and his team loses the service or the opponents win a point (red card).

(ii) For a serious offence a penalty is recorded on the score sheet and this automatically entails loss of the point or service by the offender's team (red card). In the case of a second offence by the same player, the referee may disqualify him for the rest of the set or the match (red and yellow cards).

The referee shall disqualify (without prior warning) any player who addresses derogatory remarks to officials, opponents or spectators (red and yellow cards).

RULE 5
The Teams

1. *Players' Strip*

(*a*) The clothing of a player shall consist of a jersey, shorts and light and pliable shoes (rubber or leather soles without heels). It is forbidden to wear a head-gear or any article (jewels, pins, bracelets, etc.) which could cause injuries during the game. If requested, the referee may allow one or more players to play without shoes.

(*b*) Players' jerseys must be marked with numbers of between 3 in to 6 in (8 to 15 cm) high on the chest and numbers 6 in (15 cm) high on the back. The width of the material forming the number shall be $\frac{3}{4}$ in (2 cm). In International matches, the captain shall wear on the left-hand side of his chest a badge $3\frac{1}{2}$ by $\frac{1}{2}$ in (8 by 1.5 cm) of a different colour from that of his jersey.

(*c*) Members of a team must appear on court dressed in clean, presentable strips of the same colour. If the weather is cold, they may play in numbered training suits.

2. *Composition of Teams and Substitution*

(*a*) The number of players in a team, under all circumstances, is 6. A complete team, including substitutes, may not exceed 12 players. Before a match begins, the names of all players and substitutes must be entered on the score sheet. Players not so listed may not take part in the match.

(*b*) Substitutes and coaches must be on the side of the court opposite the referee. Substitutes may warm up outside the playing area, provided they return to their designated place afterwards.

(*c*) Substitution of players is made when the ball is dead upon request from the captain or coach of a team to the referee or umpire. A team is allowed a maximum of six substitutions per set. Before entering the game, the substitute must report in playing strip to the scorer and be ready to take his place immediately he has been authorised to do so. If the substitution is not completed immediately, a time-out is charged to the team.

In the case of a team having already exhausted its allotted number of times-out, the team is penalised by loss of service or the opponents are awarded a point.

The captain or coach asking for the substitution shall indicate to the referee and scorer the number(s) of the player(s) involved. When substitution has been completed, the team may not request a new substitution until play has resumed and the ball is dead again.

(*d*) Any player beginning the set may, in that set, be replaced only once by a substitute. The original player may go back on court during the same set. However, he must re-enter in the rotational position he previously occupied and must then stay on court for the rest of that set.

Furthermore, no other player except the one originally withdrawn may enter the set to take the place of the substitute. A substitute leaving the game may not re-enter it again in the same set. If a team becomes incomplete through injury to any player, and if all other substitutes have been used, he can then replace the injured player even if the substitute has already played in another position.

If a team becomes incomplete as a result of a player being sent off, and all normal substitutions have been carried out, the team loses the set in progress, but retains the points it has scored.

3. *Position of Players*

At the time the ball is served, players of both teams must be within their own courts in two lines of three players. The three players at the net are front-line players, occupying, from right to left, positions 2, 3 and 4, while the three players in the back are back-line players, occupying, from right to left, positions 1, 6 and 5.

The positions of the players on the court must conform to the rotational order recorded on the score-sheet: namely, in the front line, 3 must be between 2 and 4, and in front of 6. In the back line, 6 must be between 1 and 5, and behind 3. Thus 2 must be in front of 1, and 4 must be in front of 5.

As soon as the ball is served, players are allowed to move anywhere within the playing area, except under the net into their opponents' court. The rotation order indicated on the official score-sheet must be adhered to until the end of the set.

Before the start of a new set, rotation order may be changed, provided it is indicated on the score-sheet prior to the start of the set.

4. *Error in Positioning of Player*

When a team is found to be out of position, play must be stopped and the error corrected. All points made by the team whilst in the wrong position must be cancelled. If the team at fault is serving at the time of the discovery of the error, a side-out (change of service) will be called. All points scored by opponents are retained. If it is not possible to determine when the error first occurred, the team at fault shall resume its correct position and shall be penalised by loss of service or by the award of a point to its opponents.

RULE 6
Team Coaches, Managers and Captains

1. Team coaches, managers and captains are responsible for team discipline.

2. The coach or captain (but not a "player coach" on court) has the right to request a time-out or substitution. During a time-out, the coach is permitted to speak to players, but may not enter the court. At no time during play may coaches or managers contest decisions of the referee.

3. The captain is the only player on the court who may speak to the officials.

III. OFFICIALS AND THEIR DUTIES

RULE 7
Officials of the Match

A match is conducted by the following officials: a referee, an umpire, a scorer, and 2 or 4 linesmen.

Once the starting line-up has been given to the scorer, no alterations are to be permitted, unless caused by an error of any official.

RULE 8
The Referee

The referee controls the game (located above one end of the net) and his decisions are final. He has authority over all players and officials from beginning to end of the match. This includes periods of halt in the play. He has power to settle all questions, including those not specified in the rules.

He may overrule the decisions of other officials, if he believes them to be wrong. He must be located approx. 20 in (50 cm) above one end of the net in order that he can clearly see the play.

In accordance with Rule 4, the referee penalises bad behaviour of players, coaches and managers.

NOTE. *Immediately after the whistle stops play, the referee shall indicate, with the use of hand signals, the nature of the fault committed and the team which has service.*

RULE 9
The Umpire

The umpire (assisting the referee) takes up position on the other side of the court facing the referee.

1. He blows his whistle when a player has crossed the centre line or has illegally played the ball within the attack zone.

2. He points out any contact of the ball with the antennae and whenever the ball passes outside them.

3. He times the duration of times-out.

4. He supervises the conduct of substitutes and coaches on the bench.

5. He authorises substitutions at the request of team coaches or captains.

6. He judges contacts with the net, except those over or near to the top of the net.

7. He checks that the rotational order and positions of the receiving team are correct at the time of each service.

8. He calls the attention of the referee to any unsporting actions.

9. He verifies at the beginning of each set that the initial positions of each team correspond exactly to the order of rotation as shown on the score-sheet.

10. He watches for contact of the ball with any foreign objects.

11. He gives his opinion to the referee in all matters when requested to do so.

NOTE. *The ball is considered to be "dead" when either official blows his whistle.*

RULE 10
The Scorer

The scorer's position is on the opposite side of the court to the referee and behind the umpire. His duties are as follows:

1. Before the game he enters on the score-sheet the names and numbers of the players and substitutes and obtains the signatures of the coaches and captains authorised to make substitutions.

2. He records the score as the game progresses, carefully noting substitutions and the number of times-out requested during each set.

3. At each new request for a time-out, he shall announce the number of times-out that have been requested during that set by each team.

4. After the toss and before each set, he records on the score-sheet the position of the players on court (the rotation order). The position of the team serving first is recorded first on the score-sheet. He shall not give the respective formations of the teams to anyone except to the officials when so requested.

5. During the set, he shall see that the rotation order is observed.

6. He announces the changing of ends after each set and after the eighth point scored by one of the teams in the deciding set.

7. During stoppages in the game, he points out to officials the number of requests for times-out.

8. At the end of the match, he presents the score-sheet to the referee and umpire for signature.

RULE 11
The Linesmen

At least two linesmen are placed diagonally in opposite corners of the playing area, other than the service areas, at a minimum distance of 1 m indoors and 3 m outdoors. Each linesman watches the side-line and the end-line nearest him. The linesman is responsible for signalling when the ball is "out" by raising the flag, and when the ball is "in" by lowering the flag.

The linesman signals to the referee when:
— errors are made by a player when serving;
— the ball touches the antennae;
— the ball does not pass over the net completely between the antennae or their indefinite extension;
— the ball which is "out" was contacted by a player of the receiving team beforehand.

IV. RULES OF THE GAME

RULE 12
Duration of Game and Choice of Ends

1. A match is played to the best of 3 or 5 sets.

All International matches are to be played to the best of 5 sets.

2. The captains toss a coin to decide ends and service. The winner may choose either the end he prefers or the right to serve first.

3. Before the start of the deciding set, the referee tosses again for the choice of ends or service.

4. Teams must change ends after each set, except when the following set is the decider. Ends of the court in the deciding set are chosen after the second toss.

5. When the teams have won the same number of sets and one team has 8 points in the deciding set, teams must automatically change ends. Service, however, is continued by the player who was serving at the time of the change.

If the change of ends was not made at the correct time, it will take place as soon as the omission is noticed by the referee or the captains. The score, however, is not affected.

6. (a) A time-out may be granted by the referee or umpire only when the ball is dead. When the captain or coach requests a stoppage he must indicate whether this is for a time-out or a substitution. If he indicates neither, the referee will presume it is a time-out.

(b) During a time-out players may not leave the court to speak to anyone, except to receive instructions from the coach, who, however, may not enter the court.

(c) Each team may take two times-out per set, each limited to 30 seconds. Two successive times-out may be requested by one or other team without the game recommencing. A time-out may be followed immediately by a substitution requested by either team and a substitution can be followed immediately by a time-out.

(d) If, in error, a third time-out is requested, it shall be refused and the captain or coach making the request shall be cautioned. If the offence is repeated during the same set, the offending team will be penalised with the loss of service or the opponents will be awarded a point.

(e) Following the substitution of a player, play will resume immediately and no one, including the coach, is allowed to advise players during a substitution.

(f) *In the case of injury*, an interruption of 3 minutes is allowed, which will not be counted as a time-out. This is only allowed when the injured player cannot be replaced. Play must stop as soon as the referee is aware of the injury. The point must be replayed.

(g) Between sets a maximum interval of 2 minutes is allowed; this shall be 5 minutes between fourth and fifth sets. The interval includes the time spent in changing ends and recording rotational orders on the score-sheet.

7. If, during an International match, circumstances (such as bad weather, failure of equipment, etc.) prevent a match from being completed, the following shall apply:

(a) If the game is resumed on the same court after one or more periods not exceeding 4 hours, the score in the interrupted set stands and the game resumes where it left off;

(b) If the match is resumed on another court, the score of the interrupted set is annulled, but the results of the sets already completed remain as they are. The cancelled set will be replayed under the same conditions as before the interruption.

(c) If the delay exceeds 4 hours the match shall be replayed completely, whatever court is chosen.

RULE 13
Beginning the Game and Service

1. Service is the act of putting the ball into play. This is done by the right-hand back-line player who hits the ball with his hand (open or closed) or any part of the arm, in order to send the ball over the net into the opponents' court.

The server stands in the service area and hits the ball. At this moment of contact the service is completed. The ball is struck after having been thrown in the air or released from the hand. The server is not allowed to strike a ball resting on his other hand. After striking the ball, the player may land on the line or inside the court, so long as at the moment of impact he was behind the back-line and within the service area.

If, after having been thrown or released from the hand, the ball falls to the ground without being hit or contacted, the service must be taken again, but the referee should caution delays of this nature.

The service is considered good if the ball passes over the net without touching it, and between the antennae.

Service must be made immediately after the referee has whistled. If service is made before the whistle, it must be taken again.

2. A player continues to serve until his team commits a fault.

3. The referee will blow his whistle and signal "change of service" when one of the following service faults occurs:

(*a*) the ball touches the net;

(*b*) the ball passes under the net;

(*c*) the ball touches the antennae or does not pass over the net completely between the antennae or the extension of the antennae;

(*d*) the ball touches a player of the serving team or any object before entering the opponents' court; or

(*e*) the ball lands outside the limits of the opponents' court.

4. If the service is made by the wrong player, the referee shall whistle "change of service" and that side shall lose all the points scored whilst the wrong player was serving. The players of the team that was at fault shall revert to their correct positions.

5. Serving in each new set is begun by the team which did

not serve first in the preceding set, except in the case of the deciding set when service is decided by the toss of a coin.

6. Any act which, in the opinion of the referee, delays the game, shall be penalised.

7. At the moment of service, it is illegal for players of the serving side to wave their arms, jump or group in twos and threes with the aim of forming a screen to mask the server's action.

RULE 14
Change of Service

1. Service is changed when the serving team commits a fault.
2. Service will change sides when a "side-out" is called.

RULE 15
Rotation

1. On change of service, the team to serve will rotate one position clockwise before serving.

2. At the beginning of a new set, players may change their positions provided the scorer has received the new line-up before the set begins.

RULE 16
Contacting the Ball During Play

1. Each team is allowed a maximum of three successive contacts of the ball in order to return the ball to the opponents' area, with the exception of contacts while blocking (Rule 17, 4 (a), (b)).

2. The ball may be hit with any part of the body above, and including, the waist.

3. The ball can contact any number of parts of the body down to the waist, provided that contacts are simultaneous, and that the ball is not held, but rebounds cleanly.

4. A player who contacts the ball, or is contacted by it, is considered to have played the ball.

5. When a ball rests momentarily in the hands or arms of

a player, it is considered to be held. The ball must be cleanly hit.

Scooping, lifting, pushing or carrying the ball shall be considered as holding. A ball hit cleanly with both hands from below is considered as "good".

6. A player contacting the ball more than once with any part of the body, with no other player having touched it in between, will be considered to have committed a "double hit". (*Exception:* blocking—Rule 17, 4(*c*).)

RULE 17
Simultaneous Contacts and Blocking

1. When opposing players contact the ball simultaneously above the net, the player of the team opposite to that receiving the ball is considered as having touched it last. After such a simultaneous contact by two opposing players, the team whose side the ball enters has the right to play the ball three times.

If, after a simultaneous contact, the ball lands on the playing area, the team in whose court the ball lands is penalised. However, if the ball lands outside the court, it is the other team that is at fault.

If the ball is simultaneously held by opposing players, it is a double fault and the point is played again.

2. If two or more players of the same team attempt to play the ball, and it is contacted by only one of them, it will count as only one contact.

A player may play the ball whilst in contact with a player of his own team without, however, using him as a means of support to reach a ball. A player is allowed to hold back a player who is about to commit a fault.

When two players of the same team contact the ball simultaneously, it is counted as two contacts (except in the case of a "block": see 4 below).

3. It is a double fault, and the point shall be played again, when two opposing players simultaneously commit a fault.

4. (*a*) Blocking is the action at the net of attempting to intercept the ball coming from the opponents' side. Any player is considered as having the intention to block if he places any

part of his body (above the waist) above the height of the net while in a position at the net.

Blocking can be performed by any or all of the front-line players. Any attempt to block is considered as an actual block only if the ball is contacted by one or more blockers.

The team which has effected an actual block shall have the right to three more contacts to return the ball to the opponents' area.

(*b*) Any player participating in a block in which the ball is contacted shall have the right to make a successive contact. However, such contact shall count as the first of the three hits allowed to the team.

(*c*) If the ball contacts one or more players in the block, it shall be counted as one contact for the team, even if these contacts are not made simultaneously by the players in the block.

(*d*) The back-line players may not block at the net, but may retrieve any ball in any other position near or away from the block.

(*e*) The blocker(s) may reach over the net. However, the blocker(s) shall not contact the ball over the opponents' area until after the completion of the opponents' action which sends the ball towards the blockers' side.

5. When the ball, after having touched the top of the net as well as the opponents' block, returns to the attackers' side, the players of this team have the right to three hits.

RULE 18
Play at the Net

1. When the ball touches the net between the antennae in the course of play (other than when served) it is considered to be good and play continues.

2. To be good, a ball must cross the net completely between the antennae or their indefinite extension.

3. A ball hitting the net completely between the antennae may be played again.

If the ball was contacted three times by a team and then touches the net without crossing it, the referee shall stop play, but only after the ball has been hit the fourth time or made contact with the ground. (*Exception:* Rule 17, 4 (*a*) (*b*).)

4. If the ball is hit into the net so hard that the net contacts an opponent, such contact shall not be considered as a fault on the part of the latter.

5. It is a double fault if two opponents simultaneously touch the net.

RULE 19
Hands Passing Over the Net

1. During the block, touching the ball with the hands over the net in the opponents' court, before opponents' attack is completed, is a fault.

2. The passing of the hands over the net, after an attack, is allowed.

RULE 20
Crossing the Centre Line

1. Contact of any part of a player's body with the opponents' court during play constitutes a fault. Touching the opponents' court with one's foot (feet) is not a fault provided that some part of the foot (feet) still remains in contact with or above the centre line. It is not a fault to enter the opponents' court after the referee has whistled to stop play.

2. Crossing the vertical plane of the net with any part of the body with the purpose of interfering with or distracting an opponent while the ball is in play, is a fault. Crossing the vertical plane of the net without touching an opponent or the opponents' court is not a fault.

RULE 21
Back Line Players

1. Back line players may not direct a ball from within the attack area into the opponents' court unless the ball is below the height of the net. From behind the attack line, they may hit the ball into the opponents' court in any way permitted by the

rules. A back line player, attacking from the back court, may land on or in front of the attack line, provided that his take-off for the attack was clearly behind the attack line.

2. Back line players may not take part in a block.

3. As the attack line extends indefinitely, a back line player may not hit a ball into the opponents' court from above the height of the net if he finds himself to be outside of the court, but within such extended limits of the attack area.

RULE 22
Ball Out of Play

1. A ball touching the antennae or the net outside of the antennae is considered as being hit out.

2. The ball is considered to be out if it touches the ground or any object outside the playing area. A ball touching any line is in.

3. The referee's whistle stops all play. The ball is then "dead".

RULE 23
Point or Side-Out

A team loses service, or its opponents gain a point, when:

(1) the ball touches the ground;

(2) a team plays the ball more than 3 times consecutively (Rule 16.1). (*Exception:* Rule 17.4 (*a*), (*b*).)

(3) the ball is held or pushed (Rule 16.3, 5);

(4) the ball touches a player below the waist (Rule 16.2, 3);

(5) a player touches the ball twice in succession except when blocking (Rule 16.6);

(6) a team, at service, is out of position (Rule 5.4);

(7) a player touches the net, vertical side markers or antennae (Rule 2.1, 3; 18.3);

(8) a player completely crosses the centre line (Rule 20.1);

(9) a player spikes the ball above the opponents' court (Rule 19.2).

(10) a back-line player, in the attacking area, hits the ball

into the opponents' court from above the height of the net (Rule 21);

(11) a ball does not pass over the net completely between the antennae (Rule 18.2 and 13.1, 3(*c*));

(12) a ball touches the ground or an object outside the court (Rule 22.2);

(13) A ball is played by a player who, in turn, is assisted by a player of his own team as a means of support;

(14) a player receives a personal warning (Rule 4.4);

(15) a team, after a referee's warning, receives deliberate instructions from team officials or substitutes (Rule 4.3(*g*));

(16) when faults are committed on both sides of the net, only the first will be penalised. The point is played again if the faults are committed simultaneously (Rule 17.3 and 18.5);

(17) a player reaches under the net and touches the ball or an opponent when the ball is in the opposing court (Rule 20.1);

(18) a player persistently delays the game (Rule 13.6);

(19) players are illegally substituted (Rule 5.2*c*, 2*d*);

(20) a third request is made for time-out for rest after previous warning (Rule 12.6*d*);

(21) when the second time-out is extended beyond 30 seconds (Rule 12.6);

(22) delaying of substitution after having used the two times-out (Rule 5.2*c*);

(23) a player leaves the court without the referee's permission during stoppages of play (except between sets) (Rule 4.3*f*);

(24) a player stamps his feet or makes gestures aimed at intimidating an opponent (Rule 4.3*g*);

(25) a team blocks in an illegal manner (Rule 17.4).

In addition to the above, the serving team loses service in the following cases:

(26) if service is not made from the service area (Rule 13.1);

(27) if the server crosses or touches the back line as the service is hit (Rule 13.1);

(28) if the service crosses the net with the help of another player on the serving team's side (Rule 13.3*d*);

(29) if service is not made in order of rotation (Rule 13.4);

(30) if the service is made incorrectly (Rule 13.1, 3);

(31) if the players wave arms, jump or form groups of two

or more, the purpose of which is to form a screen to mask the server's action (Rule 13.7).

RULE 24
Scoring and Results of the Game

1. It is a fault when a team fails to return the ball over the net correctly. This fault will be penalised by the opposition winning a point or service.

2. A set is won when a team has scored 15 points and has at least a 2 points lead over its opponents.

If the score is tied 14–14, the set continues until one team has a lead of 2 points (e.g. 16–14 or 17–15 or 18–16, etc.)

3. The game shall be forfeited by a team which refuses to play after the referee has asked for the game to be started: the score will be 15–0 for the set and 3–0 for the match. This does not apply to a team becoming incomplete because of injury to players. See Rule 5.2*d*.

RULE 25
Decisions and Protests

1. The decisions of the referee cannot be appealed against during the match.

2. Any dispute concerning interpretation of the rules must be resolved on the spot by the referee. Only the captain of the disputing team may speak to the referee.

3. If the explanation of the referee, requested by the captain, is not judged satisfactory, the captain may appeal to a higher authority. The referee continues to control the game and shall later make out a report concerning the protest.

The Rules of
Water Polo

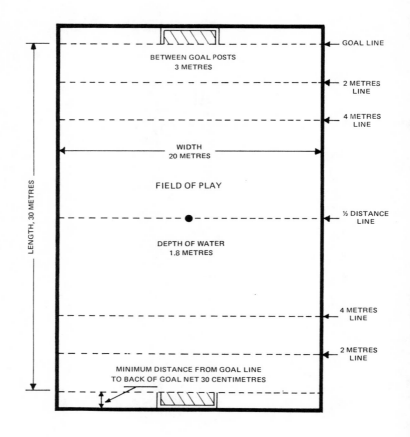

Water Polo

RULE 1

1. The promoting Club or Organisation shall be responsible for correct measurements and markings of the field of play and must provide all stipulated fixtures and equipment.

RULE 2
Field of Play and Measurements

2. (See diagram opposite.)

3. The uniform distance between the respective goal lines is 30 m. The uniform width of the field of play is 20 m. The depth of water must nowhere be less than 1.80 m. For matches in Olympic Games, World Championships and International Competitions the field of play shall be of full measurements as above.

4. For matches played by women, the maximum measurements are 25×17 m.

5. Distinctive marks must be provided on both sides of the field of play to denote the goal line, lines 2 m and 4 m from that line, and half distance between the goal lines. These markings must be clearly visible throughout the game. As uniform colours the following are recommended for these markings: goal line and half distance line white, 2 m from goal line red, 4 m from goal line yellow. A red or any other visible coloured sign shall be placed on the goal line, 2 m from the corner of the field of play on the side of the goal judge (or on the side opposite the timekeeper if there are no goal judges). The boundary of the field of play at both ends is 0.30 m behind the goal line.

6. Sufficient space must be provided to enable the referees to have free way from end to end of the field of play. Space must also be provided at the goal lines for the goal judges.

RULE 3
Goals

7. The goal posts and crossbar must be of wood, metal or synthetic (plastic), with rectangular sections of 0.075 m, square with the goal line and painted white. The goal posts must be fixed, rigid and perpendicular at each end of the playing space, equal distances from the sides and at least 0.30 m in front of the ends of the field of play or of any obstruction. Any standing or resting place for the goalkeeper, other than the floor of the bath, is not permitted.

8. The inner sides of the goal posts must be 3 m apart.

9. The underside of the crossbar must be 0.90 m above water surface when the water is 1.50 m or more in depth, and 0.40 m from the bottom of the bath when the depth of the water is less than 1.50 m.

10. Limp nets must be attached to the goal fixtures to enclose the entire goal space, securely fastened to the goal posts and crossbar and allowing not less than 0.30 m clear space behind the goal line everywhere within the goal area.

RULE 4
The Ball

11. The ball must be round and fully inflated and with an air chamber with a self-closing valve.

12. The circumference must not be less than 0.68 m nor more than 0.71 m.

13. It must be waterproof, without external strappings and without a covering of grease or similar substance.

14. The weight of the ball must not be less than 400 nor more than 450 g.

RULE 5
Flags

15. The referee must be provided with a stick 70 cm long, fitted with a white flag on one end and a blue flag on the other, each flag to be 35 × 20 cm.

16. Each goal judge must be provided with a red flag and a white flag, each $35 \times 20\,cm$, mounted on separate sticks $50\,cm$ long. One of the secretaries must be provided with a white flag and a blue one, to signal re-entrance of excluded players, and the other with a red flag with which to signal third Personal Faults (Rule 19/122). These flags also shall be of the dimensions prescribed above.

RULE 6
Caps

17. One team must wear dark blue and the other white caps, except goalkeepers, who must wear red caps. Caps must be tied with tapes under the chin. If a player loses his cap, it must be replaced at the next stoppage of the game. For Olympic Games and World Championships, caps must be fitted with malleable ear protectors and it is recommended that they be used for all other competitions.

18. Caps must be numbered on both sides, numbers being $0.10\,m$ in height.

19. The goalkeeper shall wear cap No. 1 and the other caps shall be numbered 2 to 13. A substitute goalkeeper shall wear the goalkeeper's cap. No player is allowed to change his cap number without a referee's permission.

RULE 7
Teams

20. Each team shall consist of 7 players, one of whom will be the goalkeeper and wear the goalkeeper's cap, and no more than 6 reserves who may be used as substitutes. Prior to taking part in a match, the players must discard all articles likely to cause injury. The referee shall satisfy himself that the players observe this condition. A player failing to comply must be dismissed from the game. Players must wear trunks with separate drawers or slips underneath. When a player is dismissed from the game in accordance with this paragraph a reserve player may immediately take his place.

21. Players shall not be allowed to have grease, oil or any

similar composition on the body. If the referee ascertains before starting the game that such substance has been used he must order the offending substance to be removed immediately. Should this offence be detected after the game has started, the player concerned must be ordered from the water for the whole game, and a substitute may enter immediately within 2 m from the corner of the field of play at his own goal line at the point nearest the goal-judge (or on the side opposite the time-keeper if there are no goal-judges).

22. The Captains must be playing members and be responsible for the good conduct and discipline of their respective teams.

23. Prior to the commencement of the game the Captains must, in the presence of the referee, toss for choice of ends or colours. The winner to have the choice of ends or colours.

RULE 8
Officials

24. 1. For Olympic Games and World Championships, the officials shall consist of two referees, two goal-judges, time-keepers and secretaries.

2. For all other competitions there must be at least a secretary, a time-keeper and either (*a*) two referees, or (*b*) one referee, and two goal-judges. However, it is recommended that two referees be used for all competitions. Each time-keeper and secretary may have assistants as needed.

3. The officials shall have powers and duties as specified below except that if a competition is held with two referees without goal-judges, the referees shall assume the duties specified for goal-judges in Rule 8 paras. 38–41 inclusive except that it shall not be necessary for them to make any of the flag signals specified in those rules.

Referees

25. The referees are in absolute control of the game. Their authority over the players is effective during the whole of the time that they and the players are within the precincts of the bath.

26. Each must be provided with a shrill whistle with which to start and re-start the game and to declare goals, goal throws, corner throws (whether signalled by the goal-judge or not) and infringements of the rules.

27. All decisions of the referees on questions of fact are final and their interpretation of the rules must be obeyed during the game.

28. 1. A referee may refrain from declaring a foul if, in his opinion, such declaration would be an advantage to the offending team.

2. NOTE. *It is important that the referees shall apply this principle to the full extent. For example: to declare a foul in favour of a player who is in possession of the ball and making progress towards his opponents' goal, or whose team is in possession of the ball, is considered to give an advantage to the offender's team.*

29. He may alter his decision providing he does so before the ball is again in play.

30. He has power to order any player from the water in accordance with the appropriate Rules, and should a player refuse to leave the water when so ordered, the game must be stopped.

31. He may stop the game at any time if, in his opinion, the behaviour of the players or spectators or other circumstances prevent it being brought to a proper conclusion.

32. If the game has to be stopped, the referee must report his actions to the competent authority.

Time-keepers

33. The time-keepers must be fully acquainted with the Rules and each must be provided with a Water-Polo Stop-Watch and a shrill whistle.

34. 1. The duties of the time-keepers shall be (*a*) to record on the watch the exact periods of actual play and the intervals between the periods, as provided by these Rules, (*b*) to record the respective periods of exclusion of any player or players who may be ordered from the water in accordance with these Rules, and (*c*) to record the periods of continuous possession of the ball by each team (Rule 16/93).

2. NOTE. *The time-keeper recording the 35 seconds shall reset the clock only when the ball is put into play.*

35. All signals to stop play must be by whistle. Play is resumed when the ball leaves the hand of the player taking a free throw, goal throw, corner throw or penalty throw, or when the referee throws the ball in for a neutral throw.

36. 1. A time-keeper must signal by whistle the end of each period, independently of the referee. His signal takes immediate effect except as stated in Rule 20/133. The last minute of any game and of any extra time shall be audibly announced.

2. NOTE. *It is acceptable for the time-keeper to give this signal other than by whistle, provided that his signal shall be distinctive, acoustically efficient and readily understood.*

37. The time-keepers must be near to a referee.

Goal-judges

38. The goal-judges must take up position opposite a referee and they must mutually agree upon ends. They must stand directly level with the goal line and stay there for the whole game.

39. Their duties are to signal with the white flag for a goal throw (see Rule 13), with a red flag for a corner throw (see Rule 14), with both flags for a goal (see Rule 12) and with a red flag for an improper re-entry of an excluded player (see Rule 8/ 119.2 and 121.2.1).

Their further duty is to throw in a new ball when the original ball goes outside the field of play. Goal-judges shall each have a supply of balls (see Rule 4).

When the original ball goes out of the field of play in a manner resulting in a goal throw or corner throw, the goal-judge shall give a new ball immediately to the goalkeeper for each goal throw or to the nearest member of the attacking team for each corner throw.

40. Goal-judge shall be responsible to the referee for the correct score of each team at their respective ends.

41. Goal-judges should exhibit the red flag to indicate to the referee that players are correctly positioned on their respective goal lines, according to Rule 11/53.1, but the referee's whistle to start or re-start the game takes immediate effect.

Secretaries

42. The duties of the secretaries shall be (1) to maintain a record of all players, the score, all Major Fouls (time, colour and cap number) and to signal the award of a third Personal Fault (Rule 19/122) to any player by a signal with the red flag and a whistle immediately upon such award; (2) to control the periods of exclusion of players and to signal permission for re-entry upon expiration of their respective periods of exclusion by raising the flag corresponding with the colour of the player's cap; (3) to signal any improper entry (including after a flag signal by a goal-judge of an improper re-entry), which signal stops play immediately.

RULE 9
Time

43. The duration of the game shall be four periods of 7 minutes each, actual play. The teams shall change ends before commencing a new period. There shall be a 2-minute interval between periods. Time starts when a player touches the ball at the start of any period of the game. At all signals for stoppages the recording watch must be stopped until play is resumed.

RULE 10
Goalkeepers

44. While within the 4 m area, the goalkeeper is exempt from the following clauses of Rule 16, viz: Standing and walking; striking at the ball with clenched fist; jumping from the floor; touching the ball with both hands at the same time.

45. He must not go or touch the ball beyond the half-distance line. The penalty for his doing so is a free throw to the nearest opponent to be taken from where the offence occurred.

46. He must not throw the ball beyond his opponents' 4-m line. The penalty for his doing so is a free throw to the nearest opponent to be taken from where the ball crossed the line.

47. Ruling: Throwing includes the ball bouncing off, or being punched by, the goalkeeper.

48. When a goalkeeper is penalised for holding or pushing off from the bar, rail or trough at the end of the bath, the free throw must be taken from the 2-m line opposite the point at which the foul occurred.

49. If a goalkeeper, taking a free throw or goal throw, releases the ball and, before any other player has touched it, regains possession and allows it to pass through his own goal, a corner throw must be awarded. If in the same circumstances he releases the ball, and after another player has touched it regains possession and allows it to pass through his own goal, a goal must be awarded.

50. Should a goalkeeper retire from a game through accident, illness or injury, Rule 22/140 shall apply.

51. If, when a goal throw is awarded, the goalkeeper is out of the water, the nearest defending player must take the throw. In this case, for the purpose of the throw, the limitations and privileges of a goalkeeper will apply. In any other circumstances, a player defending the goal shall not be subject to a goalkeeper's limitations and privileges. (See Rulings 14/71 and 20/130).

52. A goalkeeper who has been replaced by a substitute may, if he returns to the game, play anywhere.

RULE 11
Starting

53. 1. At the commencement of each period of play, the players must take up positions on their respective goal lines about 1 m apart and at least 1 m from either goal post. More than two players are not allowed between the goal posts. When he has ascertained that the teams are ready, the referee shall give the starting signal by a blast on his whistle and immediately afterwards release or throw the ball into the centre of the field of play.

2. NOTE. *If the ball is thrown giving one team a definite advantage, the referee should call for the ball and declare a neutral throw between the two players. Time shall commence when one player touches the ball.*

After a Goal

54. After a goal has been scored, players must take up positions anywhere within their respective halves of the field of play, behind the half-distance line, when a player of the team not having last scored shall re-start the game from the centre of the field of play. Upon the referee signalling by one blast of the whistle, the ball must be put into play promptly by passing it to another player of his team who must be behind the half-distance line when he receives it.

55. Ruling: Actual play is resumed when the ball leaves the hand of the player making the re-start.

56. A re-start made improperly must be retaken.

57. Ruling: When the start or re-start is from the goal line, no portion of a player's body, at water level, may be beyond the goal line; and when the re-start is from the centre, no part of a player's body may be beyond the half-distance line.

RULE 12
Scoring

58. A goal is scored by the ball passing fully over the goal line between the goal posts and subject to the following conditions:

59. A goal may be scored by any part of the body, except the clenched fist, provided that at the start or re-start of the game the ball has been played by two or more players. The team to which they belong or the place in the field of play from where the goal is scored is immaterial.

60. Any attempt by the goalkeeper to stop the ball before it has been played in this way does not constitute "playing" and should the ball cross the goal line or hit the goal post or goalkeeper, the goalkeeper must be awarded a goal throw.

61. Dribbling the ball through the goal posts is permissible.

62. Should a foul occur before the foregoing conditions have been complied with, Rules 16, 17, 18, 19, 20 and 21 operate.

RULE 13
Goal Throw

63. The referee must signal by whistle immediately the ball crosses the goal line.

64. When the entire ball passes over the goal line, excluding that portion between the goal posts, having last been touched by one of the attacking team, a goal throw is awarded to the defending goalkeeper, to be taken from any place within the 2 m area. (See also Rules 16 (94) and 17 (107).)

65. A goal throw taken improperly must be re-taken.

66. Ruling: In the event of a goalkeeper being out of the water, another player must take the throw from the goal line, when the limitations and privileges of a goalkeeper will apply.

RULE 14
Corner Throw

67. The referee must signal by whistle immediately the ball crosses the goal line.

68. When the entire ball passes over the goal line, excluding that portion between the goal posts, having last been touched by one of the defending team, a corner throw is awarded to the opposing team, to be taken at the 2 m mark on the side where the ball goes out.

69. The throw is taken from the 2 m mark.

70. When a corner throw is taken, no player (except the defending goalkeeper) may be within the 2 m line.

71. Ruling: Should a defending goalkeeper be out of the water when a corner throw is awarded, another player of his team may take up a position on the goal line, but without the limitations and privileges of a goalkeeper.

72. If a goalkeeper, taking a free throw or goal throw, releases the ball and before any other player has touched it, regains possession and allows it to pass through his own goal, a corner throw must be awarded.

73. A corner throw taken improperly must be re-taken.

74. Ruling: If a corner throw is taken before the players have left the 2 m area, the throw must be re-taken.

75. If a player taking a free throw passes the ball towards his own goalkeeper, and before any other player has touched it, the ball crosses the goal line or enters the net, a corner throw must be awarded. An attempt by the goalkeeper to stop the ball is not regarded as "touching" for the purposes of this rule.

RULE 15
Neutral Throw

76. 1. When one or more players of each team commit a foul at the same moment which makes it impossible for the referee to distinguish which player offended first, he must take the ball and throw it into the water as near as possible to the place where the incident took place, in such a manner that the players of both teams have an equal opportunity to reach the ball after it has touched the water.

Clauses 105, 106 and 107 must be applied.

2. All neutral throws awarded within the 2 m area are to be taken on the 2 m line opposite the point at which the incident took place.

77. Ruling: If from a neutral throw the referee is of the opinion that the ball has fallen in a position to the advantage of one team, he must take the throw again.

RULE 16
Ordinary Fouls

78. It is a foul (for goalkeepers' exceptions see Rule 10):

79. To advance beyond the goal line at the start or re-start of the game, before the referee has given the signal.

80. To assist a player at the start or re-start or during a game.

81. To hold on to, or push off from, the goal posts or their fixtures. To hold on to the rails, except at start or re-start. To hold on to, or push off from, the sides or ends during actual play.

82. To take any active part in the game when standing on the floor of the bath; to walk when play is in progress.

83. To take or hold the ball under water when tackled.

84. To strike at the ball with clenched fist.

85. To splash in the face of an opponent.

86. To touch the ball before it reaches the water when thrown in by the referee.

87. To jump from the floor of the bath to play the ball or tackle an opponent.

88. Deliberately to impede, or prevent the free movement of, an opponent unless he is holding the ball. Swimming on the shoulders, back or legs of an opponent constitutes impeding. "Holding" is lifting, carrying, or touching the ball. Dribbling the ball is not considered to be "holding".

89. To touch the ball with both hands at the same time.

90. To push, or push off from, an opponent or to simulate being fouled.

91. 1. To be within 2 m of the opponents' goal line or to remain there except when behind the line of the ball.

2. Ruling: It is not an offence if the player taking the ball into the 2 m area passes the ball to his associate who is behind the line of the ball and who shoots at the goal immediately before the first player can leave the 2 m area.

92. To waste time.

93. Ruling: 1. For a team, even with fewer players than their opponents, to retain possession of the ball for more than 35 seconds without shooting at their opponents' goal, is deemed to be wasting time, and a free throw shall be awarded against the player who last touched the ball before this foul is signalled.

2. Should a team shoot at goal as above and regain possession upon the ball rebounding or being in any other manner kept in play the measurement of 35 seconds shall immediately recommence from 35.

3. Time recommences from 35 when the ball comes into the possession of the opposing team or immediately the ball is put into play after a major foul.

(Ruling: The ball does not leave the possession of the holding team merely by being touched in flight by an opponent player, provided that it is not deflected into the possession of the opponent team.)

4. Time recommences when the ball comes into the possession of a team as the result of a "neutral throw".

5. If at expiration of the 35 seconds the ball is in flight and crosses the goal line in accordance with Rule 12, 13 or 14, or becomes out of play as provided by Rule 21, or if a neutral throw is to be taken, the resultant goal, goal throw, corner throw, free throw or neutral throw shall not be allowed, and the foul of wasting time shall be punished.

6. At expiration of the 35 seconds the free throw shall be taken by the opposing player nearest the point at which the game is stopped and undue delay by any member of the penalised team shall be punished as a Major Foul.

7. It is always permissible for the referee to penalise a foul under 16/92 before the period of 35 seconds has expired.

94. For the goalkeeper to throw the ball beyond his opponents' 4-m line or to go or touch the ball outside his own half of the field of play.

95. To take a penalty throw otherwise than in the prescribed manner.

96. To delay unduly when taking a free throw.

97. Ruling: The time allowed for a player to take a free throw is left to the discretion of the referee. It must be reasonable and without undue delay but does not have to be immediate.

98. Except as provided by Rule 10 (48) or 17 (100), the punishment for an ordinary foul shall be a free throw to the opposing team to be taken by any one of their players.

RULE 17
Free Throws

99. The referee must blow his whistle to declare fouls and exhibit the flag corresponding in colour to the caps worn by the team to which the free throw is awarded.

100. A free throw awarded for an ordinary foul committed within the 2 m area must be taken from the 2 m line opposite the point at which the foul occurred. With this exception, and the exception in Rule 21.134.2, free throws are to be taken from the point at which the foul occurred. Should the game be stopped through illness or accident or other unforeseen reason,

the team in possession of the ball at the time is awarded a free throw at that point when time is resumed.

101. Ruling: The responsibility for returning the ball to the player who is to take the free throw is primarily that of the side to which the free throw is awarded. The opponents have no duty to do this, but no player may deliberately throw the ball away to prevent the normal progress of the game. (See also Rule 18/118).

102. Ruling: *A goalkeeper awarded a free throw must take the throw himself and the throw is subject to the limitations and privileges of a goalkeeper.*

103. The throw must be made to enable other players to observe the ball leaving the hand of the thrower. It is permitted to dribble the ball before passing to another player.

104. As soon as the ball leaves the hand of a player taking a free throw, it is in play. In the meantime all players are allowed to change position.

105. Except as provided by Rule 10/49, in all cases of a free throw, corner throw, or neutral throw, at least two players (excluding the defending goalkeeper) must play or touch the ball before a goal can be scored.

106. Ruling: To touch the ball means to touch intentionally.

107. Except as provided by Rule 10/49, an attempt by the goalkeeper to stop the ball from an attacking player, before it has been touched or played by a second player, is not regarded as touching and should the ball cross the goal line or hit the goal posts or the goalkeeper, the goalkeeper must be awarded a goal throw.

108. If, before a goal throw, corner throw, free throw, penalty throw or neutral throw is taken, an offence against Rule 16/85, 16/88, 16/90 or Rule 18 is committed by a member of the team not in possession of the ball, the offender shall be ordered from the water for a period of 45 seconds actual play, or until a goal has been scored, whichever period is the shorter, and the original throw maintained. If a member of the team in possession of the ball commits the offence a free throw shall be awarded to the opponent team and a Personal Fault shall be recorded against the player committing the offence. (See Rule 19/122).

2. NOTE. *If simultaneous fouls are committed by players from opposing teams, both players shall be evicted from the water for 45 seconds actual play, or until a goal has been scored, and the original throw shall be maintained.*

3. Ruling: In the special circumstances described in this paragraph, an offence against Rule 16/85, 16/88 or 16/90 shall be deemed to be a Major Foul and a Personal Fault shall be recorded against the player committing the offence.

109. A free throw taken improperly must be re-taken.

RULE 18
Major Fouls

110. It is a Major Foul for a player:

111. To hold, sink or pull back an opponent not holding the ball.

112. To kick or strike an opponent or make disproportionate movements with that intent.

113. 1. To commit any foul, within the 4 m area, but for which a goal would probably have resulted.

2. NOTE: *In addition to other offences it is a Major Foul within the meaning of this paragraph to pull down the goal, or to play with the ball with clenched fist or with both hands in the 4 m area with the object of preventing a goal from being scored. A penalty throw must be awarded.*

3. Ruling: When the goalkeeper or any other player pulls over the goal completely with the object of preventing a goal, the player has shown disrespect and must be excluded from the remainder of the game (Rule 18 (115)). A substitute may enter the game within 2 m from the corner of the field of play on the side of the goal-judge (or on the side opposite the time-keeper if there be no goal-judges), under his goal line after the expiration of 45 seconds of actual play or when a goal has been scored, whichever period is the shorter. The eviction of the offending player is in addition to awarding the Penalty Throw.

114. To persist in any ordinary foul. (This refers to the same player having persisted.)

115. To refuse obedience to, or show disrespect for, the referee. The offending player shall be excluded from the

remainder of the game and a substitute may enter the game at his own goal line at the point nearest the goal-judge after expiration of 45 seconds actual play or when a goal has been scored, whichever period is the shorter.

116. 1. To commit an act of brutality against another player or an official. A free throw *must* be awarded to the opponent's team and the offending player *must* be excluded from the remainder of the game and *must not be substituted.*

2. NOTE. *"Brutality" includes deliberately striking or kicking.*

3. This rule (with the exception of a free throw) is also applicable if this happens during the interval between two periods of play.

117. To be guilty of misconduct. Misconduct is violence, the use of foul language, persistent foul play, etc.

118. 1. To interfere with the taking of a free throw, penalty throw, corner throw or goal throw. 2. "Interference" includes (i) deliberately to throw the ball away to prevent the normal progress of the game, and (ii) any attempt to play the ball before it leaves the hand of the thrower.

119. 1. For an excluded player to re-enter or a substitute to enter the water improperly.

2. NOTES: (1) *Improper entry is to enter or re-enter:* (a) *without permission of the Secretary,* (b) *by jumping or pushing off from the side or wall of the bath or field of play,* (c) *from any place other than prescribed by Rule 121/2(a)*;

(2) When this offence occurs during the last minute of the final quarter of any game, or during the last minute of any of the two periods of extra time (Rule 23), the offender shall be excluded for the remainder of the game without substitution and a Penalty Throw shall be awarded to the opponent team.

3. Ruling: Entry at any time of a player not entitled under the rules to participate at that time (except for a player awaiting the passage of a 45 second exclusion period to be entitled to participate and except in the situation described in Rule 121 (c)) shall cause such player to be excluded from the remainder of the game with immediate substitution when appropriate, and one penalty throw will be awarded to the opposing team.

4. Ruling: At any time when a player awaiting the passage of an expulsion period enters illegally with the object of pre-

venting a goal, it is deemed to constitute a violation of Rule 18/ 113, and after the player has left the water to complete the original exclusion period, a penalty throw shall be awarded to the opposing team. This penalty takes precedence over the penalty otherwise provided under Rule 11/119 (expulsion or penalty throw).

120. Except as otherwise expressly provided in this Rule, Rule 17/108 or Rule 20 the punishment for a Major Foul is:

121. 1. The offending player *must* be ordered from the water for a period of 45 seconds actual play or until a goal has been scored, whichever period is the shorter, and a free throw to be taken by a player of the opponent team after the excluded player has commenced to leave the water and the referee has signalled the free throw to be taken. The penalty period will start upon the taking of the free throw. If the player leaving the water intentionally interferes with the play, it shall constitute an additional major foul and a penalty throw shall be awarded.

2. NOTE: (a) *After expiration of 45 seconds actual play the excluded player himself must re-enter within 2 m from the corner of the field of play on the side of the goal-judge, under his goal line, and without affecting the alignment of the goals.*

(b) *In cases of simultaneous fouls by members of both teams the offending players shall be excluded as above and a neutral throw be taken.*

(c) *If a player is excluded and there are not 3 Personal Faults recorded against him, and at the end of his exclusion period a substitute player enters in his place, this is deemed to be an offence against Rule 18/115.*

RULE 19
Personal Faults

122. 1. A player committing a Major Foul anywhere in the field of play shall be awarded a Personal Fault, and upon being awarded a third such Personal Fault in any one game he shall be excluded from the remainder of the game and a substitute may enter at his own goal line at the point nearest to the goal judge after expiration of 45 seconds actual play or after a goal has been scored, whichever period is the shorter. See Rule 20/124.

2. If such third Personal Fault results from a foul requiring the award of a Penalty Throw, the entry of the substitute shall be immediate and before the Penalty Throw is taken. If such third Personal Fault results from a violation of Rule 17/108 by a member of the team in possession of the ball, the entry of the substitute shall be immediate.

RULE 20
Penalty Throw

123. Should a player be fouled within his opponents' 4 m area according to Rule 18/112 or 18/116 or commit a foul according to Rule 18/113, 18/119-2 or 18/121, a Penalty Throw *must* be awarded against the offender's team. The referee must announce the offender's number to the secretary.

124. When a Penalty Throw is awarded, the offending player shall be ordered from the water only if the offence is so serious as to justify ordering from the water for the remainder of the game. (Rule 18/116, 18/119-2 and 19/122.)

125. A penalty throw may be executed by any player of the team to which it is awarded, except the goalkeeper, and the player taking the throw may elect to do so from any point on his opponents' 4 m line.

126. 1. The player taking the throw must await the signal of the referee which shall be given by whistle and by simultaneously lowering the respective flag from a vertical to a horizontal position. The player must have possession of the ball and immediately throw it with an uninterrupted movement directly at the goal (see Rule 16/95). Should the ball rebound from the goal posts or crossbar it remains in play. It is not necessary for the ball to be played by any other player before a goal can be scored.

2. Ruling: A Penalty Throw may commence by lifting the ball from the water or with the ball held in the raised hand. It is permissible for the ball to be taken backwards from the direction of the goal in preparation for the forward throw at the goal, but the throw shall commence immediately upon the signal, and continuity of the movement shall not be broken before the ball leaves the thrower's hand.

127. All players, except the defending goalkeeper, or the other player according to Rule 20/130, must leave the 4 m area until the throw is taken, and no player may be within 2 m of the player taking the penalty throw.

128. The goalkeeper must take up a position anywhere on the goal line, and the referee will withhold the signal to throw until satisfied on this point.

129. Ruling: No portion of the goalkeeper's body, at water level, may be beyond the goal line.

130. Ruling: Should the defending goalkeeper be ordered from the water before or after the award of a penalty throw, another player of his team may take a position on the goal line before the throw is taken, but without the privileges and limitations of a goalkeeper.

131. A player must take a penalty throw as described. The penalty for not complying shall be a free throw to the player's nearest opponent.

132. If the taking of a penalty throw is interfered with, or Rules 20/127 and 20/128 are not complied with, the offender or offenders must be punished in accordance with Rule 18/115 and the throw must be re-taken.

133. If at precisely the same time as the referee awards a penalty throw or before a penalty throw is completed, the time-keeper whistles for an interval or full-time, the shot at goal must be allowed and should the ball rebound into the field of play from the goal post, crossbar or goalkeeper, it is dead.

NOTE: *When a penalty throw is to be taken in accordance with this paragraph all players except the defending goalkeeper and the player taking the penalty throw shall leave the water.*

RULE 21
Out of Play

134. 1. Should a player send the ball out of the field of play at either side, a free throw is awarded to the opposing team, to be taken nearest the place where the ball left the field of play.

2. Should the ball go out of the field of play between the goal line and the 2 m line the free throw must be taken from the 2 m mark on the side where the ball went out.

135. Should the ball strike or lodge in an overhead obstruction, it must be considered out of play, and the referee must stop the game and throw the ball into the water under the obstruction. In that case, the ball may not be played until it has touched the water. Should the ball rebound from the goal posts or crossbar or from the side of the field of play at water level, it remains in play, except as provided by Rules 12/60 and 17/107. If the ball rebounds from the side of the field of play above water level, it is considered to be out of play.

RULE 22
Leaving the Water and Substitutes

136. A player must not leave the water or sit or stand on the steps or sides of the bath during a game except: (*a*) during an interval; (*b*) in case of illness or accident; or (*c*) by permission of the referee.

137. A player infringing this rule must be deemed guilty of misconduct. A player having left the water legitimately may re-enter at his own goal line by permission of the referee.

138. In the case of accident or illness, the referee may, at his discretion, suspend the game for not more than three minutes. It shall be the duty of a referee to instruct the time-keeper where any 3 minute stoppage for injury shall commence.

139. When a player has cramp, he must leave the water as quickly as possible and the game must proceed as soon as the player is out of the water. A substitute is not allowed.

140. In the event of a player retiring from the game through accident or injury, the referee may permit his immediate substitution by a reserve. The referee shall refuse such permission only if he considers the request unjustified. The player so retiring shall not be allowed at any time to re-enter the game. Otherwise a player may be substituted only: (*a*) In accordance with provisions of Rules 7/20, 7/21, 18/115 or 19/122, (*b*) during the interval between periods of play, (*c*) after a goal has been scored or (*d*) prior to the commencement of extra time. Note: During extra time the provisions of (*a*), (*b*) and (*c*) above shall apply.

141. A substitute shall not be allowed for a player who has

been ordered from the water according to Rule 18/116 and 18/119–2.2.

142. A substitute must be ready to replace a player without delay; if he is not ready the referee may re-start the game without him, in which case he may not take part in the match until the next stoppage.

143. Ruling: In case of accident, illness or injury, a substitute takes his position in the water where the accident occurred and will take the free throw or corner throw which may have been awarded the injured player, but should there be no substitute, another player shall take the throw.

144. The Captain, coach or team manager must notify the referee of substitutions.

RULE 23
Extra Time

145. Should there be level scores at full time (Rule 9) in any game for which a definite result is required, any continuation into extra time must be after 5 minute interval. There shall then be played two periods of 3 minutes each actual play, with an interval of 1 minute for changing ends.

146. This system of extra time shall be continued until a decision has been reached.

147. A player who has been ordered from the water by the referee—but not for the rest of the game—shall resume with his team for extra time only when his penalty time has expired or a goal has been scored.

The foregoing Rules were effective as from 31 January 1981. The A.S.A. Water Polo Referees' Handbook, *which contains the Rules together with notes, comments and instructions for referees, is available from the Amateur Swimming Association, Harold Fern House, Derby Square, Loughborough, Leicestershire, price £2.30, including p. & p.*